Be Brave and Arise
My Life Quest As a Bahá'í Man

S. M. Alexander
with the Voices of Many Men

Be Brave and Arise
ISBN: 978-1-940062-11-2

Publisher: Marriage Transformation LLC
Printer: Lightning Source (Ingram); United States of America

© 2020 Marriage Transformation LLC; all international rights reserved. No part of this book may be electronically shared, scanned, uploaded, or reproduced by any means, without the written permission of the publisher. Violations are regarded as theft of the author's and publisher's intellectual property. *Thank you for respecting this legal copyright. Your integrity with this law spreads a spirit of loving respect throughout the world and makes us very happy.* If you wish to share the book, please direct people to our website or an online or in-person bookstore where they can purchase a copy. Quoting small portions in study groups, newsletters, and media is permitted. The publisher welcomes inquiries about use.

This publication provides helpful and educational information about life. If expert assistance is required, the services of a competent professional counselor should be sought.

Cover Design: Steiner Graphics

Cover Photo: Xijian, istockphoto.com

Dedication

This book is dedicated to The Báb, Who began a new spiritual era in the world in 1844 that called forth amazing brave heroes, and to Bahá'u'lláh, the One The Báb promised would arise shortly after Him, Who empowers and inspires all men to begin the quest of living a transformed, spiritual life of service to others.

Some Book Usage Suggestions

Who is this book for?

- This is primarily for men age 15 and up for individual or group study. It can be useful across various stages of your life and accompany you on your spiritual journey and exploration from wherever you are now. It will empower you to explore many aspects of your life and establish your choices on a strong spiritual foundation.
- This book may also be a useful tool when parenting, guiding, mentoring, or collaborating with men, for exploring their spiritual choices with them, and for encouraging them to live a life of bravery and integrity. Fathers may find it beneficial to read the book with their sons and discuss it together.
- Much of the content could benefit women as well, but the stories are generally from men to other men.

Enhancing your experience

- Each chapter has Actions that you can take to enhance your learning. Engage in the ones that are useful to you, and feel free to create your own as well.
- You may find it useful to create an electronic or written journal to record your responses and experiences with the Action sections and your insights from the Reflection Questions.
- You may often benefit from adding in physical activities that enhance and reinforce your learning. Many life lessons and confidence-building will come to you as you actively engage in life, and many physical experiences can aid your learning and growth mentally, emotionally, and spiritually.
- While the book is laid out in a linear way, each chapter is generally self-contained, and you may find it useful to go at times to the chapters of most relevance to your life in the moment.

Based on the Bahá'í Faith's teachings

- This book takes the approach that you are already at least somewhat familiar with these teachings, and you may already be a Bahá'í.

- You could be in any state or stage with your spiritual journey, connection to God, and beliefs and find benefit.
- If you are unfamiliar with the Bahá'í Faith, please see "Appendix A: What Is the Bahá'í Faith?".

Sources of the content

- Other than the content that is directly from the Bahá'í teachings or from another book, the perspectives in *Be Brave and Arise* are those of the author and those who shared stories.
- Stories are real experiences or composites of real experiences edited to make them clear and anonymous, as well as ones from authors. Stories are indicated throughout in *italics*.

Author's note

This book is humbly offered in service to others. No book is ever complete or perfect, and your input and further stories are welcome. [See the Contact section in the Appendices]

Be Brave and Arise
Navigation Aid for My Quest
Mapping Locations
(aka Table of Contents)

My Life Quest ... 1
Mapping and Packing for My Quest ... 4

Part 1: Beginning My Journey

1. Exploring the Current Reality of My Life ... 21
2. Being a Spiritual Man—An Adventure ... 29
3. Navigating Spiritual Manhood—Some Preparation ... 39
4. Creating a Support System—The Value of a Safety Net ... 47

Part 2: Challenging Myself—Growing My Light Force

5. Understanding My Best and Building from My Not-Yet-Best ... 61
6. Developing Spiritual Habits—Connecting to God's Light ... 72
7. Reducing Resistance and Aligning with Positive Action ... 83
8. Developing My Character—Increasing My Light ... 98

Part 3: Building Health and Well-Being on My Quest

9. Striving for My Mental Health ... 115
10. Striving for My Emotional Health ... 128
11. Striving for My Physical Health ... 149
12. Striving for My Sexual Health—Some Context ... 162
13. Striving for My Sexual Health—Spiritual Principles and Challenges ... 171
14. Striving for My Sexual Health—
    Building Understanding and Strengths ... 182
15. Striving for My Sexual Health—Grappling with Dark Forces ... 202

Part 4: Questing Through Life's Challenges

16. Handling the Adulting Stuff ... 219
17. Learning and Growing from Difficulties ... 230
18. Cleaning Up My Messes and Going Forward ... 239

Part 5: My Bahá'í Community Life—Shining God's Light in the World

19. Engaging with the Bahá'í Community ... 248
20. Making My Community Service Choices ... 260
21. Contributing to Respect, Justice, and Unity ... 273

Part 6: Thriving with Others on My Journey

22. Building Relationships with My Parents and Family ... 289
23. Fostering Healthy Relationships with My Friends ... 302
24. Establishing a Happy Relationship with a Partner ... 313
25. Creating My Marriage, Fatherhood, and Family ... 330

Part 7: Bravely Arising to Create My Future

26. Directing the Course of My Life ... 343
27. Learning and Working As Worship ... 351
28. Continuing the Quest for Spiritual Manhood ... 360

Appendices:

Appendix A: What Is the Bahá'í Faith? ... 369
Appendix B: Forming a Book Study Group ... 373
Appendix C: Additional Guidance for Youth
 (approximately ages 15-30) ... 376

Ending:

Quotation References ... 380
Acknowledgements ... 395
Author Biography and Contact Information ... 395

Be Brave and Arise

My Life Quest

You are on a quest, the journey of life, and you have a choice of being conscious or unconscious about your goals and your purposes during that journey. A quest is about searching, seeking, and having adventures on the way to a significant outcome.

You live in a world with few and inconsistent moral standards, and most behaviors, at least at the level of media, are portrayed as acceptable. Then you encounter the Bahá'í Faith, which can feel at times like it has an almost impossible number of standards to achieve. You have the ability, consistently a little each day, to build your capacity to live a life in alignment with the Bahá'í teachings, if you choose to:

- Be brave
- Arise and act

You may not know yet the personal satisfaction, self-confidence, and empowerment that comes from striving to achieve personal integrity with clear, purposeful goals. You may not yet have in place people to support your progress lovingly and compassionately. This book will increase your vision for how to achieve these. It's based on the author's current understanding, and it's humbly offered as a light on your journey. All the concepts in this book are evolving with time and research, and you will see how they fit with your life.

No matter in what spiritual state you are now, you can choose to gradually incorporate spiritual principles into your life, form a vision of where you want to go, and begin the journey toward your goals. Making spiritually based choices can empower you to live a life with:

- Purpose
- Happiness
- Material prosperity
- Well-being
- Integrity
- Coherence

As you go through the sections of this book, you will grow in self-understanding and self-respect, as well as make increasingly positive choices for all aspects of your life. This book will accompany you with focused encouragement and support as you seek to understand and empower yourself and as you experience parts of the quest such as:

- Pursuing education and a profession
- Forming a marriage and family
- Building community

It will assist you to build your capacity for living and for serving others based on the Bahá'í teachings:

"When his life is oriented toward service to Bahá'u'lláh, and when every conscious act is performed within this frame of reference, he will not fail to achieve the true purpose of his life."[1] On behalf of the Universal House of Justice

Many men find that spiritual values, a search for truth, and a hunger to belong to something greater than themselves protects them from a natural fear of failure and the difficulties of the world. Bahá'u'lláh says:

"He must search after the truth to the utmost of his ability and exertion, that God may guide him in the paths of His favor and the ways of His mercy. For He, verily, is the best of helpers unto His servants. … In this journey the seeker becometh witness to a myriad changes and transformations, confluences and divergences. He beholdeth the wonders of Divinity in the mysteries of creation and discovereth the paths of guidance and the ways of His Lord. Such is the station reached by them that search after God, and such are the heights attained by those who hasten unto Him."[2] Bahá'u'lláh

A man provides his thoughts:

"When I hear 'Be Brave' I feel empowered and ennobled. It honors the weight of the dark forces I face in the world each day, as we are truly heading out into a horrific and dangerous battlefield. Nothing other than true heroism, self-effacement, fearlessness, and ultimate detachment seem to be called for in this day when the forces of darkness think they are winning the battle of life.

"The call to be brave and arise also tells me that I have great opportunity for heroism, and for achieving our ultimate objective which is nearness to God. I appreciate that someone believes I can handle the raw truth and has

faith in my inner strength. It's a call to arise to something greater than myself, regardless of what I perceive my strengths to be, and it's a call to nobility. And that empowers me. The content of this book is a call to the Kingdom, a call to pass through this earthly battlefield and come out on the other side, to the other realm, having gained the tools I will need for the rest of a mighty journey."

Here is Bahá'u'lláh's promise:

"He that hath Me not is bereft of all things. Turn ye away from all that is on earth and seek none else but Me. I am the Sun of Wisdom and the Ocean of Knowledge. I cheer the faint and revive the dead. I am the guiding Light that illumineth the way. I am the royal Falcon on the arm of the Almighty. I unfold the drooping wings of every broken bird and start it on its flight."[3] Bahá'u'lláh

Developing an approach to your life based on the Bahá'í teachings is a process and a journey that calls you to be brave and arise. Welcome to your quest!

Mapping and Packing for My Quest

This is an "action" book. Each chapter and activity calls you to be brave and arise to take charge of your life and dedicate it to positive accomplishments and services as best as you can. Where the activities provided do not fit your personal quest, please develop your own that do.

People learn and travel through life in different ways and use approaches unique to them. You will apply your knowledge of yourself as you utilize this book.

Creating my map

What follows is book content laid out in words. However, it may be empowering for you to create a map on paper, a computer, or mobile device that includes the elements that match what you want to achieve in your life quest. At this stage, you are creating an initial version of your map. You will be wise to flexibly adjust it as you travel on the journey.

Step 1: Review the chapter summaries below.

1 – Exploring the Current Reality of My Life
Challenge: Sometimes it's very difficult to sort out what's good or bad in me and in the world.
Opportunity: I and my life are like a lot of different puzzle pieces, and I'm not sure what the picture will look like over my life journey, but I'm eager to find out.
Summary:
- It's good to do some planning of my life journey.
- Much of society is a mess, and so are many families, but I can be involved in making a better world, and there are many efforts already underway.
- Roles of men and women are changing and often confusing to me; men have a powerful role to play.
- It's better for me to be part of the army of light rather than being swayed by the powers of darkness.
- It's great to get to know myself well so I can make wise choices; service is an excellent way to build self-knowledge and learn new skills.

2 – Being a Spiritual Man—An Adventure
Challenge: I struggle at times being enthusiastic when I foresee a life and

spiritual journey that I suspect will have mountains, pitfalls, and danger.
Opportunity: I want to know how to handle myself and thrive during my life and spiritual journey.
Summary:
- I can be in any state and at any stage and begin to make progress forward.
- It will take time and experience for me to fully be a "spiritual man", thriving in all aspects of my life.
- Spiritual maturity for Bahá'ís begins at age 15; age 21 is another important transition when I can vote and be voted for in Bahá'í elections.
- Living life by new teachings not fully accepted in the world takes being brave, asking courageously for assistance or accompaniment as needed, and choosing to participate in community building.
- I don't have to do everything at once or be perfect at any of it; life and growth are a process toward excellence.

3 – Navigating Spiritual Manhood—Some Preparation
Challenge: Sometimes it takes courage just to get out of bed, and even more to take steps forward.
Opportunity: Often I don't know the right directions and how to find the correct landmarks toward achieving spiritual manhood, but I'm willing to seek and discover them to the best of my ability.
Summary:
- I can be brave and humble in arising to meet the challenges of life—and I am not alone.
- Sometimes it's a tug-of-war figuring out Who is ultimately in charge, but it's usually best if it's God and not me; I do what I'm responsible for, but He's there to guide and help me.
- My positive thoughts breed positive words and actions.
- My negative thoughts breed negative words and actions.

4 – Creating a Support System—The Value of a Safety Net
Challenge: I want to be strong enough to live my life on my own and by myself, otherwise I feel like I'm being weak.
Opportunity: Connecting myself to others provides relationships to sustain me; others can offer potential directions and assistance when I'm on my life quest and I'm feeling as if I'm lost in the woods without a compass.

Summary:
- The Bahá'í teachings speak of powerful Covenants that I can connect with that protect unity.
- Following the Bahá'í teachings and laws is empowering and contributes to living a life of integrity; however, carrying out these actions consistently is hard at times and a process that takes prayerful effort and time.
- Choosing to be a Bahá'í is a big decision that can be a stage of my journey when I am ready, but it doesn't mean that I'm instantly perfect.
- Living life relying only on myself is really, really difficult, so it's good to find people I trust to mentor and guide me, and this may include my father or a father figure.

5 - Understanding My Best and Building from My Not-Yet-Best
Challenge: Sometimes I resist looking too closely at myself, so I don't trigger self-importance or the despair that comes from not feeling good enough to meet other people's standards.
Opportunity: Striving to live a life of integrity and growth can empower me to be my best self.
Summary:
- Doing a daily checkup and cleanup keeps my life and relationships ever improving.
- Understanding myself, including my character, comes from observing my thoughts, actions, and interactions with others.
- Keeping my eyes on my own behavior stops me comparing myself to others.
- Whew, integrity is tough—always trying to live up to high standards takes a lot of effort—but the rewards are amazing.

6 - Developing Spiritual Habits—Connecting to God's Light
Challenge: Sometimes developing habits feels like a lot of work and not much fun.
Opportunity: I want to feel the joy of success as I strive to be stronger and more consistent with spiritual practices.
Summary:
- My soul, like my physical body, needs conscious attention and care.
- Practices like daily prayer, meditation, and reading the Bahá'í teachings keep my soul strong and healthy.

- There are special Obligatory Prayers, one of which is to be said daily along with special instructions.
- Meditation connects me with insights I can apply to my life and ideas I can use to serve others.
- Sharing about the Bahá'í teachings will become a natural and regular part of my life as I pray, read, grow, and become excited about them.

7 – Reducing Resistance and Aligning with Positive Action

Challenge: Sometimes it's very, very, very comfortable just to be the way I am now.

Opportunity: As I bravely arise to improve myself, I will discover strengths inside of me I never knew I had, and I can build new ones that will be valuable to me and others.

Summary:
- I can allow many things to get in the way of motivating myself to improve; peer pressure can be a difficult obstacle.
- My behavior is a free-will choice, and I have prayer, the Bahá'í teachings, and a support "team" to help me make excellent choices.
- God and my own efforts can transform my behavior and expand my capacities.
- Improving aspects of myself takes courage, humility, and perseverance, and this effort brings benefits like self-respect, happiness, and better relationships.
- I can be a champion for equality, so women and men both achieve their potential, and our capacities are expanded in the process.

8 - Developing My Character—Increasing My Light

Challenge: Sometimes it feels like my lower nature really wants to win, and sometimes it does.

Opportunity: As I develop my character, I like myself better, and others enjoy being around me and appreciate my contributions.

Summary:
- I'm a God-created noble human being, and I'm on a lifetime quest to keep growing as a noble being.
- I have a higher nature and a lower nature, and I'm healthiest and most contributing when I choose the high road.
- It's a bit overwhelming that I have lots, and lots, and lots of character qualities to keep track of and understand, but it's great to see all the good inside of me and the potential for more.

- When I assess, understand, and develop my character, I am powerful in fighting the spiritual battles between my lower and higher natures, and I have effective access to changing my less-desirable behaviors.
- Having many character strengths gives me the ability to navigate life with integrity and respect for myself and others; when I tell the truth and don't cheat or steal, it's amazing how much people trust me.

9 – Striving for My Mental Health

Challenge: When I'm faced with people and happenings that are #%&!, my head feels full of pounding hammers, and I only want to escape.

Opportunity: I cope, survive, and thrive when I recognize that I'm a noble human being, and I practice self-respect, encouragement, and primarily keep positive thoughts in my mind.

Summary:
- Courage, resilience, and flexibility empower me to be healthy mentally.
- There are many mental challenges facing people today, and I am not immune just because I'm striving to be a spiritual man.
- Part of practicing self-respect is acknowledging when I am struggling, and it's a courageous strength to ask for assistance as appropriate.
- Seeking accompaniment from competent mental health professionals is wise as needed.
- Respecting myself is a vital link to happiness and excellent behavior.
- Self-criticism, perfectionism, and criticism from others can sabotage my progress.
- Engaging in learning something new can be a positive mental-strengthening step.

10 – Striving for My Emotional Health

Challenge: Sometimes it's difficult to know how I feel and express it; at other times, there are so many conflicting feelings inside that I'm confused about what's happening and why.

Opportunity: I can maintain my emotional health in our challenging world, including processing the complexity of feelings, seeking assistance from others as needed.

Summary:
- With greater knowledge and practice, I can identify, understand, and express my own feelings.
- I can listen to and strive to understand the feelings of others.

- Understanding feelings increases my effectiveness in conversations with others and in mutual problem-solving.
- The Nonviolent Communication method assists me in preserving unity while expressing feelings.
- Living a spiritual life is a powerful source of joy for me.
- Laughter and humor enrich my life.
- Being thoughtful of others and doing acts of kindness for them contributes to me being emotionally healthy.

11 – Striving for My Physical Health

Challenge: Physical danger and illnesses abound from vehicle accidents, altercations, and choosing to put substances in my body that cause harm; I often eat and sleep whenever I feel like it.

Opportunity: I can make choices that respect my body as the temple of my spirit and that preserve my well-being in ways that contribute to health for a lifetime.

Summary:
- Maintaining my physical well-being through excellent nutrition, exercise, and sleep keeps my body strong and functional, and this also contributes to my mental, emotional, and spiritual health.
- Taking care of my body supports me in being involved in life and in service to others.
- There are many dangerous sources of influence in the world that can have a negative effect on men's health and lives, and I can prevent many of them from harming me.
- Making self-respectful choices by not misusing or abusing alcohol or drugs keeps destructive poisons out of my body and keeps my mind functioning clearly; there are many sources of help if I struggle with this, such as counselors, support groups, Spiritual Assemblies, and medical professionals.

12 - Striving for My Sexual Health – Some Context

Challenge: Sex feels so good that I'm not sure I want anything to do with changing my behavior.

Opportunity: To have a long-term, healthy, and happy marriage that includes sexual intimacy with my partner, I'm willing to consider carrying out spiritually based principles and approaches.

Summary:
- Sex is a unifying and pleasurable physical, mental, emotional, and spiritual experience within marriage between two consenting adults, one female and one male.
- Powerful hormones affect attraction and sex, and they can contribute to bonding two individuals together as one entity; I will need to carefully navigate this, as attraction is important but it's best to achieve this connection within marriage.
- Sex is not an effective way of getting to know someone well; in fact, it could interfere with clarity about someone's character.

13 - Striving for My Sexual Health—Spiritual Principles and Challenges

Challenge: When something like sex is so physical, it's hard for me to think of it in spiritual terms.

Opportunity: I can apply many character qualities toward my sexual health, with chastity as one of the most important.

Summary:
- Chastity is a powerful protector of my well-being and for healthy sexual expressions with my marriage partner; it liberates me from harm and many potential tests.
- The morals of society frequently do not align with the Bahá'í teachings about sex, which makes this a challenging issue for many Bahá'í men of all ages, including me.

14 - Striving for My Sexual Health—Building Understanding and Strengths

Challenge: Sexy images, people, messages, and media surround me, and it's a very strong temptation to participate in some way.

Opportunity: I can use spiritual tools to direct my thoughts and actions at appropriate times toward spiritually and mentally stimulating topics, service activities, work accomplishments, and life goals.

Summary:
- I can apply qualities like acceptance, detachment, and self-discipline to aid me in staying focused on healthy expression of my sexual energy within marriage with my partner and not in other ways that can be harmful or unhealthy.
- I can direct the energies of my body, mind, heart, and soul toward positive and creative endeavors and many purposes and services to others.

- Sexual energy is appropriate to consciously release when I choose with a willing marriage partner.

15 - Striving for My Sexual Health—Grappling with Dark Forces
Challenge: Sexual influences tempt me constantly, and I often give in.
Opportunity: I can begin to gradually adjust my habits so I'm less exposed to and influenced by the over-emphasis on sex in the culture around me.
Summary:
- It's good for me to be an ever-evolving person and take on more responsibilities as I can, no matter what age I am.
- Being an adult can have light aspects to it when I remember to laugh and be appropriately playful.
- It's fun and empowering to learn new skills that can contribute to my life and others.
- I'm a complex human being, and so there will always be many aspects of my self and my life to develop and balance.
- Assessing my progress encourages me to be in action, as I then clearly see my growth.

16 - Handling the Adulting Stuff
Challenge: Sometimes I don't want to act like an adult, and sometimes I equate being an adult with a giant weight of responsibility to carry around.
Opportunity: I'm excited to be taking on the adulting that's coming my way, and I'm learning to approach it gradually and in a balanced way one day at a time.
Summary:
- It's good for me to be an ever-evolving person and take on more responsibilities as I can, no matter what age I am.
- Being an adult can have light aspects to it when I remember to laugh and be appropriately playful.
- It's fun and empowering to learn new skills that can contribute to my life and others.
- I'm a complex human being, and so there will always be many aspects of my self and my life to develop and balance.
- Assessing my progress encourages me to be in action, as I then clearly see my growth.

17 – Learning and Growing from Difficulties
Challenge: When faced with difficulties, I sometimes make unwise or

unhealthy choices in response that make the situations worse.
Opportunity: I can use difficulties as opportunities to learn and grow; they especially strengthen my character.
Summary:
- Difficulties can build my spiritual muscles and prompt me to strive for growth and well-being.
- Life works best if I'm responsible for my own development, and that means distinguishing what battles are mine to grapple with and which ones belong to others.
- Every problem generates learning that I can use in new circumstances and with new people.
- I'm grateful I don't have to go through challenges alone, since I can ask others to consult and pray with me, as well as assist and accompany me.

18 – Cleaning Up My Messes and Going Forward
Challenge: It's often easier to pretend nothing happened, avoid dealing with an issue in a timely way, or to hide what I've done instead of addressing it.
Opportunity: I like the feeling of freedom that arises and how light I feel when I keep my life "cleaned up" daily.
Summary:
- When I contribute to difficulties, I can handle the results with understanding, regret, forgiveness, and making amends.
- Cleaning up my "messes" keeps me going forward, increases my self-respect, draws respect from others, builds character, and often protects unity with others.
- I can resiliently bounce back from difficulties and keep bravely living my life in a powerful way.

19 - Engaging with the Bahá'í Community
Challenge: Sometimes I love being involved with people who are following the Bahá'í teachings; sometimes it seems like all they want me to do is work, work, and work.
Opportunity: I can study the Bahá'í teachings, learn what's involved in community life, and make my own balanced and at times sacrificial choices for involvement and contribution.
Summary:
- No matter what experiences I have had in the past with participating, I can change the nature and quality of my experiences now and going forward.

- My voice is a vital contribution to community consultations.
- It's important to participate in 19-Day Feasts, contribute to the Bahá'í Fund, and serve others as ways of building unity and contributing to universal participation.
- I can strive to have a good relationship with the local and national Spiritual Assemblies, and I can build my capacity to serve on such institutions.
- Bahá'u'lláh, 'Abdu'l-Bahá, and Shoghi Effendi guide and inspire the elected Bahá'í institutions, and these entities are more than just a group of individuals.
- The community and institutions are in the process of maturing, so they won't always function the way I want or think they should; my own responsibility is to build unity and love, as well as grow and contribute my skills, talents, and abilities.

20 – Making My Community Service Choices

Challenge: There are so many improvements to do world-wide, that I could serve 24 hours, 7 days a week, and it would still feel like an insignificant drop in an ocean of problems.

Opportunity: Serving others is an opportunity to be involved with great people in tackling several community issues at once.

Summary:
- Service is a broad term that encompasses a wide variety of activities of daily life, so I am likely already involved in service; I can also choose to do more.
- The Universal House of Justice provides regular Plans that encourage me to set the priorities for my service; at this time, there are four core activities that are high priority.
- It takes courage for me to be involved in serving others and in sustaining my efforts.
- Who I am as a spiritual being internally must be in harmony with who I am externally and with my words and actions, so I am authentically the same person in all areas of my life.
- It's wise to balance Bahá'í community service with many other aspects of my life, including personal prayer and meditation as well as family life.

21 - Contributing to Respect, Justice, and Unity

Challenge: It's easy to look at media and what's happening around me and think that everything going on is bad #%&!.

Opportunity: It's like taking a refreshing shower in a waterfall to see millions of people taking proactive, positive actions to increase light in the world, just like me.
Summary:
- There's a lot of muck in the world, and it takes a high level of awareness and commitment to a spiritual path to avoid stepping into it and to maintain my self-respect.
- I can act to address social issues.
- The more I bring people together and contribute to them having unified relationships, the better the world will be.
- Backbiting and gossip are highly destructive to unity.
- Saying prayers for protection and urgent aid can be vital during my activities, as can using the power of the Greatest Name as a brief prayer; once I learn to pronounce the various forms of the Greatest Name and memorize them, I have instant access to help anytime, anywhere.

22 - Building Relationships with My Parents and Family
Challenge: It's very difficult at times to see examples of well-functioning and happy families, and sometimes I notice what looks like a good family is messed up underneath the surface.
Opportunity: I can be grateful when there are good things happening in my family, build unity when I can, and take constructive steps to deal with or heal from the bad, so I don't carry on negative patterns to the next generation.
Summary:
- Families are a mix of different people and relationships of varying degrees of closeness, functionality, and unity.
- I can love and appreciate the positive qualities of my family members.
- Qualities such as respect, courtesy, and love can bring my family closer.
- If being with my family feels more traumatic than a unified gathering, I can determine what spiritual principles to apply to protect my well-being.
- I can often influence family members toward unity (when it's safe and healthy).
- I can reach out for help if my family's functioning has negatively affected me.

23 - Fostering Healthy Relationships with My Friends
Challenge: Sometimes it seems like busy-ness and all our electronic devices

and social media make it hard to really connect with friends in person.
Opportunity: I can have conversations on meaningful topics with my friends and with new potential friends, and ensure we encourage each other's best efforts in life.
Summary:
- Friends add richness and enjoyment to my life.
- It's possible for friends to influence me in positive or negative ways.
- I must make a conscious effort and invest time for my friendships to last.
- Building true friendships with others is a key part of the Bahá'í focus on building vibrant communities.
- Friendship is a foundation element for relationships and marriages.
- Avoiding timewasters like excessive screen time or video games can free up time for me to connect with friends and be in action together.

24 - Establishing a Happy Relationship with a Partner
Challenge: It's confusing to navigate relationships, and it's often difficult for me to feel like I can succeed at them.
Opportunity: Success in relationships (and marriage) can be possible if I prepare myself, especially my character, and learn from the large body of spiritual and scientific knowledge about what makes them work well.
Summary:
- It's vital for me to focus on key components of relationship success such as character, friendship, and spiritual connection; being skillful with equality and consultation are also essential.
- Spending time with friends can be a good way for me to get to know others as potential partners.
- Dating is a possibility if I care about the person, I'm building a friendship with them, we are practicing chastity, and I'm considering whether they have potential as a marriage partner in the future.
- Courtship is when I get serious about a person, I want to deeply learn about them and them about me, and we figure out together whether being marriage partners is a good choice.
- Cohabitation is common in society, as people often see it as a way to prevent divorce, but "trial marriages"— where a couple lives together without marriage—are not part of the Bahá'í teachings, and these situations can also cause other problems; this unstable situation is particularly risky for any children involved.

- When I'm serious about preparing for marriage by building knowledge and skills, it will prevent problems later and contribute to me having a stronger marriage.

25 - Creating My Marriage, Fatherhood, and Family
Challenge: I have a lot of skepticism about marriage and see many couples living together or divorcing, so it's tough for me to have confidence and trust in getting and staying married myself.
Opportunity: When I look at the encouragement in the Bahá'í teachings to marry, and when I study the research about its benefits, I feel hopeful I can marry and establish a family.
Summary:
- Ideally, I have a respectful relationship with my parents, and that's a good foundation for when my relationship partner and I ask them for consent for us to marry each other.
- It enhances our success in marriage if we both have excellent characters, a strong friendship, attraction, a commitment to create an eternal union of our souls, and a wish to raise children together.
- As a father, I'm a vital member of the family unit, and I'm responsible for working in partnership with my wife and for ensuring our children are educated spiritually and intellectually.
- I and my wife can create a family that is more than the sum of the people in it, because it's unified, and its members practice kindness, respect, and loyalty.

26 - Directing the Course of My Life
Challenge: There seems to be so many choices that I often think it would be easier to just let someone else make the decisions for my life; at other times I rebel, because everyone has an opinion about what I should do.
Opportunity: With the help of God, others, and the gifts of prayer, meditation, and consultation, I can make wise decisions for my life.
Summary:
- I can, with help from God and others, direct how and where my life goes.
- It's easy to get overwhelmed with all the choices for what to do with my life, so it's empowering to prioritize based on spiritual principles.
- I have an inner drive and passion to learn and make beneficial choices.
- I can use prayer, meditation, and consultation for determining my life choices.

- As I make decisions, the power of commitment fuels my ability to bravely carry them out.

27 – Learning and Working As Worship
Challenge: There are thousands of possible degrees and professions, and it's overwhelming trying to make choices.
Opportunity: I know myself well and what interests me, so I'll begin or continue with my education and profession, watch for signs I'm on track with my choices, and see where God, meditation, and consultation with others steer me.
Summary:
- It's vital for me to be literate, learn new knowledge, and tune into what's happening in the world.
- Education of all types contributes to me being successful in my profession.
- Learning what my various aspirations throughout life are, what truly calls me to be in action, is an unfolding process that comes from prayer, meditation, consultation, observation, and experience.
- My work contributes to my family and community and to my self-respect.
- I can behave ethically with good moral choices in my work and service.
- I respect Bahá'í Holy Days by commemorating them and not working on them.

28 - Continuing the Quest for Spiritual Manhood
Challenge: The forces of darkness are powerful, and I often wonder if fighting with my sword of light and inner strength will be enough to resist them.
Opportunity: The more I'm consistent with aligning my choices with the Bahá'í teachings and living a life of integrity on the eternal journey to become my best self, the more my light shines.
Summary:
- Life is a long and eternal journey that requires my best and bravest efforts.
- Part of my quest is to live my life with high integrity and coherence.
- Some services are especially vital for me while I am a youth (15-30 years old), and I can serve in many ways throughout my life.
- When I have a clear mission in life, it empowers and inspires me to be in action.

Step 2: Draw my map.

Possible approaches for your journey:

1. Go in order, chapter by chapter.
2. Go first to one or two chapters that seem of most interest to you (you can review the chapter summaries above to identify these) and pause to assess how you want to approach the rest.
3. Create a "map" or a systematic approach for your quest.

Example:
    1 - Exploring the Current Reality of My Life
    3 - Navigating Spiritual Manhood—Some Preparation
    5 - Understanding My Best and Building from My Not-Yet-Best
    9 - Striving for My Mental Health
    12-15 Striving for My Sexual Health
    17 - Learning and Growing from Difficulties
    20 - Making My Community Service Choices
    23 - Fostering Healthy Relationships with My Friends

Whatever way you approach your journey, it is good to read the content, do the activities, and use the reflection questions.

Step 3: Pack my backpack for the journey.

As you study the content of this book and navigate your life quest, you will notice there are aspects that you want to carry with you, remember, focus on, develop, and use. These will aid you as you determine your goals, clarify how to best live your life, and engage in serving God and others. What you place in your backpack could include these items below.

A Spiritual Compass: This symbolic tool prompts you to look at your map each day and visualize how your thoughts and actions will align with God's Will for you. A compass helps you head in a good direction. When you use a compass, your feet are grounded in your current reality, and you are looking for spiritual guidance for where to go next.

Practical tools: If you were going on a journey, you would pack food, water, a jacket, a hat, a source of light, and a way to rest and sleep. On a spiritual journey you could pack prayers, quotations, and a way to make notes. You may include artistic tools and materials, like painting supplies or a musical instrument.

Adding along the way: As you pursue your quest, you will find additional items to add to your backpack. Some possibilities are:

- Quotations that inspire you
- Character strengths
- Areas for focused growth
- Reminders of behaviors to practice
- New skills you want to develop or keep practicing
- New goals to set

How you "tuck them into the pack on your back" will be up to you—setting electronic reminders, highlighting passages, printing key pages, writing notes all over the book, or anything else that helps you put this content into practice in your life. You may use a written or electronic journal. You may find a time management or goal-setting app for a mobile device that aid you in tracking your progress.

You may also share your map, study, and do activities with others, as well as engage others in discussing the content. Joining with fellow travelers and gaining their viewpoints can enhance your learning and growth.

Step 4: Begin my quest.

This book is a vital call to action:

> "Your entire life changes the day that you decide you will no longer accept mediocrity for yourself. When you realize that today is the most important day of your life. When you decide that now matters more than any other time because it is who you are becoming each day based on the decisions that you are making and the actions that you are taking that is determining who you are going to be for the rest of your life."[4]
> Hal Elrod

Part 1: Beginning My Journey

Be Brave and Arise

1 – Exploring the Current Reality of My Life

Challenge: Sometimes it's very difficult to sort out what's good or bad in me and in the world.

Opportunity: I and my life are like a lot of different puzzle pieces, and I'm not sure what the picture will look like over my life journey, but I'm eager to find out.

Summary:
- It's good to do some planning of my life journey.
- Much of society is a mess, and so are many families, but I can be involved in making a better world, and there are many efforts already underway.
- Roles of men and women are changing and often confusing to me; men have a powerful role to play.
- It's better for me to be part of the army of light rather than being swayed by the powers of darkness.
- It's great to get to know myself well so I can make wise choices; service is an excellent way to build self-knowledge and learn new skills.

More:

It's a tough time to be a person—and a man

At the beginning of a journey, it's good to understand as much as possible about:

- Your starting point
- Potential difficulties you may encounter and how to handle them
- The tools and navigation guides that will be useful
- Possible side trips and destinations ahead of you

The journey will not be simple or easy. It will require you to regularly call on your bravery and your vision of the future to stay in motion. You may pause and rest, and you may experience detours. Some planning will benefit you, but there is no way to plan for all that happens in life. Your commitment to keep arising and staying moving forward will keep you on your quest. The chapters ahead will guide you.

You live in a unique and challenging time in history when the roles and strengths of men seem to be constantly redefined. Historic and unhealthy patterns of male supremacy are still present in many spheres of activity, but they are being challenged. Women are going through their own adventure with redefining roles and ways of interacting with men. It can be confusing and difficult for everyone as humanity strives to transform into new ways of operating with new understandings.

One challenge in society that may also be a factor in your life is the social isolation that comes from significant time spent with video games, TV and movies, pornography, and internet use. It takes considerable effort and bravery to step out into the world and forge a purposeful life of worshipping God, friendships, service to others, education, work accomplishments, and marriage and family.

The daily media is fully of dreary and dire news about the state of the world, men, and families. You live in this world, so you know it's often challenging. It's timely for you to be lifted up to new approaches, so you can resist being pulled down by the dark forces of a disintegrating world order. Here is a call to action:

> "Men must come to realize that under current conditions of inequality, the development of *their* full potential is not possible. It is they who must find the moral courage to convey and model new understandings of masculinity and who must challenge and question the narrow roles that society and the media have assigned to them. In the final analysis, it is not enough to create space in the current social order for women to play their rightful role. Rather, the goal is for women and men to work shoulder-to-shoulder, each as the helpmate of the other—in the context of family, work, community, and international affairs—to construct a society which allows for the flourishing of all."[5] Bahá'í International Community

You have a unique contribution to make in the world as you learn to balance justice with compassion and grow in integrity and accountability. You can contribute much to a world going through transformation. You and many other men are needed on the quest to move beyond the negative forces in the world and be strong, spiritual, wise, and contributing. The greater your connection to spiritual guidance, the more you have a personal connection with God and Bahá'u'lláh, the more you will succeed on your journey and live a high-value life.

Be Brave and Arise

Align with the army of light versus the powers of darkness

The following is about the state of the world:

"Bahá'ís are encouraged to see in the revolutionary changes taking place in every sphere of life the interaction of two fundamental processes. One is destructive in nature, while the other is integrative; both serve to carry humanity, each in its own way, along the path leading towards its full maturity. The operation of the former is everywhere apparent—in the vicissitudes that have afflicted time-honored institutions, in the impotence of leaders at all levels to mend the fractures appearing in the structure of society, in the dismantling of social norms that have long held in check unseemly passions, and in the despondency and indifference exhibited not only by individuals but also by entire societies that have lost any vital sense of purpose. Though devastating in their effects, the forces of disintegration tend to sweep away barriers that block humanity's progress, opening space for the process of integration to draw diverse groups together and disclosing new opportunities for cooperation and collaboration. Bahá'ís, of course, strive to align themselves, individually and collectively, with forces associated with the process of integration, which, they are confident, will continue to gain in strength, no matter how bleak the immediate horizons. Human affairs will be utterly reorganized, and an era of universal peace inaugurated. Such is the view of history that underlies every endeavor pursued by the Bahá'í community."[6] Universal House of Justice

"Yet there is reassurance in the knowledge that, amidst the disintegration, a new kind of collective life is taking shape which gives practical expression to all that is heavenly in human beings."[7] Universal House of Justice

Examples of destructive forces of darkness that can influence you in negative ways are racism, materialism, pornography, greed, abuse of women and children, and drugs. Dark forces include "the passions of the world—its admiration for power, its adoration of status, its love of luxuries, its attachment to frivolous pursuits, its glorification of violence, and its obsession with self-gratification. It must be realized that the isolation and despair from which so many suffer are products of an environment ruled by an all-pervasive materialism."[8] (Universal House of Justice) It takes powerful positive examples from parents, mentors, and people you see on a regular basis, as well as your own inner spiritual strength, to counter these forces and rise above them. Prayer and collaborating with community building are also vital.

The reality that we live in Shoghi Effendi variously calls:

- The Formative Age[9]
- The Age of Transition[10]
- The Age of Frustration[11]

There is a compelling call from the Bahá'í teachings to be part of "the army of light" that vanquishes "the powers of darkness on the battlefield of the world". This analogy does not refer to your physical abilities, but rather your spiritual ones. When you amplify the powers of "light", you aid the Divine teachings to illumine humanity. You become part of the growing movement toward global peace and the oneness of the human family. You draw on bravery, also known as courage, to stay in action, regardless of what challenges arise.[12] 'Abdu'l-Bahá

Someone shares his thoughts:

"Spiritual warrior-type qualities, besides courageously teaching others about the Bahá'í Faith, are your courage to do the right thing when others are pressuring you do to otherwise, which is an oft-overlooked but fundamental leadership quality. These qualities also include your ability to experience negativity, violence, or abuse without passing it on to those who are weaker or on to the next generation. Words like 'integrity', and 'moral courage' or 'moral leadership' are great, but not as clear. Maybe what I mean is that I want men to be able to show 'tenacious gentleness'."

The Bahá'í teachings sound these calls to turn toward the light:

"O Son of Spirit! The best beloved of all things in My sight is Justice; turn not away therefrom if thou desirest Me, and neglect it not that I may confide in thee. By its aid thou shalt see with thine own eyes and not through the eyes of others, and shalt know of thine own knowledge and not through the knowledge of thy neighbor. Ponder this in thy heart; how it behooveth thee to be. Verily justice is My gift to thee and the sign of My loving-kindness. Set it then before thine eyes."[13] Bahá'u'lláh

"O Son of Man! I loved thy creation, hence I created thee. Wherefore, do thou love Me, that I may name thy name and fill thy soul with the spirit of life."[14] Bahá'u'lláh

"O Son of Man! Wert thou to speed through the immensity of space and traverse the expanse of heaven, yet thou wouldst find no rest save in submission to Our command and humbleness before Our Face."[15] Bahá'u'lláh

"We must not only be patient with others, infinitely patient!, but also with our own poor selves, remembering that even the Prophets of God sometimes got tired and cried out in despair! ... He urges you to persevere and add up your accomplishments, rather than to dwell on the dark side of things. Everyone's life has both a dark and bright side. The Master ['Abdu'l-Bahá] said: turn your back to the darkness and your face to Me."[16] On behalf of Shoghi Effendi

Who I am now

You may have changed so much in your life or become so busy that sometimes you may lose track of who you are or are becoming. You may also be uncertain how to even determine who you are. It's best to strive for self-understanding and to use your experiences to observe your own personality, character, words, and actions. The quotations below talk about how to accomplish this.

"The more we search for ourselves, the less likely we are to find ourselves; and the more we search for God, and to serve our fellow-men, the more profoundly will we become acquainted with ourselves, and the more inwardly assured. This is one of the great spiritual laws of life."[17] On behalf of Shoghi Effendi

"It is not merely material well-being that people need. What they desperately need is to know how to live their lives—they need to know who they are, to what purpose they exist, and how they should act towards one another; and, once they know the answers to these questions they need to be helped to gradually apply these answers to every-day behavior. It is to the solution of this basic problem of mankind that the greater part of all our energy and resources should be directed...."[18] On behalf of the Universal House of Justice

A man comments about his growing self-discovery:

> "The idea of finding myself felt difficult and abstract when I was 15. I grew up knowing that I was created noble and my purpose was to continue to develop the qualities and attributes of God through my interactions with others and finding ways to serve in my community. However, I didn't realize how much I was being shaped by the conversations at school, the music I listened to, and the common acceptance of lying to get out of trouble or taking things that didn't belong to oneself. I was constantly making decisions, often unconsciously, about the person I wanted to be and how I wanted others to see me.
>
> "I played football in high school and continued to play throughout college. It was through sports that I developed strong friendships that will last a lifetime and a sense of discipline and focus. I was also constantly surrounded by violent behavior, both on and off the football field, more cursing than I thought was possible, and frequent invitations to watch pornography. My ideas, beliefs, and practices were tested daily. Being surrounded by the loving guidance of my parents, insights from older siblings, and strong examples to look up to encouraged and helped me along my path."

Knowing yourself can give you access to understanding reality and to making beneficial choices:

> "Indeed, the expenditure of enormous energy and vast amounts of resources in an attempt to bend truth to conform to personal desire is now a feature of many contemporary societies. The result is a culture that distorts human nature and purpose, trapping human beings in pursuit of idle fancies and vain imaginings and turning them into pliable objects in the hands of the powerful. Yet, the happiness and well-being of humanity depend upon the opposite: cultivating human character and social order in conformity with reality. Divine teachings shed light on reality, enabling every soul to investigate it properly and to acquire, through the exercise of personal discipline, those attributes that are to distinguish the human being. 'Man should know his own self,' Bahá'u'lláh states, 'and recognize that which leadeth unto loftiness or lowliness, glory or abasement, wealth or poverty.'"[19] On behalf of the Universal House of Justice, including a quotation from Bahá'u'lláh

Be Brave and Arise

You may or may not consider yourself a Bahá'í at this stage, or you may be undecided. That's okay, because it's a big deal, a big choice, and it takes time to figure out your beliefs and choices. This book will walk you through some of this process, and you might find clarity as you try out practices like prayer and following the Bahá'í teachings. In the final analysis, however, whether to be a Bahá'í is a choice between you and God.

Action

1. Draw, take photos, write, record a video, or use some other creative medium to create a self-portrait that begins to answer these questions: "Who am I? Who am I becoming?" Consider what is inside you, what you are involved in, and the life happening around you. This self-portrait will give you insights for what you are learning, what is difficult in your life, what you have accomplished, what your strengths and growth areas are, what brings you joy, and what challenges potentially lie ahead. Below is a list to prompt thought, but don't let it restrict you.

   - Who I am striving to be
   - Upcoming events
   - Education
   - Profession
   - Favorite activities, service choices, and high priorities for time
   - Best friends
   - Family members
   - Current fears, stresses, and worries
   - Wounds in the middle of healing
   - Significant current tests and difficulties
   - Common irritants
   - Purpose(s) in life
   - Strengths as a relationship partner or husband
   - Philosophies/practices of parenting
   - Life dreams
   - Religious beliefs and activities
   - Basic philosophy of life
   - Favorite music, games, movies, TV shows
   - Most special times in life
   - Childhood traumas/stresses
   - Major aspirations and hopes

- What prompts prayer to happen
- What I would do with a major sum of money
- What I do to re-charge energy
- Dream vacation spot

After you have spent time with a good first effort, set it aside for a few days. You may then have further ideas to add. When it feels quite complete, share it with someone who knows you well and ask if they have anything else to contribute. Set a reminder to re-visit this project in a year and see what you notice at that time.

2. Connect with a family member who knows you well and request them to share 2-3 stories about you. What was your response to the stories? Did you gain any new knowledge about yourself?

3. Go outside when it's fully dark with a strong flashlight with different settings. As you turn on each setting, reflect on the power of the light to dispel the darkness. What insights did you gain?

Reflection

1. What do I find difficult about being a man in this time?
2. How do I feel when I'm aligned with the powers of light?
3. What problems in the world most negatively affect me?
4. How does my life go when I align with the forces of darkness?
5. How can I live in this world according to spiritual teachings when few around me are doing so?
6. What protects me from the forces of darkness?
7. What do I think about having a general plan and direction for my life?
8. How can knowing myself improve my ability to fully live life?
9. When I describe myself to others, what are some important facets that I share?

2 – Being a Spiritual Man—An Adventure

Challenge: I struggle at times being enthusiastic when I foresee a life and spiritual journey that I suspect will have mountains, pitfalls, and danger.

Opportunity: I want to know how to handle myself and thrive during my life and spiritual journey.

Summary:
- I can be in any state and at any stage and begin to make progress forward.
- It will take time and experience for me to fully be a "spiritual man", thriving in all aspects of my life.
- Spiritual maturity for Bahá'ís begins at age 15; age 21 is another important transition when I can vote and be voted for in Bahá'í elections.
- Living life by new teachings not fully accepted in the world takes being brave, asking courageously for assistance or accompaniment as needed, and choosing to participate in community building.
- I don't have to do everything at once or be perfect at any of it; life and growth are a process toward excellence.

More:

Beginning from where I am now

The challenge in front of you, no matter what your age or circumstances, is to step onto the spiritual path, steadfastly stay on it as best as you can, and come back to it if you wander off. You will undoubtedly be tested with difficulties during your lifetime, and at times these will cause detours and opportunities for learning and growth.

As everyone has different levels of knowledge and understanding, strengths, and weaknesses, some portions of this book may already seem obvious to you. Other aspects will be powerfully enlightening. At this moment, you could be in any possible state and yet choose to align yourself more fully with Bahá'u'lláh's teachings. Perhaps you:

- Were raised as a Bahá'í and attended children's classes and Junior Youth Spiritual Empowerment group meetings, and have assumed that you will always be a Bahá'í

- Were raised as a Bahá'í, but never really embraced and followed the teachings independently
- Just became a Bahá'í, and no one else in your family is a Bahá'í
- Have wandered away from participating in Bahá'í activities and some tests have you turning back to your beliefs
- Have included drinking alcohol and drugs into your lifestyle, and you might be wondering how they will affect your future
- Have a positive public Bahá'í face and a private life at variance with the teachings
- Come from a religious or non-religious background
- Aren't sure whether you really want to be a Bahá'í, but it would upset your family if you said so
- Are afraid that someone will find out you aren't as good as you look, and you are fearful of revealing your perceived inadequacy or failures
- Are feeling lost and unsure of what to do in life and service
- Struggle with speaking to or treating others as well as you would like
- Serve as an animator for a Junior Youth Spiritual Empowerment group, and you want to be a more powerful example for those in the group and be able to guide them well
- Struggle with being treated with injustice due to prejudice, and you are angry at times, and feeling pulled down spiritually
- Have started working and have very little time for prayers and observing Bahá'í laws
- Have a circle of friends who are not into spirituality and that do not encourage such types of conversations and actions
- Don't feel worthy of coming to Bahá'í activities or spending time with other Bahá'ís, because you have made life choices that contradict the Bahá'í teachings
- Are in a relationship with someone who doesn't like talking about spiritual matters
- Want to be married or improve your marriage and struggle to apply the Bahá'í teachings
- Know what you want to do but need some encouragement and accompaniment

Striving for spiritual adulthood

At the age of 15, Bahá'u'lláh calls those who believe in Him to take a mighty step toward spiritual adulthood. At that point, childhood moves into the rear-view mirror. Each person is called to new personal responsibilities and to take charge of the progress of their soul.

Before age 15 you can prepare yourself for this transition, and once you are over 15, you can begin aligning yourself with these responsibilities. Here is guidance:

> "While some opportunities for service in the Administrative Order are clearly reserved for those who are over twenty-one years of age, at age fifteen the individual has the privilege of affirming, in his own name, his faith in Bahá'u'lláh. The importance of attaining spiritual maturity at the age of fifteen is that it marks that point in life at which the believer takes into his own hands the responsibility for his spiritual destiny.
>
> "The following extract from a Tablet of 'Abdu'l-Bahá links the attainment of maturity with the deepening of one's understanding and comprehension of the realities of life, and the enhancement of one's very capacity for understanding:

> 'Know thou that before maturity man liveth from day to day and comprehendeth only such matters as are superficial and outwardly obvious. However, when he cometh of age he understandeth the realities of thing and the inner truths. Indeed, in his comprehension, his feelings, his deductions and his discoveries, every day of his life after maturity is equal to a year before it.'

> "While parents may grieve at some of the choices their children make, at the age of maturity a son or daughter is then essentially responsible for the decisions he or she takes and becomes answerable to God accordingly. Parents should continue in every way possible to help, encourage, and guide their children, but they should recognize clearly the basic change in accountability that has occurred."[20] On behalf of the Universal House of Justice

Here is how Shoghi Effendi describes the parallel process humanity faces in striving for manhood:

> "The long ages of infancy and childhood, through which the human race had to pass, have receded into the background. Humanity is now experiencing the commotions invariably associated with the most turbulent stage of its evolution, the stage of adolescence, when the impetuosity of youth and its vehemence reach their climax, and must

gradually be superseded by the calmness, the wisdom, and the maturity that characterize the stage of manhood. Then will the human race reach that stature of ripeness which will enable it to acquire all the powers and capacities upon which its ultimate development must depend."[21] Shoghi Effendi

Your participation is vital for the well-being of this emerging world civilization:

"A civilization befitting a humanity which, having passed through earlier stages of social evolution, is coming of age will not emerge through the efforts exerted by a select group of nations or even a network of national and international agencies. Rather, the challenge must be faced by all of humanity. Every member of the human family has not only the right to benefit from a materially and spiritually prosperous civilization but also an obligation to contribute towards its construction. Social action should operate, then, on the principle of universal participation."[22] Office of Social and Economic Development

Another transition time is the age of 21. The Bahá'í Faith does not have clergy and instead has elected institutions to guide community life. At 21, Bahá'ís are eligible to vote and be elected to serve on 9-member councils called Spiritual Assemblies. You could also be appointed to serve in other positions. It takes thought and effort to build your skills and capacity in the years between 15 and 21 and beyond, so that you can perform services well. Here is some guidance:

"If we but turn our gaze to the high qualifications of the members of Bahá'í Assemblies, as enumerated in 'Abdu'l-Bahá's Tablets, we are filled with feelings of unworthiness and dismay, and would feel truly disheartened but for the comforting thought that if we rise to play nobly our part every deficiency in our lives will be more than compensated by the all-conquering spirit of His grace and power. Hence it is incumbent upon the chosen delegates to consider without the least trace of passion and prejudice, and irrespective of any material consideration, the names of only those who can best combine the necessary qualities of unquestioned loyalty, of selfless devotion, of a well-trained mind, of recognized ability and mature experience."[23] Shoghi Effendi

Be Brave and Arise

When you bravely commit to take on spiritual responsibilities, you position yourself for greater effectiveness and more coherence in your education, profession, marriage and family life, community life, and service to others. You can more effectively tap into a greater portion of your God-given potential. You can speak and act in ways that show self-respect and respect for others, keys to your happiness in the present and in the future. This commitment contributes to you staying in positive action.

Growing spiritually

You may already feel connected to the Bahá'í spiritual path, or you may need more time and experiences. It's your unique spiritual journey. A man shares parts of his spiritual journey:

"Love: Is there any greater and more pure motivation for action in our existence? I'm not casually referring to a conscious selfless or generous act, but the deeper inspiration that precedes the choice; the wellspring within—our origin. The particle of light inside that is—and connects us to—God. In our journey, if we rediscover this subtlety of our soul, it's about as close to paradise as I can illustrate through my limited capacities.

"For me, there was a light which illuminated my soul so brightly that this aspect was instantly evident and distinguishable. For the first time in my walk through life, I experienced the outstretched hand of God gracefully cupping mine, then gently joining it with the beautiful spirit in His other. I had met and was attracted to a woman who told me over the phone that she was a Bahá'í, and I instantly recognized the blessing with clarity and certitude.

"Less than a minute after hearing this, I read a sign that said: 'Adopt-A-Highway—Bahá'í Faith.' I received this Divine wink and exited as planned. Upon arriving at my destination, I opened my laptop and immediately searched online for Bahá'ís. The following day I met with a vibrant, but soft-spoken gentleman. We talked for an hour about the Faith in general and specific aspects of dating and marriage, as I had read a book called 'Fortress for Well-Being' about marriage before we met. At the close of our time together, I asked him a single question: "Would you state that your marriage is complacent or thriving?" At the time, he responded that it was thriving.

"A few weeks later, I witnessed the blooming of this gentleman's soul unveil a level of humility I rarely encounter. It was palpable. He began expressing appreciation, vulnerably noting that his initial answer was somewhat reflexive. He proceeded to detail how the question lingered and prompted him to have a deep conversation with his wife. This helped them

see complacency had set in, and he had been overlooking aspects of his relationship. He was very grateful. I found a model in this gentleman—who is now one of my closest friends—to aspire to, and this was a factor that invited me into the Faith, which I have now joined."

Another man tells about his journey:

"I had the opportunity to travel a lot with my family while growing up, seeing different places and experiencing different cultures. Although I was raised Catholic-Christian, I was quite interested in learning about different world religions and understanding how we are all to live together harmoniously. In university, I had many opportunities to develop as an athlete, as well as study, however later I felt that I had been missing out on spiritual guidance. Discovering the Bahá'í Faith and taking opportunities to learn more about spirituality, as well as practicing these principles through service opportunities with friends and family, and through organized community activities, has led to much spiritual growth. I hope youth discover the importance and value of spiritual growth in shaping a brighter future for them and all of us."

Thank God it's a journey

Consider this perspective about becoming a man:

"The journey into manhood starts with taking responsibility for our own lives and actions. Taking responsibility means not indulging in the modern cult of victimhood, and not whining about the bad things that have happened to us and the lucky breaks we didn't get. Things don't just happen to us. They happen because of the way we react to and interact with our environment. How we react and interact reveals how we feel about ourselves. How we deal with our own issues shows how we expect to be treated, and whether we are optimistic or pessimistic, active or passive, problem solvers or complainers, and so on."[24] Howard J. Fox

The journey involves stretching your world outward:

"... [I]f a man should live his entire life in one city, he cannot gain a knowledge of the whole world. To become perfectly informed he must visit other cities, see the mountains and valleys, cross the rivers and traverse the plains."[25] 'Abdu'l-Bahá

You are also likely to keep defining for yourself what it means to be a man. Here is one man's reflection:

"I feel like most guys don't associate manhood with 'body hair' or 'huge appetite', because people typically situate their personal experiences as normal, and compare others to that. When most guys think 'man', they think of culturally defined attributes like physically strong, able to take charge, defend, be violent if needed, be sexy, be confident, and be competent."

So, how would you know that you are growing and changing spiritually and ready to take on spiritual manhood? A good way to explore this is through quiet reflective time. Here is a start: For the next 10 minutes (or more if you can), shut off your phone, take out your earbuds, turn off videos, and find a very quiet place to be, ideally in nature. It's okay to move if you need to but turn inward and listen. After the quiet period, consider:

- Did the noise in my head fade away?
- Could I be comfortable with silence or just nature sounds?
- Did I pick up any inner yearning vibrations of my heart and soul?
- Did it seem more possible to tune into Bahá'u'lláh and God and feel Their immense love for me?
- Did I have any inspiring thoughts?
- Did prayerful conversation arise naturally?

A man reflects about his own journey as well as what he sees happening in the world:

"In my early twenties while I was studying at university, I went on a week-long brown rice fast and had a spiritual awakening. Up to that time I had been an avowed atheist. This experience propelled me on a path of search which nine years later led me to accept the Bahá'í Faith.
"In addition to having been an atheist, I also did not believe in marriage, and a mentor shifted my orientation to relationships with the opposite sex. This adolescent period for me was a massive shift that put me on a track that I can be forever grateful for. I can now attribute this shift to the spiritual

susceptibilities that, according to researcher Lisa Miller, increase during these years and also to having a mentor.

"Many young men are following Jordan Peterson's work. The greatest number of these are intelligent young men who credit him with changing their lives. Many of these were atheists who gained new respect for religion and the need to take responsibility for their lives. He challenges them to new ways of thinking about topics like marriage, family life, finding your calling, and individuation.

"Now it's clearly emphasized in the Bahá'í community that young people can benefit hugely through the Junior Youth Spiritual Empowerment Program and the participation of older adolescents in tutoring the younger participants. These programs are exactly in line with what Dan Siegel, author of Brainstorm, who describes at length the research on the huge changes that take place in the adolescent brain, sees as something that our societies should provide all young people during this period."

Below is how Bahá'u'lláh instructed a son. It's a good thing there is a lifetime to strive for this behavior!

"Be generous in prosperity, and thankful in adversity. Be worthy of the trust of thy neighbor, and look upon him with a bright and friendly face. Be a treasure to the poor, an admonisher to the rich, an answerer to the cry of the needy, a preserver of the sanctity of thy pledge. Be fair in thy judgment, and guarded in thy speech. Be unjust to no man, and show all meekness to all men. Be as a lamp unto them that walk in darkness, a joy to the sorrowful, a sea for the thirsty, a haven for the distressed, an upholder and defender of the victim of oppression. Let integrity and uprightness distinguish all thine acts. Be a home for the stranger, a balm to the suffering, a tower of strength for the fugitive. Be eyes to the blind, and a guiding light unto the feet of the erring. Be an ornament to the countenance of truth, a crown to the brow of fidelity, a pillar of the temple of righteousness, a breath of life to the body of mankind, an ensign of the hosts of justice, a luminary above the horizon of virtue, a dew to the soil of the human heart, an ark on the ocean of knowledge, a sun in the heaven of bounty, a gem on the diadem of wisdom, a shining light in the firmament of thy generation, a fruit upon the tree of humility. We pray God to protect thee from the heat of jealousy and the cold of hatred. He verily is nigh, ready to answer."[26] Bahá'u'lláh

Be Brave and Arise

Bahá'u'lláh also reminds you of God's mercy and grace on the journey in this prayer:

"My God, Whom I worship and adore! I bear witness unto Thy unity and Thy oneness, and acknowledge Thy gifts, both in the past and in the present. Thou art the All-Bountiful, the overflowing showers of Whose mercy have rained down upon high and low alike, and the splendors of Whose grace have been shed over both the obedient and the rebellious.

"O God of mercy, before Whose door the quintessence of mercy hath bowed down, and round the sanctuary of Whose Cause loving-kindness, in its inmost spirit, hath circled, we beseech Thee, entreating Thine ancient grace, and seeking Thy present favor, that Thou mayest have mercy upon all who are the manifestations of the world of being, and to deny them not the outpourings of Thy grace in Thy days.

"All are but poor and needy, and Thou, verily, art the All-Possessing, the All-Subduing, the All-Powerful."[27] Bahá'u'lláh

Action

1. Take a video of people walking along a path or road. If their faces will show, please ask their permission first. Reflect on where they might be going to and why and reflect on your own spiritual journey so far. Where are you now? Where are you going?

2. Decide on one aspect about the Bahá'í Faith that you want to know more about, research it, and arrange for a group discussion about the topic, in person or over the internet.

3. Choose one aspect from the advice Bahá'u'lláh gave His son that you want to strengthen. Identify three specific actions you will take in the upcoming week to carry these out. Reflect on your progress at the end of the week. Then choose another aspect from the quotation and keep going.

4. Plant and tend a vegetable garden or other growing plants as a metaphor to reflect on the process of personal growth toward an important goal.

Reflection

1. What is my current state and stage of my spiritual life?
2. What is my current stage in seeking spiritual knowledge? What are my beliefs? What attracts me about living a spiritually based life?
3. What are some attributes of a "spiritual man"?
4. How does looking at my life as a journey of growth and development empower me?
5. How can I begin my journey when I often feel like I'm facing the task of climbing a tall, rugged mountain?
6. What qualities will reinforce my process?
7. When I consider the possibility of growing to be a Bahá'í or becoming stronger in practicing my spiritual beliefs, what are my thoughts, concerns, and joys?

3 – Navigating Spiritual Manhood—Some Preparation

Challenge: Sometimes it takes courage just to get out of bed, and even more to take steps forward.

Opportunity: Often I don't know the right directions and how to find the correct landmarks toward achieving spiritual manhood, but I'm willing to seek and discover them to the best of my ability.

Summary:
- I can be brave and humble in arising to meet the challenges of life—and I am not alone.
- Sometimes it's a tug-of-war figuring out Who is ultimately in charge, but it's usually best if it's God and not me; I do what I'm responsible for, but He's there to guide and help me.
- My positive thoughts breed positive words and actions.
- My negative thoughts breed negative words and actions.

More:

It takes courage and humility

Navigating your life journey well requires many character strengths. Two that may be particularly supportive are courage and humility. Striving to be a spiritual warrior, having confidence in God's help, and working for the betterment of global society, require both for sure. Consider these potential definitions:

> "Courage is taking brave and bold action voluntarily, defending what is right, or facing and completing a worthwhile challenge, even when experiencing fear, resistance, uncertainty, opposition, hardship, or possible danger."[28] S. M. Alexander

> "Humility is seeing the strengths, imperfections, needs, abilities, accomplishments, failures, and all other aspects of oneself and others in modest and realistic perspective; acting consistently according to principles, morals, and values rather than ego; and being willing to accept the knowledge, skills, and help of others."[29]

There is much striving, effort, service, and flexibility needed on the part of everyone in this world to live, grow, and accomplish important purposes. When you look at yourself, what qualities and strengths do you have that seem particularly suited to this time in history? What capacities will you need to develop so that you are a full participant in life, family, education, work, and service?

Free will and God's will

Humility also enables you to turn to God, to a Higher Power, in honor and praise and to ask for help and guidance. Turning to God as Chief Navigator powerfully and accurately guides the journey of your life. When you humbly recognize Him in that way, it aligns your choices to His guidance. When instead you insist you are solely in charge of all aspects of your life and can control all outcomes, usually trouble follows.

Being controlling often reflects a distrust not only in others but also in God. Turning your will over to the Will of God becomes a battle, and you may not want to see yourself as giving in. Here is an alternate perspective:

> "If it be Thy pleasure, make me to grow as a tender herb in the meadows of Thy grace, that the gentle winds of Thy will may stir me up and bend me into conformity with Thy pleasure, in such wise that my movement and my stillness may be wholly directed by Thee."[30] Bahá'u'lláh

Often underneath a wish to be in control is a deep—possibly unrecognized or unadmitted—fear of being found out to be inadequate, unworthy, or wrong. So, you may feel an intense need to be in charge and be right at times. When this occurs, there is no way to explore options, consider alternatives, defer to another, have more than one person be right about part of a matter, and so on. The creative experiences of praying, meditating, and consulting are blocked. Here are quotations that may expand your understanding of free will and God's Will:

> "Man's physical existence on this earth is a period during which the moral exercise of his free will is tried and tested in order to prepare his soul for the other worlds of God, and we must welcome affliction and tribulations as opportunities for improvement in our eternal selves. … [E]very human being is beset by such inner promptings as pride, greed, selfishness, lustful heterosexual or homosexual desires, to name a few which must be overcome, and overcome them we must if we are to fulfil

the purpose of our human existence."[31]   On behalf of the Universal House of Justice

"There are two factors, God's Will and our free will: we are not puppets, if we make mistakes we have to pay for them. ... [T]here are calamities for testing and for punishment—there are also accidents, plain cause and effect!"[32] On behalf of Shoghi Effendi

You are still responsible for taking action and doing your best. Following God's will includes:

- Aligning with spiritual guidance in the teachings
- Praying and meditating for inspiration
- Prayerfully consulting with others

The power of my thoughts

When you're navigating through your life journey, how you direct your thoughts has a powerful effect on the quality of your life and the outcome of your experiences. What you think about yourself, others, and everything else affects your perceptions, which in turn often affect your words, actions, and reactions.

When you think something negative, it causes your mood to darken, and you tend to see faults in yourself and others instead of noble qualities. In contrast, when your thoughts are positive and uplifting, your mood rises, and you're more likely to feel joyful and see positive aspects of your situation and the people you interact with.

As you become conscious of your thoughts and their effects, you can also begin to see what might be ego-driven and what is spiritual. For example, if a person thinks, "I have so much to do that my relationship partner and family are just going to have to wait", this may be the ego in charge.

Once you observe and recognize your thoughts, you then need to assess their validity and fact-find. Here are ways to do that:

"God has endowed man with reason that he may perceive what is true. If we insist that such and such a subject is not to be reasoned out and tested according to the established logical modes of the intellect, what is the use of the reason which God has given man? The eye is the organ of sense by which we view the world of outer phenomena; hearing is the faculty for distinguishing sounds; taste senses the properties of objects, such as bitter, sweet; smell detects and differentiates odors; touch reveals attributes of matter and perfects our communication with the outer world; yet after all, the circle and range of perception by the five senses is exceedingly limited. But the intellectual faculty of man is unlimited in its sphere of action."[33] 'Abdu'l-Bahá

Once you begin questioning whether the focus of your thoughts is true, you can then assess whether a spiritual principle might apply to shift your focus. For example, in the case of the person above, they could instead have their thoughts be, "My work is important, but so are relationships and service to others. It makes sense for me to moderate my work." This shift in thinking shifts the focus and the actions that follow.

In the absence of facts, human beings can, will, and do make up anything in their minds to fill in the gap. They then add significance or meaning to those thoughts and react to each other or other people based on them. Problems then arise because they speak and act based on what they have imagined and without fully understanding a situation. They might jump prematurely to conclusions; for example, seeing a relationship partner with another male and thinking they are being unfaithful. Below are some quotations about aspects of thoughts:

"O Thou the Compassionate God. Bestow upon me a heart which, like unto glass, may be illumined with the light of Thy love, and confer upon me thoughts which may change this world into a rose garden through the outpourings of heavenly grace."[34] 'Abdu'l-Bahá

"The reality of man is his thought, not his material body. The thought force and the animal force are partners. Although man is part of the animal creation, he possesses a power of thought superior to all other created beings.

"If a man's thought is constantly aspiring towards heavenly subjects then does he become saintly; if on the other hand his thought does not soar, but is directed downwards to center itself upon the things of this world, he grows more and more material until he arrives at a state little better than that of a mere animal."[35] 'Abdu'l-Bahá

"I charge you all that each one of you concentrate all the thoughts of your heart on love and unity. When a thought of war comes, oppose it by a stronger thought of peace. A thought of hatred must be destroyed by a more powerful thought of love. Thoughts of war bring destruction to all harmony, well-being, restfulness and content. Thoughts of love are constructive of brotherhood, peace, friendship, and happiness."[36] 'Abdu'l-Bahá

Some people react in their thoughts to something that happens and imagine negative scenarios for how they will respond. For example, they might imagine a parent becoming ill or dying when he or she schedules a medical test. Alternatively, they might dwell on something small and build up a high level of anxiety or fear of failure. Bahá'u'lláh often encourages people to be conscious of their unproductive thoughts and to seek protection from them:

"Praise be unto Thee, O our God, that Thou hast sent down unto us that which draweth us nigh unto Thee, and supplieth us with every good thing sent down by Thee in Thy Books and Thy Scriptures. Protect us, we beseech Thee, O my Lord, from the hosts of idle fancies and vain imaginations. Thou, in truth, art the Mighty, the All-Knowing."[37] Bahá'u'lláh

When thoughts seem to escalate in a negative direction or spin out of control, you can fill your mind with spiritual content or focus your attention in more positive directions. Examples include:

- Sing or listen to a Bahá'í quotation or prayer set to music (there are many available on the internet)
- Play a musical instrument
- Repeat Alláh'u'Abhá (God the All-Glorious) a few times [See Chapter 21.]
- Think of a memorized prayer or quotation
- Pray
- Sit and read spiritual guidance or something else uplifting
- Be out in nature or some peaceful place
- Do some type of vigorous activity or sport
- Carry out a thoughtful act of kindness for someone

The Bahá'í teachings encourage the power of positive thoughts. They can have a strong effect on your mood, accomplishments, relationships, and more. Consider the guidance below.

"If you desire with all your heart, friendship with every race on earth, your thought, spiritual and positive, will spread; it will become the desire of others, growing stronger and stronger, until it reaches the minds of all men."[38] 'Abdu'l-Bahá

[You will find additional content on this topic in Chapter 9, "Striving for My Mental Health".]

My potential spiritual destiny

As you navigate forward, you will begin to look to new outcomes in your life. You can fulfill an amazing spiritual destiny. Consider the vision in these quotations:

> "From amongst all mankind hath He chosen you, and your eyes have been opened to the light of guidance and your ears attuned to the music of the Company above; and blessed by abounding grace, your hearts and souls have been born into new life. Thank ye and praise ye God that the hand of infinite bestowals hath set upon your heads this gem-studded crown, this crown whose lustrous jewels will forever flash and sparkle down all the reaches of time.
> "To thank Him for this, make ye a mighty effort, and choose for yourselves a noble goal. Through the power of faith, obey ye the teachings of God, and let all your actions conform to His laws."[39] 'Abdu'l-Bahá

"Lift up your hearts above the present and look with eyes of faith into the future! Today the seed is sown, the grain falls upon the earth, but behold the day will come when it shall rise a glorious tree and the branches thereof shall be laden with fruit. Rejoice and be glad that this day has dawned, try to realize its power, for it is indeed wonderful! God has crowned you with honor and in your hearts has He set a radiant star; verily the light thereof shall brighten the whole world!"[40] 'Abdu'l-Bahá

"For any person, whether Bahá'í or not, his youthful years are those in which he will make many decisions which will set the course of his life. In these years, he is most likely to choose his life's work, complete his education, begin to earn his own living, marry, and start to raise his own family. Most important of all, it is during this period that the mind is most questing and that the spiritual values that will guide the person's future behavior are adopted. These factors present Bahá'í youth with their greatest opportunities, their greatest challenges, and their greatest tests—opportunities to truly apprehend the teachings of their Faith and to give them to their contemporaries, challenges to overcome the pressures of the world and to provide leadership for their and succeeding generations, and tests enabling them to exemplify in their lives the high moral standards set forth in the Bahá'í writings. Indeed, the Guardian wrote of the Bahá'í youth that it is they 'who can contribute so decisively to the virility, the purity, and the driving force of the life of the Bahá'í community, and upon whom must depend the future orientation of its destiny, and the complete unfoldment of the potentialities with which God has endowed it.'"[41] Universal House of Justice

Action

1. Choose one action that requires courage, pray for help to come from many sources and wisdom as you plan it, carefully consider your approach, consult with others as needed, and carry it out. Some examples might be:

    - Talk to someone new about a topic you are passionate about
    - Set up a job interview and prepare for it
    - Stand up respectfully to someone's prejudice in a way that gives them new perspectives
    - Ask a neighbor if they want your service with a specific task
    - Request a raise in salary from a manager at work or reach out to a new customer for your business
    - Defend someone from bullying
    - Request a parent or partner listen to your plans for your future

    Reflect afterward on what increased your courage and what the outcome of your words and actions were both internally for you and outwardly with the others involved.

2. Choose a positive quotation that reminds you of the importance of turning toward the will of God. Read it every morning and evening for a week and observe the effect on your mind, spirit, and actions. Consider recording your voice reading it, putting it to music, creating dance steps,

or developing some other physical action to reinforce the effect of the words.

3. Choose one or two ways of replacing negative thoughts with something uplifting and try the practice out every day for a week. Reflect on the effect of this practice and what methods you want to use going forward. You may reinforce your practice if you choose a specific physical action to do at the same time as doing the replacing. Examples: open your hand with the palm up or touch the side of your head.

Reflection

1. How can I courageously progress with my quest to be a Bahá'í man and not give up?
2. When am I able to be humble?
3. When am I able to rely on God?
4. When does it become difficult to turn my will over to God?
5. How can I cooperate with God instead of fighting Him?
6. When do positive thoughts empower me? What builds my self-confidence?
7. How could compassion apply in overcoming a fear of failure? What is the result when I practice compassion toward myself and others during times of struggle?
8. When do I let negative thoughts sabotage me? How can I prevent this from happening?
9. What is very effective in turning my thoughts from negative to positive?

4 – Creating a Support System—
The Value of a Safety Net

Challenge: I want to be strong enough to live my life on my own and by myself, otherwise I feel like I'm being weak.

Opportunity: Connecting myself to others provides relationships to sustain me; others can offer potential directions and assistance when I'm on my life quest and I'm feeling as if I'm lost in the woods without a compass.

Summary:
- The Bahá'í teachings speak of powerful Covenants that I can connect with that protect unity.
- Following the Bahá'í teachings and laws is empowering and contributes to living a life of integrity; however, carrying out these actions consistently is hard at times and a process that takes prayerful effort and time.
- Choosing to be a Bahá'í is a big decision that can be a stage of my journey when I am ready, but it doesn't mean that I'm instantly perfect.
- Living life relying only on myself is really, really difficult, so it's good to find people I trust to mentor and guide me, and this may include my father or a father figure.

More:

Clinging to the Covenant during the wild ride of life

God, the loving Creator of all, has promised humanity that we will never be without Divine Guidance. Each of the Founders of the world's major religions have offered that Guidance to help the world of humanity advance, according to our readiness. But a covenant is a two-way promise, and humanity's part in this miraculous and divine equation is to follow the Divine Guidance to the best of our ability.

Bahá'u'lláh—the most recent One to bring God's guidance to humanity—has provided us with a new religious system that is the means for our own personal salvation, and it will lead to true unity, peace, and justice in the world. The more faithful we are in following Bahá'u'lláh's guidance, the greater will be our ability to practice unity in all parts of our lives, including within our marriages and families, and to facilitate the unity of the entire human race. It's really quite profound!

'Abdu'l-Bahá describes the Covenant as the "Universal Balance" and as the "Magnet of God's grace". In the same paragraph, He says:

> "The power of the Covenant is as the heat of the sun which quickeneth and promoteth the development of all created things on earth. The light of the Covenant...is the educator of the minds, the spirits, the hearts and souls of men."[42] 'Abdu'l-Bahá

There is another kind of covenant recognized in the Bahá'í Faith. Bahá'u'lláh set up a system that safeguards the unity of its followers instead of them dividing up into disputing factions. He promised in a written Covenant that this system would provide ongoing Divine guidance to humanity, past the point of Bahá'u'lláh's life on this earth. This Covenant ensures the integrity of the Divine guidance that flowed from Bahá'u'lláh to all mankind: first through 'Abdu'l-Bahá (His appointed successor and interpreter, The Center of the Covenant), then through Shoghi Effendi (the Guardian), and it is now shared and illuminated through the institution of the Universal House of Justice. This institution asks us to be conscious of the "exceptional and glorious stage in humanity's spiritual evolution initiated by the Covenant" and speaks of this consciousness as being "the wellspring of the most exquisite celebratory joy."[43] Universal House of Justice

Maintaining unity amongst ourselves, then, is part of our commitment to Bahá'u'lláh and His Covenant to protect the unity of the Bahá'í Faith. A global Administrative Order has emerged from this guidance and leadership.

As you powerfully align with the unifying forces of this Covenant, and as you understand and follow the Bahá'í teachings, you are empowered to make better choices in all aspects of your life. To the best of your ability, you will live a life of integrity and coherence that includes your beliefs, actions, words, feelings, and commitments aligning with spiritual reality. Consider this guidance:

> "No doubt very great responsibilities rest upon the shoulders of all the Bahá'ís...for they are the custodians of the teachings and order of Bahá'u'lláh. They will find themselves tested from within and without, but tests, like a storm that shakes a tree, only drive its roots deeper and make it more determined to live and grow."[44] On behalf of Shoghi Effendi

Be Brave and Arise

As you develop a spiritual relationship with the protagonists of the Covenant—The Báb, Bahá'u'lláh, 'Abdu'l-Bahá, Shoghi Effendi, and the Universal House of Justice—it empowers your spiritual manhood. You are linked to the limitless stream of guidance for your life. Here is one man's perspective about the Covenant:

"When you fall in love with Bahá'u'lláh, you will find yourself attracted to 'Abdu'l-Bahá. When you fall in love with 'Abdu'l-Bahá, you will find yourself attracted to Shoghi Effendi. When you fall in love with Shoghi Effendi, you will want to know all about the Universal House of Justice. When you come to understand the function of the Universal House of Justice, you will come to love the entire Administrative Order.

"Love grows into faith and trust. You will naturally want to follow the guidance of Bahá'u'lláh and the Institutions He established, even when their instructions run counter to your desires. In return, the spiritual qualities you love will flow back into your soul allowing it to live forever. ...

"When I was a young Bahá'í, for example, the only thing I knew about Shoghi Effendi was that he wrote that section in 'The Advent of Divine Justice' about chastity. I never gave myself the chance to fall in love with him as a source of love and inspiration the way I did with Bahá'u'lláh and 'Abdu'l-Bahá. I fooled myself into thinking that chastity was a 'Shoghi Effendi Law' rather than a law of Bahá'u'lláh. This allowed me to mentally break the link between Bahá'u'lláh and Shoghi Effendi, and from there it was easier to break the law. Now that I am... married, and chastity has taken on a more subtle meaning, I find that I am often awed and inspired by the tenderness and sensitivity with which Shoghi Effendi presented Bahá'u'lláh's laws to an immature Community. It was the shame of my own disobedience that cut me off from the healing understanding he had to offer. [See Chapters 12-15 on "Striving for My Sexual Health".]

"One last clarification of the Covenant: It is not enough to fall in love with Bahá'u'lláh as a really nice, really smart guy. Bahá'u'lláh claims to be a Manifestation of God. He claims to know us and our spiritual needs better than we know ourselves. If you never really come to understand and love Bahá'u'lláh as The Divine Physician, then there will be very little to bind you to the laws of the Covenant when they don't suit your personal desires."[45]

A man reflects on his choices:

"Late in my high school years and in the first part of university, I pulled myself out of the Bahá'í community. It didn't seem like my parents were living according to the teachings, and I thought if I disconnected, I could have a space where my character and who I was could develop before anything else. Intentionally, I did not restrict myself to any boundaries. I felt I had learned the restrictions from blindly following people in my family.

"Naturally, this led to some unhealthy habits such as drinking, smoking cigarettes and weed, using pornography, and having multiple sexual partners, sometimes to excess. Through further reflection on my noble goals, and assessing the people I surrounded myself with, I pivoted back to the Faith. This time I knew in my heart and had strong confidence in the importance of the laws of God. I also found a Bahá'í who I could talk to for support. Within a few months, I pulled out of the crowd that I was spending a lot of time with, eliminated drinking and smoking, and ended an unhealthy relationship. Explicit images took the longest to move past, and I still fall back occasionally. I have spent a lot of time watching different TED.com talks, documentaries, reflecting on this topic, and conditioning my spirituality to have my thoughts in check.

"I'm glad that this experience has contributed to my firmness in the Covenant and new understanding. I wish though that somehow, I could have achieved this without going through an 'astray-phase'. My experiences have been a challenge in that I had to share them somewhat with potential relationship partners, and they are now somewhat negatively affecting me early in a marriage to someone with few life experiences like this. I think if I'd been involved more in community service or done a year of service away from home, I might have made better choices."

Here is a perspective to consider:

"I think it's important to say that when we look at the Bahá'í teachings and laws that they are aspirational. None of us (except 'Abdu'l-Bahá) gets all of it right all the time. We humans are a work in progress. The important thing is to strive to do our best, connect with others, and pray. We try each day to stay connected with God and with each other, and we each do our best and make our contributions."

Here is encouraging guidance:

"Turn thy sight unto thyself, that thou mayest find Me standing within thee, mighty, powerful and self-subsisting."[46] Bahá'u'lláh

"Bahá'ís must make the utmost effort to uphold Bahá'í standards, no matter how difficult they may seem at first. Such efforts will be made easier if the youth will understand that the laws and standards of the Faith are meant to free them from untold spiritual and moral difficulties in the same way that a proper appreciation of the laws of nature enables one to live in harmony with the forces of the planet."[47] On behalf of the Universal House of Justice

This point of following laws and teachings keeping you free from misery is a vital one. You don't have to do everything the hard way!

Turning to God and Bahá'u'lláh

Part of your support system is developing the practice of turning to God and Bahá'u'lláh with all your struggles and joys until it becomes an automatic or innate part of who you are. When a test comes, especially when it involves you or people close to you behaving in ways that don't align with the Bahá'í teachings, your own relationship with Bahá'u'lláh can provide protection. Sometimes you may have to fiercely and courageously defend your connection to keep it intact. Pause for a moment and consider Who Bahá'u'lláh is for you as you read these words:

"... [R]eflect with due solemnity upon the redemptive purpose of the life of the most precious Being ever to have drawn breath on this planet."[48] Universal House of Justice

"... [T]his is a special time for a rendezvous of the soul with the Source of its light and guidance, a time to turn to Bahá'u'lláh, to seek to obtain a deeper appreciation of His purpose, to renew allegiance to Him. This is a time of retreat to one's innermost being, to the dwelling-place of the Spirit of Baha, that interior to which He summons us when He says: 'Turn thy sight unto thyself, that thou mayest find Me standing within thee, mighty, powerful and self-subsisting.' This is a time for recommitment to the Covenant, for rededication to duty, for revitalizing the energy for teaching, the 'most meritorious of all deeds.'"[49] Universal House of Justice

Part of turning to God and Bahá'u'lláh is regular prayer. You can use your own words as spiritual conversation and also regularly read the revealed prayers from books or that you access electronically through websites or apps.

Below is guidance about praying.

"Shouldst thou recite any of the revealed prayers, and seek assistance from God with thy face turned towards Him, and implore Him with devotion and fervor, thy need will be answered."[50] 'Abdu'l-Bahá

"The believers, particularly the young ones, should therefore fully realize the necessity of praying. For prayer is absolutely indispensable to their inner spiritual development, and this…is the very foundation and purpose of the religion of God."[51] Shoghi Effendi

"You have asked whether our prayers go beyond Bahá'u'lláh: It all depends whether we pray to Him directly and through Him to God. We may do both and also can pray directly to God, but our prayers would certainly be more effective and illuminating if they are addressed to Him through His Manifestation, Bahá'u'lláh.

"Under no circumstances, however, we can, while repeating the prayers, insert the name Bahá'u'lláh where the word 'God' is used. This would be tantamount to a blasphemy."[52] On behalf of Shoghi Effendi

"… We must not be rigid about praying; there is not a set of rules governing it; the main thing is we must start out with the right concept of God, the Manifestation, the Master, the Guardian—we can turn, in thought, to any one of them when we pray. For instance you can ask Bahá'u'lláh for some thing, or, thinking of Him, ask God for it. The same is true of the Master or the Guardian. You can turn in thought to either of them and then ask their intercession, or pray direct to God. As long as you don't confuse their stations, and make them all equal, it does not matter much how you orient your thoughts."[53] On behalf of Shoghi Effendi

Here is one man's story about his challenges and successes with prayer after wandering away from the Bahá'í teachings and coming back:

"I struggled a lot when I was younger, coming back into the Bahá'í Faith. When I would pray, I just didn't feel worthy. I felt a lot of shame, and I would try and pray, and it would be like the prayers got stuck in my throat. As I would try and pray, I would be like, 'God isn't even listening to this. Why would He? He doesn't even care. Who cares about my stupid little prayer?! I'm such a failure.' It was such an immature idea of God, this big Daddy-Father Figure God as opposed to this all-inclusive Energy that vibrates every molecule, and that vibration is Love itself and that by praying we are harmonizing our inner vibrations with the outer vibrations of the Universe, and Light, and Love, and music and song and power and oxygen and leaves. My re-definition of spirituality is to re-affirm those ideas of God, the Creator, and not scowling Daddy God, disapproving God."[54]

As you develop the ability to turn to God in prayer, it strengthens your muscles of respect for authority, which depending on your age and circumstances, could include your parents, the government, Bahá'í Spiritual Assemblies, and the Universal House of Justice. It's not easy to respect authority in a world where many examples of abuse of authority exist. What is most important is learning to trust in Bahá'u'lláh's wisdom when He asks you to obey His laws and do your best to follow them from the age of 15 onward. You will grow to know the Bahá'í teachings as you read books, participate in community life, and use websites like www.bahai.org.

Turning to my father

Everyone has a father who participated in giving them life. How involved he has been in your life and how healthy he was or is in his functioning with you, are influencing factors in who you are. If you have a good relationship with your father now, he may be a key part of your support system.

Many men who experience an absent father can find father-like guidance from another relative, foster father, or other male adult, so you can also look to that relationship to understand your journey with manhood. These men may also be part of your support team. Where it says "father" in this section, please look at your biological father and anyone who has played a fathering role with you.

You may find it easy to follow authority and obey laws. Alternatively, you might feel strong rebellion and resistance to being "told" by others what to do. Sometimes this relates to a person's relationship with a parent, especially a father. Here is one man's view:

"Let's face it. Most of us have God, Parents, and Authority all squashed together in our hearts and our subconscious minds. Unless our parents did a perfect job when we were experimenting with counter-dependence at the age of two, we have doubts about any God/Parent/Authority figure being able to love us when we disagree with them. When we become Bahá'ís, that love/hate relationship often gets transferred onto the Assembly and/or any symbolic member of the Community. The ironic thing, of course, is that every institution is made up of individuals who have their own issues with God/Parent/Authority."[55]

Who your father was or was not for you growing up also shaped and influenced your view of yourself and your perceptions about your masculinity. Consider this perspective:

"Your father had traits that you liked, and traits that you did not like. He did things you approved of, and things of which you did not approve. You may have respected him, or you may have been embarrassed to be his son. He was good or bad in his marriage, his fathering, his work, and his ethics. No matter what the story is or was for you, you were molded by this relationship. You became the man you are today because you adopted the things you admired about him, or because you rejected those things you didn't like about him. Maybe you didn't want to be like him but you didn't make the effort to be different, and now you do those same things he did that you hated so much. … We become the men we are today because of, and in spite of, our fathers. …

"A man is not a complete man until he has come to terms with his relationship with his father. This is a major part of making the transition from being a boy to becoming a man. You do so when you acknowledge what you've gotten from your father, when you celebrate the good things you've received and admit the bad ones as well. Forgive your father for not being perfect, and finally meet him as the man you have become instead of as his boy. The act of forgiveness frees both of you. The son becomes free to be a man, the father knows his son has finally become a man."[56] Howard J. Fox

Below, a man observes his challenges with growing up with an alcoholic father and the effect on his spiritual life now.

"When you see the rage, remorse, and self-destruction in the person you are supposed to look up to, you don't see somebody taking care of themselves and improving day by day but rather deteriorating. That's imprinted on you. And on the other hand, you don't have the dad saying, 'You've got this'. They drag you down and tell you stuff that's awful. As an adult, it makes it hard to trust, and that includes God and it includes male authority figures, even Bahá'u'lláh. You can believe it for everyone else, but you count yourself out. I have to periodically strip the Faith down to its essence and re-learn it. The feeling of faith is not something I can ever take for granted, and I have to constantly re-build that."[57]

Understanding your father's life, including his strengths and weaknesses, can give you insights into yourself. As in the story above, seeking this understanding can also influence how you handle your spiritual life and who you turn to for wise input. A father reflects on the process of raising boys and his own son to manhood:

"Many boys and men struggle to cope with their identity in a world that can easily confuse males. Primarily, many don't know how to relate to girls and women at a time when gender roles are being redefined. Coupled with that, they appear to be frightened of commitment in a world where so many marriages are short-lived, and Bahá'ís are meant to see marriage as an eternal bond. It's also a world where faith is often marginalized by secular thinking. Although religious girls and women face the same challenge of trying to live spiritually in a material-obsessed world, males seem to struggle more with this challenge.

"So, boys must face up to this battle early on. They need male mentors, especially their fathers, but also their mothers, who have a good take on the forces impacting modern society. Importantly, they need to see their own parents living what they preach—remaining happily married and together, and demonstrating what equality looks like in their daily lives. Hopefully, they see their fathers making sacrifices for their wives' careers; see their fathers playing a strongly active role within the family, not just playing the part of the family breadwinner; and they see their fathers fully respecting their mothers. Hopefully, too, they witness both parents' commitment to a spiritual way of life, accept prayer as a normal thing, and see the difference between their parents' lifestyle and that of others'.

"Boys also need to be treated differently from girls. Girls mostly do what they are told in Bahá'í children's classes; boys are less compliant. At least, that was my observation when our children were going through childhood and early adolescence. The girls were generally happier and more relaxed about performing in front of an audience.

"Boys tend to be more physical, and physical pursuits are not just simply meaningless rough and tumbles. They can be in a different kind of classroom where they learn in a physical way. Boys don't generally like to be put into a classroom straitjacket. My own son, for example, hated being in a choir or drama presentation. He was much happier making things with wood, doing practical things, or riding a motorbike, even though the latter was a big test for his parents who feared for his life. Interestingly, it was a wise police officer who helped mature his behavior by showing him pictures of fatal motorbike crashes. But we had enough faith in him to let him have a motorbike. We didn't try to crush that interest. In pursuing their interest in physical activities, boys are likely to meet like-minded but wiser men who can be a big influence on them. Learning doesn't take place only by reading books and studying on an iPad or excelling in academic studies. In the same way, spiritual teachings can be learned by doing physical things—in some ways, for some boys, that is their preferred method of learning.

"In an especially significant way, it's important for boys to rebel. Not just by riding a motorbike but maybe by rebelling against their parents' faith, the one they dearly want their sons to follow. Adolescence can be a time of rebellion and seeking independence, and suppressing this may draw teenage boys away permanently from their parents' faith.

"With all of this, I'm trying to get across the point that boys need to find in their own lives the role models who can prepare them for grown-up relationships in a world of stunning change. For Bahá'ís, the best examples are their parents and their Bahá'í community, but Bahá'ís don't have a monopoly on wisdom, and boys can learn much from people outside their faith community. Nevertheless, Bahá'ís have a faith which is better equipped for the modern, changing world and it's their responsibility to equip their children for that world."

Where others can step in

Part of your spiritual journey is having a support "team" of people also committed to living a spiritually based life. They can share life wisdom from their experiences, provide a positive model of how to live life, give you ideas for applying spiritual principles to your circumstances, and offer new insights about your life and choices.

Be Brave and Arise

Supportive people in your life might include one or more of those listed below if they are striving to be warriors of the light.

- Friends
- Parents
- Siblings
- Older youth
- Leader at work
- Spiritual community
- Youth group
- Bahá'í Spiritual Assembly
- Teacher
- Doctor
- Coach
- Social worker
- Support group
- Counselor

It's likely you will have many mentors of a variety of ages and skills throughout your life, some for brief periods and some for longer stretches of time. People have many responsibilities in their lives, so respect their time and availability. If they cannot meet with you, then please go on and ask someone else. When you look at who is in your life now, you could:

- Make a list of your current challenges in one column. In a second column, note the names of trustworthy people or groups you see who might have insights about each of these challenges or who may have lived through similar ones and have wisdom to share.
- Approach a person or group and request that they meet with you to consult about something from your life; if they agree, set a date and time.
- If possible, pray with those you meet with, share bravely and honestly with them that you are looking for solutions to a problem, and consult with them about it; come to an agreement for your next steps.
- Pray for courage and move forward.
- Stay in communication with those you met with to share your progress and to consult about potentially changing course as needed.

Those who see the best in you, encourage you, respond to your questions and requests, and aid you to achieve your best are priceless treasures. More often you will be looking to a man to mentor and guide you through your journey. However, it's also good to consider having a female guide at times in developing relationship and character strengths and for learning how to treat females with respect and equality. You may also think about others that *you* could mentor or support, as this provides a powerful way for both of you to grow spiritually and socially.

Be Brave and Arise

Remember that it takes courage and humility to ask someone to accompany you. It can also take perseverance to find people to assist you in a world full of busy people. As you value support from others, pray for it, and seek it, you are most likely to achieve it.

Action

1. Use computer tools, videos, or art or building supplies and create a visual representation of your spiritual journey so far and your connection to the Covenants. Imagine what you would like your spiritual life to be in the future and add that in. This quotation may inspire you: "... [M]an must travel in the way of God. Day by day he must endeavor to become better, his belief must increase and become firmer, his good qualities and his turning to God must be greater, the fire of his love must flame more brightly; then day by day he will make progress, for to stop advancing is the means of going back."[58] 'Abdu'l-Bahá

2. Identify the areas of your life where support or assistance from others would be valuable. Take action to locate people and make the necessary arrangements to meet and collaborate.

3. Find a recent letter or quotation from the Universal House of Justice (some are in this book) and identify an action you can take in response to it and carry out the action. What was the outcome? If you find it difficult to study the guidance by yourself, please gather a group and study it together, using this encouragement:

"It is heartening to note that the friends are approaching the study of the messages of the Universal House of Justice related to the Plan with such diligence. The level of discussion generated as they strive to put into practice the guidance received, and to learn from experience, is impressive. We cannot help noticing, however, that achievements tend to be more enduring in those regions where the friends strive to understand the totality of the vision conveyed in the messages, while difficulties often arise when phrases and sentences are taken out of context and viewed as isolated fragments. The institutions and agencies of the Faith should help the believers to analyze but not reduce, to ponder meaning but not dwell on words, to identify distinct areas of action but not compartmentalize. We realize that this is no small task. Society speaks more and more in slogans. We hope that the habits the friends are forming in study circles to work with full and complex thoughts and to achieve understanding will be extended to various spheres of activity."[59] Universal House of Justice

Resources Note: As you reflect throughout the book on actions to take in your life, good references for you are collections of letters from the Universal House of Justice. For example, extensive guidance is published in a book called *Framework for Action, Selected Messages of The Universal House of Justice and Supplementary Material, 2006-2016*. The entire book is available for download at this link: https://www.bahai.org/library/authoritative-texts/the-universal-house-of-justice/framework-action/.

Reflection

1. What is my understanding of the Covenants? How do they influence my life? Influence unity?
2. Reflecting on my current choices and the state my life is in: What do I yearn to be different so that my present and my future as a man are powerful and effective?
3. What is currently challenging me in my spiritual life?
4. How can I know whether the Bahá'í Faith is a good choice for me?
5. Who will my support team include now? In the future?
6. How could my father (or father-figure) assist me on my journey? What healing work do I need to do around that relationship?
7. How is my support team a safety net to catch me when I slip and fall? Do I need to strengthen it?
8. How can I draw on the strengths of others and not try to navigate alone?
9. Are there people who look to me at times for support and guidance? What do I learn from mentoring them?

Part 2: Challenging Myself— Growing My Light Force

5 - Understanding My Best and Building from My Not-Yet-Best

Challenge: Sometimes I resist looking too closely at myself, so I don't trigger self-importance or the despair that comes from not feeling good enough to meet other people's standards.

Opportunity: Striving to live a life of integrity and growth can empower me to be my best self.

Summary:
- Doing a daily checkup and cleanup keeps my life and relationships ever improving.
- Understanding myself, including my character, comes from observing my thoughts, actions, and interactions with others.
- Keeping my eyes on my own behavior stops me comparing myself to others.
- Whew, integrity is tough—always trying to live up to high standards takes a lot of effort—but the rewards are amazing.

More:

Establishing a daily practice of accountability

To be successful in your quest to be a spiritual man, it's wise to keep improving yourself. Bahá'u'lláh requires everyone to review their behavior and spiritual efforts daily. In the beginning of establishing this practice, you may be resistant, concerned that doing this self-review will trigger shame or feelings of failure. You may simply have to trust that this is a wise practice until you begin to see how it helps you grow.

Initially, if it feels unnatural or overly difficult to assess yourself daily, experiment to determine what timing works best for you. Be cautious about allowing too much time between your actions and your review, as you may forget details of what you did well, or you may justify or forget any negative actions. Gradually increase the frequency until you achieve a daily practice. Here is the guidance:

"Bring thyself to account each day...to give account for thy deeds."[60]
Bahá'u'lláh

"Every day, in the morning when arising you should compare today with yesterday and see in what condition you are. If you see your belief is stronger and your heart more occupied with God and your love increased and your freedom from the world greater then thank God and ask for the increase of these qualities. You must begin to pray and repent for all that you have done which is wrong, and you must implore and ask for help and assistance that you may become better than yesterday so that you may continue to make progress."[61] 'Abdu'l-Bahá

A man shares how he began bringing himself to account and how this has evolved in his life over time:

"I started off by looking at all the bad things I had done during the day, feeling bad about them, promising to try and do better, and going to sleep each night. After a few months of this, I began to feel really bad about myself. After all, I was looking at all the things I was doing wrong. I would count the sweets I had, the helpings of ice cream, or root beer, forgetting the vegetables I had enjoyed. Then, a month or so later, I realized that if I were an accountant, and all I was looking at was my expenditures, I'd be a pretty lousy accountant. I needed to take into account all the good things I had done, too. So began my daily look at all the good things I had done, all the bad things I had done, all the really good things I had done, and all the really not so good things I had done during the day. As long as the bad things were balanced by the good stuff, I was feeling pretty ok with myself.

But somehow, way in the deep recesses of my brain, I began to look at it all as some sort of cosmic balance. Bad things taken care of by the good? Well, if I have a few extra good things in the balance, then I can have some fun with the less than good things, right? I can enjoy that extra helping of ice cream. Not quite. This led to my pausing throughout the day and thinking to myself, 'Oh, I'm going to have to account for this at the end of the day. Do I still want to do it?' And this, naturally, led to a change in my own behavior. ... [That] is when my life really began to change.

What about now? Well, the basics haven't really changed all that much, except that a lot of my questioning during the day is more habitual by now. I try not to judge myself, leaving that to God, but still try to judge my own actions. One thing, though. that has changed is my actual looking back over my day in a more detailed sort of way. Now, at least once a day, I try to actively recall as much as I can about my day. I think about how I woke up, whether I was refreshed or not, and what I did when I got out of bed. I think about washing up, making breakfast, what I ate. I think about walking my son to the bus, and what we discussed on the way. I actually try to go through most of my steps, my thoughts, my reactions. I try to consciously recall my entire day and look back at it objectively, remembering what I did, what I enjoyed, and what I would like to do in the future. And I find that I am more aware of my life. I remember more of what I have done. ...

"Taking the time to actively look back on my day has given me a greater awareness of the continuity of my life. It has helped me see where I have come from, where I am heading, and led me to a greater appreciation of what I truly value. ... Too often, I think we live unconsciously, letting the days drift by, unaware of any particular one, but taking the time to bring myself to account every day has helped me to be more aware of each day". [62]

This can be your daily focus:

- See where you succeeded with your spiritual goals and where you appreciate your progress and successes
- Think about where you may have made a mistake or a choice you regret
- Assess where you may have hurt or harmed others
- Consider how to address issues or consequences; you might have a mess to clean up and a request to make to God for grace, mercy, forgiveness, and guidance

The benefits from a daily review can be that you:

- Feel encouraged by how you chose and carried out your words and actions
- Learn from those experiences
- Make better choices the next time
- Become aware of choices you may make automatically
- Improve your overall physical, mental, emotional, and spiritual well-being
- Clarify what to be grateful for in your life

As you look at your interactions with others, there are these reminders:

"Lay not on any soul a load which ye would not wish to be laid upon you, and desire not for anyone the things ye would not desire for yourselves. This is My best counsel unto you, did ye but observe it." [63] Bahá'u'lláh

"Never is it the wish of 'Abdu'l-Bahá to see any being hurt, nor will He make anyone to grieve; for man can receive no greater gift than this, that he rejoice another's heart. I beg of God that ye will be bringers of joy, even as are the angels in Heaven."[64] 'Abdu'l-Bahá

When you get stuck in only seeing errors or negative behavior when you do a daily review, consider this:

"There is nothing more harmful to the individual—and also to society than false humility which is hypocritical, and hence unworthy of a true Bahá'í. The true believer is one who is conscious of his strength as well as of his weakness, and who, fully availing himself of the manifold opportunities and blessings which God gives him, strives to overcome his defects and weaknesses and this by means of a scrupulous adherence to all the laws and commandments revealed by God through His Manifestation."[65] On behalf of Shoghi Effendi

Someone comments:

"I'm focused on the present moment, staying true to myself, whole within my own core, doing an accounting every day and doing the work around that. I'm grateful to be getting better acquainted with myself through the process too. I'm finding that through natural reflection following community service, honest sharing and humble learning occurs, in a palatable way. I feel an acceptance for who I am, as I am, which fosters the natural desire to be better and work on those areas to improve myself."

Examining how I treat others

During your daily review of your words and actions, notice how well they reflected character strengths. Were you able to be truthful? Courteous? Dependable? Respectful? Character qualities interact and balance each other, increasing your ability to treat others well. The story below illustrates how humility and compassion can effectively balance purposefulness, orderliness, excellence, and dependability.

"A group of eye doctors worked on a project to improve their overall performance through values-based leadership. They realized enhancing their humility and compassion would improve their ability to listen to patients, nurses, and fellow doctors.

"One of the most skilled doctors in the group struggled to interact well with others. He was easily purposeful, orderly, excellent, and dependable with surgery. However, others avoided him and would not listen to him, because he was often truthful to the point of being insulting. He was convinced he was right, his ideas were the best, and people should be willing to hear the complete truth.

"Concerned about the dynamics of what was happening, a team member suggested the doctor try being compassionate and consider other people's feelings before giving advice or criticism. He also encouraged the doctor to practice humility and let others speak and present ideas first, which might make it easier for them to listen to his. With reflection and practice, the doctor saw the wisdom in these new approaches. With improved character-based interactions, he began being included in more discussions with colleagues. More patients also sought his services."

Often when you look back on an interaction with someone, you quickly spot where you could have practiced a character quality like flexibility more effectively. Sometimes, however, you might feel uncertain about how you went wrong. You may get clarity by asking yourself some direct and in-depth questions related to whatever quality seems to be appropriate. For example, you might consider the questions below about how you practice the quality of truthfulness, as well as the helper quality of compassion.

- When communicating, am I careful to stick to the facts and not make up details?
- Do I withhold important information, or do I leave out key details because they might affect how others view me?
- Do I justify lying under some circumstances? When? Why?
- When I'm truthful, do I sometimes hurt others' feelings by forgetting to be compassionate?
- Do I take enough time to search for the truth when solving problems, instead of rushing to an easy solution?

Below is another example of questions to ask yourself during self-review after participating in a social activity, this time about friendliness and its helper qualities of respect and unity.

- Was I friendly to only a few people and ignored or stayed away from those I did not know?

- Did I include respect in reaching out to someone new?
- Did I misuse friendliness in a self-centered way to impress others?
- Was I sensitive about including everyone to build unity?
- Did I pretend to be friendly to gain something from someone?
- Did I have a meaningful conversation with someone? How did the person respond?

You can also ask yourself these more general questions:

- How well did I meet my behavior and character goals today (or this week…)?
- What character qualities did I practice well?
- When did my actions cause hurt feelings or some other negative outcome?
- What could I have done better?
- What did I have control over? What factors could I not control?
- What do I want to do differently tomorrow?

A trusted friend or relative may also assist you in reflecting on your behavior, not with the intent to criticize, but with the goal of mutually determining what and how you can improve.

[See Chapter 8, "Developing My Character".]

My mission: A high level of integrity

The world needs your example of living the Bahá'í teachings with integrity. Integrity is achieving a state of balance and wholeness in your life and character, by acting in accord with civil laws and deepest beliefs, highest values and principles, and commitments. It includes aligning your words and actions.

Throughout your life, people will ask you to live up to or achieve certain standards of behavior. Parents, teachers, employers, and relationship or marriage partners all likely have their perspectives on how you should behave, and hopefully these are positive goals. The media throws in yet other perspectives. Spiritual teachings add in another standard, which may or may not align with what others want from you. Part of being a spiritual man is becoming clear about your standards for yourself that you will strive to meet, and hopefully you use spiritual teachings as your best behavior guide. The more you align your words and actions with your chosen standard, the greater your sense of inner integrity or wholeness.

One way to assess your level of integrity is to notice the effect in your life and on your soul as you give your word to carry out actions and then keep your promises through deeds. Here is guidance:

"In all matters, great or small, word must be the complement of deed, and deed the companion of word: each must supplement, support and reinforce the other."[66] Shoghi Effendi

Here are some examples:

- When you say, "I'll call you tomorrow", you do it
- You commit to work with someone on a task, and you show up or contact the person to re-schedule
- You pay your bills when they are due and strive to minimize debts
- You are on time for appointments
- You commit to saying your Daily Obligatory Prayer and achieve the goal [See Chapter 6 "Developing Spiritual Habits".]

As you strive for integrity, you will keep your word more and more each day. When you see you cannot carry out something you promised to fulfill, then be in communication so that a new agreement is reached. This keeps your life in a better state of integrity. Here is one person's experience:

"At one point in my adult life I was taking a nine-month training course and was assigned an integrity coach to guide me throughout. Each day I had to look at my commitments and whether I was keeping them, or if something was missing. If something was undone, I had to address it. Once a week I checked in with my coach to review progress, and together we built reminders and processes into my life, so I didn't lose track of what I promised. It was like being in an intense physical exercise training program for getting ready to run a marathon. I had many muscles to stretch and strengthen to ensure my word and my actions aligned. While it was very challenging learning these practices, they have served me well in my work and community service ever since."

Be Brave and Arise

Bahá'u'lláh's counsel to you is in the quotation below.

"Beware, O people of Bahá, lest ye walk in the ways of them whose words differ from their deeds. Strive that ye may be enabled to manifest to the peoples of the earth the signs of God, and to mirror forth His commandments. Let your acts be a guide unto all mankind, for the professions of most men, be they high or low, differ from their conduct."[67] Bahá'u'lláh

This quotation contains a be brave and arise opportunity in it:

"How often the beloved Master ['Abdu'l-Bahá] was heard to say: Should each one of the friends take upon himself to carry out, in all its integrity and implications, only one of the teachings of the Faith, with devotion, detachment, constancy and perseverance and exemplify it in all his deeds and pursuits of life, the world would become another world and the face of the earth would mirror forth the splendors of the Abhá Paradise. Consider what marvelous changes would be effected if the beloved of the Merciful conducted themselves, both in their individual and collective capacities, in accordance with the counsels and exhortations which have streamed from the Pen of Glory."[68] Shoghi Effendi

Assessing how you are doing with practicing integrity can be part of your daily self-review. Consider these perspectives from two authors:

"A person's word can have value and power or it can be cheap and meaningless. Persons of integrity have a reputation for keeping their word. What creates a strong reputation for integrity is behavior that is congruent, or consistent, with what we say. People listen to those who keep their word, and people organize their own behavior around promises made. ... When [people] keep their word to each other, predictability results, which creates security and trust. They can rely on each other."[69] S. G. Bender

"A person has integrity when there is no gap between intent and behavior...when he or she is whole, seamless, the same—inside and out. I call this 'congruence.' And it is congruence—not compliance—that will ultimately create credibility and trust.

"People who are congruent act in harmony with their deepest values and beliefs. They walk their talk. When they feel they ought to do something, they do it. They're not driven by extrinsic forces, including the opinions of others of the expediency of the moment. The voice they listen and respond to is the quiet voice of conscience. … When you consistently demonstrate inner congruence to your belief system and to principles, you inspire trust in both professional and personal relationships. People feel you are strong, solid, and dependable, and that you are committed to live in ways that are certain to bring positive results and validate their confidence in you."[70] Stephen M. R. Covey

Living a life of integrity takes practice and isn't easy. It's also exhausting at times, and then you must take time to breathe, balance your well-being, and simplify your life where possible. You will notice there are many opportunities in your life to be out of integrity. You will also notice, however, that as you strengthen these muscles, your self-respect, confidence, and trustworthiness grow. You feel happier with who you are, as well as with how others treat and trust you.

Eyes on my own choices

Staying focused on your own behavior and responsibility is important, as is not comparing your journey to that of others, positively or negatively. Here is guidance:

"If we Bahá'ís cannot attain to cordial unity among ourselves, then we fail to realize the main purpose for which the Báb, Bahá'u'lláh and the Beloved Master lived and suffered. In order to achieve this cordial unity one of the first essentials insisted on by Bahá'u'lláh and 'Abdu'l-Bahá is that we resist the natural tendency to let our attention dwell on the faults and failings of others rather than on our own. Each of us is responsible for one life only, and that is our own. Each of us is immeasurably far from being 'perfect as our heavenly father is perfect' and the task of perfecting our own life and character is one that requires all our attention, our will-power and energy. If we allow our attention and energy to be taken up in efforts to keep others right and remedy their faults, we are wasting precious time."[71] On behalf of Shoghi Effendi

Of course, this focus on your own responsibilities is different than the importance of looking toward the example of others such as 'Abdu'l-Bahá.

He is the best source as our Exemplar. At times, however, you can also benefit from the example of a teacher or mentor, as well as that of other members of Bahá'u'lláh's family, such as His daughter Bahíyyih Khánum, who had an excellent character.

With courage and detachment, you can step back and act as an independent observer of your life and behavior. When you are too close to a situation, you can see only a small portion of it. Close to a mountain, you might see only a handful of rocks and a few trees, but from a mile away, you can see all of it. You may find it useful to keep a journal and record your ongoing efforts. Self-reflection will assist you to make steady development progress.

Action

1. Create a document or chart and make notes of what is good about you, such as your talents, skills, character strengths, abilities, friendship skills, and so on. When you struggle with negative thoughts about yourself or your efforts, take this document out and remind yourself that you are a valuable human being with gifts to offer others. This reminds you to practice self-respect and it also helps you avoid the pitfall of false humility.

2. When you feel fearful, insecure, confused, or lost, turn to prayer and the Bahá'í teachings. Ask God to help you with releasing these feelings and replacing them with uplifting thoughts and joyfulness. You may find it useful to memorize a quotation and repeat it a few times, such as, "Soar upon the wings of joy in the atmosphere of the love of God."[72] Bahá'u'lláh

3. Develop a daily habit of looking back at your day and seeing both what has gone well or that you have done well, and where you need to improve. Some people find it more effective to do a personal review at night before bed, and others prefer reflecting after a night of sleep. Then you can determine what to do better. Try out different times and methods, such as reflection during prayer, writing in a journal, using a spreadsheet, drawing pictures, or listening to music and reflecting while playing it.

4. Make a list each week of your unfulfilled commitments and promises and make a plan for completing them. Ensure that you take time to

encourage and appreciate your efforts in the process. For significant accomplishments, you may also find it beneficial to celebrate in some way.

5. Act as a storyteller and tell a group about one or two of the lives of people featured in the book *Dawnbreakers*, which contains stories about the "beauty and courage and wisdom and love of the great heroes of our faith."[73] *Bahá'í World, Volume VIII*

Reflection

1. How can I get to know what's excellent in me and what needs to grow?
2. What gifts and talents do I have? How am I using them to enrich my life and contribute to others?
3. How can I know if a standard is a good one to strive for?
4. What words and behaviors of mine seem to be in alignment with the Bahá'í teachings?
5. Where am I struggling to be in alignment with the teachings?
6. What routines or physical prompts will remind me to do a daily self-review? What am I appreciating about doing this practice?
7. How am I contributing to my physical well-being? Mental well-being? Emotional well-being? Spiritual well-being? What could I be doing better?
8. What prompts me to experience inner joy? What joy, laughter, and happiness am I bringing to others?
9. What guidance has come from the Universal House of Justice in the last five years that I can apply in my life? How can I begin?

6 - Developing Spiritual Habits—Connecting to God's Light

Challenge: Sometimes developing habits feels like a lot of work and not much fun.

Opportunity: I want to feel the joy of success as I strive to be stronger and more consistent with spiritual practices.

Summary:
- My soul, like my physical body, needs conscious attention and care.
- Practices like daily prayer, meditation, and reading the Bahá'í teachings keep my soul strong and healthy.
- There are special Obligatory Prayers, one of which is to be said daily along with special instructions.
- Meditation connects me with insights I can apply to my life and ideas I can use to serve others.
- Sharing about the Bahá'í teachings will become a natural and regular part of my life as I pray, read, grow, and become excited about them.

More:

Exercising my soul

It may be easier to think of how you take care of your physical self than how to take care of your spiritual being. In a physical sense, you sleep, eat, drink, poop, shower, and exercise. If you stop doing any of these actions, there are consequences. You are exhausted, hungry, thirsty, constipated, dirty, or weak. It's similar in the spiritual sense:

> "It is incumbent upon thee, by the permission of God, to cleanse the eye of thine heart from the things of the world, that thou mayest realize the infinitude of divine knowledge, and mayest behold Truth so clearly that thou wilt need no proof to demonstrate His reality, nor any evidence to bear witness unto His testimony."[74] Bahá'u'lláh

> "... [F]or if the spiritual qualities of the soul, open to the breath of the Divine Spirit, are never used, they become atrophied, enfeebled, and at last incapable...."[75] 'Abdu'l-Bahá

When you consider the well-being of your soul, your spiritual self, then there are specific actions that keep your vitality flowing. They involve the teachings and laws of Bahá'u'lláh, such as these:

"The source of courage and power is the promotion of the Word of God, and steadfastness in His Love."[76] Bahá'u'lláh

"Bahá'u'lláh has stated quite clearly in His Writings the essential requisites for our spiritual growth, and these are stressed again and again by 'Abdu'l-Bahá in His talks and Tablets. One can summarize them briefly in this way:

- The recital each day of one of the Obligatory Prayers with pure-hearted devotion.
- The regular reading of the Sacred Scriptures, specifically at least each morning and evening, with reverence, attention and thought.
- Prayerful meditation on the Teachings, so that we may understand them more deeply, fulfil them more faithfully, and convey them more accurately to others.
- Striving every day to bring our behavior more into accordance with the high standards that are set forth in the Teachings.
- Teaching the Cause of God.
- Selfless service in the work of the Cause and in the carrying on of our trade or profession.

"These points…represent the path towards the attainment of true spirituality that has been laid down by the Manifestation of God for this age."[77] Universal House of Justice

"Your peers long to make sense of the events they see unfolding around them, both at home and on the global scene. You alone have the Message that can soothe their troubled hearts and provide them with the clarity of thought they desire."[78] Universal House of Justice

You may also be familiar with the 19-Day Fast that occurs during March of each year, when Bahá'ís abstain from food and drink from sunup to sundown. Below is guidance on this topic.

"For this material fast is an outer token of the spiritual fast; it is a symbol of self-restraint, the withholding of oneself from all appetites of the self, taking on the characteristics of the spirit, being carried away by the breathings of heaven and catching fire from the love of God."[79] 'Abdu'l-Bahá

"… [O]bligatory prayer and fasting produce awareness and awakening in man, and are conducive to his protection and preservation from tests."[80] 'Abdu'l-Bahá

When you're actively engaged in these spiritual actions, you are more likely to feel happy, creative, energetic, and in harmony with others. Through caring for your soul, you more easily spot ways to be of service to others and carry them out.

A man shares his perspectives on caring for the soul:

"What is a soul and how does one take care of it? How does one seemingly upkeep something that cannot be seen? Where is the high shelf or enclosure to keep it out of reach, ensuring it's handled only by those who understand its value? And, if it can't be touched, how do we maintain, clean, and polish it?

"Typically, something we can't see, touch, or recognize with one of our five senses tends to fade from our awareness. In our walk within this world—the human experience—we commonly lose sight of our soul-essence, as our daily lives seem to require most of our attention and effort. It begins to recede behind a wall of what we'll often call reality. Our truest self, as a fragment of light from God, fades with disconnect and distance until it eventually seemingly disappears.

"I believe a great part of our journey is rediscovering our essence and advocating its purpose with steadfastness, aligning ourselves inwardly and outwardly. Consciously choosing to step onto this path is a brave action. Most people live their lives unconsciously (which simply means they're on autopilot) rather than clearly making choices they know are congruent with their soul, their sacredness.

"At a young age I was able to discern two concurrent experiences within me, but realized one seemed to precede the other by a split-second. I understood an imperceptible part of me was often at disparity with my thoughts. It was as if there was a confident and clear understanding beyond what I was thinking or told.

"I decided that I wanted to give more credibility to what I designated as my soul, and much less of it to my thoughts. I surmised that thoughts came from my brain—a melting pot of what I think is correct, others tell me is correct, and information and impressions from nearly every aspect of the world. There's probably a lot of beliefs mixed in that aren't mine, and therefore incorrect for me.

"I knew I could not succeed at changing all these other factors, so my deeper sense—my soul—is likely where my own truths exist. I concluded that my brain is usually incorrect, and my soul is almost always correct. Alas, there is one caveat: being attuned with it. I realized that while I may enjoy the sound of a piano, it's not my full truth. More accurately, I enjoy the sound of a well-tuned piano. Otherwise, the sound is dissonant and inaccurate. Conversely, if I am not attuned to my soul and actively choosing to deeply know myself, I won't be skilled at discriminating among any other noise.

"It certainly isn't easy with all the invitations and interactions we encounter. For example, the desire to be accepted presents itself in the form of peer pressure, as we're invited into situations or choices that may not be healthy for our spiritual, emotional, or physical well-being. Instantly we are presented with a choice. When we lead with our soul—making choices from a space of knowing ourselves—we'll make choices that support the expression of not who, but what we truly are: a reflection of God's light in this world for all.

"I came to this understanding through different periods and degrees in my journey, and often find myself at the same precious landscape, but with more love, loyalty, understanding, forgiveness, and compassion for myself and others.

"There is no high shelf or encasing to keep our soul protected. The expedition in this world is in the preparation for our next. For me, the courage is in being vulnerable and open to what life offers, such as relationships, experiences, and emotions. These are the vessel and pathway to refine and express my relationship with God, while generously showing up for myself and others."

Other important ways you may take care of your spiritual well-being are:

- Being creative
- Listening to or playing uplifting music (and avoiding music with vulgar, derogatory, or hate-filled words)
- Spending time in nature, God's creation; cleaning-up the environment

- Sharing genuine humor and laughter with others
- Building excellent friendships
- Engaging in service to and with others
- Eliminating prejudiced thoughts and actions and promoting the oneness of humanity
- Promoting the equality of women and men
- Building family unity

The Universal House of Justice honors the path to take:

"How fitting that, at this hour, a generation of youth has come into its own, ready to assume growing responsibility, since its contribution to the work at hand will prove decisive in the months and years ahead. In our prayers at the Sacred Threshold, we will entreat the Almighty to sustain all those who would be a part of this immense undertaking, who prefer the true prosperity of others over their own ease and leisure, and whose eyes are fixed upon 'Abdu'l-Bahá for a flawless pattern of how to be; all this, that 'those who walk in darkness should come into the light'…."[81] Universal House of Justice

Building strength and capacity

If you want to grow into being a physically strong person, it takes almost daily exercise. In spiritual terms, this means such practices as self-assessment [see Chapter 5], prayer, meditation, and reading the Bahá'í teachings. In nature terms, if you want to grow into being a strong tree, it takes daily care of the seed and then the sapling—weeding, watering, and fertilizing it as it grows. Below is a very short selection of quotations on this topic, and you can find many more when you study the teachings.

"As for thy mention of the Obligatory Prayer: in truth, anyone who readeth this with absolute sincerity will attract all created things, and confer new life upon the world of being. This servant beseecheth his Lord to assist His loved ones in that which will deliver them from this world's vicissitudes, its preoccupations, its frustrations, and its darkness, and will adorn them with that which shall under all conditions draw them nigh unto Him. He, verily, is the All-Possessing, the Most High."[82] Bahá'u'lláh

"The obligatory prayers are binding inasmuch as they are conducive to humility and submissiveness, to setting one's face towards God and expressing devotion to Him. Through such prayer man holdeth communion with God, seeketh to draw near unto Him, converseth with the true Beloved of his heart, and attaineth spiritual stations."[83] 'Abdu'l-Bahá

"When a person becomes a Bahá'í, actually what takes place is that the seed of the spirit starts to grow in the human soul. This seed must be watered by the outpourings of the Holy Spirit. These gifts of the spirit are received through prayer, meditation, study of the Holy Utterances and service to the Cause of God. The fact of the matter is that service in the Cause is like the plough which ploughs the physical soil when seeds are sown. It is necessary that the soil be ploughed up, so that it can be enriched, and thus cause a stronger growth of the seed. In exactly the same way the evolution of the spirit takes place through ploughing up the soil of the heart so that it is a constant reflection of the Holy Spirit. In this way the human spirit grows and develops by leaps and bounds."[84] On behalf of Shoghi Effendi

"The Twin Luminaries [The Báb and Bahá'u'lláh] of this resplendent age have taught us this: Prayer is the essential spiritual conversation of the soul with its Maker, direct and without intermediation. It is the spiritual food that sustains the life of the spirit. Like the morning's dew, it brings freshness to the heart and cleanses it, purifying it from attachments of the insistent self. It is a fire that burns away the veils and a light that leads to the ocean of reunion with the Almighty. On its wings does the soul soar in the heavens of God and draw closer to the divine reality. Upon its quality depends the development of the limitless capacities of the soul and the attraction of the bounties of God, but the prolongation of prayer is not desirable.[85] Universal House of Justice

"It is striking how private and personal the most fundamental spiritual exercises of prayer and meditation are in the Faith. Bahá'ís do, of course, have meetings for devotions...but the daily obligatory prayers are ordained to be said in the privacy of one's chamber, and meditation on the Teachings is, likewise, a private individual activity, not a form of group therapy. In His talks 'Abdu'l-Bahá describes prayer as 'Conversation with God', and concerning meditation He says that 'while you meditate you are speaking with your own spirit. In that state of mind you put certain questions to your spirit and the spirit answers: the light breaks forth and the reality is revealed."[86] On behalf of the Universal House of Justice

Sharing the Bahá'í teachings with others

The subject of teaching others about Bahá'u'lláh could fill volumes, and there are many available resources. Essentially though it's about:

- learning the teachings,
- living them as best as you can, and
- while interacting with friends, colleagues, family, and others you meet, you naturally share about what you believe.

Many people don't yet know that there is a new, wonderful Faith in the world with transformative teachings, and as you become excited about this, you will want others to know about it. Below are quotations of guidance:

"Every word that proceedeth out of the mouth of God is endowed with such potency as can instill new life into every human frame…."[87] Bahá'u'lláh

"In these days, the most important of all things is the guidance of the nations and peoples of the world. Teaching the Cause is of utmost importance for it is the head corner-stone of the foundation itself."[88] 'Abdu'l-Bahá

"Let him consider the degree of his hearer's receptivity, and decide for himself the suitability of either the direct or indirect method of teaching, whereby he can impress upon the seeker the vital importance of the Divine Message, and persuade him to throw in his lot with those who have already embraced it. Let him remember the example set by 'Abdu'l-Bahá, and His constant admonition to shower such kindness upon the seeker, and exemplify to such a degree the spirit of the teachings he hopes to instill into him, that the recipient will be spontaneously impelled to identify himself with the Cause embodying such teachings. Let him refrain, at the outset, from insisting on such laws and observances as might impose too severe a strain on the seeker's newly awakened faith, and endeavor to nurse him, patiently, tactfully, and yet determinedly, into full maturity, and aid him to proclaim his unqualified acceptance of whatever has been ordained by Bahá'u'lláh. Let him, as soon as that stage has been attained, introduce him to the body of his fellow-believers, and seek, through constant fellowship and active participation in the local activities of his community, to enable him to contribute his share to the enrichment of its life, the furtherance of its tasks, the consolidations of its interests, and the coordination of its activities with those of its sister communities. Let him not be content until he has infused into his spiritual child so deep a longing as to impel him to arise independently, in his turn, and devote his energies to the quickening of other souls, and the upholding of the laws and principles laid down by his newly adopted Faith."[89] Shoghi Effendi

As you pray and read, you can spot phrases to memorize so you can share the exact words from the teachings. These can especially influence others' hearts.

The "essential requisites" of service and transforming behavior are covered in other sections of the book.

Action

1. Choose two prayers and say them consistently each day for a week. Note if they are easier or harder to say in different environments, such as in private and when others are around. Memorize the entire prayers or phrases from them that are helpful to carry in your mind. If you have not already, focus on memorizing the Short Obligatory Prayer to be said daily between noon and sunset: "I bear witness, O my God, that Thou hast created me to know Thee and to worship Thee. I testify, at this moment, to my powerlessness and to Thy might, to my poverty and to Thy wealth. There is none other God but Thee, the Help in Peril, the Self-Subsisting."[90] Bahá'u'lláh

2. After reflecting on the quotations in this chapter, explore if any of the essential requisites are missing from your life. Choose two to begin carrying out more actively over the coming week. Create a reminder system to see how you're doing over the course of the week. After you have had some success, begin adding other requisites, one at a time, gradually over time. If increasing your ability to share about the Bahá'í Faith is one of your goals, this advice may guide you: "He suggests that you daily pray to Bahá'u'lláh to let you meet a soul receptive to His

Message. The power of prayer is very great, and attracts the Divine confirmations."[91] On behalf of Shoghi Effendi

3. Research different types of meditation and experiment to see what works well for you. Some people prefer to sit quietly, and others prefer to be more active, such as doing a walking meditation or a discipline like Tai Chi. This is some guidance: "There are no set forms of meditation prescribed in the teachings, no plan, as such, for inner development. The friends are urged—nay enjoined—to pray, and they also should meditate, but the manner of doing the latter is left entirely to the individual."[92] On behalf of Shoghi Effendi

4. Once you have the habit of reading the Writings twice a day, give yourself the advanced challenge of once a day, or on some other time interval, reading something from all of the following:
    a. The Báb
    b. Bahá'u'lláh
    c. 'Abdu'l-Bahá
    d. Shoghi Effendi
    e. Universal House of Justice

    You can purchase books from many locations, and you can find many sources here to download: https://www.bahai.org/library/. There are also apps with Bahá'í prayers, books, and quotations.

5. Consider going on pilgrimage to the Bahá'í Holy Places in Israel as a place to become strongly spiritually connected and do intense prayers. Contact the Bahá'í institutions in your country for instructions on how to apply to participate.

6. Consistently pray one of the three daily Obligatory Prayers for a week, praying at a time when you are alone and private. Then put in place an ongoing reminder system so you stay consistent with saying one of them. In addition, the following is to be done each day: "It hath been ordained that every believer in God, the Lord of Judgment, shall, each day, having washed his hands and then his face, seat himself and, turning unto God, repeat 'Alláh'u'-Abhá' ninety-five times."[93] Bahá'u'lláh

The Obligatory Prayers each have specific actions to carry out along with them. Here are additional instructions for you to carry out:

a. "Ablutions are to be performed by the believer in preparation for the offering of obligatory prayer. They consist of washing the hands and face." Where there is no water for ablution, you can repeat five times: "In the Name of God, the Most Pure, the Most Pure."[94] *The Kitáb-i-Aqdas*, Notes

b. "Morning", "noon", and "evening" in the instructions for prayers means, "from morning [dawn] till noon, from noon till sunset, and from sunset till two hours thereafter".[95] *The Kitáb-i-Aqdas*, Questions and Answers

c. "The 'Point of Adoration', that is, the point to which the worshipper should turn when offering obligatory prayer, is called the Qiblih." ... "Bahá'u'lláh ordains His resting-place as the Qiblih after His passing. The Most Holy Tomb is at Bahji, 'Akká. [located in present-day Israel]"[96] *The Kitáb-i-Aqdas*, Notes

Reflection

1. What spiritual habits will empower my growth, well-being, and service to others?
2. What effect could it have on my progress with being a spiritual man if I'm regular with these habits?
3. What is the experience like for me when I say the Obligatory Prayers? How does saying them daily relate to achieving integrity in my spiritual life?
4. How do I describe my approach to and experience of prayer?
5. How could I be more prayerful every day, both in reading revealed prayers and with increasing my prayerful conversations with God and Bahá'u'lláh?
6. What meditation do I do? How could I be consistent with it? Have I ever received wonderful insights after meditating? When I raise a question with my spirit, am I specific with what I'm seeking? Are the insights I receive related to my present or more applicable to my future?
7. What differences do I notice in my life on days I pray and on days I don't pray?
8. When I live with other people, how does it affect our relationship if we pray together regularly?

9. Do I ever feel all this is too much, that the standard is too high or the demands overwhelming? Is it okay to talk about these feelings? Who can I share them with? How can I allow myself to grow gradually into Bahá'í life?

7 – Reducing Resistance and Aligning with Positive Action

Challenge: Sometimes it's very, very, very comfortable just to be the way I am now.

Opportunity: As I bravely arise to improve myself, I will discover strengths inside of me I never knew I had, and I can build new ones that will be valuable to me and others.

Summary:
- I can allow many things to get in the way of motivating myself to improve; peer pressure can be a difficult obstacle.
- My behavior is a free-will choice, and I have prayer, the Bahá'í teachings, and a support "team" to help me make excellent choices.
- God and my own efforts can transform my behavior and expand my capacities.
- Improving aspects of myself takes courage, humility, and perseverance, and this effort brings benefits like self-respect, happiness, and better relationships.
- I can be a champion for equality, so women and men both achieve their potential, and our capacities are expanded in the process.

More:

No, I don't want to improve!

You may be resistant to or fearful of making improvements in yourself, feel quite satisfied with how you are, or object to someone asking you to change. If you notice yourself thinking: "This is the way I am, and I can't (or won't) improve or change myself", your resistance may get in the way of learning and growth. It can be easy to become attached to being a certain way, and to not be comfortable making changes. However, when you overcome your uncertainties, bravely arise, and take action, new possibilities open up.

So, why change? Consider this man's response to this question as he pondered being happy with who he had become in response to his life circumstances, even though it did not work well in his marriage:

"The answer was surprisingly obvious (once I saw it). I needed to change in order to become a better person. Just because I had experienced a dysfunctional home life did not make it any less true that as human beings, we are meant to have a life of connection, interdependence, relying on others, and having them be able to rely on us. In short, we are intended to have a life of love."[97] John Buri

When you choose to improve yourself, there is a rush of self-empowered energy, and there is great satisfaction when you are successful. When others try to force you, resistance can kick in. In between those two paths is often an area where you get feedback or observe challenges that arise from your behavior choices. It takes self-honesty and discernment to process that feedback for validity and determine whether changing an aspect of yourself is wise or unwise.

The images in these quotations may give you insights into the importance of these concepts:

"O My Servant! Thou art even as a finely tempered sword concealed in the darkness of its sheath and its value hidden from the artificer's knowledge. Wherefore come forth from the sheath of self and desire that thy worth may be made resplendent and manifest unto all the world."[98] Bahá'u'lláh

"... [M]an must acquire heavenly qualities and attain divine attributes. He must become the image and likeness of God. He must seek the bounty of the eternal, become the manifestor of the love of God, the light of guidance, the tree of life and the depository of the bounties of God. That is to say, man must sacrifice the qualities and attributes of the world of nature for the qualities and attributes of the world of God. For instance, consider the substance we call iron. Observe its qualities; it is solid, black, cold. These are the characteristics of iron. When the same iron absorbs heat from the fire, it sacrifices its attribute of solidity for the attribute of fluidity. It sacrifices its attribute of darkness for the attribute of light, which is a quality of the fire. It sacrifices its attribute of coldness to the quality of heat which the fire possesses so that in the iron there remains no solidity, darkness or cold. It becomes illumined and transformed, having sacrificed its qualities to the qualities and attributes of the fire."[99] 'Abdu'l-Bahá

Someone comments on his process:

"When I'm trying to improve my character, it's hard to be objective, with all the filters and justifications I can put up. Regardless, part of my growth depends on my being honest with myself. Prayer and humility help. Reflection on life events and experiences also can be fruitful in understanding myself. The input and comments from friends—and sometimes people who don't even like me—have also been beneficial. Things that get in the way of knowing and growing my own character, like lying to myself, denial, fantasy-driven expectations, and romantic intoxication with somebody are probably also true of others. I need a heightened awareness and introspection if I want to explore my own character or someone else's character as a potential marriage partner. Detachment helps me stay away from judging myself or others and focus instead on discernment."

Ironically, your ability to improve is linked to first accepting yourself the way you are, and then also recognizing that everyone can improve. This frees you from resistance, and you can then move forward.

Handling small steps

As you understand your own thinking patterns that can interfere with development, you can begin to make adjustments. Practicing moderation assists you to start small and grow organically as your ability and capacity expand. If instead you try to address every issue or develop every aspect of yourself at the same time, typically you'll end up overwhelmed, discouraged, and unsuccessful at meeting your goals. Trying one simple straightforward improvement before attempting a complex one may increase success.

Start out with catching yourself making excuses for something you have done. Listen for blaming words in your daily speech that attempt to excuse or lay the fault for something you did onto someone else. Practice eliminating these patterns and replacing them with positive words that take responsibility for your life instead. As the Universal House of Justice wrote, "Small steps, if they are regular and rapid, add up to a great distance traveled."[100] Step by step, and day by day, brings progress.

Being honest with yourself and others and transforming your avoidance patterns will increase your self-respect and assist you to have healthy and mature relationships. The more you understand and accept yourself, the easier it will be to share yourself honestly with another person. If you resist understanding and developing yourself, others may feel uncomfortable or uncertain about being connected with you. If you are as honest with yourself as you can be, then you will be as authentic with others as you can be.

Fear of rejection, uncertainty about who you are, or self-rejection may lead you to don a mask and pretend to be someone you are not. Such pretense interferes with self-understanding and improving yourself. It also interferes with others' ability to get to know you. The painful outcome to behaving this way is described here:

> "If we wear our masks long enough, we may guard against rejection and we may even be admired, but we'll never be whole. And that means we'll never enjoy true intimacy. ... When what you do and what you say do not match the person you are inside—when your deepest identity is not revealed to others—you develop an incongruent or fragmented self."[101]
> Les Parrott and Leslie Parrott

People who pretend to be different than who they really are often focus so much on the *impression they make* on others that they don't connect with the person they are with. They may become stuck in a pattern of looking for someone else to make them feel good about themselves. You can eliminate these patterns as you get to know your character and develop your strengths. Remember, if you feel somewhat overwhelmed by self-assessment and self-development, take small steps, one at a time. [See Chapter 8, "Developing My Character".]

Remember that this is not about being a student in school trying to earn a grade, nor like being an employee going through a performance review to determine if you deserve a pay raise. Do not be overly self-critical, but neither should you ignore areas of concern. You are simply taking an opportunity to look at how you are doing compared to a standard of excellence. Gaining a realistic perspective of yourself aids you to work toward your self-improvement goals.

Resisting negative influence from others

Free will allows you to make whatever character and behavior choices you wish. You have the power to choose how you respond to and treat others, and you can resist pressure or bullying from others to behave certain unwise ways. One man said, *"Sometimes I had to make the choice to stand my moral ground about my conduct."*

As you choose words and actions that reflect character strengths, your self-respect and happiness will increase, and you will likely get along better with others. Here is some encouragement:

"The power of God can entirely transmute our characters and make of us beings entirely unlike our previous selves. Through prayer and supplication, obedience to the divine laws Bahá'u'lláh has revealed, and ever-increasing service to His Faith, we can change ourselves."[102] On behalf of Shoghi Effendi

Your behavior does not and should not depend upon the behavior of others, even though it's easy to think that way. Peer pressure can work on your mind and make it harder to see that you can behave the way you choose, not simply do what others think you should do. Bullying can also make you feel like you have no control over what happens to you. Here are some stories about these issues:

"Many people in my department at work thought it was okay to take faulty products and sell them to people in poor countries. They often made prejudiced comments about the people in those countries. For a while, I went along with setting up the shipments to happen. Then I rebelled and started speaking up with positive comments about the people in these countries and objecting to our business practices. It wasn't popular, but I slept better at night knowing I wasn't going along with what seemed like poor ethical choices."

"There must've been a fight.... The contents of Michael's backpack—dozens of loose-leaf pieces of paper, notebooks, pencils, coins—were scattered on the damp ground. Each time he bent down to pick something up, Jake kicked him. Then Jake and the jerks he hung out with would laugh like this was the funniest thing they'd ever witnessed.

"'Don't come by in the middle of a fight and think we won't see you,' Jake said. 'You freak. This is our part of the school.'

"'Yeah,' Sam laughed and pointed toward the special-ed wing. 'You belong over there with the others.'"[103] K. Kingsbury

"Especially for those that are still in school, not giving in to peer pressure can have real consequences. You can lose friendship, or status. Reduction in status can result in verbal/social victimization or isolation, and even not that infrequently, physical intimidation. Integrity, courageous leadership, and

relying on prayer for help can keep up one's spiritual strength in the face of those pressuring you to behave in uncomfortable or immoral ways.

"There's also a social dynamic in many schools, where people can lose status for being friendly to people with low status. It takes great spiritual strength and determined kindness to potentially sacrifice your own social standing to include someone new or different. You'll benefit from the relationship with someone more diverse, and from resolutely following Bahá'u'lláh and 'Abdu'l-Bahá's instructions. I gotta root for the outcast, who people find solidarity and social safety in excluding, because I was excluded so much growing up."

No matter how difficult your circumstances, individual transformation—in you and others—can and does happen. Sometimes addressing a situation requires intervention and involvement from others you trust, such as teachers, parents, counselors, or community members. Sometimes your own conviction that what is happening is unwise or unfair can result in a surge of inner confidence and commitment to strive for justice or equality.

Taking powerful action

A good place to begin your focus on personal transformation is reading many stories about 'Abdu'l-Bahá, also known as the Master, because Bahá'u'lláh has designated Him as our Exemplar. His life and choices are the guiding example for how we are to live our lives. You are asked to fix your eyes "upon 'Abdu'l-Bahá for a flawless pattern of how to be".[104] (Universal House of Justice) Here are some short stories:

> "'Abdu'l-Bahá's humility did not stem from any weakness. Once when a child asked Him why all the rivers of the earth flow into the ocean, He said, 'because it sets itself lower than them all and so draws them to itself.'"[105] Collected by A. Honnold

> "'Abdu'l-Bahá was out with His secretary [in Dublin, Ireland]. A poor, old man passed the inn and the Master asked the secretary to call him back. The man was not only ragged but filthy, but the Master took his hand and smiled at him. They talked together a moment, the Master taking in the whole figure—the man's trousers hardly served their purpose. The Master laughed gently and stepped into a shadow. The street was quite deserted. He fumbled with the clothes at His waist. When He stopped, His trousers slid down, but He drew His robe around His body and

handed His trousers to the poor man with a 'May God go with you.'"[106] Collected by A. Honnold

"Once in Egypt 'Abdu'l-Bahá obtained a carriage in order that He might offer a ride to an important Pasha, who was to be His luncheon guest. When they reached their destination, the driver asked an exorbitant fee. The Master was fully aware of this and refused to pay the full amount. The driver, big and rough, grabbed His sash and 'jerked Him back and forth', demanding his unfair price. 'Abdu'l-Bahá remained firm and the man eventually let go. The Master paid what He actually owed him and informed him that had he been honest, he would have received a handsome tip instead of only the fare. He then walked away."[107] Collected by A. Honnold

Dan Popov, one of the founders of The Virtues Project, talks about how to be in action:

"Your choices matter, so make a commitment and choose a new path, even if you are uncertain about where it will lead you. Be aware—if the path is familiar, it is not a new one. Only if you give your effort your full 100% commitment, will you be able to assess its value effectively later on. Involve others by telling them of your commitment and asking for their assistance—show them how it can benefit both of you. Call on the spiritual power of prayer and allow yourself to be guided forward.

"Your commitment and choice to take a new path in your life will likely result in four to six weeks of turmoil; it will call for conscious awareness and regular effort before it begins to feel right. At the first difficulty along the path, you may be tempted to retreat to a more familiar path, but persevere, be determined, and hold your commitment with integrity. Guidance, confirmation, and support come when you are in action. Observe what is happening and be honest with yourself. Growth is positive change. Be patient, flexible, and graceful—change will come—little by little, day by day."[108] Dan Popov

Here is guidance:

"It is neither possible nor desirable for the Universal House of Justice to set forth a set of rules covering every situation. Rather is it the task of the individual believer to determine, according to his own prayerful understanding of the Writings, precisely what his course of conduct should be in relation to situations which he encounters in his daily life. If he is to fulfill his true mission in life as a follower of the Blessed Perfection [Bahá'u'lláh], he will pattern his life according to the Teachings. The believer cannot attain this objective merely by living according to a set of rigid regulations. When his life is oriented toward service to Bahá'u'lláh, and when every conscious act is performed within this frame of reference, he will not fail to achieve the true purpose of his life.

"Therefore, every believer must continually study the sacred Writings and the instructions of the beloved Guardian, striving always to attain a new and better understanding of their import to him and to his society. He should pray fervently for Divine Guidance, wisdom and strength to do what is pleasing to God, and to serve Him at all times and to the best of his ability."[109] On behalf of the Universal House of Justice

A man outlines his journey of improving himself:

"I knew that if I wanted to have a happy and healthy life, I needed to grow. Because of the positive changes I've made, I feel happier, I sleep better at night, and I'm a better friend. I honestly don't think that I know one person who really changed because someone else asked them to and then was genuinely happy. It must come from inside. I learned mindfulness meditation, I started dance classes (to overcome insecurity issues), I went back to reflection and prayer, and more.

"Here's what I learned:

1. *Changing from a personal growth point of view (when the choice is mine and nobody else is asking me or expecting me to change) required me to leave my comfort zone and take risks. We develop defense mechanisms, and we draw imaginary lines that we're not willing to cross or that we don't let others cross. If we or others get too close to that line, or at the first sign of adversity, we come right back to our comfort zone.*

2. *The hardest thing about changing is acknowledging my own shortcomings, but positive change will occur if I have a genuine desire to improve. It's as if subconsciously it means that something is broken inside of me and needs to be fixed. If someone else asks me to change, then that feeling gets magnified.*

3. On the lighter side, I'm discovering that the beautiful thing about change is that ultimately, it's a choice. When I am brave enough to struggle through change, as in points 1 and 2 above, no matter how hard it is, how embarrassing it feels, or how much it hurts, ultimately the choice is mine. Now, if I learn something, fix something, or get any type of benefit from what I do, then the reward is totally worth the risk.

4. One more hard thing about changing habits, is that by doing so my relationships with a lot of people changed, including some of my best friends with whom I hadn't practiced the best habits. It took me a long time to realize that it was okay, even if it was tough.

"I still have more growing to do, and more change is coming. Now that I have left my ego behind much more, I have extended my comfort zone way past where it was. I have let some old relationships go, and I now surround myself with people who bring out the best in me. I am looking forward to whatever the future brings—all the new lessons, the new experiences, and everything else that 'change' may bring into my life."

Championing equality with women

It may seem strange to you to have the topic of the equality of women and men here in a chapter about making personal improvements. It's actually vital, because humanity is at a critical stage in recognizing and empowering women to be fully involved in society, and your behavior is linked with females throughout most of your activities.

Equality is not a static concept, which also contributes to the challenges of achieving it. Your understanding of it and how it's expressed in various parts of your life will evolve over time. Consider these quotations from the Bahá'í teachings:

"The world in the past has been ruled by force, and man has dominated over woman by reason of his more forceful and aggressive qualities both of body and mind. But the balance is already shifting; force is losing its dominance, and mental alertness, intuition, and the spiritual qualities of love and service, in which woman is strong, are gaining ascendancy. Hence the new age will be an age less masculine and more permeated with the feminine ideals, or, to speak more exactly, will be an age in which the masculine and feminine elements of civilization will be more evenly balanced."[110] 'Abdu'l-Bahá

"As long as women are prevented from attaining their highest possibilities, so long will men be unable to achieve the greatness which might be theirs."[111] 'Abdu'l-Bahá

A man provides his observations, experience, and encouragement:

"Many women today are acting like men used to, full of commanding insistence. Sometimes they can be forceful, even ruthless or aggressive. This can leave a Bahá'í man who is trying to be humble and meek feeling helpless at times. The key is to express how this makes you feel, even though being assertive may feel uncomfortable. The goal is to strive for Bahá'í consultation which involves honest and thoughtful sharing. Only in this way can realization of where things have come to set in.

"I think we also need to openly advocate more often for the female virtues of humility, gentleness, kindness, forgiveness, mercy, love, and care, for they are the ones that we need more of today. As we recognize these virtues, as we praise and call for them, they will reappear. Sometimes it requires new habits of mind. In the same way that we learn to elect the meek and humble rather than the proud and boastful in Bahá'í elections, we need to learn to cherish the traditionally feminine virtues. In this way these female qualities will finally gain ascendancy, leading us to peace and prosperity."

This quotation below illustrates the concept of balance between men and women:

"The world of humanity consists of two parts: male and female. Each is the complement of the other. Therefore, if one is defective, the other will necessarily be incomplete, and perfection cannot be attained. There is a right hand and a left hand in the human body, functionally equal in service and administration. If either proves defective, the defect will naturally extend to the other by involving the completeness of the whole; for accomplishment is not normal unless both are perfect. If we say one hand is deficient, we prove the inability and incapacity of the other; for single-handed there is no full accomplishment. Just as physical accomplishment is complete with two hands, so man and woman, the two parts of the social body, must be perfect. It is not natural that either should remain undeveloped; and until both are perfected, the happiness of the human world will not be realized."[112] 'Abdu'l-Bahá

Chuck Egerton, who has conducted a doctoral research study of men and masculinity called "Being and Becoming", comments on the above quotation:

"The analogy of two hands must be contemplated to fathom its brilliant simplicity. The meaning and importance of hands are something all humankind understands and relates to. We can infer from this analogy that the male hand, proud of its ability, is unconscious that the unequal female hand imposes an overall loss of capability. Men structure their lives around the assumption of this limited dexterity and expend vast resources to devise structures, aids and tools to facilitate a one-handed life. Perhaps this analogy has the power to help men realize that they are missing out by performing, enforcing and imposing a negative masculinity and holding women back from their full potential. A world with two fully functional hands (men and women) working together changes everything. Having the full use of two hands more than doubles human capacity."[113] Chuck Egerton

The Bahá'í teachings also include the metaphor of men and women being like two wings of a bird:

"The world of humanity is possessed of two wings: the male and the female. So long as these two wings are not equivalent in strength, the bird will not fly. Until womankind reaches the same degree as man, until she enjoys the same arena of activity, extraordinary attainment for humanity will not be realized; humanity cannot wing its way to heights of real attainment. When the two wings or parts become equivalent in strength, enjoying the same prerogatives, the flight of man will be exceedingly lofty and extraordinary. Therefore, woman must receive the same education as man and all inequality be adjusted. Thus, imbued with the same virtues as man, rising through all the degrees of human attainment, women will become the peers of men, and until this equality is established, true progress and attainment for the human race will not be facilitated."[114] 'Abdu'l-Bahá

Egerton also comments below on this quotation.

"What would it mean for humanity to soar on equal wings for the first time? Imagine the transformation of family life, governance, economics, the protection and use of natural resources as well as new ways of knowing, and intellectual and scientific developments. Could this be the key to the establishment of universal peace on the planet? Like two equal hands, the functionality of two equal wings adds much more than a doubling of ability. The potential benefit to human civilization is incalculable from where we stand now. Again, this analogy illustrates that the whole *is* much greater than its parts."[115] Chuck Egerton

A man reflects:

"Throughout my life, my view of equality has shifted and changed, as has the way women in my life have shifted and changed. I still find it challenging at times to navigate the complexities. I do my best to listen well, treat everyone—male or female—with respect, and when I seem to get it wrong, apologize. I think men need to stop behaving like it's a win-lose proposition to have women fully involved in all aspects of life. It's an opportunity to expand the space we operate in with more opportunities for all."

A Bahá'í International Community statement says:

"... [T]he equality of men and women is a facet of human reality and not just a condition to be achieved for the common good. That which makes human beings human—their inherent dignity and nobility—is neither male nor female. The search for meaning, for purpose, for community; the capacity to love, to create, to persevere, has no gender. Such an assertion has profound implications for the organization of every aspect of human society."[116]

The statement also says that the equality of men and women will not only affect women but will "revolutionize all facets of human society" and points out that "Men must come to realize that under current conditions of inequality, the development of *their* full potential is not possible" and that "they...must find the moral courage to convey and model new understandings of masculinity and...challenge and question the narrow roles that society and the media have assigned to them."[117]

Action

1. Carefully and deliberately reflect on the questions below about tendencies you may be falling into that can interfere with seeing issues and changing yourself, answering each one with "yes" or "no". You may also find it useful to invite a close friend, relative, or mentor into the reflection. Clarity prompts growth.

   Do I Often:
   a. Deny my need to change and grow?
   b. Blame others for my behavior and complain about their actions rather than addressing my own?
   c. Justify, make excuses for, and defend my poor behavior?
   d. Give up on growth because I feel the change process should be easier?
   e. Feel lost about how to make changes?
   f. Refuse feedback about my blind spots?
   g. Feel pride and satisfaction with how I am, without an intention to continue to grow?
   h. Hold such high standards of perfection that I give up trying to improve?
   i. Have an overly strong desire to please others—or to change myself for others?
   j. Minimize a problem I caused and tell myself that I simply committed a small or isolated offense?
   k. Justify prior behavior by convincing myself that other people are too sensitive?
   l. Think no one will ever find out there's a problem with my behavior?
   m. Lie to myself or others about my behavior?
   n. React with strong self-criticism when I see my own character weaknesses?
   o. Refuse to forgive myself, ask for forgiveness, or offer forgiveness?

2. Choose a hero (or heroine)—preferably someone from Bahá'í history—whose character, spiritual life, service, and choices you admire. Read something about their life and identify any specific behaviors of theirs that you want to emulate. Identify a specific circumstance in your life where following that person's example might inspire and assist you. Follow through with an action and assess the result. What was useful about keeping that person in mind while you acted?

3. Make one small change in your home environment to see how long it takes you to get used to it. You might move a piece of furniture, change the location of a picture hanging on the wall, or put your socks in a different drawer. Then make a different, more significant improvement in your physical space, such as organize a few drawers or a closet, paint a wall, or plant some flowers or a tree. What do you think, and how do you feel, about the changes? What do you think about the amount of effort required for the improvements?

4. Carry out an activity that takes significant patience and perseverance, such as fishing for a few hours and catching enough fish for a meal, teaching a child a new skill, learning a few phrases in a new language, or building skill in operating a new piece of machinery. What made you more successful with being patient? With persevering?

5. Changing a habit:
   a. Identify a habit you want to modify or replace.
   b. Outline the expected benefits of the change.
   c. Write specific goals for your behavior change.
   d. Make a commitment to another person; ask that person to hold you accountable and to encourage you.
   e. Plan small rewards for every week or whatever time interval is most useful.
   f. Set up other reminders or incentives for fulfilling your commitment.
   g. Set regular times on your calendar (daily? weekly?) and assess your progress toward your goal.
   h. Celebrate your achievement.

6. Make a list of the different ways you observe this quotation happening in your life: "Equality between men and women does not, indeed physiologically it cannot, mean identity of functions. In some things women excel men, for others men are better fitted than women, while in very many things the difference of sex is of no effect at all."[118] (On behalf of Shoghi Effendi) What roles do men and women play that are similar? Different?

7. Identify a project or activity that you and a woman or a group of men and women can do together. Consult about each person's abilities and how they can be applied cooperatively. Agree on ways to approach the project that will exemplify the equality of women and men. After

completion, reflect and consult peacefully together on how everyone's behavior matched spiritual principles and what might have worked better. If possible, carry out another activity and encourage and practice improved behaviors.

Reflection

1. What assists me to grow and change? How do creativity, patience, and perseverance support me in this effort?
2. What may get in the way of my ability to understand myself and my behavior very well?
3. How can I overcome my resistance to improving myself and building new capacities?
4. What personal transformation goals are most important to me? To others? How do I feel about the ways others want me to make changes?
5. How am I being affected by peer pressure? Are there other negative forces happening in my life?
6. What difficult moral choices have I had to make at school and/or work?
7. What activities can I be involved in to give me greater opportunities to practice and improve my behavior?
8. When have I successfully made a change in my behavior? What was the effect on interactions with others?
9. How could I "convey and model new understandings of masculinity"?
10. How do I react when I see women achieving higher marks in school, getting promoted, or earning more money than me?
11. What specific positive actions could I take that would balance equality with the women I interact, live, and work with?
12. How could I make it easier or possible for a woman I know to have greater opportunities with learning or work? How could it be collaborative? What would be my own learning and growth in the process?

8 - Developing My Character—Increasing My Light

Challenge: Sometimes it feels like my lower nature really wants to win, and sometimes it does.

Opportunity: As I develop my character, I like myself better, and others enjoy being around me and appreciate my contributions.

Summary:
- I'm a God-created noble human being, and I'm on a lifetime quest to keep growing as a noble being.
- I have a higher nature and a lower nature, and I'm healthiest and most contributing when I choose the high road.
- It's a bit overwhelming that I have lots, and lots, and lots of character qualities to keep track of and understand, but it's great to see all the good inside of me and the potential for more.
- When I assess, understand, and develop my character, I am powerful in fighting the spiritual battles between my lower and higher natures, and I have effective access to changing my less-desirable behaviors.
- Having many character strengths gives me the ability to navigate life with integrity and respect for myself and others; when I tell the truth and don't cheat or steal, it's amazing how much people trust me.

More:

Seeking character growth

Your ability to function well in relationships of all types and contribute to an ever-advancing civilization depends on your strength of character. You may or may not be familiar with character. Simply put, character is:

- The sum of all the qualities you develop throughout your life as you make choices about how to speak and act; character affects most of your words and actions; these qualities are also known as virtues
- The spiritual essence of who you are as a human being; the qualities of God mirrored in you
- Your moral compass or ethical strength that provides the unwavering drive to choose what is right, even when that choice could cause you

difficulties, and even if no one else is watching you or knows what you are doing

Your reputation is what others think about you. Your character is who you truly are. You have significant ability to practice character qualities with others for their benefit and yours, as well as to transform the ones that are weaker. You can build a good reputation for yourself by demonstrating character strengths. Below are quotations from the Bahá'í teachings about character and its importance:

"The light of a good character surpasseth the light of the sun and the radiance thereof. Whoso attaineth unto it is accounted as a jewel among men. The glory and the upliftment of the world must needs depend upon it."[119] Bahá'u'lláh

"The most vital duty, in this day, is to purify your characters, to correct your manners, and improve your conduct."[120] 'Abdu'l-Bahá

"The foundation-stone of a life lived in the way of God is the pursuit of moral excellence and the acquisition of a character endowed with qualities that are well-pleasing in His sight."[121] Shoghi Effendi

"The power of God can entirely transmute our characters and make of us beings entirely unlike our previous selves. Through prayer and supplication, obedience to the divine laws Bahá'u'lláh has revealed, and ever-increasing service to His Faith, we can change ourselves."[122] On behalf of Shoghi Effendi

"The great thing is to 'live the life'—to have our lives so saturated with the Divine teachings and the Bahá'í Spirit that people cannot fail to see a joy, a power, a love, a purity, a radiance, an efficiency in our character and work that will distinguish us from worldly-minded people and make people wonder what is the secret of this new life in us. We must become entirely selfless and devoted to God so that every day and every moment we seek to do only what God would have us do and in the way He would have us do it. If we do this sincerely then we shall have perfect unity and harmony with each other. Where there is want of harmony, there is lack of the true Bahá'í Spirit. Unless we can show this transformation in our lives, this new power, this mutual love and harmony, then the Bahá'í teachings are but a name to us."[123] On behalf of Shoghi Effendi

You develop and refine your character over time as you:

- Pray
- Follow the Bahá'í teachings
- Learn about character qualities
- Try out new words, actions, and activities that will strengthen your qualities, especially with family members, at work, and during community service
- Experience and overcome challenges
- Listen to your conscience and feelings of shame or guilt and take corrective action
- Make amends to others you have hurt; ask God and those you hurt for forgiveness
- Put yourself in environments and with people who encourage you to make beneficial changes and accompany you in the process

No one is perfect. You are probably strong in some character qualities and unskilled or uncertain about practicing others. You develop each quality according to your own willingness, choice, and effort. The stronger your character qualities, the better you will function in the world. Here is the challenge to remember in your life:

> "On the one hand, the high standard of conduct inculcated by Bahá'u'lláh's Revelation can admit no compromise; it can, in no wise, be lowered, and all must fix their gaze on its lofty heights. On the other, it must be acknowledged that, as human beings, we are far from perfect; what is expected of everyone is sincere daily effort."[124] Universal House of Justice

You can make your best effort to know and develop yourself before attempting serious endeavors such as marriage, parenthood, Bahá'í administrative service, and being a successful entrepreneur or worker in your chosen profession. You will also continue to grow through all these activities.

My dual natures: higher and lower

You may at times feel like there are two entities arguing inside of you, one that aligns with the light and another that aligns with the darkness. This is your conscience at work, and this image demonstrates the choices you have in life. Your higher nature and your lower nature (ego) can engage in both gentle disagreements and fierce spiritual battles. Your goal during your quest is to increasingly position your higher nature to triumph. Below are quotations about your nature.

"O Son of Spirit! Noble have I created thee, yet thou hast abased thyself. Rise then unto that for which thou wast created."[125] Bahá'u'lláh

"In man there are two natures; his spiritual or higher nature and his material or lower nature. In one he approaches God, in the other he lives for the world alone. Signs of both these natures are to be found in men. In his material aspect he expresses untruth, cruelty and injustice; all these are the outcome of his lower nature. The attributes of his Divine nature are shown forth in love, mercy, kindness, truth and justice, one and all being expressions of his higher nature. Every good habit, every noble quality belongs to man's spiritual nature, whereas all his imperfections and sinful actions are born of his material nature."[126] 'Abdu'l-Bahá

"The mission of the Prophets of God has been to train the souls of humanity and free them from the thralldom of natural instincts and physical tendencies. They are like unto Gardeners, and the world of humanity is the field of Their cultivation, the wilderness and untrained jungle growth wherein They proceed to labor."[127] 'Abdu'l-Bahá

"Self has really two meanings, or is used in two senses, in the Bahá'í writings; one is self, the identity of the individual created by God. This is the self mentioned in such passages as 'he hath known God who hath known himself etc.'. The other self is the ego, the dark, animalistic heritage each one of us has, the lower nature that can develop into a monster of selfishness, brutality, lust and so on. It is this self we must struggle against, or this side of our natures, in order to strengthen and free the spirit within us and help it to attain perfection.

"Self-sacrifice means to subordinate this lower nature and its desires to the more godly and noble side of ourselves. Ultimately, in its highest sense, self-sacrifice means to give our will and our all to God to do with as He pleases. Then He purifies and glorifies our true self until it becomes a shining and wonderful reality."[128] On behalf of Shoghi Effendi

"... [T]he complete and entire elimination of the ego would imply perfection—which man can never completely attain—but the ego can and should be ever-increasingly subordinated to the enlightened soul of man. This is what spiritual progress implies."[129] On behalf of Shoghi Effendi

"In contrast to many contemporary conceptions, the Bahá'í teachings maintain that a person must rise above certain material aspects of human nature to develop and manifest inherent spiritual qualities that characterize his or her true self. The Sacred Texts contain laws and exhortations that, in many instances, redirect or restrict behaviors that arise from impulses, tendencies, and desires, whether inborn or acquired. Some of these are physical, while others are emotional or psychological. Yet, whatever their origin, it is through their regulation and control that the higher, spiritual nature is able to predominate and flourish. Those who are not Bahá'ís may have no cause to take into account such considerations. A Bahá'í, however, cannot set aside the implications of these teachings and must endeavor to respond to the best of his or her ability, though it be little by little and day by day. In so doing, all believers face challenges, although the specific type or extent of a test may differ. They act with faith in Bahá'u'lláh's declaration, 'Know assuredly that My commandments are the lamps of My loving providence among My servants, and the keys of My mercy for My creatures', and they respond to His call, 'Observe My commandments, for the love of My beauty.'"[130] On behalf of the Universal House of Justice

If you experience excessive shame or guilt and do not take remedial action, you can interrupt your growth process. If you fall into the trap of feeling you are unworthy, or you believe lies of others about you, it aborts your personal transformation progress. If you decide to stop moving forward in fruitful ways, it can harm your well-being and functioning. This state of mind can also disrupt relationships with your loved ones, and with God. As you recognize that you are worthy of love and respect, you progress forward in life, honoring your essential nobility as a human being with a body, mind, heart, and soul.

Here is a perspective on this theme:

"Feelings of guilt and shame lead to depression and despair. This, in turn, generates a very negative self-image, and even the smallest problem can seem insurmountable. ... The distinguishing characteristic of a human being is his nobility of character. No matter what the circumstance or the condition, the underlying reality remains that of a nobility of character in the image of God Himself. Negative self-images have no place in a Bahá'í context, and self-abasement is contradictory and forbidden. Struggles and frustrations should be expected as the result of the nobility striving to express itself, and the spiritualization process in these instances must be direct towards strengthening this image of nobility, as opposed to a tendency to cripple oneself with guilt and self-flagellation."[131] Sharon Hatcher Kennedy and Andrew Kennedy

All people have a higher spiritual nature and a personal responsibility for developing it while subduing their lower, material nature. Humans have the capacity to develop an almost endless number of character strengths, the attributes of God that He has placed within us in our higher nature. However, having the capacity, courage, and strength to fully understand and develop your character will be a gradual process.

Many aspects of the lower nature can interfere with a self-improvement process, such as:

- Laziness
- Irresponsibility
- Lying
- Stealing
- Violence
- Rudeness
- Infidelity
- Unfriendliness

There are tools and principles for purifying your character with positive choices and working toward excellence. Being truthful is one of these:

"Truthfulness is the foundation of all human virtues. Without truthfulness progress and success, in all the worlds of God, are impossible for any soul. When this holy attribute is established in man, all the divine qualities will also be acquired."[132] 'Abdu'l-Bahá

Here is someone's personal reflection:

"'Truthfulness is the foundation' of all the positive character qualities because it requires us to be honest with ourselves about who we really are, what we think, and what we feel. This is an essential condition for positive change, and it's a process, not something to be achieved all at once. 'Little by little, day by day', as 'Abdu'l-Bahá said. On the other hand, deception—the opposite of truthfulness—is, I think, a defensive reaction to being hurt, criticized, and judged. We try to hide from others, thinking that we are unworthy or defective. However, God knows who we really are, what our character is, accepts us in that condition, and helps us grow. Humbly and honestly sharing with God when we act poorly is essential to allow His love and healing to reach us. Such honesty is not always easy to achieve. Somewhat counterintuitively, I have found that praying for forgiveness actually helps me know that God is all-Loving and is here to help, not to condemn."

When you are in a mode of action and learning, striving to improve yourself, you will tend to produce positive results, increasing your self-respect—even if you don't quite qualify for sainthood! It's possible to look honestly and objectively at what you are doing well and where you need to focus your self-improvement efforts without spiraling downward with criticism and an excessive focus on achieving perfection.

Engaging in being my best

As you read the Bahá'í Writings, you will see clues for what a good character looks like, such as in this example about kindness:

"He should show kindness to animals, how much more unto his fellow-man, to him who is endowed with the power of utterance."[133] Bahá'u'lláh

Self-assessment is rarely easy, but it can be very satisfying to understand yourself and feel your character muscles growing. The process can be similar and connects to bringing yourself to account daily, as you learned about in Chapter 5. Prayer, reflection, and courageous consultation with a trusted friend, relative, or mentor can assist you to gain insights. It's beneficial when you stay focused on your own behavior and responsibilities, and you don't compare yourself to others. Remember to practice moderation, as you can often make better progress with focusing on improving one or two qualities at a time.

After you interact with your parents, a girlfriend or wife, a manager at work, or a community member at a gathering, you can assess yourself by asking questions such as:

- Were my intentions, words, and actions aligned and consistent with each other?
- What did I do that was effective? What positive effect did my choices have on me and on others?
- Which character qualities did I practice well?
- Where did I misstep? What would I change if I could do it over?
- Would another character quality have made a difference if I had practiced it instead? For instance, did I practice justice, when compassion might have led to a better outcome?
- Could I have added in a second quality, such as flexibility or respect, to balance the first quality and thereby improve the situation?
- Did I behave ineffectively, or did the other person's difficulties or problems cause the negative outcome?
- If the interaction didn't go smoothly, what words or actions would I choose instead, to elicit a better outcome next time?

One man reflects on the value of character assessment:

"A truthful evaluation of our own thoughts and character is a wholesome, healing step to take, for it is only when we are honest about ourselves that we begin to change and then have a profound effect on society. Prayerfully turning our attention to our own shortcomings and telling ourselves the truth need not have a negative or destructive effect; this is the beginning of a powerful, positive process when it is motivated by the love of God and the desire to be of service to humanity."[134]

Once you see it's wise to strengthen a quality, you can begin the process. The following story illustrates the process a person went through striving to become truthful and overcome the habit of lying:

"As we grow in our understanding of the Creative Word, our flaws are shed. For example, a young man is touched by the Message of Bahá'u'lláh and becomes a Bahá'í. But he's a liar. He has always lied, because his parents

lied, as did their parents. Lying was a natural part of their lives, used as a tool to survive in a hostile society. So lying had been ingrained in the new Bahá'í. He couldn't be kept out of the Faith because of a character flaw, for it that were the case, then most of us would be barred from Bahá'í membership.

"As a Bahá'í he discovers that 'truthfulness is the foundation of all human virtues.' ('Abdu'l-Bahá, quoted in Advent of Divine Justice, p. 22) He vows to change. But how to do it?

"Realizing that through deepening and prayer he can be 'endowed with a new eye, a new ear, a new heart, and a new mind,' (Bahá'u'lláh, Gleanings from the Writings of Bahá'u'lláh, p. 267) he decides to deepen every day—in the morning and evening as Bahá'u'lláh prescribes. He reasons that he must follow what Bahá'u'lláh urges us to do, because He knows, better than anyone else, what would help him carry out his vow.

"So, he begins to deepen, making time in the morning before going to work, and making time in the evening before going to bed. He even buys an alarm clock, to make sure he gets up thirty minutes before his usual time. A week after he starts deepening, he's tested at work. His foreman asks a question, and he lies, the way he did in his pre-Bahá'í days, without hesitating an instant. But when the foreman leaves, he realizes that he lied, something he would never have concerned himself with in the past. His new awareness is not only a sign of progress in overcoming a character flaw, but also signifies the development of the young man's conscience.

"A month later—still deepening every day—he's tested again. This time he hesitates before answering a coworker, wondering if he should tell the truth or lie. He succumbs to the pull of the past and lies, and for a few minutes feels bad for not having the strength to beat back his natural inclination. Though he lied, the young man is making progress.

"He continues to deepen regularly. Three weeks later, he's faced with another test. He lies again, but this time, before he utters a word, his chest and throat tighten and he can't look at the person. Afterwards he berates himself for more than an hour for not telling the truth. Obviously, more progress.

"Three months go by. Still faithfully deepening, he's confronted by a former friend about a matter that took place before he was a Bahá'í. He wishes he could disappear. The friend senses his uneasiness and wonders if he's ill. In a way, he is ill, for the thought of lying makes him nauseous—but he lies. For the remainder of the day he's conscience-stricken, even has difficulty sleeping.

"After a year of deepening, a process he has learned to enjoy and now wouldn't think of missing, he's tested again. This time he's seized with pain *in his chest and begins to sweat. His hesitation is so long that the person he's talking to asks the question a second time. In torment, he sits down, placing his head in his hands. He wants desperately to tell the truth, yet feels the tug of the past.*

"Suddenly, he opens his eyes, looks at the foreman who is standing over him and tells the truth. The pain in his chest disappears. There's a glow in his eyes. He feels like dancing. The foreman is perplexed, wondering if the young man is on some kind of narcotic. He has never seen him so happy. It is a victory only the young man can appreciate, a feeling of liberation he has never experienced before. He is not what he was before he started deepening. He sees and hears things that he didn't see or hear before. How could he ever go back to what he was? Never! For he has sensed the fragrance of the Abhá Kingdom. But this new awareness didn't emerge instantly. It wasn't something that he obtained as one would purchase a coat to protect oneself from the cold. The potential to be what he is now was always a part of him. By deepening he simply nurtured and cultivated the seed of happiness that he was born with."[135]

The teachings remind you:

"How resplendent the luminaries of knowledge that shine in an atom, and how vast the oceans of wisdom that surge within a drop! To a supreme degree is this true of man, who, among all created things, hath been invested with the robe of such gifts, and hath been singled out for the glory of such distinction. For in him are potentially revealed all the attributes and names of God…."[136] Bahá'u'lláh

"… The inestimable value of religion is that when a man is vitally connected with it, through a real and living belief in it and in the Prophet who brought it, he receives a strength greater than his own which helps him to develop his good characteristics and overcome his bad ones. The whole purpose of religion is to change not only our thoughts but our acts; when we believe in God and His Prophet and His teachings, we find we are growing even though we perhaps thought ourselves incapable of growth and change."[137] On behalf of Shoghi Effendi

Once you develop a character strength in yourself, you can:

- Feel a sense of authenticity when you practice it

- Feel excited and enthusiastic about having a positive quality you can apply in all aspects of your life

Action

1. **Assess and Understand My Character Qualities:**

   This activity will get you started on a development process if you are not doing one currently. It's just the beginning, as you will continue to develop all your qualities throughout your life.

Instructions:
- Set up a chart on an electronic device or in a notebook of the qualities listed below to increase your understanding of some of your strengths and to identify areas for improvement. Definitions are provided to build your understanding. There are many more possible qualities that could be listed; if you have any additional ones that are important to you, then add them to the list.

- Take whatever time you need to be thorough. You may or may not be able to do this activity all at once, and you may need to make revisions at times. You can rate yourself on each character quality by using the 5-point scale provided below. Write down the number you think is accurate next to each quality. Do your best to be honest, but also don't be overly harsh with yourself.

    1: I rarely use this quality, so my words and actions can often cause problems
    2: I use this quality only occasionally, possibly causing problems
    3: I understand this quality, and am strengthening it; sometimes resulting in positive outcomes
    4: I am becoming more consistent in practicing this quality, usually with positive outcomes
    5: I practice this quality consciously and consistently (not perfectly!)

- Looking at your list of qualities again, note four that you most want to develop or build upon—at least for now. The qualities you rated 1, 2, or 3 may offer good choices, as they are in a currently weaker state. Reflect on what specific actions might strengthen them and try out a few.

Some Character Qualities from CharacterYAQ:

1. **Adherence is** following guidelines, rules, agreements, and laws created to protect relationships, safety, and order; staying faithful to promises made to others.
2. **Compassion is** demonstrating a unique capacity to listen deeply to others about their situations; understanding others' feelings; caring for others' well-being; and seeking ways to ease someone's pain and suffering in mutually satisfactory ways.
3. **Creativity is** drawing on ideas, inspiration, or imagination from many sources to develop or produce something new; being resourceful, intuitive, and solving problems in unique and beneficial ways; and immersing in a problem or situation, looking broadly for insights and connections, allowing for breakthrough ideas and solutions to emerge.
4. **Dependability is** making and keeping commitments, completing agreed tasks, honestly managing resources and money, handling information wisely, and cleaning up after mistakes.
5. **Excellence is** achieving high standards and a superior quality of work, effort, appearance, relationships, and personal development; learning and improving from experiences; and continually raising and meeting expectations.
6. **Flexibility is** being open to change and surprises, adjusting and adapting to life as it happens; being nimble in responding to different people and situations; and considering new and different approaches, methods, ideas, and viewpoints.
7. **Friendliness is** demonstrating an outgoing and positive social attitude and reaching out to connect and build relationships with people; and gracious and warm consideration for others by interacting with polite manners, respectful gestures, thoughtful actions, and tactful language.
8. **Honor is** having clear principles, beliefs, and positive intentions that guide actions to create beneficial change.
9. **Humility is** seeing and accepting one's whole self, including strengths, imperfections, abilities, accomplishments, failures, and needs in modest and realistic perspective; offering one's time, knowledge, and talents in a self-effacing way; and being willing to accept the knowledge, skills, and help of others.
10. **Joyfulness is** maintaining a happy, optimistic, and uplifting attitude; energetically celebrating the best in relationships, work, and service; and looking at the positive side of circumstances.

11. **Justice is** making careful, independent, and proactive observations of other's actions; initiating decisions, agreements, or actions based on clear facts that are free of bias or prejudice; ensuring fair rewards and appropriate natural consequences or agreed corrective actions occur; and setting appropriate boundaries in relationships.
12. **Moderation is** recognizing and avoiding extremes in use of time, words, actions, and other choices; accomplishing variety, balance, and positive outcomes in such aspects as rest, work, reflection, community service, and leisure activities; and effectively applying and adjusting a level of intensity of focus and action to both accomplish goals and protect relationships and well-being.
13. **Orderliness is** living and working with a sense of harmony; creating uncluttered, well-organized, clean, and shareable spaces; developing systems that allow for easy finding; and systematically planning improvements, tasks, and projects.
14. **Perseverance is** applying energy, effort, and resources toward worthwhile goals until achievement is attained; being committed to the long-term future benefit of actions done in the present; and using willpower to overcome challenges or adversity as they arise.
15. **Purposefulness is** pursuing and fulfilling meaningful long-term personal goals, commitments, aspirations, and needs; contributing ideas, words, and actions; and participating primarily in vital activities that contribute to desired outcomes.
16. **Reflection is** calm self-awareness, understanding, and assessment; inwardly exploring actions, circumstances, thoughts, feelings, and perceptions; seeking inspiration; and analyzing to learn the best approaches for improving situations.
17. **Respect is** interacting with all people and what they value with fair treatment, dignity, consideration, and esteem; and recognizing the best knowledge, skills, talents, and abilities of others.
18. **Self-Discipline is** maintaining the inner control to perform needed and important tasks in a timely way; consciously responding in appropriate ways; and choosing what is beneficial or productive and resisting what is harmful or distracting.
19. **Service is** acting selflessly and often sacrificially, directly or indirectly, and with positive intent; and providing time, knowledge, or resources to benefit others without expecting reward or recognition.
20. **Trust is** generously extending confidence; assuming the good intentions and actions of others; accompanying others through learning

experiences that build skills and capacities; and giving and expecting appropriate confidentiality.
21. **Truthfulness is** recognizing and accurately communicating facts and feelings; independently seeking knowledge of people, circumstances, issues, and information.
22. **Unity is** consciously looking for and strengthening points of commonality, harmony, connection, and attraction; accepting differences; and working with others to build a strong and coherent foundation for oneness, love, fairness, commitment, inclusion, cooperation, and common goals.

Source and Copyright: The definitions in this list are the copyright of CharacterYAQ™ (characteryaq.com) and S. M. Alexander, W. G. Peirce IV, and J. S. Wong. None of the definitions should be reproduced for any purpose, without written permission from the copyright holders. Thank you for your respect toward our work.

2. **My Character Development Plan:** Set up on an electronic device or in a notebook a chart that includes the elements in this example below for each quality you want to develop.

EXAMPLE
Quality to Develop: *Perseverance*
Why? *Because I often fail to finish my personal projects. Too often I allow obstacles or trying to be perfect to discourage me, I lose motivation, and I postpone action until "I have more time."*
Who Can Help or Encourage Me with This? *My friend Oscar, who told me he found some strategies for developing his virtues of perseverance, "stick-to-it-iveness," and "grit".*
Development Goal (Desired Outcome): *I'd currently rank my perseverance at a 2 out of 5. If I could get that quality, when working on my projects, up to a strength of 4, I think I could accomplish much more in life.*

Continued below.

Development Actions:	Start Date:	Assess Date:
1. *I will create actionable goals and firm deadlines for when to complete 2 personal growth projects. I will make myself accountable to Oscar or someone else for delivery of these results. I will make sure that at least 1 project is focused on service to others.*	Date	Date
2. *Talk with Oscar or other friends whenever I feel discouraged; this will help me to address the obstacles so I can keep moving forward.*	Date	Date
3. *When starting work on each project, I will take a few minutes to pray for perseverance, focus, and determination.*	Date	Date
4. *Read inspiring quotations and stories about perseverance as part of my daily practice of reading the Bahá'í writings.*	Date	Date

Signs of Improvement: *After 1 month of doing this, I completed 1 of the 2 projects, and I am 75% finished with the second project. The service component of these projects has visibly helped the children in my community take charge of improving their lives and those of others.*

New Actions to Take: *Keep up the accountability, talk to Oscar more often about this—at least once every 2 weeks.*

When the date arrives to assess your progress, look over your notes, review your behavior, and reflect on your words and actions. Determine how much you advanced toward your goal. Think carefully about how people responded to you—not only those you consulted with but also those you encountered as you strove to develop and demonstrate the quality. This assessment process will give you a sense of your progress, which you can note in the Signs of Improvement section. If you want feedback in addition to your own self-assessment, you can approach people and ask for frank but kind comments. Is anyone noticing your positive changes? Are you getting enough useful feedback and encouragement?

3. Choose a character quality from the list above in this chapter that you want to increase your awareness of. For a week—or some other reasonable timeframe—put yourself frequently in situations with other people. Track how others demonstrate or discuss the quality you chose. Where did you see it happen? How often did it happen? Did the use of it surprise you? How did you practice character qualities, too? What thoughts do you have about your observations?

4. To gain a broader view of your character, you can take research-based character assessments such as the Character Foundations Assessment developed by a Bahá'í along with a certified feedback coach available through Marriage Transformation. [See the Contact Information at the end of the book.]

5. Choose a quality that inspires you and search for quotations that increase your understanding of it. Create an artistic rendering of the quality that will be visible to you in your daily life. Consider a poster, screensaver on your computer, meme, artwork, song, poem, photo, dance, or other expression.

Reflection

1. What are the benefits of caring about the state of my character?
2. In what ways do I see myself differently when I use a spiritual lens? How could I form the habit of regular character self-assessment?
3. What interferes with knowing my own character? How can I overcome these challenges?
4. What is easy and wonderful about learning about my own character?
5. Which three of my well-developed character qualities may improve my relationships with family members? With a relationship or marriage partner?
6. Which three character qualities are weaker and cause me concern, as they might cause problems in my relationships or interactions with others?
7. What specific examples show that I already effectively practice some of my character strengths?
8. Who do I trust that knows me well and can assist me to gain further insights? How and when will I invite them to participate in this reflection process?

Part 3: Building Health and Well-Being on My Quest

Essential Note: Many aspects of your well-being are covered in the chapters in this part of the book. They are presented as separate topics to allow for focused attention, ease of reflection, and building understanding and action. However, you are one human being, and all these aspects, as well as your spiritual health (the focus throughout the book), interact and are completely interlinked and inseparable.

After you have read and acted on the various aspects presented, please spend time reflecting on the concept of coherence:

- How can I live a life where I balance my physical, mental, emotional, and spiritual well-being?
- How does looking outward and serving others contribute to my holistic well-being?

[See Chapter 20 for more on the concept of coherence.]

9 – Striving for My Mental Health

Challenge: When I'm faced with people and happenings that are #%&!, my head feels full of pounding hammers, and I only want to escape.

Opportunity: I cope, survive, and thrive when I recognize that I'm a noble human being, and I practice self-respect, encouragement, and primarily keep positive thoughts in my mind.

Summary:
- Courage, resilience, and flexibility empower me to be healthy mentally.
- There are many mental challenges facing people today, and I am not immune just because I'm striving to be a spiritual man.
- Part of practicing self-respect is acknowledging when I am struggling, and it's a courageous strength to ask for assistance as appropriate.
- Seeking accompaniment from competent mental health professionals is wise as needed.
- Respecting myself is a vital link to happiness and excellent behavior.
- Self-criticism, perfectionism, and criticism from others can sabotage my progress.
- Engaging in learning something new can be a positive mental-strengthening step.

More:

Challenges of achieving mental health

Being well-balanced mentally is a challenge at times for every human being, and it takes daily effort to strive for it. Here is one man's perspective:

"Courage is love as action—love on her silver steed, forcing change in the world, rising to challenges, negotiating life with skill, and confronting others with care and wisdom. The qualities that courage draws upon—hardiness and resilience, as well as the ability to bend and alter course when faced with difficulty, to commit oneself to a cause, and to find inner power during times of pain—are *all* associated with mental health. We need a deep, tensile strength to face the tough times in life, to speak out persuasively against injustice, and, above all, to love others wisely and well. To love at all is a risk that requires courage—we risk our safety, letting ourselves be raw and vulnerable; we accept our share of compromise and weather disappointment and despair; and above all, we are willing to confront a loved one even if what we need to say is not easy or kind."[138] Stephen Post

Remember those dark forces? They can impact your mental well-being, even when you are trying to do everything "right" spiritually. Many people today struggle with anxiety, depression, low self-worth, and a variety of mental illnesses. Family dysfunctions and abuse have an impact on many. Self-harm, including suicide, is happening at an alarmingly high rate. If you hide, withdraw, and overly focus on the problem, it will likely get worse. Here is an excerpt from a global report:

"Depression is one of the leading causes of illness and disability among adolescents, and suicide is the second leading cause of death in adolescents. Violence, poverty, humiliation and feeling devalued can increase the risk of developing mental health problems.

"Building life skills in children and adolescents and providing them with psychosocial support in schools and other community settings can help promote good mental health. Programs to help strengthen the ties between adolescents and their families are also important. If problems arise, they should be detected and managed by competent and caring health workers."[139]

Here is some guidance:

"It is too bad that young and promising men, who if they remain living can render great services to humanity, should take away their life at a moment of despair.

"The world, especially in these days, is full of woes and sufferings. We should be brave and have a stout heart. Trials and tribulations should arouse in us added vigor and greater determination and not dampen our zeal and kill our spirit."[140] On behalf of Shoghi Effendi

It's often said in 12-step support groups—where people re-connect to God and others while addressing an addiction—that no situation is too difficult to be bettered and no unhappiness is too great to be lessened. Whatever issue you are experiencing can be improved. Please reach out to people who are equipped to influence the situation in a positive direction. You may be more comfortable with helping others than in asking for help, thinking you are being weak if you lean on another person. However, the truth is that it often takes being brave and in action to reach out to others for assistance, and the goal is to lean only while you build the strength to not need to. Once you are strong, you are then positioned to be of service to others.

Self-respect—A key part of mental health

Respecting others seems like an obviously good thing for everyone to do. Respect is a well-known word and part of our everyday language. And yet, you may often behave in ways that diminish your respect for yourself. One impetus for changing this pattern is realizing that your happiness is vitally linked to self-respect. Below is some guidance on this topic.

"... [M]an's supreme honor and real happiness lie in self-respect, in high resolves and noble purposes, in integrity and moral quality, in immaculacy of mind."[141] 'Abdu'l-Bahá

"... [T]he Cause of God will derive immense benefit when it is observed that the Bahá'ís, and particularly Bahá'í youth, stand out against the laxity and depravity of the permissive society, that the exalted standards of conduct which they strive to uphold are firmly rooted in spiritual principles, giving them confidence, self-respect and true happiness."[142] On behalf of the Universal House of Justice

When you're happy, it's easier to influence happiness in others, you are more likely to find useful ways to be of service in the world, and your friendships, relationships, or marriage are stronger and more unified.

Sabotaging Factors: Unworthiness and perfectionism

There appears to be an epidemic of inner "unworthiness" in humanity today. Sometimes this can be fueled by negative comments from peers or with social media postings showing seemingly perfect people or attacking others. As people feel unworthy, they often question whether they deserve to have others respect and love them. Learning or accepting that you are a noble human being can be hard work. Sometimes this requires counseling and a good dose of common sense from professionals in the self-help field and healthy friends and family members. So many people now are "products" of poor parenting, divorce, and a lack of spiritual awareness.

Everyone is developing (or sabotaging) their capacities for knowing and loving God, themselves, and others. Insisting on perfection from yourself or others can block mutual understanding and the ability for others to love you as you truly are, including your vulnerabilities. In its essence, this means missing opportunities to build a connection of love and unity with others around you. As you develop your capacity for self-respect and love, you strengthen your ability to be of selfless service to others, which can be viewed as an excellent expression of the best of yourself.

It may seem that striving for perfection should always have a positive outcome. However, sometimes you may slip into your lower nature and be unwise and immoderate. Instead of striving for excellence, you may start demanding perfection from yourself. This can result in magnifying your faults or weaknesses and minimizing your strengths and nobility. This is often called "perfectionism". Consider this:

> "The only people who are truly free of the 'dross of self' are the Prophets, for to be free of one's ego is a hall-mark of perfection. We humans are *never* going to become perfect, for perfection belongs to a realm we are not destined to enter. However, we must constantly mount higher, seek to be more perfect."[143] On behalf of Shoghi Effendi

Life experiences, especially those that are emotionally or physically painful or abusive, may lead a person to question their value as a human being. When people grow up with a lot of criticism from parents, they can feel competent with daily responsibilities but lack confidence in their own worth. Those who instead received excessive praise from parents may be confident, but they lack the competence to work and serve others effectively. When people are exposed to a significant amount of criticism or unachievably high demands from others, they can often struggle to feel noble, worthy of love, or respected by themselves or others.

If your life is driven by perfectionism, you may:

- Experience an inner critical and judgmental voice telling you that your efforts are not good enough, even though you may be achieving positive outcomes
- Lose the ability to discern that you are doing something well
- Be hyper-conscious of never wanting to make a mistake or appear as a failure in front of others; as a result, you could lose energy and then begin to fail, or become exhausted from working so hard to appear perfect

- Resist asking others for assistance, out of strong concerns about appearing imperfect or a failure
- Stop yourself from trying something new or interesting

Indicators that this negative cycle is operating in your life occur when you frequently use words like "should," "ought," "must," "always," or "never" in relation to doing something; put excessive weight on what others will think of you; or think that you are "bad" or "wrong". Labeling your whole self as "bad" or "wrong" is a broad accusation and condemnation. It's healthier to say a particular *action* was harmful and respond appropriately to correcting your behavior. This is one person's reflection:

> "Authentic spirituality means giving up perfectionism for the rigorous process of developing ourselves one thought, one act, one day at a time."[144] L. K. Popov

Here is someone's reflection on the topic:

> "I think it's important to note that there are many types of perfectionism. One is critical and judgmental behavior toward your own self. It results in procrastination and difficulties in starting or initiating anything because there is the fear of failure and of not performing as perfectly as one would want. So, this often results in inactivity.
>
> "The other type of perfectionism is where the person is hyper-productive, an over-achiever, and they constantly perform and initiate new projects without true balance in life. They tend to be workaholics, only satisfied with the best grades in school (otherwise the world falls apart), and the best person in most situations. They have a strong urge to control many situations and people."

Below are some examples of perfectionism. Reflect to see if you have some of these negative patterns:

Standards and Fear
- Set high standards that are impossible to attain
- Have a very high fear of failure and try to hide it
- Inflexibly demand perfection all the time from self and others
- Fail to analyze the source of self-improvement standards
- Do not consider the reasonableness of meeting a standard

- Overly focus on living up to other's standards, while ignoring or not recognizing self-chosen ones
- Ignore other higher priorities

Judging and Criticizing
- Judge (and condemn!) yourself or others as unworthy of respect or love
- Criticize anything that is not perfect or does not meet high standards
- Attack or abandon your creativity, ideas, and dreams
- Doubt yourself and attempt to hide your perception of inadequacy
- Feel like an imposter when achieving something
- Avoid blame or criticism from others by harshly talking or acting toward others
- Strategize how to avoid making mistakes or having others see your errors
- Listen to others with false empathy to find and exploit their failures or to feel superior to them

These behaviors above are damaging to your self-respect, and they tend to reduce love and unity, thereby causing estrangement in your relationships. Perfectionism can also disrupt your connection with God and your spiritual life. Signs of this disruption are when you:

- Find it difficult (or impossible) to ask God or your religious community for resources and assistance
- Break away from God and stop participating in spiritual or other community activities
- Block feelings of love to or from God
- Feel paralyzed and unable to act because you do not perfectly know what the Will of God is beforehand
- Fearfully try to make perfect decisions to keep God happy and not angry with you
- Give up on self-respect and self-improvement efforts altogether

There is a high cost of living without joy. Do you erect walls or impose standards that interfere with happy and healthy relationships? Could this leave you feeling angry and alone?

It is good to remember and accept that you are always worthy of being loved by God. Reflect on the quotation below.

"O Son of Being! Love Me, that I may love thee. If thou lovest Me not, My love can in no wise reach thee. Know this, O servant."[145] Bahá'u'lláh

There is no question that God sets high standards for us and encourages us to strive toward them. However, we will never perfectly meet them. The gift in having high standards is that you get better and better, benefitting those you live with and serve. Developing your character strengths will result in a happier, love-filled life. Here is some guidance:

"The Bahá'í community...makes no claims to perfection. To uphold high ideals and to have become their embodiment are not one and the same. Myriad are the challenges that lie ahead, and much remains to be learned."[146] Universal House of Justice

"Let no excessive self-criticism or any feelings of inadequacy, inability or inexperience hinder you or cause you to be afraid. Bury your fears in the assurances of Bahá'u'lláh. Has He not asserted that upon anyone who mentions His Name will descend the 'hosts of Divine inspiration' and that on such a one will also descend the 'Concourse on high, each bearing aloft a chalice of pure light'? Step forth, then, into the arena where all His loved ones are equally summoned, equally challenged and abundantly blessed. For to teach, Bahá'u'lláh Himself affirms, is to do the 'most meritorious of all deeds'. And at this extraordinary moment in the history of the planet, nothing whatever is of more critical importance than inviting people of every sort and every gift to the banquet table of the Lord of Hosts."[147] Universal House of Justice

It's wise for you to avoid negative self-talk that weighs you down with destructive criticism. This looks like inner comments such as "I am so stupid!" or "Why don't I ever do anything right?!" If you are very self-critical—which is essentially training yourself to always see what is wrong with you—you are more likely to be critical of a relationship/marriage partner, coworkers, or others around you. You are also less likely to notice and accentuate your strengths and those of others. If negativity is an issue for you, it may be useful for you to study and strengthen the qualities of humility, mercy, and joyfulness.

A man encourages reaching out to a professional as needed:

"[At times, nothing is a] substitute for a good therapist. ... If your life is not going as well as you would like, then finding an objective, compassionate person to consult with about it will do you a lot of good. ... Having a real, live person look into your eyes and say, 'You have a right to feel that way' can break through more layers of denial and fear than a hundred books, so give it a try. Before I visited my first therapist, I was terrified. ... Consider therapy a kind of consultation on how to improve your life, the way you would bring a contractor in to help remodel your home. If you don't feel you are making progress after half a dozen sessions, change therapists. Don't give up.

"Here is a list of healthy beliefs that a good therapist will help you internalize:
- I am safe—though my body may be frail and vulnerable, my soul is strong and eternal.
- I am valuable—I matter to God and to the world. I make a difference.
- I am lovable—I am created in the image of God and reflect spiritual virtues.
- I am loving—I am attracted to the signs of God reflected in the people around me.
- I have capacities—I am not a helpless pawn of the universe. I can make choices and accomplish goals.
- *I can grow*—I am not static. I can learn and develop new skills and virtues."

"A good therapist will also support your efforts at developing honesty, forgiveness, compassion and faith."[148]

Rebounding from criticism

When others criticize you, this can also be destructive to how you feel about yourself. However, self-respect encourages you to be discerning. Are the person's words accurate and truthful, and you have action to take to change? What were the person's motives? Is there something going on in that person's life that has them behaving in a miserable way, and therefore it's good to feel compassion and forgiveness toward them?

We have this guidance about our interactions with each other:

"... Bahá'ís in their deep love for Bahá'u'lláh, should be eager to apply every spiritual precept in their own lives while at the same time exercising patience, forbearance and forgiveness in respect to the shortcomings of others."[149] Universal House of Justice

"Bahá'u'lláh also recognizes that human beings are fallible. He knows that, in our weakness, we shall repeatedly stumble when we try to walk in the path He has pointed out to us. If all human beings became perfect the moment they accepted the call of Bahá'u'lláh this world would be another world. It is in light of our frailty that 'Abdu'l-Bahá appealed to the friends everywhere to love each other and stressed the emphatic teaching of Bahá'u'lláh that each of us should concentrate upon improving his or her own life and ignore the faults of others. How many times the Master stressed the need for unity, for without it His Father's Cause could not go forward."[150] On behalf of the Universal House of Justice

When you stay stuck in the critical words others say to you and keep replaying them in your mind, it can diminish your self-respect, and you might withdraw from participation in activities where the criticizer is present. It's difficult to keep going and maintain unity when criticism is repetitive. Self-respect may prompt you to raise the issue for consultation with the person, or it may be wise to seek guidance from someone or an entity in authority, such as a manager at work or a Spiritual Assembly. Sometimes this can result in the person changing. Sometimes they are convinced they are right and insist you are wrong. Sometimes the person's heart changes if you are repeatedly kind to them, something 'Abdu'l-Bahá often demonstrated.

It's also wise to spend time with people who lift you up rather than tear you down. Sometimes people think criticism contributes to others and are not aware of its damage. There are times when clear feedback is appropriate to aid your self-assessment and growth, and it's best when offered with love and in a way that effectively supports your will to improve. Criticism, instead, is often delivered in a highly destructive way with harmful words and tones of voice. You can be brave and request that the person include respect, kindness, and tactfulness along with feedback. This will encourage your growth and progress. Stay aware, however, because sometimes removing yourself from a situation or lessening your time around some people can be an act of self-respect, love, and unity.

Bahá'u'lláh asks us to keep seeing Him when relationships are difficult:

"If any differences arise amongst you, behold Me standing before your face, and overlook the faults of one another for My name's sake and as a token of your love for My manifest and resplendent Cause. We love to see you at all times consorting in amity and concord within the paradise of My good-pleasure, and to inhale from your acts the fragrance of friendliness and unity, of loving-kindness and fellowship. Thus counseleth you the All-Knowing, the Faithful. We shall always be with you; if We inhale the perfume of your fellowship, Our heart will assuredly rejoice, for naught else can satisfy Us. To this beareth witness every man of true understanding."[151] Bahá'u'lláh

Valuing encouragement

Part of increasing self-respect includes transforming the way you talk to yourself. You can acknowledge your progress in positive ways and encourage yourself to keep improving little by little, day by day. It's wise to acknowledge and appreciate every small success you accomplish; each one adds up to large achievements. You can be fair, kind, and compassionate to yourself as well as to others.

Encouragement well delivered and received can release creativity and action in positive directions for you and others. Here are some ideas to try:

- Assist people who are discouraged, especially when they try hard or attempt something new
- Accompany others when they are following their dreams or attempting new tasks, providing demonstrations of new behavior as needed
- Express confidence in the ability of others to succeed
- Inspire the hearts of others to act with courage when they struggle with fear, uncertainty, or problems
- Notice the choices and plans others make or want to make, offering them sincere support
- Acknowledge the best in others and in their words and actions
- Build connection and unity with others through positive words

Here is some guidance:

"Each one should endeavor to develop and assist the other toward mutual advancement...."[152] Shoghi Effendi

"We can never exert the influence over others which we can exert over ourselves. If we are better, if we show love, patience, and understanding of the weakness of others, if we seek to never criticize but rather encourage, others will do likewise, and we can really help the Cause through our example and spiritual strength."[153]   On behalf of Shoghi Effendi

Learning—Vital for my progress

Globally, education for young men is in some degree of crisis. Researcher Warren Farrell, co-author of *The Boy Crisis: Why Our Boys Are Struggling and What We Can Do About It*, indicates that globally males are struggling to meet proficiency levels in core subjects like reading, math, and science. He and coauthor John Gray also share their concerns about the mental health and lack of purpose in many young males. They link much of the problem to absent or uninvolved fathers during a child's developmental years and much of the solution to more fathers being involved. Of course, educating fathers (and mothers) is also part of the solution.

Literacy and seeking knowledge and education are strongly encouraged in the Bahá'í teachings. As you assess your mental health, you can look at whether some new type of learning activity would benefit you. This may be deepening with the Bahá'í writings and/or furthering your education on a subject. One challenge with the electronic era is that you may not read a book in its entirety and just read pieces. You may benefit from reading the whole book. Many can now be downloaded from the Reference Library on www.bahai.org or found through various Bahá'í Distribution Services and bookstores. Of course, balance is necessary—some people bury themselves in books and forget to be out living life!

Learning-in-action is also becoming an increasing part of Bahá'í community culture. This gives you the freedom to study guidance, consult with others, try different approaches to determine what works the best for you at any time, reflect on the outcomes, and choose new actions. This process can occur in whatever sequence works best in any given group endeavor, but it's likely in day-to-day service that they are all happening continuously. Sometimes having an acronym helps you to remember the elements, and here is one you may find useful:

S: Study
C: Consult
A: Act
R: Reflect

Scars on your body may be a physical reminder of either poor or brave actions you took, as well as lessons learned. However, utilizing these four elements can provide wisdom that prevents bad occurrences and mental scars from happening.

Action

1. Make a list of the actions that assist me to maintain my mental well-being. Schedule three of them to happen over the coming month at whatever frequency is beneficial.

2. Reflect on whether seeing a counselor would be useful and healing for me. Locate someone to consider and set up an appointment. After the appointment, reflect on what you learned. Make a second appointment if indicated. Note that you may need to include Bahá'í insights along with those from a professional.

3. Identify what types of encouragement are useful to me from myself and from others who can accompany me regularly with encouraging words. Request someone's assistance and accompaniment.

4. Assess the scars on your body and remember how you got them. Were there actions that would have improved if you had included elements of the SCAR acronym in this chapter? Are any of the scars reminders about being courageous? When would it have been wiser to moderate risk-taking behavior? Any other insights?

Reflection

1. When has practicing self-respect had a positive effect on my life? How has treating myself poorly affected my self-respect in a negative way?
2. What do I specifically respect about myself?
3. What increases my self-respect during times when I doubt my self-worth?
4. What self-criticisms happen regularly? How do I feel when I think them? How do I behave as a result? How do others respond when I say these self-critical comments to them? What is my reaction to their responses?
5. What words can I use in my inner thoughts that are positive and respectful about myself? How do I feel when I think them? How do I behave as a result?

6. How do others respond when I speak positively and respectfully about myself? What words or tone of voice would seem egotistical instead of respectful?
7. How do I relate to or react to reading quotations that ask me to strive for a very high standard?
8. When has trying too hard to be perfect resulted in unhappiness for me or others?
9. When I think of striving for perfection, the following feelings arise in me: _____. (examples: worry, joy, anger, enthusiasm, sadness, hopelessness, contentment, frustration, excitement...). When I think of striving for excellence instead of perfection, are there any different thoughts or feelings that arise in me?
10. What transforms negative thoughts or feelings about myself and my progress and increases positive ones? When does having a sense of humor about myself bring me back to a more balanced perspective about my efforts?
11. What encouraging words would I appreciate hearing from myself? What encouraging words would I appreciate hearing at times from others? How might these words affect my progress?
12. What am I involved in that would expand with increased encouragement? How can this be accomplished?
13. How am I contributing to my mental well-being? What could I be doing better?
14. What assistance from others would be beneficial for me?

10 – Striving for My Emotional Health

Challenge: Sometimes it's difficult to know how I feel and express it; at other times, there are so many conflicting feelings inside that I'm confused about what's happening and why.

Opportunity: I can maintain my emotional health in our challenging world, including processing the complexity of feelings, seeking assistance from others as needed.

Summary:
- With greater knowledge and practice, I can identify, understand, and express my own feelings.
- I can listen to and strive to understand the feelings of others.
- Understanding feelings increases my effectiveness in conversations with others and in mutual problem-solving.
- The Nonviolent Communication method assists me in preserving unity while expressing feelings.
- Living a spiritual life is a powerful source of joy for me.
- Laughter and humor enrich my life.
- Being thoughtful of others and doing acts of kindness for them contributes to me being emotionally healthy.

More:

Expressing feelings well

You can better navigate all relationships if you develop emotional intelligence, which can be defined as your capacity to be aware of, control, and express your emotions or feelings. This is a capacity you can expand with focus and determination, although it can be more challenging for men than for women. Feelings can be confusing; it's easier to sort them out when you are observant and listening carefully to yourself and others. You will enrich your life as you increase these success factors:

- Awareness of your current and underlying feelings
- Understanding what has prompted your feelings

- Sharing with others that it works best for you when you can ease into emotions gradually rather than abruptly, which can cause a strong physical reaction and withdrawal
- Self-control and adjusting—not letting the feelings be in charge instead of you
- Being able to express intense emotions calmly, clearly, and safely, releasing or calming them through constructive physical action as needed
- Wanting others to understand your feelings and vice versa
- Being able to empathize with another's feelings
- Being able to interact easily in social and close friend or partner settings

Success in these above areas increases your capacity to be mature, compassionate, and healthy with others. Feelings influence how you:

- Perceive a situation being addressed
- Express your thoughts
- Make decisions
- Create and carry out possible solutions

This quotation addresses the feelings that come from the heart:

"... [T]he function of language is to portray the mysteries and secrets of human hearts. The heart is like a box, and language is the key. Only by using the key can we open the box and observe the gems it contains."[154] 'Abdu'l-Bahá

Generally, the quality of any consultation improves when participants acknowledge and share feelings about a topic early in the process. Expressing feelings does not mean attacking each other with anger or other strong emotions. It does mean saying what feelings are happening and why, so that understanding between you and others builds.

You will benefit from recognizing when your feelings and those of others are growing or changing in conversations or situations. It's especially important to note if negative feelings are escalating. Consider this guidance:

"It is important to note that truth emerges after the 'clash' of carefully articulated views (which may well be expressed with enthusiasm and vigor), not from the clash of feelings. A clash of feelings is likely to obscure the truth, while a difference of opinion facilitates the discovery of truth."[155] Research Department of the Universal House of Justice

If feelings are escalating and likely to cause disunity or hurtful words, it's wise to pause the consultation so everyone can calm their feelings before resuming. Escalation that triggers inner stress can interfere with clear thinking and the ability to express thoughts well.

Research at The Gottman Institute shows that these are some of the dynamics when communication between two people start and continue in a negative way:

- Harsh Start-up: Sudden, negative attack or sarcasm, a form of contempt.
- Criticism: Personality criticism or an attack on the character; example, "You are so irresponsible."
- Defensiveness: Reacts defensively and blames the other person; example, "I am not! You are always picking on me!"
- Contempt: Shows contempt for the other person through body language, sneering, sarcasm, or patronizing or self-righteous comments; example, "You're such an idiot! "Can't you do anything right?"
- Stonewalling: Withdraws to avoid communication, thereby stonewalling and shutting the other person out.
- Flooding: Recipient of harsh criticism and contempt experiences "flooding", a protective reaction where physical symptoms overwhelm the person and effective communication shuts down.[156] Summary; based on work of John Gottman, PhD, and Nan Silver

There can be many cultural and gender influences that affect expressing feelings with those around you. Here are just a few examples:

- Many men have internalized the message that they are to be strong, independent, and not display feelings, especially the "softer" ones; this is especially true in older generations.
- Men can resist expressing feelings when they are in environments where the feelings could interfere with tasks or work or might risk others thinking less of them.
- At times a female partner may be so emotionally dependent upon a man that if he expresses fear or that he is struggling with work or other large issues, she feels insecure and reacts negatively; this can discourage a man from expressing difficult feelings with her again.

- If a female friend or partner has been abused, any expression of a man's unhappiness or anger can prompt her to withdraw in fear or react back in anger; there needs to be strong reassurance of the relationship safety and connection for the partner to be able to hear and respond effectively to the negative feelings.

On the other hand, men can experience intimate relationships where their partners are supportive, and women often express frustration when a male partner doesn't say how he feels. If you work together with a female partner, you may be able to understand and express how you feel more effectively.

Expressing feelings is not an easy or straightforward landscape to navigate. However, it's vital to make progress, because Bahá'í consultation in homes and in the community includes expressing and understanding each other's feelings.

Putting words to feelings

You may not yet be skillful with the vocabulary to label your feelings. Marshall B. Rosenberg, PhD, guides people through the challenges of understanding and identifying feelings. He encourages specificity, which would have you state that you are "happy", "excited", or "relieved", rather than saying you feel "good" or "fine". This gives you more clarity as well as more information to others.

Rosenberg says that some words you might use for your feelings when your needs *are being met* are:

- Adventurous
- Affectionate
- Amazed
- Amused
- Aroused
- Calm
- Curious
- Energetic
- Fascinated
- Happy
- Mellow
- Moved
- Optimistic
- Proud
- Relaxed
- Surprised
- Thrilled
- Wonderful

He suggests the words below for your feelings when your needs *are not being met*:

- Afraid
- Angry
- Annoyed
- Anxious
- Ashamed
- Bored

- Concerned
- Confused
- Disappointed
- Discouraged
- Embarrassed
- Hurt
- Irritated
- Jealous
- Overwhelmed
- Pessimistic
- Resentful
- Sad [157]

Marshall B. Rosenberg, PhD

With some practice, you may be able to reflect and identify your feelings and name them. Alternatively, you may notice that your feelings only become clear while sharing them with others or when being physically active. You can seek feedback and questions from others to increase your awareness. When you see that you struggle with identifying feelings, it may be useful to write down an description of what is happening and then list the feelings related to it, perhaps with input from another person.

Disunity can arise when people don't honor or acknowledge each other's feelings, or someone remains silent and withdrawn for an extended period. A simple practice to encourage others to share their feelings, especially a relationship or marriage partner, can be for you to say, "Something seems to be happening with you. Can you share with me what's going on?" A follow-up practice can be to say, "Is there anything else you want to say?" This ensures the person empties their inner cup. It's good to stop at times and summarize back to each other what you think you heard. When you check for understanding in this way, you quickly correct misunderstandings and let each other know careful listening is happening.

Sharing feelings and making requests

Sometimes you are alone when processing what you are feeling. You think about what happened and how you are responding. Sometimes you discover that what occurred simply reminded you of something from the past, which can prompt you to let go of your reaction in the present. Other times, someone else is involved, and it's good to share and discuss your feelings (and yes, this will sometimes be difficult!).

When you live or work with other people, you may pick up hints that they have some feelings going on but are not talking about them. It's wise to avoid making assumptions or judgments about another's feelings and to simply inquire and honor how they feel. It's unwise and likely disunifying to:

- Tell the other person how they are feeling
- Project your own feelings onto them

- Imagine what they are thinking and feeling without verifying whether it's true
- Tell them they should or should not be having a certain feeling

People's tones of voice and the volume of their voices are also powerful cues about thoughts and feelings. If you pay close attention, you can begin to hear your own feelings. If you listen carefully, you can usually tell if another person is feeling upset, happy, angry, excited, or annoyed. When someone's words and tone of voice do not match, usually you will believe their tone, so it's good to fact-check.

As you and others increase your skill with matching tones of voice with feelings and words, you will notice that your trust in each other increases. When there is trust, you will also find it easier to offer each other gentle feedback and communicate effectively about concerns.

A couple shares their experiences:

"Over the years there are so many ways we non-verbally communicate our love and affection—a look, a smile, a touch—even when with friends. We have learned that the tone of our voice can communicate more than the words we say when we are disgruntled, anxious, frustrated, or happy. We discovered that it's better to consult about an issue when in a positive frame of mind rather than a negative one, because those feelings color the issue. That also gives us time to pray, reflect, and consider options."

At times your feelings have nothing to do with another person but rather relate to other happenings in your life. Sharing with others around you that something has caused feelings in you unrelated to them can relax everyone a bit. Some examples of other happenings could be:

- Perhaps a neighbor's accident causes some grief, in part because it reminded you of a family member passing in an accident
- Maybe a clerk was rude in a store and anger is simmering at them
- Something happened at work, and you are afraid of losing your job

Asking a friend to listen to you can increase your understanding of your feelings and calm them down. When you are in a close friendship or relationship, and the feelings are closely connected to two of you, it takes practice to convey your feelings in a constructive way that doesn't hurt each other. It may be useful to have a routine time each day or each week to check in and sort out any issues that arise.

However, sometimes feelings and issues arise and must be handled right then. A couple shares about their relationship and an experience they had:

"When we speak, we are aware of how our words include not only the idea we are trying to convey, but also how we feel about it. With this awareness, we take the time to let our speech be as skillful as it can be, while trusting that the other one will listen attentively. We speak our minds, and we let go of what we have said.

"As we listen proactively, we are aware of our own internal reactions, arising thoughts, and feelings. However, we also know that the process of consulting allows a time and space for us to present what each of us feels is needed and helpful. This allows our minds to stay relatively quiet while the other speaks. We can truly hear what is being said as we consider our own opinion and formulate a response.

"Our consultations as a couple then, are a process of being aware of our own feelings as we speak and as we listen. There is a sense of great support in knowing that we are each openly aware as we do this. For example, I recently returned home from a week-long business trip. My wife was exhausted from caring for our sick four-year-old son for three days.

"When we had a few minutes to sit and catch up with each other and consult about what would happen the next day, we needed time to share our feelings. My wife said, "I was very scared I was going to have to take him to the hospital without you here", and "I was so upset that you didn't call last night to check on us."

"With mindful listening, I was able to acknowledge her feelings of loneliness and fear about handling this challenge on her own, without jumping into being defensive. She could then hear me as I shared, "I was very frustrated that there was no cellphone signal along the route we were driving last night. I was very concerned about both of you and hoping you could feel my prayer support."

"Listening to each other's feelings helped us re-connect. We also realized that we were both too tired to consult about plans for the next day. All we needed right then was to agree on how to look after our son for the next few hours."

Rosenberg's "Non-Violent Communication" method is designed for people to share and receive observations, feelings, needs, and requests honestly and peacefully. You can read more about this method at his website or in his books to be able to use it most effectively (https://www.cnvc.org/). A summarization of the basic communication process is:

1. SEE: We observe and share the concrete actions in another person that affected our well-being.
2. FEEL: We identify and share how we feel about what we observed.
3. NEED: We notice and share the needs, values, desires, and so on that led to our feelings.
4. REQUEST: We communicate a specific request (not demand) of the other person that is clear and positive that if they carry it out will enrich our life.

Example:

1. SEE: "I'm noticing that you are getting involved in a lot of community service activities, and we are spending less time together."
2. FEEL: "I'm feeling lonely and missing you, and I'm feeling frustrated that many things we agreed to do together are not being done."
3. NEED: "I value our relationship and the time we spend together as a couple and family."
4. REQUEST: "I request that we consult together about our current commitments and before you say yes to new service activities."
5. The two of you would then discuss the request and determine solutions, which might include spending time together on an agreed date and time.

Negative feelings—What do I do with them?

If you label feelings as bad or feel shame about them, you will be tempted to ignore or suppress them, but they will be difficult to hide. The following steps may be useful instead:

1. Acknowledge and name the feeling you are experiencing
2. Determine what has caused the feeling
3. Assess or consult with others about what to do about the feeling:
   - Is there action to take?
   - Is there a problem to address with someone? Do you need to calm the feelings first?
   - Is your reaction coming from an old situation and once recognized can be released?

- Is there physical activity to do that will lessen the feeling so it's easier to think about it?
- Do you need to give yourself some time to understand what you are feeling and why?
- Is the feeling causing you or others harm?
- Is the feeling brief and temporary, or has it been with you for a while and needs professional help?

It's important to get help when your feelings are seriously troubling and unresolved. For example, if hatred is added to anger, "Action is the result. It's no longer an emotional or spiritual problem, but a physical one, such as physical, sexual, or verbal abuse; shooting; cutting, binging, and purging; excessive tattooing and body piercing; spending money you can't afford" and so on.[158] S. Gammage

Here is some guidance:

"Verily the most necessary thing is contentment under all circumstances; by this one is preserved from morbid conditions and from lassitude. Yield not to grief and sorrow: they cause the greatest misery. Jealousy consumeth the body and anger doth burn the liver: avoid these two as you would a lion."[159] Bahá'u'lláh

"Love the creatures for the sake of God and not for themselves. You will never become angry or impatient if you love them for the sake of God. Humanity is not perfect. There are imperfections in every human being, and you will always become unhappy if you look toward the people themselves. But if you look toward God, you will love them and be kind to them, for the world of God is the world of perfection and complete mercy."[160] 'Abdu'l-Bahá

"You ask how to deal with anger. The House of Justice suggests that you call to mind the admonitions found in our Writings on the need to overlook the shortcomings of others; to forgive and conceal their misdeeds, not to expose their bad qualities, but to search for and affirm their praiseworthy ones, and to endeavor to be always forbearing, patient, and merciful."[161] On behalf of the Universal House of Justice

The same feelings can be positive or negative, depending on the circumstances. Reflect on the guidance below.

"In the innate nature of things there is no evil—all is good. This applies even to certain apparently blameworthy attributes and dispositions which seem inherent in some people, but which are not in reality reprehensible. For example, you can see in a nursing child, from the beginning of its life, the signs of greed, of anger, and of ill temper; and so it might be argued that good and evil are innate in the reality of man, and that this is contrary to the pure goodness of the innate nature and of creation. The answer is that greed, which is to demand ever more, is a praiseworthy quality provided that it is displayed under the right circumstances. Thus, should a person show greed in acquiring science and knowledge, or in the exercise of compassion, high-mindedness, and justice, this would be most praiseworthy. And should he direct his anger and wrath against the bloodthirsty tyrants who are like ferocious beasts, this too would be most praiseworthy. But should he display these qualities under other conditions, this would be deserving of blame."[162]
'Abdu'l-Bahá

Here is an experience that illustrates the above quotation:

"I was in a bad mood every day after work for a few days. I slammed items on the kitchen counter. If I played sports in the evening, I was overly aggressive. When I saw my girlfriend, I was short-tempered with her. Finally, she said in exasperation, 'What are you so angry about?!' It startled me into looking at what was happening. She agreed to sit and pray and consult with me to understand the reasons behind my reaction and what actions I needed to take.
"I had been working hard for months on a project at my job, including putting in a lot of extra time. I hoped that if I did well on it, the outcome would include a pay raise. Instead, I got a brief thank you from my manager. I was angry because the situation seemed unjust. Together my girlfriend and I created a planned approach to my manager. We decided it was best for me to tone down my anger. I wanted him to listen to me instead of defensively reacting to me being angry. We wrote down the facts about the situation, so I could study them and clearly present my case. I was able to request a raise courageously and courteously. The meeting went well, and he agreed to my request."

There is a difference between feelings that arise normally every day and serious ones that occur and stay for long periods and are best addressed by a mental health professional. As indicated in Chapter 9, serious depression or thoughts of suicide need to be addressed with mental health professionals. The Bahá'í teachings also include turning to medical doctors as needed. Here is guidance to a physician:

> "Praise be to God that thou hast two powers: one to undertake physical healing and the other spiritual healing. Matters related to man's spirit have a great effect on his bodily condition. For instance, thou shouldst impart gladness to thy patient, give him comfort and joy, and bring him to ecstasy and exultation. How often hath it occurred that this hath caused early recovery. Therefore, treat thou the sick with both powers. Spiritual feelings have a surprising effect on healing nervous ailments."[163] 'Abdu'l-Bahá

The challenge of anxiety

For many people, it can be common for something specific to occur and to feel "stressed" or anxious in response. For example, if your parents are not getting along, there can be a fear of separation or divorce. If layoffs are happening at work, there can be concerns about job loss. Sometimes when something negative happens there is then escalating fear or anxiety about it happening again. Here is some of the dynamic of what is happening inside of you:

> "Stress is not something that happens to us but rather something that develops within our own thinking. From the inside out, we decide what is and what is not stressful. Events are not stressful per se; they are what we make of them."[164] Richard Carlson and Joseph Bailey

The higher the anxiety and stress level, the more it's also wise to examine whether ego is becoming a factor. There may be almost unconscious thoughts like, "If I'm this busy, I must be someone important" or "If I don't do this work myself, everything will fall apart". When people are highly stressed or very anxious about themselves, others, or world circumstances, it can negatively affect health and relationships. It becomes vital to turn to God in prayer and to others for assistance. Participating in a regular devotional gathering may be calming or uplifting.

Below is another perspective on anxiety some may find useful.

"Anxiety…is the result of a long, slow drift away from God and our spiritual potential. … Anxiety is the subconscious awareness that our longing for God is not being attended to. If we neglect our relationship with God, then we run the risk of drifting further and further away from our spiritual reality. We lose contact with the Foundation of our identity and the Source of our virtues. There is nothing in life more terrifying than this."[165] Justice St Rain

For some people, chronic anxiety is part of their lives. A man shares his response and concerns about the viewpoint in the above quotation and his own experiences:

"What this quotation says may be true for him and for many other people, but it's definitely not true for me or some of the others I know who suffer from chronic anxiety. In fact, this way of looking at it can be very damaging. It's possible to get wrapped up in a kind of obsession about one's relationship with God, thinking that we are 'not longing for Him enough', feeling as though we are 'drifting further and further away from our spiritual reality' and there is nothing we can do about it. Indeed, the feeling that 'there is nothing in life [or indeed, the afterlife] more terrifying than this' has a paralyzing effect that can cripple a person's mind for a while.

"In one of its messages the Universal House of Justice warns that 'The friends should not lose heart in their personal struggles to attain to the Divine standard, nor be seduced by the argument that, since mistakes will inevitably be made and perfection is impossible, it's futile to exert an effort…. So too is paralysis engendered by guilt to be avoided; indeed, preoccupation with a particular moral failing can, at times, make it more challenging for it to be overcome'.[166] *The specific context of this quotation is chastity, but it very much applies to anxiety as well.*

"Instead, I view anxiety as a kind of message from our lower nature. The lower nature, in this view, is not at all a bad thing in itself—it's just the complete mental, physical, hormonal, and social reality of our presence in this earthly plane of existence, as opposed to the purely spiritual side of our being that exists in another plane and then shines its light into this one. The lower nature is part of us, and as such, it's only a bad thing when it gets prioritized over our higher nature. Any part of it can become warped, broken, covered in dust, and much more, but this does not necessarily affect the source of the light of God that shines upon it. Bahá'u'lláh says that "all infirmities of body or mind" are "due to the hindrances that interpose themselves between his soul and his body, for the soul itself remaineth

unaffected by any bodily ailments.... In like manner, every malady afflicting the body of man is an impediment that preventeth the soul from manifesting its inherent might and power."[167] So, in this view, anxiety is not a spiritual disorder—it's a message from the body/mind mixture, that something is not right, and needs addressing.

"For example, last year I was hard at work completing a very difficult final assessment for my university degree. My anxiety told me that I was in big trouble, that I might fail, and that if I could not pass, the future of my family would be severely impacted. It was very hard to push through that feeling, like sticky spider webs, constantly hindering my thoughts and preventing my progress on the assessment itself. I found that fighting it with thoughts like 'No! That's not going to happen!' only made it stronger. And if, heaven forbid, I ever thought 'this anxiety is happening because I'm not detached and spiritual enough, my relationship with God is not right', I would start to feel depressed and hopeless in addition to being anxious, because the thought of God judging me for being too anxious on top of everything else was more than I could handle.

"I eventually learned to take breaks to listen to that feeling and respond to it as if it were another very noisy person living with me in my mind, a worthy being who needed validation and respect—it needed 'regulation' not 'suppression' as some of the Writings put it. 'Yes', I said to this voice of my lower nature, 'That is one possible outcome, but there are also others. What you are afraid of only happens if I quit. If I try my best and fail, there are opportunities to try again later, which, though unpleasant, do not severely impact my future. For now, let us put aside the outcome of my current effort and focus on what we can control. We don't know if I will pass on my first try, my second, or perhaps even my third; but whatever happens, I will push ever onward no matter what, and give this the best effort that I am capable of right now, limited as that may be.' By reframing it as a choice to quit or not—which I could control—rather than an outcome of passing or not—which I could not control—I was able to quiet that voice of anxiety enough that, for a while, I could actually work on the assessment, and by repeating this strategy, I could eventually get it done.

"That said though, there were definitely other factors. My wife was very understanding and helpful, not judgmental of me in the slightest. I also had the support of my professors and classmates in the university program. And of course, I knew that if I failed, I could try again—not all assessments are like that. I have post-traumatic-stress-disorder symptoms, and this definitely magnifies little anxieties into big ones, quite against my will. I'm not the only person to suffer from this or a similar mental or emotional health issue. There are others who are not able to do what I did because they don't have a helpful marriage partner or supportive learning community, nor perhaps even a second chance at their assessment.

"In this sense, then, anxiety is not 'the result of a long, slow drift away from God and our spiritual potential', but rather, it's a physical sensation like sight, hunger, sexual drive, pleasure, and many others. All of these are associated with the mind as well as the body, some more with one than the other. But just because anxiety feels mostly associated with the mind does not mean that it's not actually physical. In itself, it's never blameworthy. Rather, only the response of giving into its control in inappropriate ways, as with any other of these physical sensations, is what causes us to 'drift away from God'. That's what drifting is—seeking to alleviate a negative sensation, or stimulate a positive one, in a way that does not agree with God's purpose for us. None of them are harmful if that purpose remains at the forefront of our consciousness.

"There are, of course, many other triggers of anxiety. Sometimes I can avoid these, sometimes I can deal with them. But always keeping my spiritual purpose front and center is the compass that helps me navigate these stormy emotions. These feelings will be there—having them is not blameworthy, but rather part of the journey. What really matters is what we choose to do with these feelings. In time, we may be able to navigate ourselves to a mental space where those feelings no longer surge with the same force, or perhaps even leave us, in peace at last! But this is a journey without end, and even at that stage there will be come another test or challenge for us to face. Whatever the milestones may be, the ultimate direction is that Supreme Horizon, the Sun of Truth that shines on us wherever we are. We are not meant to 'reach' that ultimate destination, for to touch that Sun would only destroy us—only 'reach out' for it.

"Bahá'u'lláh says, 'Seek fellowship with none until thou hast found Me, and whenever thou shalt long for Me, thou shalt find Me close to thee'.[168] For us, the journey is the destination, the longing is the attainment, and to stand against the tests of the world is to pass the tests of the soul."

When you remain calm, pray, and stay in the present moment, even urgent situations can feel less stressful. Keeping control of your thoughts instead of using them to imagine disastrous outcomes prompts you to be more effective in responding to all circumstances. If you do imagine a negative outcome, then turn your mind toward how to prevent it from happening. You may also find it useful to look at your positive future goals and focus on the perseverance necessary to fulfill them. It then becomes easier to think of difficulties as temporary and as opportunities to learn and develop.

Detachment—How does it help?

Sometimes when strong feelings escalate in you, the quality of detachment can nudge you to step back, calm the feelings, and take a more neutral look at what is happening.

Below are some indicators that someone is practicing detachment well. He:

- "Empathizes with others without making their feelings his own or suffering because of the actions or reactions of others
- Thinks rationally and clearly with some emotional distance and focus; responding according to the known facts without exhibiting personal bias, strong emotions, or preconceived expectations
- Gathers information, seeks input from others, and examines the facts related to a project, situation, or person without premature judgment or participating in backbiting or gossip
- Seeks spiritual solutions to issues
- Releases desires, dreams, or expectations that are unrealistic or unattainable, grieving as needed in the process of letting go
- Accepts a present situation with equanimity, even if it's difficult, uncomfortable, or not what he would have chosen
- Frees himself from unhealthy or unwise attachment to people, incidents from the past, physical objects, and desires
- Releases overly strong fears of losing something or someone
- Bases choices on current circumstances rather than solely on previous experiences
- Understands and accepts the limitations of others and his own"[169]
S. M. Alexander

Here is someone's reflection about detachment:

"I'm in a situation with another person that's very challenging. I have come to realize part of my frustration lies in my trying to 'suppress' feelings in hopes of become detached. Now, I think the way to navigate this period is through reflection, acceptance, and gratitude. It also helps when I focus on thinking the best of the other person. Accepting that my feelings and

inclinations are natural frees me from being critical of myself and allows for honesty in my reflections on the matter. Gratitude for the test allows me to use the experience as a tool to learn about detachment, so that I can further develop this virtue."

Happiness and laughter

Many people associate spirituality with being serious all the time. However, a very effective way to bring about positive feelings and happiness throughout your life journey is through genuine humor. Your ability to be content, happy, and laughing no matter what the circumstances will be a strong spiritual power in conquering the dark forces.

'Abdu'l-Bahá, the eldest son of Bahá'u'lláh who was known at times as "The Master", is the person we are to look to as an example of how to live. There are many stories where you can read about His spiritual qualities and choices, one of which was His excellent sense of humor. He often joked and told stories. Here is an example: "In New York City a young supporter of tax-reform asked, 'What message shall I take to my friends?' The Master laughed with delighted humor: 'Tell them to come into the Kingdom of God. There they will find plenty of land—and there are no taxes on it!'"[170] 'Abdu'l-Bahá

The quotations below amplify this topic.

"… [L]augh, smile and rejoice in order that others may be made happy by you."[171] 'Abdu'l-Bahá

"Joy gives us wings! In times of joy our strength is more vital, our intellect keener, and our understanding less clouded. We seem better able to cope with the world and to find our sphere of usefulness. But when sadness visits us we become weak, our strength leaves us, our comprehension is dim and our intelligence veiled. The actualities of life seem to elude our grasp, the eyes of our spirits fail to discover the sacred mysteries, and we become even as dead beings. There is no human being untouched by these two influences; but all the sorrow and the grief that exist come from the world of matter—the spiritual world bestows only the joy!"[172] 'Abdu'l-Bahá

A description below of life in 1800's in the prison city of 'Akká, in what was then Palestine and is now Israel, illustrates how the religious prisoners used humor.

"How the Master ['Abdu'l-Bahá] loved His wonderful Father. He told of this loathsome prison. How Bahá'u'lláh would call the pilgrims together, would make them laugh at their troubles, until they forgot their stone beds, the lack of food and water. He banished the pain of their illness and the ravages of their fever. He would tell them stories and lift their hearts. He would start them to laughing so loudly that they must be cautioned for fear the sentinels would believe they were mad if they could laugh and enjoy themselves in these conditions of utter dreadfulness."[173] William B. Sears

Of course, humor also comes with a caution, as hurting hearts is not the intent:

"… [W]hile laughter should not be suppressed or frowned upon, it should not be indulged in at the expense of the feelings of others. What one says or does in a humorous vein should not give rise to prejudice of any kind. You may recall 'Abdu'l-Bahá's caution 'Beware lest ye offend the feelings of anyone, or sadden the heart of any person…' (*Tablets of 'Abdu'l-Bahá, Vol. 1*, p. 45)."[174] On behalf of the Universal House of Justice

Here is guidance about the balance for you to create in your life:

"One of the signs of a decadent society, a sign which is very evident in the world today, is an almost frenetic devotion to pleasure and diversion, an insatiable thirst for amusement, a fanatical devotion to games and sport, a reluctance to treat any matter seriously, and a scornful, derisory attitude towards virtue and solid worth. Abandonment of 'a frivolous conduct' does not imply that a Bahá'í must be sour-faced or perpetually solemn. Humor, happiness, joy are characteristics of a true Bahá'í life. Frivolity palls and eventually leads to boredom and emptiness, but true happiness and joy and humor that are parts of a balanced life that includes serious thought, compassion and humble servitude to God are characteristics that enrich life and add to its radiance."[175] On behalf of the Universal House of Justice

Here are some comments about this topic:

"I believe gratitude is key to being able to experience joy, and it's especially important to look for opportunities for gratitude during times of difficulty."

"Laughter is a healing medicine for the soul, mind, and heart. Laughter melts away imagined differences and brings to the forefront that we are actually all related in a very real way. It unites us. Joy for me is about detachment from the changes and chances of this world. Joy is a kindness to us and to others. When I am experiencing joy, I have more energy, I find life more pleasing and funnier in general. I am more compassionate and better able to empathize with others. I am able to serve others with grace and cheerfulness. I find it easier to think of others' needs and forget my own selfish wants. Others are happier around me when I am happy and joyful!"

"I have been tuning in more to what naturally boosts my level of happiness and joy. Really, I think of it as my 'joy level,' since joy—the joy that comes from accepting the will of God—is stable and always there for me to access. Whenever I feel that joy ebbing (like when I see so much injustice and disunity), I become aware that I am becoming attached to worldly things. Now I have some tools to reconnect my soul to the grace of God! Prayer and reading quotations from the Bahá'í writings and from other faiths, as well as uplifting words of other people, are among these tools. Nature is and has always been a big one for me too. Water is intensely relaxing for me, and so is being around trees and birds."

Two authors link laughter, joy, and spirituality:

> "Laughter is a spiritual practice. ... The transformative nature of any spiritual discipline comes with regular practice. When done consistently, it can eventually change our lives. If we make time to invite joy into our lives each day, we will become more aware of joy and laughter in our lives and in the world. Eventually, laughter will become an innate part of who we are."[176] S. Sparks

> "Cultivate humor as a higher path—a cosmic contentment that is truly lighthearted and full of joy. You will lighten the lives of others simply by the radiance of your good humor. Even the briefest laugh reminds us that we have available a kind of spiritual gold anytime, anywhere."[177] Stephen Post

You can begin to conquer the dark forces of depression, jealously, violence, hopelessness, and so on by drawing on the strong powers of humor, laughter, and happiness. Offering thoughtful and kind acts to others and practicing gratitude for your blessings—even if they are hard to see on some days—are also vital forces for good.

Action

1. Identify the positive and negative feelings that could arise in each of the situations listed below:

    a. There has been an injustice in your neighborhood; in your country
    b. You go out on a date to a concert for an important anniversary
    c. You have been asked to carry out a specific community service
    d. You burn and ruin a special dinner
    e. You are participating in a physical/spiritual fasting process, and a relationship partner is not
    f. You take your first vacation in five years
    g. You unexpectedly receive a large sum of money
    h. You become a parent, uncle, or grandparent

2. To expand your skill in identifying feelings, think about different scenarios from your life, and then practice a few times with saying: "When I see or hear _____ (or when _____ happens), I feel _____."

3. Make a list of what you perceive to be stressors in your life. Connected to each of them, note what your thoughts and interpretations usually are about each item. What are your insights? Then each day for a week, list three items, environments, people, or occurrences in your life that you are grateful to God for and three requests for help from Him. Thank Him for your blessings and pray to receive help. Keep in mind that you may need to be patient for the answers to come. Sometimes the answer is "no", and the reasons to be grateful for this response emerge over time. Continue with this gratitude practice if it's beneficial as a daily practice.

4. Identify two issues in your life and invite another person to take turns with you using Nonviolent Communication as a method. The receiver should first summarize back to the speaker what they understood from the communication. Then the two of you can engage in a problem-solving consultation to determine a resolution.

5. Read the story that follows and then carry out this practice of finding and sharing something funny in your day regularly for a week or so. Assess the effect of it on you and others. "It is good to laugh. Laughter is a spiritual relaxation. When [we] were in prison...and under the utmost deprivation and difficulties, each of [us] at the close of the day would relate the most ludicrous event which had happened. Sometimes it was a little difficult to find one but always [we] would laugh until the tears would roll down [our] cheeks. Happiness...is never dependent upon material surroundings, otherwise how sad those years would have been. As it was [we] were always in the utmost state of joy and happiness."[178] Howard Colby Ives

Reflection

1. How can I learn about my feelings other than happy, sad, and angry?
2. What is the benefit to me and others for understanding, expressing, and managing feelings?
3. What feelings do I experience most often?
4. How do I express those feelings?
5. In what ways would I prefer to express those feelings?
6. What feelings most often arise between me and others? How are they expressed? What needs to improve?
7. How to I react when someone expresses strong feelings with me with little or no warning?
8. What negative thoughts and feelings do I hold toward others? Am I willing to detach from them? What would I replace them with?
9. How do videogames, television shows, movies, and other media, including social media, affect and influence my emotions? What is my response when violence is a part of them? How does that affect others around me? [*Note:* Some people find watching violence decreases their inner stress, and for others, it increases it.]
10. What prompts me to feel anxiety? How can I lower this feeling and my stress level?
11. How do humor and laughter influence my emotional health? What benefits do they bring to others?
12. Am I able to share laughter and humor in a sincere way that does not include negative comments about others that may be hurtful? How do others respond when I use sarcasm, criticism, or prejudice as part of humor?

13. What are the sensitivities about humor in my culture or the society in which I live? How is it used well?
14. What ways have I been successful in uplifting others? What new ways will I try?
15. How am I contributing to my emotional well-being? What could I be doing better?

Resources Note: If you are in a couple relationship and want to better understand the emotional and communication dynamics between you, books that may be useful are: *Seven Principles for Making Marriage Work*, 2nd ed., *How to Improve Your Marriage Without Talking About It*, *The Relationship Handbook*, and *Re-Vitalizing Our Marriage*.

11 – Striving for My Physical Health

Challenge: Physical danger and illnesses abound from vehicle accidents, altercations, and choosing to put substances in my body that cause harm; I often eat and sleep whenever I feel like it.

Opportunity: I can make choices that respect my body as the temple of my spirit and that preserve my well-being in ways that contribute to health for a lifetime.

Summary:
- Maintaining my physical well-being through excellent nutrition, exercise, and sleep keeps my body strong and functional, and this also contributes to my mental, emotional, and spiritual health.
- Taking care of my body supports me in being involved in life and in service to others.
- There are many dangerous sources of influence in the world that can have a negative effect on men's health and lives, and I can prevent many of them from harming me.
- Making self-respectful choices by not misusing or abusing alcohol or drugs keeps destructive poisons out of my body and keeps my mind functioning clearly; there are many sources of help if I struggle with this, such as counselors, support groups, Spiritual Assemblies, and medical professionals.

More:

Well-being–What is it and how do I get it?

Learning how to manage your physical well-being takes time, learning, and experience. You not only need to understand the basics of how your body works, you also must learn how the presence and absence of the following aspects of life affect you:

- Healthy and unhealthy food and drinks; frequency of eating; types of food and drinks
- Exercise, fresh air, and sunshine
- Supplements
- Rest, relaxation, and sleep

Here is guidance:

> "... [Y]ou should not neglect your health, but consider it the means which enables you to serve. It—the body—is like a horse which carries the personality and spirit, and as such should be well cared for so it can do its work! You should certainly safeguard your nerves, and force yourself to take time, and not only for prayer and meditation, but for real rest and relaxation. We don't have to pray and meditate for hours in order to be spiritual."[179] On behalf of Shoghi Effendi

> "... [T]here are very few people who can get along without eight hours sleep. If you are not one of those, you should protect your health by sleeping enough. The Guardian [Shoghi Effendi] himself finds that it impairs his working capacity if he does not try and get a minimum of seven or eight hours."[180] On behalf of Shoghi Effendi

Many men have a regular fitness routine that strengthens their muscles and keeps their cardio-vascular system in good shape. You might work out at a fitness center, run, walk, or play a sport. Shoghi Effendi wrote the following in an essay before he began serving as head of the Bahá'í Faith:

> "Athletics refresh the body, tranquilize and enlighten the mind, and develop moral character. As a concrete example let us take a student in his college activities. The student who does exercise is always fresh and vigorous, he seldom gets sick and tired. His jovial character, his good disposition and his interest in life are his chief characteristics.
>
> "Moreover in exercising, the student gets animated, his blood is purified and consequently his mind becomes more apt to receive the ideas and thoughts found in his lessons. The health which he acquires will help him to work harder and he becomes more successful. A weak person seldom can endure the hardship of school-life, the trouble of memorizing and persevering in his daily lessons. Lastly when a student is busy with athletics during recess time his ideas do not deviate any more to the path of impurity, to think of such trivial things and the health and strength which he acquires will help him in overcoming such temptations. Generally a healthy person is endowed with a will stronger than that of a weak person."[181]

It also takes time, learning, and experience to determine what types of health practitioners benefit you and whether they have skills in healing with foods, supplements, and medicines. Others in your life may be ahead of you in this process and be able to help you locate practitioners. Here is some guidance:

> "When highly skilled physicians shall fully examine this matter, thoroughly and perseveringly, it will be clearly seen that the incursion of disease is due to a disturbance in the relative amounts of the body's component substances, and that treatment consisteth in adjusting these relative amounts, and that this can be apprehended and made possible by means of foods.
>
> "It is certain that in this wonderful new age the development of medical science will lead to the doctors' healing their patients with foods. For the sense of sight, the sense of hearing, of taste, of smell, of touch—all these are discriminative faculties, their purpose being to separate the beneficial from whatever causeth harm."[182] 'Abdu'l-Bahá

> "It is incumbent upon everyone to seek medical treatment and to follow the doctor's instructions, for this is in compliance with the divine ordinance, but, in reality, He Who giveth healing is God."[183] 'Abdu'l-Bahá

It's also wise to distinguish between what is a physical illness and what is something else and requires a different remedy:

> "There are two ways of healing sickness, material means and spiritual means. The first is by the treatment of physicians; the second consisteth in prayers offered by the spiritual ones to God and in turning to Him. Both means should be used and practiced.
>
> "Illnesses which occur by reason of physical causes should be treated by doctors with medical remedies; those which are due to spiritual causes disappear through spiritual means. Thus an illness caused by affliction, fear, nervous impressions, will be healed more effectively by spiritual rather than by physical treatment."[184] 'Abdu'l-Bahá

The Bahá'í teachings encourage "purity", which links to how well you keep impure substances out of your body and to cleanliness. Here are quotations about this topic:

> "Make ye then a mighty effort, that the...purity, immaculacy, refinement, and the preservation of health, they shall be leaders in the

vanguard of those who know. And that by their freedom from enslavement, their knowledge, their self-control, they shall be first among the pure, the free and the wise."[185] 'Abdu'l-Bahá

"Even in the physical realm, cleanliness will conduce to spirituality…. And although bodily cleanliness is a physical thing, it hath, nevertheless, a powerful influence on the life of the spirit. It is even as a voice wondrously sweet, or a melody played: although sounds are but vibrations in the air which affect the ear's auditory nerve, and these vibrations are but chance phenomena carried along through the air, even so, see how they move the heart. A wondrous melody is wings for the spirit, and maketh the soul to tremble for joy. The purport is that physical cleanliness doth also exert its effect upon the human soul."[186] 'Abdu'l-Bahá

"Concerning smoking; it is not forbidden in the Bahá'í teachings and no one can enforce its prohibition. It is strongly discouraged as a habit which is not very clean or very healthy. But it is a matter left entirely to the conscience of the individual and not of major importance, whereas the use of alcohol is definitely forbidden and thus not left optional to the conscience of the believer."[187] On behalf of Shoghi Effendi

What concerns come from science?

You have choices to make to consciously maintain your physical well-being as well as choices to make that can reduce physical harm. Some of this section addresses teenagers, but men of all ages can benefit from addressing these issues as well. These choices can often be a matter of life and death. From a December 13, 2018, report from the World Health Organization (WHO) on "Adolescents: health risks and solutions" come some concerning statistics:

- More than 1.1 million adolescents [male and female] aged 10-19 years died in 2016, over 3000 every day, mostly from preventable or treatable causes.
- Road traffic injuries were the leading cause of death among adolescents in 2016. Other major causes of adolescent deaths included suicide, interpersonal violence, HIV/AIDS, and diarrheal diseases.

The report continues, in part:

"Around 1.2 billion people, or 1 in 6 of the world's population, are adolescents aged 10 to 19. Most are healthy, but there is still substantial premature death, illness, and injury among adolescents. Illnesses can hinder their ability to grow and develop to their full potential. Alcohol or tobacco use, lack of physical activity, unprotected sex, and/or exposure to violence can jeopardize not only their current health, but also their health as adults, and even the health of their future children.

"Unintentional injuries are the leading cause of death and disability among adolescents. In 2016, over 135,000 adolescents died as a result of road traffic accidents. Many of those who died were 'vulnerable road users', including pedestrians, cyclists, or users of motorized two-wheelers. In many countries, road safety laws need to be made more comprehensive, and enforcement of such laws needs to be strengthened. Furthermore, young drivers need advice on driving safely, while laws that prohibit driving under the influence of alcohol and drugs need to be strictly enforced among all age groups. Blood alcohol levels should be set lower for young drivers than for adults. Graduated licenses for novice drivers with zero-tolerance for drink-driving are recommended.

"Drowning is also among the top 10 causes of death among adolescents—nearly 50,000 adolescents, over two thirds of them boys, are estimated to have drowned in 2016. Teaching children and adolescents to swim is an essential intervention to prevent these deaths.

"Harmful drinking among adolescents is a major concern in many countries. It reduces self-control and increases risky behaviors, such as unsafe sex or dangerous driving. It is an underlying cause of injuries (including those due to road traffic accidents), violence, and premature deaths. It can also lead to health problems in later life and affects life expectancy. ... Drug use among 15-19-year olds is also an important global concern. Drug control may focus on reducing drug demand, drug supply, or both, and successful programs usually include structural, community, and individual-level interventions. ...

"Physical activity provides fundamental health benefits for adolescents, including improved cardiorespiratory and muscular fitness, bone health, maintenance of a healthy body weight, and psychosocial benefits. WHO recommends for adolescents to accumulate at least 60 minutes of moderate- to vigorous-intensity physical activity daily, which may include play, games, sports, but also activity for transportation (such as cycling and walking), or physical education."[188]

My choices with alcohol and drugs

Sometimes the struggle between the dark forces and the army of light is no big deal, as it's just a small skirmish. You may have seen enough people cause problems in their lives with drinking and drugs that you do whatever you can to avoid them. You don't even feel tempted to try them out.

Other people, especially if they aren't engaged in the soul maintenance discussed in previous chapters, think there's no great harm in putting these substances in their body. They might think, "Well, everyone else is doing it, why shouldn't I?"

Remember, when you are a strong and spiritual man, you can say "no" and mean it. If instead you say, "yes", the consequences at least initially could be minor, like some silly behavior or bad judgment. For others, one exposure and repeated exposures can lead to destruction and addiction. Consequences can include driving under the influence and hurting yourself or someone else in the process, unprotected or abusive sexual encounters, and even loss of life.

There are many aspects of the global social culture that are legal. These can include drinking alcohol, depending on your age and where you live. When harmful substances are readily available, it can be confusing at times for Bahá'ís wanting to obey the teachings, which forbid using intoxicants, including alcohol. When something is legal under civil law, it can be easier to fool yourself into thinking there is no harm in it.

An exception to the prohibition against the use of alcohol and some drugs exists when a qualified physician has determined that its use is the best treatment for a medical condition, provided this is legal where the person resides, and administered in private rather than in public locations where this might send a mixed message to others. Recreational use under the guise of medical usage would, of course, not align with what's best for you in light of the guidance. Consider this:

> "Abdu'l-Bahá explains that the Aqdas prohibits 'both light and strong drinks', and He states that the reason for prohibiting the use of alcoholic drinks is because 'alcohol leadeth the mind astray and causeth the weakening of the body'.
>
> "Shoghi Effendi, in letters written on his behalf, states that this prohibition includes not only the consumption of wine but of 'everything

that deranges the mind', and he clarifies that the use of alcohol is permitted only when it constitutes part of a medical treatment which is implemented 'under the advice of a competent and conscientious physician, who may have to prescribe it for the cure of some special ailment'".[189] *The Kitáb-i-Aqdas*, Notes

Here is one person's story:

"As a young boy I was aware of a few men in our family who were heavy drinkers, and others who considered themselves social drinkers. I began drinking on weekends with school friends, perhaps seven or eight times a year, when I was about 15-years old. My drinking increased for a couple of years and then tapered off a little. At 18, I was in my first year of college and I worked 50-hour weeks. I generally went with friends two nights a week for a drink. For the most part I was a beer drinker. On the occasions when I over drank, I was a happy drunk. I did not perceive drinking to be a problem.

"I was 20-years old when I found the Bahá'í Faith. I fell in love with this Faith and declared my belief within three months. I struggled a little with giving up drinking for a few weeks. Then I made an all-out effort to quit completely. I experienced mild headaches and felt the urge to drink for about six months. Then, the urges were gone, and I never drank again.

"Over the years, I've watched a number of cousins and uncles die young because of alcoholism. I have a sister who's an alcoholic. Drinking caused a lot of problems for these dear souls. Marriages suffered as well as health. I benefited greatly by not drinking, and the benefits have been more than good health. The places that I avoid as a non-drinker, and the dignity enjoyed by not abusing my mind are just a couple. When I started to have children it also became very clear to me that I had gained an ability to provide a model for my children."

Alcohol often causes devastation to individuals and families, and professional help and support groups are wise. The impact of using some drugs can be even worse, as you will read about in the guidance below, and seeking help is vital.

"As to opium, it is foul and accursed. God protect us from the punishment He inflicteth on the user. According to the explicit Text of the Most Holy Book, it is forbidden, and its use is utterly condemned. Reason showeth that smoking opium is a kind of insanity, and experience attesteth that the user is completely cut off from the human kingdom.

May God protect all against the perpetration of an act so hideous as this, an act which layeth in ruins the very foundation of what it is to be human, and which causeth the user to be dispossessed for ever and ever. For opium fasteneth on the soul, so that the user's conscience dieth, his mind is blotted away, his perceptions are eroded. It turneth the living into the dead. It quencheth the natural heat. No greater harm can be conceived than that which opium inflicteth. Fortunate are they who never even speak the name of it; then think how wretched is the user."[190] 'Abdu'l-Bahá

You may have heard of "opioids" and the epidemic of abuse and addiction related to them. They may be made directly from opium or are synthetic variations that act in similar ways. Opioids are a class of drugs that include the illegal drug heroin; synthetic opioids such as fentanyl; and pain relievers available legally by prescription, such as oxycodone (OxyContin®), hydrocodone (Vicodin®), codeine, morphine, and many others. Before taking any medicine like this, either by doctor's prescription or handed to you from someone, be very aware whether it's chemically related to opium, be informed of the likely side effects, and have a conscious consultation with doctors about their use. Some are prescribed for very short periods, such as immediately after surgery for pain, or when a person is dying. When they are prescribed for longer periods, addiction is a high risk.

Many other drugs are also forbidden in the Bahá'í teachings due to their effect on people:

"... Bahá'ís should not use hallucinogenic agents, including LSD, peyote and similar substances, except when prescribed for medical treatment. Neither should they become involved in experiments with such substances.

"Although we have found no direct reference to marijuana in the Bahá'í writings, since this substance is derived from what is considered to be a milder form of cannabis, the species used to produce hashish, we can share with you a translation from the Persian of a Tablet of 'Abdu'l-Bahá on hashish:

'Regarding hashish you had pointed out that some Persians have become habituated to its use. Gracious God! This is the worst of all intoxicants, and its prohibition is explicitly revealed. Its use causeth the disintegration of thought and the complete torpor of the soul. How could anyone seek this fruit of the infernal tree, and by partaking of it, be led to exemplify the qualities of a monster? How could one use this forbidden drug, and thus deprive himself of the blessings of the All-Merciful?...

'Alcohol consumeth the mind and causeth man to commit acts of absurdity, but ... this wicked hashish extinguisheth the mind, freezeth the spirit, petrifieth the soul, wasteth the body and leaveth man frustrated and lost.'"[191] Universal House of Justice

"Concerning the so-called 'spiritual' virtues of the hallucinogens ...spiritual stimulation should come from turning one's heart to Bahá'u'lláh, and not through physical means such as drugs and agents.
"... [H]allucinogenic agents are a form of intoxicant. As the friends, including the youth, are required strictly to abstain from all forms of intoxicants, and are further expected conscientiously to obey the civil law of their country, it is obvious that they should refrain from using these drugs.
"A very great responsibility for the future peace and well-being of the world is borne by the youth of today. Let the Bahá'í youth by the power of the Cause they espouse be the shining example for their companions."[192] Universal House of Justice

When my choices are different

When you're consciously thinking about choosing to put alcohol and/or drugs into your body, it's wise to look ahead to possible consequences. These substances interfere with your ability to behave like the noble human being you are, and they can cause you to behave in ways that are harmful to you, others, and property. The addictive nature of them is also very dangerous and can cause you to seek ever-stronger substances, perhaps doing harmful or illegal actions to keep a supply coming. This is one person's experience:

"I grew up in a Bahá'í family, and when I turned 15, I chose to stay and became a Bahá'í. It was what other youth were doing, but it meant little to me at the time. Shortly after, I moved communities, and my connection with the Bahá'í Faith was lost. During this period, I underwent several traumatic experiences and started seeking any form of solace. The Faith was no longer a big presence in my life; but sex, drugs, and alcohol were readily available, and they were able to numb my pain for a while. As the effects of milder

addictions began to wear off, stronger and more dangerous addictions ensued.

"For almost half my life, I struggled constantly with addictions and my desire to be a better Bahá'í. My relationship with the Bahá'í community was a love-shame one; I loved to be involved in the activities, but I often felt that I could not be honest about how I lived my life. I always felt afraid to discuss these topics, or to let anyone know about my struggles due to the fear of being judged. This fear stopped me at first from receiving the assistance I needed. Eventually I found support groups, medical help, and turned to a Bahá'í community for prayer and support.

"My perceptions of the Bahá'í community interfered with my spiritual growth; had I not been as tenacious with my beliefs as I was, perhaps I would not be a Bahá'í today. Yet, from my experience, this is true of believers of many different faiths—the Bahá'í Faith is not immune to the negative forces of the outside world. People have an unbelievable ability to change, and Bahá'u'lláh reminds us to be forgiving and understanding of others. Anyone can come into the love of God, within the blink of an eye, no matter who they are."

A young man comments on his experiences with mentoring youth:

"When I talk with my youth group about marijuana—which some of them have tried, and one is trying to stop being dependent on—I focus on how it prevents spiritual growth. I let them know if weed is available and they turn to it whenever they feel bad, then each time they turn to it, they deprive themselves of that opportunity to develop their capacity to cope with bad feelings. Dependence over years or even decades can systematically deprive them of these opportunities for spiritual growth. This resonates with them, because most of them expect to be parents someday, and they understand how parenting is very challenging, and a big part of it is being able to function despite challenging feelings. With the one who's dependent, I try to emphasize that each time he uses it, he can choose to use less, and each time he uses it less, it's a victory, and good for his spiritual and brain development. I also emphasize that he's not a lost cause.

"I think it's also a concern that weed leads to physical and mental inactivity and apathy. Sometimes they think that because weed often doesn't lead to unseemly or dangerous behavior, they can conclude it must not be as bad as other drugs like opium. I remind them of the quotation from 'Abdu'l-Bahá: 'Man is, so to speak, unripe: the heat of the fire of suffering will mature him'. So, using it can get in the way of developing vital life, husband, and fathering skills, and it can prevent the development of spiritual maturity."

You might convince yourself to try a substance due to:

- Peer pressure
- A desire to lower stress or anxiety
- A wish to escape pain
- Curiosity

The following can assist you to pause and resist temptation:

- Your spiritual courage
- Self-discipline
- Being involved in spiritual activities and community service
- Having a mentor
- The nudge of the Holy Spirit on your conscience
- Prayer and holding tight to the power of the Covenant [See Chapter 4, "Creating a Support System".]

The Universal House of Justice offers this encouragement about where you can direct your energy:

"When so much of society invites passivity and apathy or, worse still, encourages behavior harmful to oneself and others, a conspicuous contrast is offered by those who are enhancing the capacity of a population to cultivate and sustain a spiritually enriching pattern of community life."[193] Universal House of Justice

If you're already struggling with substance use or abuse, you may find help in 12-Step programs, such as Alcoholics Anonymous or Narcotics Anonymous, and potentially obtain professional health counseling. There are also 12-Step programs to help family members or friends of the person affected, such as Al-Anon or Nar-Anon. Here is guidance:

"... [T]here is no objection to Bahá'ís being members of Alcoholics Anonymous, which is an association that does a great deal of good in assisting alcoholics to overcome their lamentable condition. The sharing of experience which the members undertake does not conflict with the

Bahá'í prohibition of the confession of sins; it is more in the nature of the therapeutic relationship between a patient and a psychiatrist."[194]
On behalf of the Universal House of Justice

In cases where the Bahá'í teachings are not in alignment with general evolving social mores, it may be advisable for those seeking professional counseling to find a therapist who comes from a religious background, especially a background that adheres to strong moral values. While such mental health professionals are not always easy to identify, it may be that you can find a Bahá'í or make inquiries to other religious groups that share Bahá'í values.

Resources Note: Books that may be useful are *Twelve Steps & the Bahá'í Faith: One Member's Perspective* and *Living with an Alcoholic: My Story of Healing and the Bahá'í Faith*.

Action

1. Establish or strengthen a fitness routine. If you have difficulty with regular exercise, find a buddy to do it with you, so you can mutually encourage each other and challenge each other to develop a routine.

2. Identify one food that will likely improve your health and add it to your regular diet. After about two weeks of including it, assess whether it has been beneficial. Continue to add or replace foods until most of your diet consists of ones that are healthy.

3. Choose three rules for safe driving and practice them each time you are behind the wheel of a vehicle.

4. Alcohol and Drugs:
   a. Research alcohol. Is it true that beer is less intoxicating than hard liquor? Is wine just grape juice? What do you think about having wine with dinner or at a party if everyone else is drinking it? Research the types of help available for alcohol dependence or alcoholism. What approaches seem to work the best? Consult a variety of sources in your research.
   b. Research marijuana (weed). Why is it legal in some parts of the world? What are its harmful effects? What are its useful effects

when prescribed for medical purposes? What is your opinion about using marijuana? Does the research support the idea that using it leads to the abuse of harder drugs? Consult a variety of sources in your research.
   c. Research common street drugs like heroin, cocaine, ecstasy, and prescription drugs that are often abused, like the pain killers Oxycontin or Percocet. What do these drugs do to the brain? To behavior? Once begun, why is it often so hard to stop using them? Consult a variety of sources in your research.

5. Research addiction. What is it? Can you become addicted to your phone, the internet, caffeine, video games, food, sex, and so on? [Note: Addiction to pornography is address in Chapter 15.] Why is addictive behavior so hard to stop? What is needed? Who is needed? Where can help be found? Is an addiction a disease? Does being addicted mean you are "bad"? Is it something to hide or something that needs help? Consult a variety of sources in your research.

6. Fill a glass or jar that represents your body with clear water to represent purity. Put a few drops of food coloring, water-based paint, or ink into the water to represent harmful substances. Meditate on the concept of purity and assess what you put in your body. What are your insights? Then take a shower, bath, or go for a swim, thinking as you do the activity about the concept of purifying yourself. What are your further insights?

Reflection

1. How can I ensure my body stays strong and healthy?
2. What do I see as the purpose and benefits of physical health and fitness?
3. How am I contributing to my physical well-being? What could I be doing better?
4. When and why do I harm my body?
5. What effects and outcomes have I seen from people drinking alcohol? From using or abusing drugs?
6. When have I felt pressured to participate in such activities? What empowers me to resist peer pressure?
7. What might indicate that I have become addicted to something? What steps will I take to address the issue?
8. What benefits come to me and others from maintaining my well-being?

12 - Striving for My Sexual Health – Some Context

Challenge: Sex feels so good that I'm not sure I want anything to do with changing my behavior.

Opportunity: To have a long-term, healthy, and happy marriage that includes sexual intimacy with my wife, I'm willing to consider carrying out spiritually based principles and approaches.

Summary:
- Sex is a unifying and pleasurable physical, mental, emotional, and spiritual experience within marriage between two consenting adults, one female and one male.
- Powerful hormones affect attraction and sex, and they can contribute to bonding two individuals together as one entity; I will need to carefully navigate this, as attraction is important but it's best to achieve this connection within marriage.
- Sex is not an effective way of getting to know someone well; in fact, it could interfere with clarity about someone's character.

More:

The topic of sex is complex and often controversial. It's also somewhat ironic that there is a lot of material here and in the following three chapters, so you can better learn how to give less emphasis to sex in your life! This material opens the door to this area of sexual health and brings it into the open for discussion and consultation. Ideally, this topic would be contained in one chapter, but it's subdivided for clarity and learning.

As sex has become a lucrative industry, its original pure purposes have become obscured. This chapter cannot address every related issue in depth. However, it will hopefully clarify the intended purposes of sex and assist you in viewing sex through a spiritual lens. This will assist you to balance it as part of a coherent life and not see it as such a dominant factor.

Sexual energy is normal and natural in healthy people, even if its intensity varies from person to person and over each person's lifetime. It's a powerful force that can take you by surprise. Therefore, it's good to be prepared and learn, think, talk, and pray about it.

Pornography is not sex education—scientific sources are needed to teach you how your body and that of a marriage partner works. It's also important to recognize that sex extends beyond the physical or biological aspects into the emotional and even spiritual realms. Sources like this book then assist you to develop spiritual strengths and skills that keep you on a spiritual and healthy pathway. Understanding and following God's purpose for your sexual energy will surely be part of your quest.

How sex fits within marriage

In the Bahá'í Faith, sex within marriage is a gift and a sacred means of bonding marriage partners together in unity. Sex and sexuality are not impure or unholy; sex is a natural impulse, but it belongs in a certain context: within a healthy marriage. Marriage is a divine institution, within which sexual intimacy serves as a protective, pleasurable, and unifying factor for a married couple. Here is guidance:

> "The Bahá'í teachings on sexual morality center on marriage and the family as the bedrock of the whole structure of human society and are designed to protect and strengthen that divine institution. Bahá'í law thus restricts permissible sexual intercourse to that between a man and the woman to whom he is married."[195] *The Kitáb-i-Aqdas*, Notes

Sex within marriage is often referred to as "lovemaking" because it's an expression of the feelings of love between the couple. Lovemaking can strengthen couples' spirituality by enhancing their unity. Couples can also spiritually enrich their sexual experiences by consciously practicing character qualities such as respect, trust, and flexibility. Here is a perspective on sex in marriage:

> "When we unite love with sex in its proper place, which is marriage, we have an abiding fountain of happiness and strength from which to draw. Sex can strengthen love, love can sublimate sex into a spiritual communion, a joy for the soul as well as the body."[196] R. Rabbani

Marriage has both physical and spiritual aspects, and they are often intertwined. Consider this quotation:

> "… [T]he union must be a true relationship, a spiritual coming together as well as a physical one, so that throughout every phase of life, and in all the worlds of God, their union will endure; for this real oneness is a gleaming out of the love of God."[197] 'Abdu'l-Bahá

Here is an author's perspective:

"It is important to acknowledge that God could have arranged the whole reproduction thing any way He wanted: a hidden button, a super-secret handshake, or some unique facial exchange that brought about conception. Really, He could have. But instead, He designed sex. He must have had a good reason, but what is it? The answer, in short, is that God wanted sex to be a lot more than just a really fun thing for wives and husbands to do together. And He wanted it to be more than an extremely enjoyable way to populate the planet. He had a far loftier goal in mind. God designed marital sex to be an encounter with the divine. Sexual intimacy, with all of its overwhelming emotions and heart-pounding sensations, was never intended to be experienced solely in the emotional and physical realms. Rather, it is to be a spiritual, even mystical, experience in which two bodies become one. God is present in a very real way every time this happens. Sex really is holy. It's a sacred place shared in the intimacy of marriage."[198] Tim Alan Gardner

Sexual intercourse, of course, can also lead to creating a new life—another human being with both a body and a soul who parents can raise to worship God. This is a powerful, humbling, and meaningful reality with both physical and spiritual ramifications. Here is guidance about marital sex:

"You are aware that the Bahá'í Faith recognizes the value of the sex impulse and holds that the institution of marriage has been established as the channel of its rightful expression. In letters written on his behalf, Shoghi Effendi made the following statements: 'The sex instinct, like all other human instincts, is not necessarily evil. It is a power which, if properly directed, can bring joy and satisfaction to the individual.' Further, the Bahá'í standard 'does not preclude the living of a perfectly normal sex life in its legitimate channel of marriage.' With regard to the importance that should be placed on the physical aspect of marriage in comparison to its moral and spiritual aspects, a letter written on behalf of the Guardian stated:

'The institution of marriage, as established by Bahá'u'lláh, while giving due importance to the physical aspect of marital union, considers it as subordinate to the moral and spiritual purposes and functions with which it has been invested by an all-wise and loving Providence. Only when these different values are given each their due importance, and only on the basis of the subordination of the physical to the moral, and the carnal to the spiritual, can such excesses and laxity in marital relations as our decadent age is so sadly witnessing be avoided, and family life be restored to its original purity, and fulfil the true function for which it has been instituted by God.'

"Bahá'ís are, understandably, influenced by the forces of society, including contemporary beliefs about sexual practices. As believers come to more deeply understand the principles that have been set forth in the Bahá'í teachings, they will be able to obtain a more balanced and healthier view of sexual relations within marriage. That itself will help Bahá'í married couples to avoid or to resolve many difficulties in a world with an exaggerated emphasis on, and distorted view of, sex. Of course, a number of sexual problems can well have medical aspects, and in such cases recourse should certainly be had to the best medical assistance. Moreover, a letter written on behalf of Shoghi Effendi explained: 'Sex is a very individual matter,' and 'some people are more passionate by nature than others'."[199] On behalf of the Universal House of Justice

The spiritual and physical are very interlinked in marriage, and couples pray and consult to understand the balance in their relationship and home. It's an amazing blessing when you have a partner you can talk to about anything and consult to create your marriage together. Here are some of the physical aspects, all of which can have spiritual dimensions:

- Working cooperatively in the kitchen
- Taking care of each other during illnesses
- Enjoying all the layers of touch and sexual intimacy
- Sharing intimate space in bedroom and bathroom
- Giving birth
- Parenting

Some success factors with sex in marriage are not about touch:

"There are two key factors related to satisfying sex: emotional connection and conversations about sex. The second one often gets overlooked, but research shows that only 9% of couples who can't talk comfortably about sex report sexual satisfaction. By talking about sex, couples develop a "script" or "playbook" for how to please one another emotionally and sexually. ... That's why it's vital for couples to not only prioritize sex in the relationship, but also to learn how to talk about sex comfortably on a consistent basis. How can you make it more comfortable? Sharing your likes and dislikes about sex isn't a difficult task in itself, but being that vulnerable (even with your soulmate!) can make it a very difficult task. To make it more comfortable, try to think about sex as a physical expression of your friendship. At its core, the goal of sex is to become closer friends and have fun together. This reframing makes it a friendship issue, which is easier to address than a sexual issue."[200] Get Lasting

Married couples can also draw on science for positive experiences to occur:

"... [F]or some people, sexual desire—the urge to become sexual—doesn't *precede* feeling aroused; it actually follows it. In other words, some people rarely (or never) find themselves fantasizing about sex or feeling sexual urges, but when they're open to becoming sexual with their spouses anyway, they often find the sexual stimulation pleasurable, and they become aroused. Once aroused, there is a desire to continue. And that's every bit as much 'sexual desire' as the more traditional view of things."[201] M. W. Davis

This is a perspective about what affects a woman to become aroused or instead keep the "brakes" on:

"Context is made of two things: The circumstances of the present moment—whom you're with, where you are, whether the situation is novel or familiar, risky or safe, etc.—and your brain state in the present moment—whether you're relaxed or stressed, trusting or not, loving or not, right now, in this moment. The evidence is mounting that women's sexual response is more sensitive than men's to context, including mood and relationship factors, and women vary more from each other in how much such factors influence their sexual response."[202] E. Nagoski

The Bahá'í teachings encourage learning about sexual expression in partnership together in marriage—lovingly and with compassion. Couples are wise to study and consult about the topic of sex before and during marriage to ensure they know the healthy actions and skills that will benefit them. Remember that pornography is not a healthy source for study. [More on this topic is in Chapter 15.]

The complexity of sexual relations in marriage cannot be fully covered here. For more information, please determine what you need to know and visit www.marriagetransformation.com and access other resources.

Healthy attraction and connections

Physical intimacy, including sexual touch and intercourse, is the norm in dating relationships in many parts of the world, for people of all ages. When two people care for each other, the desire to express their affection physically pulls strongly on their hearts, often speeding them toward each other. In such situations, personal moral standards, religious beliefs, and being involved with a supportive spiritual community can act as an internal and external braking system that empowers a couple to wisely wait until the ideal time for physical intimacy. Within marriage, couples can relax and appreciate their mutual attraction in new ways, and their intimacy draws them closer together.

Someone comments about timing:

"Learning to integrate our spiritual values with our sexual desires is best done during adolescence when that conflict naturally arises. Similarly, learning to attract a partner without becoming unchaste is also best learned at the outset. This is partly because we live in a sexualized society and need to negotiate a world full of flirtation, seduction, and manipulation. We can't really hope to avoid this, and so we need to learn how to handle ourselves from a young age."

For some people, attraction becomes obvious even in early encounters. However, for others it becomes more evident after getting to know and appreciate someone's mind, heart, and soul. Sexual intimacy while you and a partner are getting to know each other, or as a method of getting to know each other, increases the difficulty of objectively assessing a partner, their character, and their potential complementarity for marriage.

According to Dr. Mark Laaser, an expert on sexual addiction, sex releases a chemical cocktail—which includes adrenaline, dopamine, serotonin, and oxytocin.[203] These neurotransmitters produce very powerful emotions and feelings of pleasure, which can cloud people's ability to clearly see each other's character and to notice incompatibilities and future problems that would threaten the health of a long-term committed relationship or marriage. The mix of chemicals and hormones that cause feelings of emotional closeness, however, is a good contribution to marriage.

Sex is, of course, an intimate physical act, but it also has mental, emotional, and spiritual components and effects. One of you may think that having sex means you're in a committed relationship, while the other could be focused only on enjoying the physical experience and a temporary connection. A man says:

"If the relationship then ends and you felt bonded to that person, you may feel quite betrayed, and at the same time, may still want intimate physical affection. This desire could be a trap and unwise cycle in subsequent relationships. There could be a strong draw toward physical contact without knowing a partner well, and unhappiness is the likely result."

It's important to know that there's a spark of attraction between you and a potential marriage partner. Sometimes there is an assumption one should be so chaste as to not even be aware if there is attraction, or if someone is "pleasing" to you, which can result in a marriage with little sexual activity or even aversion instead. Consider this guidance:

> "As for the question regarding marriage under the Law of God: first thou must choose one who is pleasing to thee, and then the matter is subject to the consent of father and mother."[204] 'Abdu'l-Bahá

Someone shares their observations about attraction:

"I've seen how going overboard and avoiding anything even remotely close to flirting has resulted in not knowing how to show genuine interest toward the opposite sex. That's how we were brought up in my community, where chastity was so overemphasized that we have a generation of people who don't know how to approach the opposite sex and start a natural process of getting to know someone.

"It's been hammered into our heads that easy-familiarity (kissing and touching many people) and flirting are dirty and bad. And yet the reality is that showing a healthy type of interest, and experiencing some chemistry, is crucial for attraction and interest to build and for anything romantic to ever start between two people. Otherwise you end up not married at all or end up in a marriage with someone who feels like your sister.

"These topics need to be discussed in balance. Personally, I think there's nothing wrong with showing healthy interest, so that both people perceive a

green light and feel approachable. No one is going to show a green light if they are stuck in feeling like they are doing something wrong. As a result, nobody approaches anyone, and what is supposed to be a natural process now has a dirty label on it and marriages don't happen. As a worldwide community, I hope we start learning about genuine and authentic approaches to showing interest in each other."

An attraction mixed with sexual urges can become a challenge when it moves into "intensity". Here is one man's view of the difference between intensity, which is unwise and needs to be unlearned, and intimacy, that is a vital part of healthy marriages:

"... [S]weaty palms, racing heart, weak knees and tingling groin [can be what] many interpret as a sign from God that they have finally met their soul mate. The belief that these intense sensations are signs of love is almost universal in our culture. ... It is often our bodies that make decisions for us without our consent. In the world of physical sensation, the choice is experienced as being between intimacy and intensity. With your body in a state of hyper-sensitivity (which can be enhanced through anything that boosts your adrenaline, even if it's dangerous or unwise), sexual activity can be ecstatic, overpowering and exhausting. When movies depict wild passionate sex, this is the experience they are trying to capture. This kind of sex might feel powerful and overwhelming, but does it feel loving? ...

"If we want to enjoy having sex with a safe, loving, supportive and appropriate partner, we will need to replace our fascination with intensity with an appreciation for intimacy. ... We can choose to make the deeper, sweeter, more enduring sensations of intimacy the ones we strive for."[205] Justice St Rain

The author goes on to say that intimacy "involves a feeling of knowing and being known; of caring and being cared for, and of physical, mental and spiritual closeness." He indicates key foundation elements are trust, honesty, safety, good character, commitment, and perseverance.[206]

Action

1. Research what is involved in creating healthy sexual experiences within marriage. Does what you found align with the Bahá'í teachings? Are there additional factors that could apply?

2. Examine the concept of attraction by holding two magnets close to each other. What strengthens their connection? What lessens it? Do a second experiment by taking two lengths of tape about 10-inches long. Wrap them in a circle around each of your hands with the sticky side facing out. If each circle represents individuals who marry without having sexual experiences with other people and you touch them together, how well do they "stick"? Take them apart and lightly place the sticky sides a few times against carpeting or the floor, symbolizing relationships with many people. Now test how well the two pieces of tape stick together. What are your insights?

Reflection

1. What do I think I know about sex? What expectations and assumptions do I have about it? How will I verify all of this for accuracy?
2. Why might it be best for me to only have sex within marriage with my partner?
3. What do I look forward to about sexual experiences in marriage?
4. How can I and my partner have positive sexual experiences in marriage?
5. How could pornography use interfere with these positive experiences?
6. How can I build my strength to resist sexual temptations outside of being in a healthy marriage?
7. What are my observations about intensity versus intimacy?
8. What do I notice most attracts me to women?
9. How can I put more emphasis on knowing someone's character without sexual attraction distracting me?

13 - Striving for My Sexual Health— Spiritual Principles and Challenges

Challenge: When something like sex is so physical, it's hard for me to think of it in spiritual terms.

Opportunity: I can apply many character qualities toward my sexual health, with chastity as one of the most important.

Summary:
- Chastity is a powerful protector of my well-being and for healthy sexual expressions with my marriage partner; it liberates me from harm and many potential tests.
- The morals of society frequently do not align with the Bahá'í teachings about sex, which makes this a challenging issue for many Bahá'í men of all ages, including me.

More:

Liberating myself through chastity

Bahá'u'lláh as the Divine Physician prescribes chastity as the armor against the harmful influences related to sex in society, with a protective layer of purity and holiness added in. He (and The Báb, and 'Abdu'l-Bahá, and Shoghi Effendi, and the Universal House of Justice!) asks you to trust Him that it's like a superpower of health and protection. Sexual acts outside of the proper context can increase the risk of contracting sexually transmitted diseases, result in an unplanned pregnancy, or cause feelings of guilt or shame. This is true whether you are single or married. Someone says:

"Personally, I think that chastity has protected me from many situations I might not have wanted to fall into. I've seen how much it costs society when people are not chaste. Therefore, I think it's important to better educate our society, especially the youth, about chastity, and why it's a good principle."

Chastity is a complex topic, far beyond abstinence. It's about making positive choices rather than just saying "no" to intercourse or other sexual or intimate physical contact. It can be defined as maintaining sexual purity and reserving sexual attraction, thoughts, responses, and intimacy as a special and respectful gift to share with a marriage partner. Chaste actions include faithfulness to one's chosen partner and keeping one's thoughts and words pure and focused on each other rather than outside to others.

Below is some guidance about chastity and dating:

> "... [T]here is nothing in the Bahá'í Writings which relates specifically to the so-called dating practices prevalent in some parts of the world, where two unmarried people of the opposite sex participate together in a social activity. In general, Bahá'ís who are planning to involve themselves in this form of behavior should become well aware of the Bahá'í Teachings on chastity and, with these in mind, should scrupulously avoid any actions which would arouse passions which might well tempt them to violate these Teachings. In deciding which acts are permissible in the light of these considerations, the youth should use their own judgment, giving due consideration to the advice of their parents, taking account of the prevailing customs of the society in which they live, and prayerfully following the guidance of their conscience. It is the sacred duty of parents to instill in their children the exalted Bahá'í standard of moral conduct, and the importance of adherence to this standard cannot be over-emphasized as a basis for true happiness and for successful marriage."[207] On behalf of the Universal House of Justice

A man shares his struggles:

"Chastity is not a common word you hear in daily life, and even within the Bahá'í community, many people of all ages are struggling with it. You may think 'Everyone is doing 'it', why shouldn't I? What's wrong with sex? I'm just being human. I will try to follow Bahá'í law in other areas, but in this area, it's impossible!"

It's often difficult, but it's not impossible. Being a spiritual man, a spiritual warrior of light, means donning that "armor", so you and any others you are involved with are not vulnerable in many ways that can derail your lives. It's also not impossible to have a good marriage where one or both of you have previously had sex with others. However, it can cause difficulties:

- Jealousy
- More difficulty bonding with each other

- Physical effects from diseases
- Performance comparisons

Consider this:

"Chastity—one of the rarest of all...gems in the world to-day—means to conserve your personal sex powers, so intimate in nature, capable of conferring so much beauty on your life, for their proper expression which is with your life partner, your mate, the one who with you will share home, children and all the glad and sad burdens of living. The decency, the spiritual cleanliness of marriage, the essential humanness of it, are enhanced a thousandfold by chastity on the part of both men and women, previous to their unions. Their chances of successful marriage are also far greater, for they will then share with each other, in every way, the new life they have embarked upon. Comparisons will not be drawn, over-emphasized appetites on the part of one or the other will not have been cultivated which might mar it, and above all, they will have put sex into its proper place, where instead of stampeding the emotional nature of the individual (as it does at present to so marked a degree), it will fulfill its natural function in rounding out life and contributing to its normality and healthfulness."[208] R. Rabbani

The passages below offer more explanation and insight into chastity. The standards in the Bahá'í teachings are very high, but they are also balanced with reason. As with any high moral standard, you benefit from striving, with sincere motivation, to reach the standard, while also having compassion and understanding for yourself and others when you may fail to reach it. It's the sincere, daily effort to strive for the standard which results in long-term spiritual and moral growth, which often happens gradually.

> "A chaste and holy life must be made the controlling principle in the behavior and conduct of all Bahá'ís, both in their social relations with the members of their own community, and in their contact with the world at large. ... It must be upheld, in all its integrity and implications, in every phase of the life of those who fill the ranks of that Faith, whether in their homes, their travels, their clubs, their societies, their entertainments, their schools, and their universities. ... It must be closely and continually identified with the mission of the Bahá'í Youth, both as an element in the life of the Bahá'í community, and as a factor in the future progress and orientation of the youth of their own country.

"Such a chaste and holy life, with its implications of modesty, purity, temperance, decency, and clean-mindedness, involves no less than the exercise of moderation in all that pertains to dress, language, amusements, and all artistic and literary avocations. It demands daily vigilance in the control of one's carnal desires and corrupt inclinations. It calls for the abandonment of a frivolous conduct, with its excessive attachment to trivial and often misdirected pleasures. It requires total abstinence from all alcoholic drinks, from opium, and from similar habit-forming drugs. It condemns the prostitution of art and of literature, the practices of nudism and of companionate marriage, infidelity in marital relationships, and all manner of promiscuity, of easy familiarity, and of sexual vices. It can tolerate no compromise with the theories, the standards, the habits, and the excesses of a decadent age. ...

"It must be remembered, however, that the maintenance of such a high standard of moral conduct is not to be associated or confused with any form of asceticism, or of excessive and bigoted puritanism. The standard inculcated by Bahá'u'lláh seeks, under no circumstances, to deny anyone the legitimate right and privilege to derive the fullest advantage and benefit from the manifold joys, beauties, and pleasures with which the world has been so plentifully enriched by an All-Loving Creator."[209] Shoghi Effendi

Here is a personal perspective on the challenges of following the guidance above:

"The quotations about chastity were hard to listen to as a teenager, and they are still hard to listen to now as an adult. Not that I think it's a bad idea, but because it was/is the easiest to 'fail' at. Sexual urges are the ultimate animal instinct, and to overcome this basically on your own is close to impossible, especially when we don't truly understand our own status as spiritual beings. It's hard enough to meet someone you like, then to be rejected (or you reject them) because of sex is hard to accept in our current times.

"What Shoghi Effendi is asking of us is in my opinion revolutionary. He has strongly emphasized chastity, and he is asking us to choose wisely how we conduct ourselves, including where we go, who we hang out with, what we talk about, and so on. Frankly, it's hard, and it's going to get harder. Because it's revolutionary, whoever tries to accomplish this new form of dating, this new form of character-based-relationship-building (not just on

an emotional love high), and strives to be perfect at it is frankly a pioneer in the subject, and if I may add, nothing comes easy for pioneers.

"Dating can be wonderful and horrifying because it's the perfect testing ground for your own character. It doesn't matter where you meet each other and in what context you date (although some ways are easier than others admittedly). You will still spend the time and experience emotions trying to judge between reality and desires. Ultimately, I think that in dating, you are learning how to judge between your material and spiritual desires—and it hurts when your vain imaginings are being burnt away.

"The thing to remember is though, no matter what happens, you need to learn to ask God to forgive you. The feeling of 'guilt' I think is the most hindering emotion you can hold onto, especially when building relationships. It's hard on yourself, but it's hard on others who must see you suffer and to suffer along. If you're totally honest with yourself, and you can let go of your guilt and fears of failing, maybe dating won't be so scary or daunting."

Sometimes chastity can feel like an abstract concept, or it becomes the overly simplistic and inaccurate "just don't have sex". The following concrete statements may assist you to better understand some of the nuances about it:

"A man practices chastity effectively when he:

- Moderates and restrains the power of attraction to others, channeling it moderately and appropriately only with a chosen partner; avoids excessive flirting or contact in person or through electronic media
- Abstains from sexually and physically arousing and intimate acts before marriage or outside of marriage with someone other than his wife
- Regards sexual intercourse as a spiritual act of unity that is only consummated within marriage
- Releases passion appropriately with his marriage partner, understanding what is sexually pleasurable and connecting to her and meeting her needs as much as possible as well as his own
- Speaks, dresses, and moves modestly to avoid inviting inappropriate attention, touch, and sexual attraction; respects appropriate privacy
- Strives to keep his mind from holding onto sexual thoughts and also to control his sexual desires and impulses, other than appropriate ones related to his wife

- Chooses respectful entertainment and activities for others and himself; avoids telling or listening to jokes or stories with sexual content
- Builds and maintains strong platonic friendships with both men and women, keeping appropriate boundaries and avoiding sexual innuendos, domination, or seduction
- Treats the bodies, minds, hearts, and souls of others with equality, respect, and gentleness
- Fills his life with worthwhile purposes and service, placing less focus, emphasis, and importance on sex, especially prior to marriage

"A man needs to strengthen chastity when he:

- Has sex outside of marriage, which can threaten health, well-being, jobs, or family unity
- Sees sex as the primary way to achieve happiness or to have a relationship
- Acts in a sexually seductive manner or engages in arousing or sexual touch outside of marriage
- Values a partner's physical attributes more than her character qualities; views anyone as a sex object instead of as a whole person
- Uses substances such as alcohol or drugs, in part because they reduce his sexual inhibitions [Note: If someone is not practicing chastity and is also drinking or taking drugs, he will find it more difficult to discern whether a partner has given clear consent for any type of physical contact.]
- Views sex as a game, spectator sport, diversion, opportunity for conquest, imposition of power, something to brag about, way to become acquainted, or as a means of self-centered relaxation
- Pursues pleasure through sexually stimulating entertainment or activities with others besides a wife (in person or through electronic media)
- Engages in excessive sexual fantasies, particularly about a non-marriage partner; views or participates in pornography; masturbates; or becomes addicted to sexual pleasure
- Abuses others sexually by forceful or manipulative behavior, threats, or violence

"A man misuses (to excess or in the wrong time or place) the strength of chastity when he:

- Rejects or disparages his own natural sexuality and sensuality or that of others, acting as if sex is something dirty or wrong rather than a spiritual gift contributing to the unique bond that unites a married couple
- Fails to communicate affectionate feelings verbally to a partner/wife and physically to a wife
- Judges, condemns, gossips, or backbites about the sexual activities of others or himself"[210] S. M. Alexander

We are all responsible for our own choices and lives, and we are asked to use mature judgment, look to the truth in the Bahá'í teachings, draw on the advice of those we trust and who know us well, and look at the greater context of our society. We live with the consequences of our choices—whether they relate to sex or anything else. Here is a man's story:

"During a time that I should've been studying the Bahá'í Writings and praying more, I was seduced to have sex with a new friend. I was dazzled by her good qualities, and I had a lot to learn from her. We started having sex on the premise that it was casual. But she wanted more, and I found that if sex was made available, I couldn't stop myself from continuing.

"We ended up in a relationship. I was never very happy in it, because our conversation styles didn't mesh. What's worse, she became verbally abusive. I tried to quit having sex with her many times, but each time, I would slip up after a while and we'd be 'together' again.

"After two or three years, with the advice of a trusted friend, I had nearly mustered up the volition to quit the relationship for good. But she was nice for a couple of days, and even though we didn't really enjoy talking to each other, I started seriously considering that I 'should' propose marriage to her. That week, she suddenly got angry and spent a few days berating me for reasons out of my control. I was finally able to leave the relationship for good.

"Now, nearly two years later, I still get shaky if I see her, and during hard times, I feel lonelier than I ever felt before I met her. When I was with her, I could cuddle with her to cope with challenges and stress, and now I have nothing but that memory. Dealing with loneliness and certain life challenges is much harder than it was before I first got involved. Friends tell me to find a partner to make myself feel better, and that's what people seem to frequently do. But I'm resolved not to have sex again unless I'm married. I also don't want to use another person like a drug again.

"Men don't frequently talk about it with each other, certainly not in groups. But I've talked with enough guys individually to know that the end of a guy's first loving and sexual relationship is typically devastating. However, I'm really glad I get to be alone rather than permanently attached to someone who isn't right for me."

As with any choice, when you make a positive one, you strengthen your spiritual muscles and increase your self-respect. You have the confidence that comes from making difficult decisions and good choices that allow you to bravely move forward in a positive way. When instead you step away from the teachings and act in ways that don't align with them, there is a negative effect on you. The light inside of you becomes dim with a potential mix of guilt, shame, and fear.

There are always consequences when we choose actions that would bring sadness to Bahá'u'lláh's heart and that don't follow His teachings. Being a spiritual man means that you do your best each day to make good choices, take responsibility for your actions, seek God's forgiveness when you don't reach the standard, learn from your experiences, correct the situation or address the consequences as best as you can, and determine how to go more powerfully forward.

A man comments on his experiences:

"As a teenager, I was aware that the influence of peers and media worked against the divine standard of chastity that the Holy Books call us to. I met with some success in the struggle with desire as a result, but still some failure. I decided to impose a financial cost any time I failed, so I set an amount to give to the Bahá'í funds. I paid a large amount at one point, and the happy news is that the thought of paying again has helped keep me chaste ever since, now going on a decade! I also call to mind the horror of being responsible for the killing of an unborn child due to abortion and of risking exposure to sexually transmitted diseases. I think these practical measures, thanks to the love and the fear of God, helped to keep me on the straight path."

Someone offers this conclusion:

"Chastity seems like the surest way for a strong marriage and commitment to one another. I like the guidance given on behalf of the Universal House of Justice in this quotation:

> 'For the individual, who both contributes to and draws strength from the environment that is the Bahá'í community, adhering to Bahá'í law is endowed with meaning and, though perhaps still difficult on occasion, does not pose the insurmountable challenge that you fear it will.'[211] On behalf of the Universal House of Justice

"It gives me a lot of strength to know that I have the Universal House of Justice's confidence that I can practice chastity without being overly challenged."

Bahá'í teachings and society

The topic of sex often ignites many emotions and has aspects that become a pitfall for many. We live in an oversexualized world that objectifies especially women, but also men at times. Yet we are called to uphold high standards, all of us, because that's what Bahá'u'lláh is guiding us to. We are motivated to do so if we feel we are beings of light who want to create a new culture of having a good sex life in marriage, not beings of sin, living like animals and who constantly need to suppress our impure thoughts. If we are creating this new culture and context, we can fill our minds and lives with positive, purposeful activities and put sex in its best place within a healthy marriage. Here is some guidance:

> "One of the outcomes of the rising tide of materialism and consequent reorientation of society, over more than a century, has been a destructive emphasis on sexuality. Sexuality has become a preoccupation, pervading commerce, media, the arts, and popular culture, influencing disciplines such as medicine, psychology, and education, and reducing the human being to an object. It is no longer merely a part of life but has become the defining element of a person's identity. Thus, our civilization has exalted sex and sexuality to a level of importance far beyond its proper place in our lives. Sex has also been wrenched out of its proper context. On the one hand, our current culture suffuses every aspect of our lives with sex, but on the other, it isolates

the sex act from its natural corollaries of marital life and the bearing and rearing of children."[212] On behalf of the Universal House of Justice

Action

1. Go out on a date with an agreed standard of chaste behavior set ahead of time. Reflect on the outcome together.

2. Create a purification ceremony, alone or together with others. Some elements could include:
   - Build a fire in a safe place
   - Write down on paper all the thoughts and behaviors related to sex that you want to detach from, improve, or ask God to forgive; if other people are present, you might have a general discussion about what you each wrote down, but "confessing" sins to others that abases you is not to be part of the experience
   - Crumple the paper(s) into a ball and throw it/them into the fire
   - While the paper(s) are burning, read or sing the verses of the "Long Healing Prayer"

3. Explore whether having a support team and additional resources could assist you on your quest through the topic of sex and put them in place. Consider:

   a. Trustworthy friends and relatives
   b. Seeking appropriate medical and psychological resources as needed
   c. Reading books on or off the topic
   d. Consultation with trusted advisors, such as parents, an Auxiliary Board member, or a representative of a Spiritual Assembly

   If you decide one or more of these is useful, proceed with your outreach and requests.

Reflection

1. What have been my perceptions about the concept of chastity? What new insights have I now gained from this chapter?
2. What have I observed about chastity and sex in the society around me? How is media affecting my perceptions?

3. How have my experiences affected my view of sex? Do I have anything to resolve from previous experiences? How could I address these?
4. What can I do that empowers me to practice chastity before marriage? After marriage?
5. What do I consider good guidelines for myself around chaste behavior when I am in a couple relationship?
6. What would support me going back to living a chaste and holy life if I've made or were to make choices that don't align with the teachings?

14 - Striving for My Sexual Health—Building Understanding and Strengths

Challenge: Sexy images, people, messages, and media surround me, and it's a very strong temptation to participate in some way.

Opportunity: I can use spiritual tools to direct my thoughts and actions at appropriate times toward spiritually and mentally stimulating topics, service activities, work accomplishments, and life goals.

Summary:
- I can apply qualities like acceptance, detachment, and self-discipline to aid me in staying focused on healthy expression of my sexual energy within marriage with my partner and not in other ways that can be harmful or unhealthy.
- I can direct the energies of my body, mind, heart, and soul toward positive and creative endeavors and many purposes and services to others.
- Sexual energy is appropriate to consciously release when I choose with a willing marriage partner.

More:

Some current difficulties

You are building your understanding of the concept of chastity and how it could apply to your life. However, even when you are committed to chastity, there can be ongoing challenges to carrying it out. Sex is one of the most difficult aspects of Bahá'í life for many men (and women too!). The standard of chastity until marriage is not the current cultural norm, and neither is the essential aspect of faithfulness within marriage. In fact, much of television, movies, books, and music seem to praise having sex frequently and with many different partners. They portray it as an end that should be pursued and is associated with masculinity. Add to that an acquaintance who thinks it's a great thing to text you photos of a classmate's breasts, an invitation to a party you know won't be healthy, and friends who urge you to access the latest porn site on your mobile phone, and the dark forces can feel like they are swirling around you with high intensity.

Navigating in a world where sex is perceived as a "normal" component of encounters and dating, and people tally up and brag about (lie about?) their "conquests" heightens the intensity even more. Media implies that making very fast decisions about the long-term viability of a relationship based on strong physical attraction or sexual experiences is a reasonable route to take, which is misleading. Taking the time to know someone's character and build a close friendship is far more effective.

Here is a sharing from a woman after a difficult experience with a Bahá'í man:

"I befriended a Bahá'í man in his early 40's from another country, and due to the distance, we communicated mainly through texts and phone calls. We flirted some and got to know each other. He had been a Bahá'í for a few years, and he served on a Bahá'í institution, so I assumed he was likely well-grounded in the teachings. After some months of chatting, we decided to meet in person, but I soon realized that his only intention was to have 'fun' with me. It all became very awkward when he actively sought to be sexually close to me and was less interested in getting to know me. He mentioned that he had observed other Bahá'ís being loose with the laws about chastity, and that this made him think it's not a big deal to have sex before marriage.

"I felt sorry for him that he was exposed to such an environment. However, I also felt very disappointed that he took advantage of me living here alone to test whether I would be willing to go against the laws. It was scary, but I'm very glad he didn't try to force me into having sex with him. I was able to get away from him safely.

"Some of my fellow single Bahá'í women friends have also mentioned to me that they have had similar encounters with Bahá'í men. They also tell me they have been approached by married Bahá'í men with suggestive photos of themselves. I thought I would have to justify waiting for sex after marriage if I was dating someone who wasn't a Bahá'í, but now I can see this is a big test to overcome among Bahá'ís as well."

Here is more sharing about the current challenge:

"I have many single Bahá'í friends—both men and women—and some of them have high libidos, so it's very hard for them to not have sex and wait. Many of them are also aware of what the teachings say about the topic, but they disagree with it and say that they for sure want to find out about whether there's sexual compatibility. They don't want to risk finding out about major problems after marrying. For them the idea of waiting and not

making sure about sexual compatibility is an absurd and even naïve thought."

One problem with this line of thinking is that sex before marriage is not necessarily a predictor of sexual satisfaction within marriage. People sometimes behave differently when having an affair than when in the daily routines of married life. It's also impossible to practice marital unity and the spiritual unity that comes through marital sexual experiences if you are not actually married.

A man comments on his struggles:

"What I began to notice in my life was that I had a different standard when dating a Bahá'í or a non-Bahá'í. With the Bahá'ís I was trying to be chaste and trying not to have sex. But when dating a non-Bahá'í, especially since it's so common in my country, it seemed almost as if I had to have sex with them. It was easier to just give in and be fully physical, as they weren't bound by the Bahá'í laws. It took me awhile to notice that this double standard was really messing with my head and conscience. I also started to realize it was going to interfere with me finding a life partner who loved Bahá'u'lláh and was making chaste choices."

Shoghi Effendi provides this balance:

"… [B]y holiness…is meant attachment to God, His Precepts and His Will. We are not ascetics in any sense of the word. On the contrary, Bahá'u'lláh says God has created all the good things in the world for us to enjoy and partake. But we must not become attached to them and put them before the spiritual things. Chastity in the strict sense means not to have sexual intercourse, or sexual intimacies, before marriage. In the general sense it means not to be licentious. This does not mean we Bahá'ís believe sexual relations to be impure or wrong. On the contrary they are natural and should be considered one of God's many blessings. … Sex is a very individual matter, some people are more passionate by nature than others, and might consequently suffer more if forced to be continent. But when the world becomes more spiritual there will not be such an exaggerated emphasis on sex, as there is today, and consequently it will be easier for young people to be chaste and control their passions. A man of noble character and strong willpower, could certainly remain faithful to his wife during a long absence!"[213] Shoghi Effendi

The Bahá'í Faith teaches that the current culture is way off track. Someone said, "I have Bahá'í friends who won't follow the teachings on chastity, because they think we as humanity aren't there yet. It will be easier in the future to be chaste, but not for now". Living in that dichotomy is a real challenge, as this misguided nature of society is a force to be reckoned with. You may think, "What do I tell my friends about my beliefs around sex? How do I behave? How should I behave? How do I respond to a woman who pushes me to have sex with her? Will my friends think I'm weird if I follow Bahá'í laws?" Here are responses to youth, but this guidance is good for all ages:

> "We…can sympathize with the problems that Bahá'í youth face when trying to live up to the Bahá'í standards of behavior. It is, perhaps, natural that in the bewildering amoral environment in which Bahá'í youth are growing up they feel the need for specific instructions on which intimacies are permissible and which are not. However, we feel it would be most unwise for any Bahá'í institution to issue detailed instructions about this.
>
> "The Bahá'í youth should study the teachings on chastity and, with these in mind, should avoid any behavior which would arouse passions which would tempt them to violate them. In deciding what acts are permissible to them in the light of these considerations the youth must use their own judgment, following the guidance of their consciences and the advice of their parents.
>
> "If Bahá'í youth combine such personal purity with an attitude of uncensorious forbearance towards others they will find that those who may have criticized or even mocked them will come, in time, to respect them. They will, moreover, be laying a firm foundation for future married happiness."[214] Universal House of Justice

"As to chastity, this is one of the most challenging concepts to get across in this very permissive age, but Bahá'ís must make the utmost effort to uphold Bahá'í standards, no matter how difficult they may seem at first. Such efforts will be made easier if the youth will understand that the laws and standards of the Faith are meant to free them from untold spiritual and moral difficulties in the same way that a proper appreciation of the laws of nature enables one to live in harmony with the forces of the planet."[215] On behalf of the Universal House of Justice

A few men share their perspectives:

"It's worth mentioning that chastity means refraining from any action that stimulates sexual arousal outside of its proper use in marriage. This includes sexual vices, fetishes, or anything to stimulate the sex drive that is not as intended, such as an erotic massage. This list could be endless. You may not initially realize why this is important; however, the misuse of the sex drive corrupts the mind and the body, which eventually corrupts our thoughts and soul. Even just visualizing something sexually stimulating is dangerous, and this is partially what's referred to in the Bahá'í writings as 'vain imaginings'."

"The decision of a couple to wait for sex until marriage involves not only refraining from sexual behaviors but also cultivating in their bodies, minds, hearts, and souls the character quality of chastity. In the Bahá'í teachings, chastity means not only refraining from sex outside of marriage, but also from any other actions, thoughts, or words that we might, in prayerful consideration and good conscience, conclude are impure or unchaste, because they stimulate sexual impulses. I heard someone describe chastity as striving to see people as God sees them, or with God's eyes, rather than seeing them in terms of what they can do for us. I liked that description, how positive it is, how it follows from the idea that we are created noble."

"Many interactions and experiences suggest to me that having sex with a woman who you're not permanently committed to is virtually always unkind and disrespectful to her. It's sort of politically incorrect to suggest this. Women and men are basically the same intellectually and spiritually and so forth—but the one area that it actually makes sense we'd be different is how we're wired when it comes to matters related to reproduction, and I think it should be okay to acknowledge that."

It's actually unkind and disrespectful to you too.

Many men these days feel homosexual urges or identify as homosexual or bisexual. The Bahá'í teachings on sex can present a strong test. Human sexuality is a very complex subject with yet incomplete scientific research about potential causes or treatments. Some countries accept homosexuality and legalize gay marriage. Other countries put men in jail or severely punish them. Below is brief guidance on this topic, and more is available from Bahá'í institutions, so you can reach out to them if you need more information.

"The purpose of the Faith of Bahá'u'lláh is the realization of the organic unity of the entire human race, and Bahá'ís are enjoined to eliminate from their lives all forms of prejudice and to manifest respect towards all. Therefore, to regard those with a homosexual orientation with prejudice or disdain would be against the spirit of the Faith. Furthermore, a Bahá'í is exhorted to be 'an upholder and defender of the victim of oppression', and it would be entirely appropriate for a believer to come to the defense of those whose fundamental rights are being denied or violated.

"At the same time, you are no doubt aware of the relevant teachings of the Faith that govern the personal conduct of Bahá'ís. The Bahá'í Writings state that marriage is a union between a man and a woman and that sexual relations are restricted to a couple who are married to each other. Other passages from the Writings state that the practice of homosexuality is not permitted. The teachings of Bahá'u'lláh on personal morality are binding on Bahá'ís, who strive, as best they can, to live up to the high standards He has established."[216] On behalf of the Universal House of Justice

"The Bahá'í attitude towards the condition of homosexuality differs from its attitude towards those who engage in homosexual practices. The Guardian [Shoghi Effendi] states that a Bahá'í who faces this challenge must strive daily to come closer to the Bahá'í standard and, in this process, should be treated with tolerance and receive help, advice, and sympathy. In one instance he encouraged the believers in question to adhere to their Faith and not to withdraw from active service because of the tests they experienced. In this connection, it may be helpful to consider that the challenge of striving to live a chaste and holy life is one that confronts every Bahá'í who is seeking to align his life with the principles of the Faith."[217] On behalf of the Universal House of Justice

An excerpt from a talk provides this additional perspective:

"Sexual desire does not define human beings. A long-term relationship with one person is not the cause of human happiness. And no one is the living model for the society God wants us to create. To think about the world in this way is a really bad idea. ... [T]he whole cultural framework, our whole perception of heterosexuality and homosexuality and of human nature as fundamentally material, sexual, and acquisitive is a bad idea. Our culture's way of thinking about sexuality flattens, narrows, and diminishes what it is to be human; it distorts us. Furthermore, it interferes with the process of imagining and creating a just society, because it naturalizes oppressive gender roles, acquiesces in the loss of social responsibility of members of a community for each other. It freezes attention on the simple question of what do people do with desire, blocking out consideration of any other dimension of what might be just or unjust about society."[218] H. Hanson

Controlling my sexual energy

You now have a good understanding of the spiritual principles and the challenges in consistently applying the teachings. Now it's time to powerfully learn how to navigate this part of your life. You can be successful. The message that men, especially young men, often interpret from both social and religious sources is that sexual energy is bad and wrong. Since it's a natural part of being a male and a person, and as noted below is a creation of God, this sets up an inner conflict that's difficult to deal with. Part of your success is linked to recognizing these key points:

"While recognizing the Divine origin and force of the sex impulse in man, religion teaches that it must be controlled, and Bahá'u'lláh's Law confines its expression to the marriage relationship."[219] On behalf of the Universal House of Justice

Here is a perspective on the topic of sexual control:

"We often pay lip-service to this principle, but many Bahá'ís attempt to obtain control of their sexual feelings through complete suppression, perhaps unaware that there may be more creative ways of channeling these feelings keeping within the Bahá'í framework. This perhaps is a natural reaction to the excessive misuse of the sex instinct so prevalent in our society, especially among youth where sex can be unconsciously viewed not only as a means for physical gratification but also as a vehicle to obtain secondary gains such as friendship, love, self-confidence, and acceptance so desperately needed during adolescence. When sex is pursued in this way, it generates conflict and profound unhappiness.

"In a Bahá'í context, sex is viewed as primarily a spiritual phenomenon that uses the tool of the body for expression. The Báb writes:

'As this physical frame is the throne of the inner temple, whatever occurs to the former is felt by the latter. In reality that which takes delight in joy or is saddened by pain is the inner temple of the body, not the body itself.'[220]

"Unquestionably, the body, with all its senses, experiences pleasure through sex, but it is the soul that translates this experience into meaningful fulfillment. Sex is a very powerful force with enormous potential to bond two individuals on a very deep level. When illumined with the light of spirituality as a physical expression of a spiritual union, sex augments love, unity, companionship, dignity, and is a source of happiness and upliftment. Divorced from spirituality and a true understanding of God's purpose for man, the individuals involved run a serious risk of being left with unwanted attachment, estrangement, and abasement.

"The Bahá'í teachings explain that union and oneness are essential attributes of the Creator and that the principal generating impulse of creation is to manifest this oneness at increasingly more advanced levels. ... It is indeed a powerful testimony to the beauty of God's creation that all the elements exist within human beings for this union to occur—the diversity and uniqueness of individuals; the complementarity of male and female qualities; and final the power of attraction, including the force of sexuality."[221] Sharon Hatcher Kennedy and Andrew Kennedy

Consider this man's views:

"Consciously controlling our sexual energy is not a negative act. It's not suppression or something that diminishes our masculinity. It's about taking charge of our sexual energy and directing its flow in ways that can benefit us and others. When we direct it toward our marriage partner in healthy ways, we move that relationship forward."

Here is some guidance:

"Outside of marital life there can be no lawful or healthy use of the sex impulse. The Bahá'í youth should, on the one hand, be taught the lesson of self-control which, when exercised, undoubtedly has a salutary effect on the development of character and of personality in general, and on the other should be advised, nay even encouraged, to contract marriage while still young and in full possession of their physical vigor. Economic factors, no doubt, are often a serious hindrance to early marriage, but in most cases are only an excuse, and as such should not be overstressed."[222] On behalf of Shoghi Effendi

One benefit of being in control of your sexual energy is that you can "have profound and enduring friendships with many people, both men and women, without ever sullying that unique and priceless bond that should unite man and wife."[223] On behalf of the Universal House of Justice

A breakthrough in scientific research in recent years is challenging the myth that sex is an uncontrollable drive—a myth that influences many of the often coercive or violent sexual patterns in society. Shifting to understand this new information may prompt you to do a mental "re-set" about what you experience in your body as needs, desires, and drives:

"A drive is a biological mechanism whose job is to keep the organism at a healthy baseline—not too warm, not too cold, not too hungry, not too full. ... Appetite is the classic example of a drive. Hunger for food drives foraging and eating, and then when you feel full, you stop eating. ... Hunger and thirst are motivational systems that push you to do the things you have to do in order to avoid dying. The uncomfortable ("aversive") internal states of thirst, exhaustion, and cold push you out into the world, to go meet a need, so that you can return to a baseline, and that baseline is all about staying alive. When you hear 'drive,' think 'survive.'"[224] E. Nagoski

Nagoski goes on to say that no one ever died from not having sex: "There is no baseline to return to and no physical damage that results from not 'feeding' your sexual desire." Rather, the human reproductive system motivates us by pulling us toward an attractive external stimulus, what can also be called an "incentive motivation system". When a man conceptualizes sex as a need that must "be fed" for survival, it "fosters men's sense of sexual entitlement," which reinforces a culture in which sexually pushing or assaulting women has become frequent. But in reality, sex is not a human need—it's a wish or want that men can consciously choose to regulate and control.[225] Obviously, if this view is taken to excess, population growth would completely stop. The point is that sexual activity is wisest when fulfilled within marriage and when you are making conscious, healthy, wise, and respectful choices with your sexual energy.

A man asks, "So how do we manage when sexual energy is so powerful?" This is a good question. Some ideas to consider are in the next section.

You may be thinking that it takes a tremendous amount of energy to suppress sexual urges before marriage, and that's likely true. Even within marriage, sex may be less frequent than you wish at times, and it may stop completely for short or long periods due to factors like menstruation, childbirth, prostate issues, or illness. Your and your wife's libidos will have natural ebbs and flows over a lifetime. It's also good to have strategies for your sexual energy if at times you feel attraction to someone other than your partner and want to stay faithful.

Building my strength and self-control

The Bahá'í teachings give you hope for making progress with self-control:

"The power of God can entirely transmute our characters and make of us beings entirely unlike our previous selves. Through prayer and supplication, obedience to the divine laws Bahá'u'lláh has revealed, and ever-increasing service to His Faith, we can change ourselves."[226] On behalf of Shoghi Effendi

"The believers, if they are true to God's Covenant, should be endeavoring all the days of their lives, with the aid of the grace and bounty of God, to overcome their weaknesses and to gradually transmute their imperfections into perfections. But while this endless individual regeneration is progressing, the community must continue to expand and consolidate. While we are engaged, as individuals, in perfecting our lives, we should lend our wholehearted support to the furtherance of the interests of the Faith."[227] Universal House of Justice

Here are one man's thoughts on this topic:

"Striving daily to purify our thoughts and not indulge our minds in sexual thoughts is important in preventing non-useful desires or unhealthy habits from growing. When it feels like the energy wants to come out like a powerful firehose though, I end up wondering where to direct it? If I had a powerful amount of water in the hose in my hands, I could damage whatever I point it at. If I turn off the valve, the pressure will build and burst the hose. Or, I could direct it toward crops in danger of dying of drought and save them.

"For me, learning to exercise control over my sexual energy has 'saved' me. Both when I've been single and when I've been married and sex wasn't happening for some reason, it helped me stay sane and healthy. I was able to practice acceptance, detachment, and redirection so I could focus my thoughts and energies into professional excellence, managing a staff effectively, and making unique and valuable contributions as an employee. My strengthening ability to shift my energies helped me keep my family together and guide our children into worthwhile activities. Later it helped me create a new business to serve others."

As with any type of personal growth, daily effort is required to practice chastity. Individuals will make the best choices they can to avoid situations that arouse passions and cause temptation. Some may spend time in groups and in community service along with a partner. Some may have a supportive buddy to call and talk to when temptations arise, or they prefer to do some type of vigorous physical activity together.

Here are reflections from two people:

"In addition to group settings, I think it's really important to spend enough alone time getting to know the person you're dating and considering marriage with. It's just a totally different dynamic compared to a group setting or spending time in a public place compared to a private spot. It comes down to how much you trust yourself, as well as transparency. It also requires open dialogue and mutually agreeing where to draw the line. Both the man and the woman should contribute to holding up to the agreed standard. Mature people should be able to spend time alone together, but it's of course wise to think whether to watch a movie while sitting side-by-side on a couch or instead laying together on a bed. Depending on who you are, you might be able to do both, but only you know how you'll handle the situation. So, self-knowledge is key."

"Getting to know someone before marriage through group settings, electronic means, and in public places first is best, because such activities are 'safer,' as in fewer temptations. It's good to gradually get to know if we want to have a relationship with, and potentially marry a partner. The question of perspectives on chastity may certainly come up if a Bahá'í is dating someone who is not Bahá'í or not familiar with the Bahá'í guidance. The other partner might have a different 'concept' of when to allow or bring intimacy into a relationship, even if they are part of a religion that teaches no sex before marriage. However, even if someone 'knows' the religion advocates chastity,

one must be sure that the person actually intends to observe it. What I'm trying to say is that we must walk the walk not just talk the talk.

"When a Bahá'í dates someone who is not familiar with the Bahá'í guidance, it's probably best for the Bahá'í to be honest and upfront relatively early on, about how and more importantly why the Bahá'í Faith advocates its position. This will avoid confusion later, because a large school of thought in society at this time may find the concept of no sexual intimacy before marriage strange. A relationship partner may not understand why the Bahá'í doesn't want to have sex, and they may pressure him to participate.

"Admittedly, I gave in for a while, but it led to a lot of ongoing emotional upheaval as a young university student, which later led me to have to end the relationship. Yes, hindsight is 20/20, and that's one case where I wish I had been firm all along. These days, when we see the woes that single parents go through, the court systems, and children out of wedlock, it's easy to see how very costly it is not to be chaste, and it's the kids who suffer most. As Bahá'ís if we know kids in such situations, we can reach out to them and contribute to them having fulfilling childhoods, and we learn a lot ourselves too."

It may benefit you to have a more concrete example of how to apply self-control. Visualize your God-given sexual energy as being contained in a reservoir in front of a power-generating dam:

Step 1, Recognize and Accept: The character quality of "reflection" will assist you to recognize that sexual energy is present in your body and to respect it as part of one's God-given human nature.

Step 2, Detach and Control: The quality of "detachment" (see details below) helps you recognize that you can release your attachment to the sexual expression of your energy and direct it toward other worthwhile purposes , just as a hydroelectric dam uses the energy of moving water to generate and release electrical power.

Step 3, Self-Discipline, Moderation, and Purposefulness: These qualities allow you to guide your energies, dynamically balance them and keep them from becoming extreme, and direct them toward goals, just as water flows through a dam and continually supplies power to others. This is not permanent; you don't lose your ability to feel sexual energy. It's a temporary re-direction of your energy toward a purposeful goal. Self-discipline may guide your attention for several minutes, hours, or even days, depending on the skill level and capacity you intentionally build.

Step 4, Perseverance: With the quality of "perseverance", you then achieve your goals, or discover other, even more relevant, goals.

Every healthy person has the capacity to make conscious decisions and to restrain or release their sexual energy as appropriate. It's a dynamic process that you manage coherently physically, mentally, emotionally, and spiritually. To the extent that your life purposes are clear, you can focus toward fulfilling them and place less emphasis on sex. Where there is a healthy expression of your energy, it becomes consistently beneficial and additive to society. Your watchword can be: "Therefore strive that your actions day by day may be beautiful prayers. Turn towards God, and seek always to do that which is right and noble."[228] 'Abdu'l-Bahá

One of the most challenging concepts in the above steps is that of "detachment". Here are some perspectives about it:

"I implore Thee with a throbbing heart, with streaming tears and a yearning soul, and in complete detachment from all things, to make Thy lovers as rays of light across Thy realms, and to aid Thy chosen servants to exalt Thy Word, that their faces may turn beauteous and bright with splendor, that their hearts may be filled with mysteries, and that every soul may lay down its burden of sin."[229] 'Abdu'l-Bahá

"All emotions are energy that can be used by us in many different ways. We can train ourselves to use the energy, instead of just feeling it and reacting unconsciously."[230] H. Dobbs

"Detachment is crucial to the process of seeking. If we can detach ourselves from our own expectations, we can see more clearly; if we can detach ourselves from a certain end product, we can find equanimity and spiritual contentment in the process. Remember, we are constantly drawn to our ego's desires but these are a chimera. With detachment we are enabled to let go of these distractions and keep ourselves on a path that leads us to our goal."[231] Raymond Switzer

Here are some specifics for how you can understand and strengthen this quality:

"Detachment is stepping back to gain a different perspective on what is happening and placing less importance on worldly concerns, while selflessly letting go of one's feelings, hopes, desires, and attachments.

"Someone practices Detachment effectively when he:

- Thinks rationally and clearly with some emotional distance and focus; responding according to the known facts without exhibiting personal bias, strong emotions, or preconceived expectations
- Gathers information, seeks input from others, and examines the facts related to a project, situation, or person without premature judgment or participating in backbiting or gossip
- Seeks spiritual solutions to issues
- Releases desires, dreams, or expectations that are unrealistic or unattainable, grieving as needed in the process of letting go
- Accepts a present situation with equanimity, even if it's difficult, uncomfortable, or not what he would have chosen
- Frees himself from unhealthy or unwise attachment to people, incidents from the past, physical objects, and desires
- Releases overly strong fears of losing something or someone
- Bases choices on current circumstances rather than solely on previous experiences
- Understands and accepts the limitations of others and his own

"Someone needs to strengthen Detachment when he:

- Reacts emotionally and speculates about possible outcomes or explanations; jumps to conclusions rather than pausing to determine the facts of the matter accurately
- Attaches himself emotionally to someone or something so strongly that he abandons good judgment or uses that person to reinforce his unwise conclusions or behavior
- Depends excessively upon others in ways that negatively affect their well-being or his own
- Jumps in to prevent a problem or crisis so quickly that it prevents learning experiences for others

- Holds onto objects, paperwork, situations, and people even when doing so interferes with effective functioning or achieving one's higher goals in life
- Focuses on material possessions and actions while ignoring spiritual principles or choices

"Someone misuses (to excess or in the wrong time or place) the strength of Detachment when he:

- Fails to consider with sensitivity the well-being of others
- Isolates himself from others, treating them in a cool, distant, and unloving way
- Acts as if he has no opinions or needs
- Disposes of belongings, objects, or property without regard for value, sentiment, or usefulness to others or himself
- Neglects personal responsibilities or denies involvement in situations"[232] S. M. Alexander

It's good to be aware that some actions can short-circuit a person's sexual energy, stopping it from being usable for positive purposes. This happens with introducing something negative like pornography, infidelity, or abusive sex. The energy can no longer be properly and beneficially directed until after these factors are effectively addressed and removed from your energy experience. [These topics are addressed in more detail in Chapter 15.]

Making positive choices

You can assess the decisions you make about many aspects of your life, including sexual ones, with these steps:

- Be aware that you make decisions about the actions you take that affect your life; it's not random
- Pray to make beneficial choices
- Look at the potential results of your decisions, including the impact on others, before you firmly make them, asking yourself, "Would this decision be beneficial or harmful?"
- Re-assess any current decisions you are making
- Move forward

- Reflect on the outcomes and any changes you will make in future decisions

Then it takes practice to make good decisions.

You can strengthen your skill in learning how to manage your choices and energy consciously and respectfully. Begin with self-preparation actions as needed, such as ensuring your body is in good shape with regular and enough rest and sleep, good nutrition, exercise, and cleanliness. Even more important are likely to be mental and spiritual preparation actions, such as, visualization, prayer, and meditation to strengthen your connection with God. Here are some details about these:

Visualization: Visualize mental images of a new and improved condition or situation.

Prayer:
"… [P]ray, and…supplicate the Almighty that He may give you a fuller measure of His grace; that through it your spiritual energies may be quickened…."[233] On behalf of Shoghi Effendi

Meditation; conscious connection to souls who have passed on:
"The spirit of man is itself informed and strengthened during meditation; through it affairs of which man knew nothing are unfolded before his view. Through it he receives Divine inspiration, through it he receives heavenly food. … This faculty brings forth from the invisible plane the sciences and arts. Through the meditative faculty inventions are made possible, colossal undertakings are carried out; through it governments can run smoothly. Through this faculty man enters into the very Kingdom of God."[234] 'Abdu'l-Bahá

"The inspiration received through meditation is of a nature that one cannot measure or determine. God can inspire into our minds things that we had no previous knowledge of, if He desires to do so."[235] On behalf of Shoghi Effendi

Some people are most comfortable praying and meditating while sitting still. Others prefer to move. For example, you can pray and meditate while walking or boating. You may also find disciplined practices useful, such as yoga, Qi Gong, Tai Chi, or martial arts.

A man shares his experience:

"I needed ideas and methods to accomplish a large project that I'd never done before. Each morning I sat outdoors with my coffee, with my thoughts and soul reaching out to the souls of people who have passed from this world. In addition to Bahá'u'lláh, I thought specifically of people with the expertise that I needed, such as Albert Einstein, Nikola Tesla, and W. Edwards Deming. I also asked for help from people I had worked with in the past. The flow of inspiration was more like a flood. I almost couldn't write it down fast enough. The energy that manifested made it difficult to even sit still. It was breathtaking!"

You will also likely find it useful to identify, strengthen, and both leverage and apply the character qualities that seem to best suit your goal. Some possibilities are adherence, compassion, self-discipline, reflection, moderation, creativity, purposefulness, perseverance, and flexibility. [See Chapter 8, "Developing My Character".]

Then you can deliberately apply your attention and energy in the focus areas outlined below.

Focus Area 1: Physical Choices [*For awareness:* Some exercise and sports activities can increase testosterone, which may increase the desire for a sexual outlet.]
Examples:
- Brisk walking or running
- Doing sit-ups or push-ups
- Rowing a boat
- Taking care of an animal
- Developing an adventure experience
- Improving nutrition
- Getting adequate sleep

Focus Area 2: Mental Choices
Examples:
- Carrying out written communications with someone
- Finding a new strategic approach to a problem
- Planning for a major financial expenditure
- Fostering networking among coworkers
- Taking a new approach to learning something new

Focus Area 3: Emotional/Creative Choices
Examples:
- Composing a song or poem and sharing it
- Comforting a friend going through a difficulty
- Painting or other artistic project
- Celebrating an achievement or special occasion
- Making amends for an error
- Encouraging people to smile or laugh

Focus Area 4: Spiritual Choices
Examples:
- Serving as a study circle tutor
- Animating a junior youth group
- Carrying out a social action outreach/community service
- Teaching someone about the Bahá'í Faith
- Pioneering in your country or internationally
- Praying with a friend
- Doing an anonymous good deed
- Planning an interfaith devotional/prayer meeting
- Advocating for fair treatment for a person or group
- Expanding personal prayer or meditation practices

Be aware that you will be most effective throughout all the activities in these focus areas if you maintain a strong conscious connection with God. Ideally that feeling of connection also increases as you go through the stages.

The more you redirect your energy into activities with a spiritual focus, and the more you attune to Bahá'u'lláh and God in the process, the more powerful and humbling the outcome will be. You will know your efforts are working well when you feel strong energy coming to you from Bahá'u'lláh, God, and those in the Abhá Kingdom. Remember, however, that you are building new spiritual muscles, and it will take time, patience, and perseverance to achieve this new level of discipline.

Here is guidance:

"The duty to obey the laws brought by Bahá'u'lláh for a new age, then, rests primarily on the individual believer. It lies at the heart of the relationship of the lover and the Beloved; 'Observe My commandments, for the love of My beauty,' is Bahá'u'lláh's exhortation. Yet what is expected in this connection is effort sustained by earnest desire, not instantaneous perfection. The qualities and habits of thought and action that characterize Bahá'í life are developed through daily exertion. ...

"The friends should not lose heart in their personal struggles to attain to the Divine standard, nor be seduced by the argument that, since mistakes will inevitably be made and perfection is impossible, it is futile to exert an effort. They are to steer clear of the pitfalls of hypocrisy, on the one hand—that is, saying one thing yet doing another—and heedlessness, on the other—that is, disregard for the laws, ignoring or explaining away the need to follow them. So too is paralysis engendered by guilt to be avoided; indeed, preoccupation with a particular moral failing can, at times, make it more challenging for it to be overcome."[236] On behalf of the Universal House of Justice

Action

1. Research the potential beneficial well-being effects for you of participating in regular exercise and/or sports. At what point would engaging in additional exercise and sports become a negative well-being issue? How do these types of activities affect your ability to manage life stresses? Your testosterone level? Your sexual energy?

2. Choose a focus topic and apply prayer and meditation toward it for at least 15 minutes three days in a row. Make notes of any ideas or thoughts that emerge. At the end of the third occurrence, assess what inspiration has arisen. Would it benefit you to share this inspiration with another person and consult with them about how to carry out an action, or about ideas that came to you?

3. Identify and carry out an artistic project. Notice the flow of your energy toward the project. Were you able to stay focused on being creative without any sexual thoughts arising? What helped you to focus? What would have increased your ability to focus if that was a difficulty?

4. Identify a service to others that you want to begin or increase. What qualities do you want to strengthen? What new skills do you want to learn? How will you best benefit those you wish to serve? How will you practice chastity and hold pure thoughts during this service?

5. Carry out a presentation and discussion with youth on the material in this and the previous two chapters. Include an element from the arts if possible.

Reflection

1. What do I see as my current challenges with sexual health?
2. What is going on in the society around me that prompts me to increasingly strengthen and protect myself?
3. What will assist me to consistently make healthy choices related to my sexual energy?
4. How can I strengthen the qualities of acceptance, detachment, and self-discipline? How will these reinforce my efforts to practice chastity?
5. How are visualization, prayer, and meditation assisting me? What do I want to increase?

15 - Striving for My Sexual Health— Grappling with Dark Forces

Challenge: Sexual influences tempt me constantly, and I often give in.

Opportunity: I can begin to gradually adjust my habits so I'm less exposed to and influenced by the over-emphasis on sex in the culture around me.

Summary:
- I can choose to limit mental fantasies and eliminate masturbation, as these don't support my overall personal or relationship health and my commitment to practicing chastity.
- Dark forces such as infidelity, pornography, sexual harassment, sexual assault, and sexual abuse can mis-direct my sexual energy and cause harm to others and to me.
- It's possible and vital to bravely ask for and receive effective help to heal from dark-forces experiences and move forward in a healthy way in my life.
- It takes self-discipline, significant courage, and perseverance to resist and overcome the dark forces, but it's possible to accomplish.

More:

Understanding masturbation

Masturbation may begin with someone being curious about how their body works. However, if you are masturbating, it's not the best use of your sexual energy, and it can become something you depend on for the feelings it generates. Sometimes people masturbate thinking it will make the urge for sex go away. Instead it seems to increase the desire in the body for more. A man comments about masturbation:

"I find that chastity within marriage is quite comparable to chastity outside marriage: it's not just about a 'list of things that you can and can't do'; it's about leading a life characterized by pure thoughts, sincere intentions, and a praiseworthy conduct. A friend of mine shared his own layman's take on this: 'Masturbation is energetically wrong, you're losing energy. Whereas when you make love you are exchanging energy—yin and yang.'

"The puritanical approach which seems to be the hallmark of how many religious parents deal with sex may also be making their children feel that sex is the ultimate goal. With sex being completely 'veiled' from them as they grow up, children can be involuntarily programmed into believing that sex is the last stage in a progression of intimacy, while it's not. Sex is simply one form of intimacy; it is a manifestation of a higher, deeper emotional connection. It should be regarded as simply one facet of the all-important sphere of love."

The Universal House of Justice quotes a letter on behalf of Shoghi Effendi:

"Amongst the many other evils afflicting society in this spiritual low water mark in history, is the question of immorality, and over-emphasis of sex...."

Then the Universal House of Justice goes on to say:

"This indicates how the whole matter of sex and the problems related to it have assumed far too great an importance in the thinking of present-day society.

"Masturbation is clearly not a proper use of the sex instinct, as this is understood in the Faith. Moreover it involves, as you have pointed out, mental fantasies, while Bahá'u'lláh, in the *Kitáb-i-Aqdas*, has exhorted us not to indulge our passions and in one of His well-known Tablets 'Abdu'l-Bahá encourages us to keep our 'secret thoughts pure'. Of course many wayward thoughts come involuntarily to the mind and these are merely a result of weakness and are not blameworthy unless they become fixed or even worse, are expressed in improper acts. ...

"Your problem, therefore, is one against which you should continue to struggle, with determination and with the aid of prayer. You should remember, however, that it is only one of the many temptations and faults that a human being must strive to overcome during his lifetime, and you should not increase the difficulty you have by over-emphasizing its importance. We suggest you try to see it within the whole spectrum of the qualities that a Bahá'í must develop in his character. Be vigilant against temptation, but do not allow it to claim too great a share of your attention. You should concentrate, rather, on the virtues that you should develop, the services you should strive to render, and, above all, on God and His attributes, and devote your energies to living a full Bahá'í life in all its many aspects."[237] Universal House of Justice

Below an author provides insights into how the mind functions.

"The mind is a creature of habit. It thrives upon the *dominating* thoughts fed it. Through the faculty of will-power, one may discourage the presence of any emotion, and encourage the presence of any other. Control of the mind, through the power of will, is not difficult. Control comes from persistence, and habit. The secret of control lies in understanding the process of transmutation. When any negative emotion presents itself in one's mind, it can be transmuted into a positive, or constructive emotion, by the simple procedure of changing one's thoughts."[238] Napoleon Hill

Another author once responded in a letter to a man about the topic of masturbation, and there may be useful concepts in his viewpoints for you to consider.

"For me the real evil of masturbation would be that it takes an appetite which, in lawful use, leads the individual out of himself to complete (and correct) his own personality in that of another (and finally in children and even grandchildren) and turns it back: sends the man back into the prison of himself, there to keep a harem of imaginary brides. And this harem, once admitted, works against his ever getting out and really uniting with a real woman. For the harem is always accessible, always subservient, calls for no sacrifices or adjustments, and can be endowed with erotic and psychological attractions which no real woman can rival. Among those shadowy brides he is always adored, always the perfect lover: no demand is made on his unselfishness, no mortification ever imposed on his vanity. In the end, they become merely the medium through which he increasingly adores himself. ... And it is not only the faculty of love which is thus sterilized, forced back on itself, but also the faculty of imagination.

"The true exercise of imagination, in my view, is (a) To help us to understand other people (b) To respond to, and, some of us, to produce, art. But it has also a bad use: to provide for us, in shadowy form, a substitute for virtues, successes, distinctions etc. which ought to be sought *outside* in the real world—e.g. picturing all I'd do if I were rich instead of earning and saving. Masturbation involves this abuse of imagination in erotic matters (which I think bad in itself) and thereby encourages a similar abuse of it in all spheres. After all, almost the main work of life is to *come out* of our selves, out of the little, dark prison we are all born in. Masturbation is to be avoided as *all* things are to be avoided which retard this process. The danger is that of coming to *love* the prison."[239] C. S. Lewis

Splitting attention to a different partner

When someone chooses to connect with a person other than their relationship or marriage partner in an intimate way mentally, emotionally, visually, or physically/sexually, they are being unfaithful. It can be easy to rationalize this behavior when there is an infatuation with someone outside the couple. However, everyone has responsibility for their life, body, and decisions.

Individuals being unfaithful to their marriage partner is a profound issue that cuts deep into the integrity of the marriage bond and results in the other partner feeling betrayed. Trust is strongly affected. Honoring the marriage requires a level of self-awareness and honesty, as well as a deep understanding about maintaining healthy boundaries within the context of the marriage. The power of discernment and self-accountability are spiritual capacities people learn to develop by being tested. Most people do not set out to begin an affair or choose it. It's the mini choices along the way that are not initially perceived as betrayal that can lead to a bigger problem. Couples can prevent infidelity when they encourage the development of openness in the marriage that includes setting clear boundaries, not based on jealousy or mistrust, but a healthy loving bond.

A man provides his experience:

"I participated as a youth in many Bahá'í activities and felt connected to the community. However, as time went on, I noticed how troubled my parent's marriage was. It came out that Dad, who was a well-known Bahá'í, had been unfaithful to Mom. I was full of anger toward him. I was angry at myself that I couldn't protect my mother from this pain. I don't feel the same way toward the Faith now. His behavior and my belief in God have bashed each other inside of me. I'm not sure I'll ever have the same level of belief again."

Another man took a different path:

"When I was a teenager, I counseled my father not to cheat on or leave my stepmother, as he had done with my mother. My father heeded my advice and changed. He died a few years later, and I was happy that he had improved his life first. This experience has helped me make positive spiritual choices in my life as well, and I'm now happily married and committed to being faithful to my wife."

Another form of infidelity occurs when people engage in an emotional affair. This can be defined as non-sexual behavior that involves sharing intimate feelings and thoughts with an extramarital partner, and secrecy that violates the explicit or implicit expectations of the relationship (for example: secretly sending flowers to an extramarital partner and expressing feelings of romantic attraction; secretly spending a large amount of one-to-one time together in non-sexual encounters). Emotional affairs, which can often begin through encounters at work or through an internet or social media connection, can also lead to physical infidelity.

If the infidelity ends, it can be possible for a couple to re-build trust, usually along with educational and professional help. There are extensive books, websites, and counselors that can assist couples who have experienced emotional or physical infidelity heal and rebuild. Divorce is not an automatic occurrence if a couple is willing to:

- End the unfaithful actions
- Honestly assess what happened
- Accept how they each may have contributed to the situation
- Make key positive changes in their behaviors
- Forgive
- Rebuild trust
- Establish the marriage on a stronger and healthier basis

If the infidelity is before marriage, then you have a choice of seeing this behavior as a character issue that stops the relationship, or you can get help and your partner's assurances of future fidelity and go forward. Below is guidance:

"The question you raise as to the place in one's life that a deep bond of love with someone we meet other than our husband or wife can have is easily defined in view of the teachings. Chastity implies both before and after marriage an unsullied, chaste sex life. Before marriage absolutely chaste, after marriage absolutely faithful to one's chosen companion. Faithful in all sexual acts, faithful in word and in deed.

"The world today is submerged, amongst other things, in an over-exaggeration of the importance of physical love, and a dearth of spiritual values. In as far as possible the believers should try to realize this and rise above the level of their fellowmen who are, typical of all decadent periods in history, placing so much overemphasis on the purely physical side of mating. Outside of their normal, legitimate married life they should seek to establish bonds of comradeship and love which are eternal and founded on the spiritual life of man, not on his physical life. This is one of the many fields in which it is incumbent on the Bahá'ís to set the example and lead the way to a true human standard of life, when the soul of man is exalted and his body but the tool for his enlightened spirit. Needless to say this does not preclude the living of a perfectly normal sex life in its legitimate channel of marriage."[240] On behalf of Shoghi Effendi

The effects of pornography

Pornography through the internet has become affordable, accessible, and anonymous, making it a highly dangerous dark force. It can seriously disrupt your spiritual quest. Frequent use of and addiction to pornography have become widespread, which has resulted in:

- Misconceptions that many sexual acts are pleasurable that are not
- Seeing violent and abusive acts portrayed as normal
- Demeaning, objectifying, and dominant attitudes toward women
- Twisted views of children in sexual roles
- Reduced ability to function emotionally and sexually with a partner
- Distancing from higher, spiritual selves

Men's response to pornography, often including excessive masturbation, is resulting in serious health issues. These are also causing relationship issues. Some examples are:

- Numbing of the response to pleasure over time
- Erectile dysfunction

- Delayed or premature ejaculation
- Hyper-reactivity to pornography
- Willpower erosion
- Self-focused; anxiety about interacting with others

Using pornography or other sexual vices to masturbate, which doesn't involve a relationship partner, creates habits of thought and action that can get in the way of a healthy, loving relationship and/or marriage. It's a form of infidelity.

Here are comments from a professional on what can happen between partners when one is using pornography and becomes sexually addicted:

> "If your partner seems like they want more and more and more over a period of time, that would be a sign of possible escalation. Or if it's not just a matter of frequency, they will constantly want a certain level of variety.
>
> "Another symptom—albeit somewhat counterintuitive—is if they seem to become bored with you or tired of you. If they are not as sexually demanding or initiating, it could be because they are going to other places in their mind (looking at pornography or internet sites) or masturbating more frequently. In the worst-case scenario, they're actually having sexual encounters with other partners.
>
> "Sexuality will become dissatisfying to them in some extreme way. There may be too much absence of it, which we oftentimes refer to as sexual anorexia, or there's too much sexual demand in it. There's too much boredom, or there's too much anger and aggression.
>
> "When you're engaged in an act of sexuality, intuitively most people can tell whether their partner is actually emotionally present in the room. If their mind is elsewhere, you know that's a good symptom that your partner is struggling with something.
>
> "Trust your own intuition, which a lot of people have tried to turn off. They say, 'Oh, I love him, and I don't want to confront him.' If you are somewhat co-dependent to begin with, you know you will deny your own awareness and intuition. There is a level of denial that exists for some people that they simply have to get past. ...
>
> "One of the things we have found is that if the partners are aware of the addiction before marriage, and if the addict has been honest about the addiction, then the chances that they can survive even acts of infidelity in the marriage is a lot greater.

"If an addict and partner—despite whatever level of fear, anxiety, or co-dependency they have going into the marriage—can get honest about their sexual struggles, I think it's much more likely that the two people can be each other's companions and intimate partners.

"If they are struggling with this issue prior to marriage or in marriage, there are a lot of resources, healing options, and great therapists who can help. I personally believe infidelity is something that cannot only be survived, but if the couple gets the right kind of help, they can learn how to turn it into something that will allow their marriage to thrive."[241] Mark Laaser

If you are struggling with your response to pornography, educating yourself and accessing help are vital. Here are some resources:

- https://fightthenewdrug.org
- https://brainheartworld.org/
- https://bahaiteachings.org/porn-affecting-us-can
- https://www.yourbrainonporn.com/

There is persistent, widespread social harm occurring with the systematic spread of pornography using sexual images of men, women, and children to wider and younger audiences. Therefore, it's also wise for you to think about how to address the issue systemically over time, both in your own life and in your family, community, and society. How can you contribute to reducing the demand for it? In your own personal behavior, you can consider the following:

- Not communicating to women and children the expectation that they must look sexually "hot".
- Increasing modesty in clothing choices worn in public.
- Not posting sexy photos of yourself and others on social media.
- Not buying or subscribing to publications or media with revealing photos of women.
- Blocking internet sites with pornography on your computer or mobile device.
- Using email filtering services that segregate sexy junk email and make it easily deleted.

- Striving to keep your marriage and family intact and functioning well, such that sex occurs only with your wife, and your children are together with you.

Some possibilities to reduce the societal demand for pornography include:

- Initiating community-building and family-strengthening efforts that engage children, youth, and adults in developing their characters and learning how to make good moral choices.
- Involving people of all ages in being of service to others to reduce loneliness and self-focused activities.
- Offering factual sex, healthy relationships, and marriage education in homes, schools, and centers of community activity at appropriate ages.
- Monitoring and limiting what children and teens are exposed to on their screens.

This won't be an easy problem to solve, but it can be done over time, particularly as people begin to regard themselves as noble, spiritual human beings and obtain the education and help needed to make healthy choices.

Stopping sexual harassment, assault, and abuse

Sexual energy directed in a way that causes harm to others has become a significant dark forces global problem. Harassment, assault, and abuse can occur between people of any gender and any age. You or people you know may have been on the receiving end or in a perpetrating role, either of which likely needs professional help.

What counts as harmful behavior keeps being re-defined, and these terms explained below have legal definitions and implications depending on where and when the actions happen. However, these general descriptions below will give you some understanding of the concepts. All of them are serious disruptions of a life-journey based on spiritual principles. They are compiled for your information from many sources simply so you can expand your understanding of the concepts and do a review of your behaviors. If you are involved in any of them, you will need to consult a legal expert for specific guidance for your situation.

Sexual harassment can be considered as potentially occurring when peers or supervisors do or condone the examples of the actions below where the participation of the recipient is coerced or consent absent:

- Unwelcome sexual advances
- Requests for sexual favors
- Discussing sexual relations/stories/fantasies at work, school, or in other inappropriate places
- Exposing oneself or performing sexual acts on oneself in front of others
- Unwanted sexually explicit photos, emails, or text messages
- Verbal harassment of a sexual nature, including jokes referring to sexual acts or sexual orientation
- Deliberate or repeated offensive verbal comments or gestures of a sexual nature

Sexual harassment generally applies when:

a. submission to such conduct is made either explicitly or implicitly a term or condition of a person's job, pay, or career;
b. submission to or rejection of such conduct by a person is used as a basis for career or employment decisions affecting that person; or
c. such conduct has the purpose or effect of unreasonably interfering with an individual's work performance or creates an intimidating, hostile, or offensive working environment; and is so severe or pervasive that a reasonable person would perceive, and the victim does perceive, the environment as hostile or offensive

Sexual assault is generally indicated by intentional sexual contact with the use of force, threats, intimidation, or abuse of authority, or when the victim does not or cannot consent. It includes actual physical engagement, not just words. Behaviors could include:

- Unwanted fondling or sexual touching
- Attempted rape
- Forcing someone to perform sexual acts, such as oral sex or penetration of the perpetrator's body
- Penetration of any part of someone's body, also known as rape, including forcible sodomy (defined as anal sex)

Sometimes consent can seem confusing when the recipient shows observable sexual responses to touch that don't seem to match a verbal indication of unwillingness. These physical responses do not automatically constitute consent, as biological responses can occur in the absence of mental and emotional agreement. [For more on this topic, refer to the topic of "sexual non-concordance" in E. Nagoski, *Come As You Are*, Chapter 6.]

Sexual abuse can generally include any of the harassment or assault behaviors above, but the actions are usually between those who know each other, such as relatives, friends, or someone like a teacher or coach. Relatives can include a relationship or marriage partner or parent. Consent is coerced or absent. Often the perpetrator is older, stronger, and has some authority over the targeted person. Manipulation or threats are likely part of the situation. Children can be gradually accustomed to sexual touch and convinced that they must submit. Where the actions are between unmarried relatives, it's also known as "incest".

Those who have experienced sexual harassment, assault, or abuse can struggle with:

- Physical effects such as headaches, fatigue, sleep disturbance, and eating disturbance; withdrawal from places or organizations associated with the incident(s)
- Mental effects such as anxiety, depression, panic attacks, post-traumatic stress, and substance abuse
- Emotional reactions such as anger, fear, shame, and guilt
- Confusion about sexuality and healthy sexual functioning
- Spiritual reactions such as withdrawal from participation or obsessive participation, inability to pray, and feeling unworthy of love and acceptance
- Sexually acting out through such actions as viewing or taking inappropriate photos, participating in casual sexual activity, dressing inappropriately, or unconsciously re-enacting the trauma
- Doing actions to others like what was done to them

It's vital that you be tuned into the importance of consensual touch and avoiding behavior that might look or feel pressuring or predatory toward others. These can result in someone feeling harassed, assaulted, or scared about being forced to participate in acts they don't really want. In some circumstances, especially if the actions come to you from other men, you may be tempted to characterize someone's behavior as bullying or hazing, but it often is part of this topic of negative sexual actions.

Laurie Halse Anderson, a speaker and author about sexual topics, has found that female teenagers will speak to her easily, but sometimes it's a bit harder for males. Here is what she says:

"The boys want to talk, too. Some want a private conversation; others ask bold questions in front of their classmates.

"Those who want to talk to me alone wait until the last student leaves the auditorium or track me down in the library office, where I'm eating lunch. A few have been victims of sexual violence themselves. Many more have been targeted by bullies at school. Others come for advice about situations they don't know how to deal with.

"We sit in a quiet corner. The boy, sweating, fidgeting, eyes downcast, tells me his story. Sometimes he tells of a girl, a friend who has been raped. He wants to know the best way to help her because since it happened, she has been cutting herself, skipping school and getting high to avoid the pain. He wants to kill the boy who hurt his friend. He wants to help and doesn't know how.

"And then there are the half-confessions. No boy has ever come out and admitted to me that he raped someone, but a few have said, 'I might have pushed things too far,' or 'Well, we were drunk,' or 'Things got out of hand and... she refused to talk to me after that night.' They don't look me in the eye as they say this. They are not proud of themselves. Their confused shame is heart-breaking and infuriating. ... These boys have been raised to believe that a rapist is a bad guy in the bushes with a gun. They aren't that guy, they figure, so they can't be rapists.

"Why should they think otherwise? Their parents generally limit conversations about sex to 'don't get her pregnant' lectures. They learn about sex from friends, and from internet porn, where scenes of non-consensual sex abound. No one has ever explained the laws to them. They don't understand that consent needs to be informed, enthusiastic, sober, ongoing and freely given.

"This is only made worse by the other question I get most often from these teenage boys in the classroom: *Why was the rape victim so upset?* They explain, *The sex only took a couple minutes, but she's depressed for, like, a year.* They don't understand the impact of rape.

"When a boy says these things, the girls in the class are shocked, and the teacher is appalled. They are stunned to discover how many of the guys don't have a clue. So was I, at first. But I quickly learned that reacting with anger and judgment did not help anyone. Instead, I discuss the studies that show that 94% of women who are raped experience PTSD symptoms. Nearly a third of victims still have those symptoms 9 months after the rape, and 13% of women who are raped attempt suicide. Facts like that make an impact. I share resources like the Rape, Abuse & Incest National Network (RAINN) website (www.rainn.org) with the teacher, and encourage the staff to follow up my visit with presentations from mental health professionals and police officers. ...

"Teenage boys are hungry for practical conversations about sex. They want to know the rules. They want to be the good guy, the stand-up, honorable dude. Their intentions might be good, but their ignorance is dangerous. Our society has begun talking a bit more openly about these issues, but that doesn't mean teenage boys suddenly have all the information they need."[242] Laurie Halse Anderson

It's not within the scope of this book to fully address this issue, which is in the arena of professional counseling. Sometimes the matter needs to be addressed at an institutional level, such as at a university or company, if multiple people are involved. However, it's important to mention that since sexual abuse experiences are widespread in society, being part of a religious community is not a guaranteed prevention or cure. There are Bahá'ís and people of all faiths who are affected by this grave moral failing.

Here is guidance on the topic of sexual abuse and incest:

"It is difficult to imagine a more reprehensible perversion of human conduct than the sexual abuse of children, which finds its most debased form in incest. At a time in the fortunes of humanity when, in the words of the Guardian, 'The perversion of human nature, the degradation of human conduct, the corruption and dissolution of human institutions, reveal themselves . . . in their worst and most revolting aspects,' and when 'the voice of human conscience is stilled,' when 'the sense of decency and shame is obscured,' the Bahá'í institutions must be uncompromising and vigilant in their commitment to the protection of the children entrusted to their care, and must not allow either threats or appeals to expediency to divert them from their duty. A parent who is aware that the marriage partner is subjecting a child to such sexual abuse should not remain silent, but must take all necessary measures, with the assistance of the Spiritual Assembly or civil authorities if necessary, to bring about an immediate cessation of such grossly immoral behavior, and to promote healing and therapy."[243] On behalf of the Universal House of Justice

This is a brief recounting of a man's experience:

"A neighbor who was a close friend of my parents repeatedly trapped me in his home and sexually fondled and raped me when I was a teenager. It really screwed me up. For a while I gained a lot of weight, hoping that I would be ugly to him, but it didn't make a difference. I drank a lot of alcohol to deaden the pain. I ended up with eating disorders, depression, and suicide thoughts and attempts.

"I found a woman and married her, thinking this might heal me, but I sexually and emotionally abused her. It took me a long time to get the help I needed to straighten out my thinking and my life. I sought inpatient and outpatient psychiatric and psychological treatment, found sobriety through Alcoholics Anonymous and Overeaters Anonymous, and I achieved a level of recovery over time. After some healing, I found the Bahá'í Faith, and being involved in community service helped me further my healing. My first marriage didn't survive, but I was able to re-marry successfully."

Trauma from perpetrating or receiving harassment, assault, or abuse can disrupt a healthy sex life in marriage. Therefore, it's vital to the well-being of the individuals and the marriage for people to heal, often with professional assistance, ideally at any point it occurs or as soon as it's recognized.

It's also important to note that many people who have experienced sexual assault or abuse have gone on to have happy, healthy marriages. They often benefit from counseling, personal healing work, self-acceptance, forgiveness, and a compassionately loving, patient, and caring marriage partner.

Perpetrators of assault and abuse are under the jurisdiction of legal authorities, who have a responsibility to protect the well-being of others and ensure the matter is handled properly. If you have been assaulted or abused, or you witness these, please report it to the authorities. The individuals involved will, of course, require professional counseling and medical help to heal and recover.

If you are someone who has perpetrated such assault or abuse toward children or adults, it's vital to your well-being and to those you have injured that you seek assistance as soon as possible. If you are experiencing impulses to behave sexually toward a child or minor, *please* talk to a friend, professional counselor, Auxiliary Board member, or an institution such as a

Be Brave and Arise

Spiritual Assembly. You didn't choose to have these impulses, but you are responsible for being brave and arising to talk to someone about it as soon as you can, in order to keep you and those around you safe. You do not need to go through this alone.

Action

1. Gather a group of peers or youth and study and discuss Chapters 12-15 on striving for sexual health together. Is having an adult or a professional present as a resource a wise idea? What new insights did participants gain?

2. If you are struggling with pornography, or with other sexual vices or fetishes, access the resources listed in this chapter, research the topic, and please seek help. You may also find it wise to consult with a doctor who specializes in sexual health.

3. The chapter includes a quotation that says, "many wayward thoughts come involuntarily to the mind and these are merely a result of weakness and are not blameworthy unless they become fixed or even worse, are expressed in improper acts". Spend 20-30 minutes consciously noticing your thoughts and which ones pass on out and which ones seem to become "fixed" and stuck in your mind. Identify something that might interrupt thoughts that want to linger, such as saying one of the forms of the Greatest Name [See Chapter 21] or playing spiritually based music. For an addition 15 minutes, take this interrupting action when a thought enters your mind that is unworthy of your nobility.

4. Gather a group of men together to talk and make commitments about how you will each treat and interact with women. Consider opening and closing the discussion with a "drumming circle". If you don't have access to musical drums, then create ones with household objects like pans, boxes, trash cans, and so on.

Reflection

1. What can I do, whether single or married, to strive to make my thoughts as pure as possible? How can I try to have any impure thoughts that do arise pass through my mind quickly and leave?
2. What, if any, is my experience with masturbation? What is my plan to keep myself from falling into a habit of doing it or to overcome the habit?
3. What, if any, is my experience with pornography? What is my plan to keep myself from falling into a habit of consuming it? If needed, what will I do to overcome the habit or addiction?
4. When, if ever, have I seen or experienced sexual harassment? What was the outcome? Are there still any remedial actions that are wise for me to initiate?
5. What, if any, are my observations and experiences related to sexual abuse or violence? What have I done to address them? What more do I need to do?
6. What will I concentrate on in my life instead of focusing so much on sex, if this is what is happening in my life?
7. What benefits could happen from seeking professional help for one or more of the issues raised in this chapter? How can I find an appropriate counselor?

Part 4: Questing Through Life's Challenges

16 - Handling the Adulting Stuff

Challenge: Sometimes I don't want to act like an adult, and sometimes I equate being an adult with a giant weight of responsibility to carry around.

Opportunity: I'm excited to be taking on the adulting that's coming my way, and I'm learning to approach it gradually and in a balanced way one day at a time.

Summary:
- It's good for me to be an ever-evolving person and take on more responsibilities as I can, no matter what age I am.
- Being an adult can have light aspects to it when I remember to laugh and be appropriately playful.
- It's fun and empowering to learn new skills that can contribute to my life and others.
- I'm a complex human being, and so there will always be many aspects of my self and my life to develop and balance.
- Assessing my progress encourages me to be in action, as I then clearly see my growth.

More:

Ever-evolving stages and phases

Everyone develops strengths and abilities at different rates and in unique ways. Maturing is a process that unfolds over time and has factors that affect the body, mind, heart, and soul of everyone. Here is how 'Abdu'l-Bahá describes the process:

"From the beginning to the end of his life man passes through certain periods or stages each of which is marked by certain conditions peculiar to itself. For instance during the period of childhood his conditions and requirements are characteristic of that degree of intelligence and capacity. After a time he enters the period of youth in which his former conditions and needs are superseded by new requirements applicable to the advance in his degree. His faculties of observation are broadened and deepened, his intelligent capacities are trained and awakened, the limitations and environment of childhood no longer restrict his energies and accomplishments. At last he passes out of the period of youth and enters the stage or station of maturity which necessitates another transformation and corresponding advance in his sphere of life-activity. New powers and perceptions clothe him, teaching and training commensurate with his progression occupy his mind, special bounties and bestowals descend in proportion to his increased capacities and his former period of youth and its conditions will no longer satisfy his matured view and vision."[244] 'Abdu'l-Bahá

A man reflects about maturation:

"In general, it's important to incorporate very genuinely the understanding that: (a) the Bahá'í model of maturation, or in other words the Bahá'í model of a life journey, does not necessarily coincide with what older Western generations coming from a Judeo-Christian background would recognize as maturation, and (b) that even the model of those generations is out of step with what those in subsequent generations must contend with.

"I think the Bahá'í model of a life journey entails mental and spiritual stages, and while they may coincide with physical or bodily stages, they do not necessarily coincide with material stages such as job status or how many possessions a person has. In a future Bahá'í world, perhaps all the stages will coincide; but in our era and into the long foreseeable future, they will not and perhaps cannot. That said, I think matters like managing hygiene and having a fitness program can still be mapped onto the life journey. Maintaining some order in one's physical life, such as brushing one's teeth daily, or one's spiritual life by at least doing the Short Obligatory Prayer once per day, do help keep a man going forward, even when everything else is falling apart.

"But—and this is important—although Bahá'u'lláh does prescribe the need for professions specifically and employment generally, He does not prescribe how and by when one is to achieve these, nor even what achieving these would really look like. Of course, the Bahá'í Writings do imply certain things, namely accruing enough professional and financial stability to support one's family and to donate to the funds of the Faith. For me, the path has not been easy or straight, as work and education have been intermingled, and I married 'late'. My maturity has built over time, and yet I still feel like there is quite a journey ahead of me."

The Universal House of Justice provides this perspective on the maturing process:

> "While it is right to expect great things from those who have so much to give in the path of service, the friends must guard against adopting a narrow outlook on what development to maturity entails. Freedom of movement and availability of time enable many youth to serve in ways that are directly related to the needs of the community, but as they advance further into their twenties, their horizons broaden. Other dimensions of a coherent life, equally demanding and highly meritorious, begin to make stronger claims on their attention. For many, an immediate priority will be further education, academic or vocational, according to the possibilities before them, and new spaces for interaction with society open up. Moreover, young women and men become acutely conscious of the exhortations of the Supreme Pen to 'enter into wedlock' that they may 'bring forth one who will make mention of Me amid My servants' and to 'engage in crafts and professions'. Having taken up an occupation, youth naturally try to contribute to their field, or even to advance it in light of the insights they gain from their continued study of the Revelation, and they strive to be examples of integrity and excellence in their work. Bahá'u'lláh extols those 'that earn a livelihood by their calling and spend upon themselves and upon their kindred for the love of God, the Lord of all worlds.' This generation of youth will form families that secure the foundations of flourishing communities. Through their growing love for Bahá'u'lláh and their personal commitment to the standard to which He summons them will their children imbibe the love of God, 'commingled with their mother's milk', and always seek the shelter of His divine law. Clearly, then, the responsibility of a Bahá'í community towards young people does not end when they first start serving. The significant decisions they make about the direction of their adult lives will determine whether service to the Cause of God was only a brief and memorable chapter of their younger years, or a fixed center of their earthly existence, a lens through which all actions come into focus."[245] Universal House of Justice

Creating a multi-faceted life

As you grow and mature, you will at times focus more on one or another aspect of life. The goal overall, however, is to end up being a multi-faceted human being involved coherently in various aspects of life. Guidance is below.

> "Bahá'ís should seek to be many-sided, normal and well balanced, mentally and spiritually. We must not give the impression of being fanatics, but at the same time we must live up to our principles."[246] On behalf of Shoghi Effendi

Often "adulting" is a gradual process of taking on more and more responsibilities, and of course it's reasonable to take these commitments seriously and to carry them out well. They are part of what makes life work better for you and others. However, being an adult does not have to be synonymous with being deadly dull. Remember from Chapter 10, that happiness, joy, and humor can be very beneficial. Here are perspectives that may contribute to understanding balance:

> "Playfulness...[can sound to some people] frivolous and shallow, distracting and irrelevant, inefficient and unproductive. That's because we live in a technological culture that worships busyness and activity. Under the guise of saving time, we now are inundated with e-mail...and cellular phones. We end each day smothered by the demands of our time and are greeted each new morn with more to do, not less. Play? There's no time to play. How can we play when the mountain of work and problems we are faced with each day get higher and deeper? How can we play when the world is overcome with poverty, famine, and war? Play is an expression of God's presence in the world; one clear sign of God's absence in society is the absence of playfulness and laughter. Play is not an escape; it is the way to release the life-smothering grip of busyness, stress, and anxiety. Playfulness is a modern expression of hope...."[247] Michael Yaconelli

> "The key to effective play...has less to do with *what* we do and more to do with the *spirit* in which we do it. If we approach a moment with a lighthearted attitude, many endeavors can become playful. In fact, playfulness can be an addition to activities and situations normally seen as everyday routine, like washing the car. The benefit: Playfulness adds a spark of energy to almost anything we do.
> "Play adds the element of enjoyment to our activities by pulling us toward being present in the moment. It may include a degree of spontaneity, creativity, humor, excitement, challenge, or silliness. A

playful heart brings a measure of lightness, even in moments filled with seriousness."[248] Robert S. Paul

"The most relaxing recreating forces are a healthy religion, sleep, music, and laughter. Have faith in God—learn to sleep well—love good music—see the funny side of life—and health and happiness will be yours."[249] Dale Carnegie

As you go through this book and live your life, you will gradually gain your own perspective of the man you want to be. Hopefully, it will be one who can at times "lighten up" life for himself and others.

Building my skills

It's likely that you have a goal of leaving home and living successfully on your own, if you have not yet done so. If you have already been living on your own, you can still review where skill-building would be wise. Your success in developing a good "toolbox" full of abilities links to your ability to manage many aspects of life. As a teenager and young adult, the more you can learn the necessary skills and knowledge from parents, education, and others, the easier your transition to independence will be. As an adult already on your own, you can look where increasing your skills will contribute to efficiency, helpfulness, and equality in your home and family.

You (or your parents) may be tempted to use your education or professional responsibilities as an excuse to not do work at home, but this will handicap your ability to learn necessary skills. Parents, roommates, or a marriage partner may prefer to avoid your whining or resistance to doing household tasks. They may also prefer their own way of doing the task. Asking them to detach from "perfection" and take the time to teach you how to do the task well, may be part of the solution. Then, of course, you must humbly do your best. You may also tactfully communicate with anyone you are living with that there is more than one way of accomplishing a task, and not just one "right" way.

As you look at what is involved in living as an independent adult, you can make a list of what you need to learn. Consider these points:

- Can you organize and decorate your living space?
- Can you do your own laundry without everything turning out grey or some unwanted color?
- Can you shop for food and create several different and nutritious meals?

- Can you clean and sanitize a toilet and bathroom?
- Can you organize your finances and pay bills on time?

Asking your family, roommates, relationship or marriage partner, friends, or mentors for opportunities to learn as well as requesting accompaniment in the process, will serve you well going forward in most circumstances. There is this guidance as a target: "The home should be orderly and well-organized."[250] 'Abdu'l-Bahá

Financial management is a key area for skill-building. However, many people don't have training in effectively managing their money, and you may need to seek help from experts. Management involves:

- Paying bills
- Opening and maintaining bank and investment accounts
- Determining your needs versus your wants
- Exercising discipline in spending and saving
- Managing your credit
- Giving to the various Bahá'í funds and Huqúqu'lláh*
- Applying spiritual principles; for example, being generous with your funds is a sacred and beautiful act. Philanthropy is a valued characteristic that contributes to the physical, mental, emotional, and spiritual well-being of others and your own personal growth as well.

Alex Mazloom, who with his wife Nazila Shokohi, established www.mindtreasures.org as a financial education service, offers his opinions of what worked for his family:

"My wife and I encourage teaching finances to children and helping them develop good habits from young ages. Kids these days are exposed to material things almost from birth. I see so many children in their strollers with a phone or tablet in front of them. While we cannot isolate children from this environment, we can teach them young. Providing an allowance from young ages and helping children to save for the things they want to have is essential. Allowance should not be tied to chores, since we all must continue to be responsible for our affairs. It does not have to be limited to money either, as it can be in the form of stickers or rewards that can be exchanged for other things. Sharing also must be nurtured from young ages. The education must continue through their teenage years with more complex elements such as investing and credit."

Here is useful guidance:

"... [V]oluntary giving fosters an awareness that managing one's financial affairs in accordance with spiritual principles is an indispensable dimension of a life lived coherently. It is a matter of conscience, a way in which commitment to the betterment of the world is translated into practice."[251] Universal House of Justice

* *Note:* Huqúqu'lláh was established by Bahá'u'lláh and is also known as the Right of God. This is an offering to the Bahá'í Faith of a percentage of one's increase in wealth after determining and deducting one's needful expenses. The Right of God is used by the Universal House of Justice of the Bahá'í Faith for various purposes, including charity.

What progress am I making?

Progress forward in life links to many factors, some of which you can control, some of which are harder to influence. Some factors are:

- Your physical, mental, emotional, and spiritual health
- Material and other resources
- Age
- Goals
- Education
- Profession
- Life and family circumstances

All of these can affect your ability to develop yourself, your motivation to grow further, and timing.

Here is a description of one aspect of maturity:

"*Psychological maturity* is a broad term that defines how well and in what manner a person copes with life and is able to relate well to others and the environment. There are numerous factors that determine your current level of maturity and adjustment, most notable being the quality of your early family life, the types of losses or challenges you've had to face so far in your life, your degree of optimism or pessimism, and even biology (some people have a nervous system that makes them more or less vulnerable to stress)."[252] Paul Coleman

There are many elements of maturing or "adulting", and there is an activity below for personal reflection on many of them. Building this understanding contributes to your conscious plans for progress.

Action and Reflection

1. Review and reflect on each aspect of your life below, considering how important it is for you. Consider the level of importance that the item has in your life right now—low, medium, or high priority—and how often you currently successfully carry out each activity: never, rarely, sometimes, often, or high consistency. Identify where more learning or practice would be beneficial and pursue both.

    Daily Living and Well-Being
    a. Eat regular, balanced, and nutritious meals
    b. Practice healthy self-care, including exercise and cleanliness
    c. Seek medical care when needed, such as dentist, medical assessments, and treatments
    d. Get enough sleep each night
    e. Organize home or living space
    f. Clean and maintain personal living space/home
    g. Arrange reliable transportation

    Education, Work, and Financial Management
    a. Go to school and/or work; completing appropriate tasks in a timely manner with a positive outlook and an attitude of service
    b. Take the necessary steps to be self-supporting
    c. Manage finances well, including paying bills on time, maintaining savings, and managing credit and debts

    Intellectual Matters
    a. Learn about the world at large, staying informed about current events, but not overly focusing on them
    b. Participate in ongoing learning activities and experiences
    c. Engage in problem-solving discussions as needed
    d. Express thoughts openly and honestly, staying aware of the impact of words and modifying them as needed with respect, kindness, or tactfulness

Handling and Expressing Emotions
a. Recognize feelings as they arise
b. Manage feelings with balance and wisdom
c. Effectively express feelings
d. Take personal responsibility rather than blaming others or making excuses when something doesn't go smoothly
e. See and interact with other adults as equals, not as a parent-substitute or as a child
f. Address and heal issues from the past, and as needed in a timely way in the present
g. Practice joyfulness and confidence, even when life is difficult
h. Respond constructively to stressful events, maintaining the ability to continue functioning
i. Demonstrate resilience after difficulties occur

Social and Community Interactions
a. Interact in unity, and as healthy and safe, with family members
b. Interact positively with friends and neighbors
c. Engage with others in community-building activities
d. Take occasional breaks for fun and relaxation
e. Ensure laughter, humor, and storytelling happen with others
f. Offer hospitality to others
g. Build knowledge and skills for achieving a healthy and loving present or future relationship or marriage
h. Manage activity levels to accommodate natural energy (Example: If I am an introvert and need time alone to recharge, or if I am an extrovert and need time with others to recharge), and adjust to the natural energy patterns of those close to me

Spiritual Matters
a. Believe in God (a Higher Power)
b. Have faith and trust in God
c. Pray regularly, both during difficulties and in times of ease; say prayers according to my beliefs or religion
d. Turn to wise and spiritual sources for insights and guidance
e. Meditate and reflect to achieve deeper understanding, fulfill spiritual teachings, and share insights with others
f. Regularly read sacred scriptures or other books with spiritual content—with reverence, attention, and thought
g. Participate in spiritually based activities

h. Demonstrate respect for self and others
i. Strive to improve the conditions of the world, addressing issues that affect others
j. Recognize opportunities to be of thoughtful service to others, and then do so willingly and with a positive spirit
k. Observe, reflect on, and improve the quality of thoughts, words, actions, and character with a focus on ongoing personal transformation
l. Regularly feel and express gratitude for blessings
m. Share insights and beliefs with others
n. Seek guidance from and show truthfulness and respect to institutions, such as Spiritual Assemblies, the Universal House of Justice, and the Continental Board of Counsellors and their representatives

2. Learn how to repair or do maintenance on some part of the home where you live, and carry out the repair well, with assistance from others as needed.

3. Learn how to check the fluids and tires of a vehicle you use regularly or maintain your transportation in other ways as needed.

4. Find a recipe that appeals to you, shop for the ingredients, and make the meal. Invite someone to share it with you.

5. Learn how to fully clean and sanitize a bathroom and practice on one you use regularly.

Reflection

1. What are some of the qualities and activities I particularly associate with being an adult? When I reflect on these, am I viewing them in a realistic way?
2. What feelings arise as I consider what is involved with adulting? What am I resisting? What is wise to accept and deal with? Who could I talk with about my thoughts and feelings?
3. What are some of my current strengths in managing the details of my life? Who is benefiting from these strengths? In what ways?

4. What are three areas in which I want to make significant improvement? Who will benefit from these improvements? What system will I use to observe my progress with this effort?

17 – Learning and Growing from Difficulties

Challenge: When faced with difficulties, I sometimes make unwise or unhealthy choices in response that make the situations worse.

Opportunity: I can use difficulties as opportunities to learn and grow; they especially strengthen my character.

Summary:
- Difficulties can build my spiritual muscles and prompt me to strive for growth and well-being.
- Life works best if I'm responsible for my own development, and that means distinguishing what battles are mine to grapple with and which ones belong to others.
- Every problem generates learning that I can use in new circumstances and with new people.
- I'm grateful I don't have to go through challenges alone, since I can ask others to consult and pray with me, as well as assist and accompany me.

More:

Difficulties—A reality of life

Life has challenges and difficulties. It just does. You can pray to be spared from major ones, but tests are part of life on earth, and they can be a means of waking you up and strengthening your faith. How you respond and make use of them in ways that foster your physical, mental, emotional, and spiritual growth is what's vital to address and improve. Here are perspectives on the purpose of difficulties:

"Tests are benefits from God, for which we should thank Him. Grief and sorrow do not come to us by chance, they are sent to us by the Divine Mercy for our own perfecting."[253] 'Abdu'l-Bahá

"The mind and spirit of man advance when he is tried by suffering. The more the ground is ploughed the better the seed will grow, the better the harvest will be. Just as the plough furrows the earth deeply, purifying it of weeds and thistles, so suffering and tribulation free man from the petty affairs of this worldly life until he arrives at a state of complete detachment. His attitude in this world will be that of divine happiness. Man is, so to speak, unripe: the heat of the fire of suffering will mature him."[254] 'Abdu'l-Bahá

"Naturally there will be periods of distress and difficulty, and even severe tests; but if that person turns firmly towards the Divine Manifestation, studies carefully His Spiritual teachings and receives the blessings of the Holy Spirit, he will find that in reality these tests and difficulties have been the gifts of God to enable him to grow and develop."[255] On behalf of Shoghi Effendi

It can be especially difficult to navigate a test when you don't see any good reason for it, and when you wish that something different were happening instead. Perhaps you are not accepted into the university of your choice, you lose a job, a child dies at a young age, or there is a pandemic. Reaching a point of contentment with the Will of God can take you through grieving and angry resistance, but with time, prayer, meditation, consultation, and love, you can persevere and trust in God's greater wisdom. This is the goal:

> "The first and foremost duty prescribed unto men, next to the recognition of Him Who is the Eternal Truth, is the duty of steadfastness in His Cause. Cleave thou unto it, and be of them whose minds are firmly fixed and grounded in God. No act, however meritorious, did or can ever compare unto it. It is the king of all acts, and to this thy Lord, the All-Highest, the Most Powerful, will testify....
>
> "The virtues and attributes pertaining unto God are all evident and manifest, and have been mentioned and described in all the heavenly Books. Among them are trustworthiness, truthfulness, purity of heart while communing with God, forbearance, resignation to whatever the Almighty hath decreed, contentment with the things His Will hath provided, patience, nay, thankfulness in the midst of tribulation, and complete reliance, in all circumstances, upon Him. These rank, according to the estimate of God, among the highest and most laudable of all acts. All other acts are, and will ever remain, secondary and subordinate unto them....
>
> "The spirit that animateth the human heart is the knowledge of God, and its truest adorning is the recognition of the truth that 'He doeth whatsoever He willeth, and ordaineth that which He pleaseth.' Its raiment is the fear of God, and its perfection steadfastness in His Faith.

Thus God instructeth whosoever seeketh Him. He, verily, loveth the one that turneth towards Him. There is none other God but Him, the Forgiving, the Most Bountiful. All praise be to God, the Lord of all worlds."[256] Bahá'u'lláh

Powerfully taking on the challenges

Often the way people respond to difficulties may not feel very enlightened. It can be easier to whine and complain or try to escape them than to handle them in a positive way. However, there are many spiritual benefits to tests and how you respond to them. They are often an opportunity to re-examine your spiritual life and re-connect to God and faith in an authentic way. They are designed for you to become a better person. Consider these quotations:

"Meditate profoundly, that the secret of things unseen may be revealed unto you, that you may inhale the sweetness of a spiritual and imperishable fragrance, and that you may acknowledge the truth that from time immemorial even unto eternity the Almighty hath tried, and will continue to try, His servants, so that light may be distinguished from darkness, truth from falsehood, right from wrong, guidance from error, happiness from misery, and roses from thorns."[257] Bahá'u'lláh

"The more one is severed from the world, from desires, from human affairs, and conditions, the more impervious does one become to the tests of God. Tests are a means by which a soul is measured as to its fitness, and proven out by its own acts. God knows its fitness beforehand, and also its unpreparedness, but man, with an ego, would not believe himself unfit unless proof were given him. Consequently his susceptibility to evil is proven to him when he falls into the tests, and the tests are continued until the soul realizes its own unfitness, then remorse and regret tend to root out the weakness. The same test comes again in greater degree, until it is shown that a former weakness has become a strength, and the power to overcome evil has been established."[258] 'Abdu'l-Bahá

When problems happen or you make a mistake, it's an opportunity to learn and strengthen your wisdom and good judgment. However, wisdom also comes from studying and internalizing spiritual teachings, so sometimes you can prevent damaging results when you pay attention in advance:

"In exasperating situations, we must find the time to pause and reflect if we are not afterwards to regret our words and actions. The Golden Rule, 'Do unto others what you would have them do unto you' or 'Do not do to others that which you do not wish done to yourself' is a useful guideline for action."[259] M. Sefidvash

Part of your life journey includes determining who a test belongs to. Sometimes you may try to rescue or manage other people's tests for them, which often interferes in their learning and development. If you focus on your own challenges and inner battles in learning to live by spiritual principles, you will achieve your own victories and growth. Of course, you can still compassionately offer to help or accompany others, but it's good to be clear and wise in the process that you aren't doing for others what is vital they do for themselves. What can look initially like kindness to another person can result in handicapping them over time. Here is some guidance:

"Ultimately all the battle of life is within the individual. No amount of organization can solve the inner problems or produce or prevent, as the case may be, victory or failure at a crucial moment. In such times as these particularly, individuals are torn by great forces at large in the world, and we see some weak ones suddenly become miraculously strong, and strong ones fail—we can only try, through loving advice...to bring about the act on the part of the believer which will be for the highest good of the Cause. Because obviously something bad for the Cause cannot be the highest good of the individual Bahá'í."[260] On behalf of Shoghi Effendi

The teachings encourage you in these ways:

"... [A]s we suffer these misfortunes we must remember that the Prophets of God Themselves were not immune from these things which men suffer. They knew sorrow, illness and pain too. They rose above these things through Their spirits, and that is what we must try and do too, when afflicted. The troubles of this world pass, and what we have left is what we have made of our souls; so it is to this we must look—to becoming more spiritual, drawing nearer to God, no matter what our human minds and bodies go through."[261] On behalf of Shoghi Effendi

"Life in this world is a succession of tests and achievements, of falling short and of making new spiritual advances. Sometimes the course may seem very hard, but one can witness, again and again, that the soul who steadfastly obeys the Law of Bahá'u'lláh, however hard it may seem, grows spiritually, while the one who compromises with the law for the sake of his own apparent happiness is seen to have been following a chimera: he does not attain the happiness he sought, he retards his spiritual advance and often brings new problems upon himself."[262] Universal House of Justice

As you go through difficulties, your self-confidence grows, and you resiliently gain a mental toughness that helps you push through the next one that comes. You learn what you can do, and this spreads to all areas of your life.

Utilizing learning in action

The Universal House of Justice encourages the culture of the Bahá'í community to be one of acting and then learning. This makes it easier to relax and not try so hard to be perfect. You can step forward in courage to try something new with less worry about failure or criticism from others. It's also easier to accept a mistake if you gain learning from it. Here is guidance about "learning in action":

> "… [T]he friends participate in an ongoing process of action, reflection, study, and consultation in order to address obstacles and share successes, reexamine and revise strategies and methods, and systematize and improve efforts over time."[263] Universal House of Justice

Remember from Chapter 9 this SCAR acronym that could potentially assist you to recall the various inter-related and synergistic elements of learning in action and that scars can result from being bravely in action:

S: Study
C: Consult
A: Act
R: Reflect

How does SCAR relate to learning in action for you?

This is someone's perspective:

"You need to understand with compassion that being alive is hard work. It's okay to have a cushion to sit down on instead of a hard rock though. You think better, think further. I believe in Maslow's hierarchy of needs, but I also believe in miracles. So, if a person lives without all the basics in life, do I believe their spirit is capable of having transcendental experiences? Of course I do. But do I think it's the best way, the efficient way to train a human? No I don't. Hardships and tests and difficulties do wake us up, but is it the only way to wake up? Very few of us trust the route of love, understanding, and education, waking up by learning it, and getting it."

While you are becoming a spiritual man, the following can be your attitude:

"See difficulties as learning opportunities that will expand your talents and capacities. Remind yourself that you can positively influence much of what happens in life. See yourself as capable and as an active participant in your world. Even when a problem has aspects that cannot be changed, trust that if you are resourceful, you will be able to use the situation to learn new ways of responding to it. Welcome change and challenge. Have faith that greater life meaning and satisfaction will emerge from each stressful situation."[264] Stephen Post

Even when you know the standards for how to best behave as a spiritual man, both individually and with others, you will still struggle to meet them at times. Our goal as human beings is always to strive for excellence, but perfection isn't possible. Here is some encouragement:

"He is very happy to see that you have put into practice one of the most encouraging precepts of 'Abdu'l-Bahá in which He said that we should try and make every stumbling-block a stepping-stone to progress. In the course of your past life you have all stumbled very gravely; but, far from being embittered or defeated by this experience, you are determined to make it a means of purifying your natures, improving your characters, and enabling you to become better citizens in the future. This is truly pleasing in the eyes of God."[265] On behalf of Shoghi Effendi

Failures, which happen to everyone, teach humility and trust in the mercy and forgiveness of God. They provide opportunities to ask for assistance, make amends, and learn new ways of speaking and acting. Problems give you opportunities to strengthen your character and make better choices the next time. Addressing issues rather than hiding from them produces a life of high integrity.

Getting a hand up from others

As has been mentioned throughout the book, you can bravely turn to others for support when you have challenges, or to prevent challenges. Often the insights from others dramatically change the outcome. Here is some guidance:

> "When a believer has a problem concerning which he must make a decision, he has several courses open to him. If it is a matter that affects the interests of the Faith he should consult with the appropriate Assembly or committee, but individuals have many problems which are purely personal and there is no obligation upon them to take such problems to the institutions of the Faith; indeed, when the needs of the teaching work are of such urgency it is better if the friends will not burden their Assemblies with personal problems that they can solve by themselves. A Bahá'í who has a problem may wish to make his own decision upon it after prayer and after weighing all the aspects of it in his own mind; he may prefer to seek the counsel of individual friends or of professional counselors such as his doctor or lawyer so that he can consider such advice when making his decision; or in a case where several people are involved, such as a family situation, he may want to gather together those who are affected so that they may arrive at a collective decision. There is also no objection whatever to a Bahá'í asking a group of people to consult together on a problem facing him. It should be borne in mind that all consultation is aimed at arriving at a solution to a problem and is quite different from the sort of group baring of the soul that is popular in some circles these days which borders on the kind of confession that is forbidden in the Faith."[266] Universal House of Justice

A man reflects:

> "I think being raised with a strong Bahá'í foundation was what gave me the tools to navigate the negative influences. Even with that though, I did fall down a lot and gave in to many of those pressures. But having the Faith was

what made me strong enough to pull myself back out. The junior youth and youth groups have become a powerful tool for helping young people get through that age with more strength. The hardest thing can be feeling like you are alone in life, and for youth to be surrounded with quality friends and other youth going through the same things, and studying how to handle the pressures, is so helpful. It's impossible to 'protect' young people from the pressures. Inevitably they will be exposed to them in some form, but the most important thing is addressing the negative influences and talking about how to handle them.

"Sometimes people think talking about negative forces in the world might make them more likely to happen, but I think talking about them directly makes them feel less daunting. It's also important to hear that making a mistake isn't the end, because I've known many people that made one mistake and then felt they were no longer good enough to be a Bahá'í. I think society creates the idea that we are born pure and then become less pure as we make mistakes. But in the Faith, it's through tests that we become more pure. And God knows we will fail. He sends us the same test over and over at a greater degree until that weakness becomes a strength. If God knows that and loves us even when we fall down, then as parents, peers, friends, and Bahá'ís we need to help people feel that as well."

Action

1. Invite a small group of trusted people to hold a reflection gathering and consultation about your life. The goal will be to identify challenges that you are tripping over and capture learning opportunities and devise solutions. Carry out the solutions and re-assess the situation(s).

2. Identify two lessons you have learned from difficulties and share them by creating a challenging learning activity for junior youth, youth, or others.

3. Set up and carry out a camping expedition with others that includes many elements of "roughing it". Look ahead to some of what may happen and plan for the challenges that you can. Experience the trip and assess the learning together with the others who participated, including a review of the character qualities that the group members applied and strengthened.

4. Identify a new sport, fitness workout, or martial art that you want to learn. Begin lessons or training and notice the difficulties involved. What are you learning? What is beneficial? What stops you from wanting to continue participating? How can you address any difficulties that are occurring?

5. Plan and go on a challenging hike with a small group. Look ahead and plan for safe passages. Work together to traverse the rougher areas. Afterward, reflect together on how you handled the difficulties involved.

Reflection

1. How do I generally respond to tests and challenges that arise?
2. When do I rely on avoidance or turn to alcohol, drugs, sex, or other means of trying to ignore or forget what is happening?
3. What would I like to improve about my responses to difficulties?
4. What have I learned from a difficulty in the past?
5. When have I successfully used learning from a difficult situation to improve actions in a new situation?
6. What specific character qualities have I strengthened or am I currently strengthening from working through a difficulty? [Refer back to Chapter 8 for a list of possible qualities.]
7. When have I successfully reached out and received assistance from a person, group, or institution when a problem was happening? What in my life now would benefit from doing this outreach?

18 – Cleaning Up My Messes and Going Forward

Challenge: It's often easier to pretend nothing happened, avoid dealing with an issue in a timely way, or to hide what I've done instead of addressing it.

Opportunity: I like the feeling of freedom that arises and how light I feel when I keep my life "cleaned up" daily.

Summary:
- When I contribute to difficulties, I can handle the results with understanding, regret, forgiveness, and making amends.
- Cleaning up my "messes" keeps me going forward, increases my self-respect, draws respect from others, builds character, and often protects unity with others.
- I can resiliently bounce back from difficulties and keep bravely living my life in a powerful way.

More:

Reconnecting with God through forgiveness

In your life quest as a Bahá'í man, it's wise to keep your life as "cleaned up" as possible, no matter what the size of the issue. It's good to gain confidence with cleaning up the small, daily matters that arise, so that you are more skilled when big matters occur. Resolving issues includes being effective at:

- Observing your words and actions
- Reflecting to understand what happened and why
- Acknowledging to yourself your errors and where your words or actions caused problems
- Regretting what happened
- Seeking forgiveness from God
- Admitting honestly what happened to any others involved, taking appropriate responsibility, apologizing as needed, but avoiding abasing yourself
- Cleaning up and resolving whatever problems you have caused or whatever consequences you are partially responsible for
- Learning from what occurred and from the clean-up process

- Applying the learning to further personal growth and in new circumstances
- Respecting yourself and acknowledging your efforts to grow
- Being resilient in picking up and going on to work with, relate to, and serve others

The longer you stay stuck in whatever poor choice you made and its consequences, the deeper the hole you will dig. You become emotionally and mentally stuck in denial or in the past, and this influences future choices with relationships, work, and community involvement. You may even withdraw from participating in activities or avoid people who were involved in a situation. Making efforts to resolve the past and resiliently go forward will empower you to have a better future. You are lighter and happier when not dragging unresolved issues along with you. With practice, the process will likely become smoother and faster. Consider this:

"Wherefore, hearken ye unto My speech, and return ye to God and repent, that He, through His grace, may have mercy upon you, may wash away your sins, and forgive your trespasses. The greatness of His mercy surpasseth the fury of His wrath, and His grace encompasseth all who have been called into being and been clothed with the robe of life, be they of the past or of the future."[267] Bahá'u'lláh

Here is a reflection about the concept of "repenting":

"... [R]epentance is about conduct—you realize you've done something wrong, you resolve to change it in the future. ...Inside each of us is some spark of God—the real us. ... Sin, evil, murder—all those things have the ability to cover up our true selves. [Repenting]...means turning back to the part of God that's gotten concealed. When you repent, usually, you feel sad—because of the regret that led you there. But when you talk about [repentance], about making that connection with God again—well, it makes you happy. ... Happier even than you were before, because your sins separated you from God...."[268] J. Picoult

Once you are clear that you regret your part in what happened, asking for forgiveness from God reconnects you with Him, and you can draw on that strength to do the next actions. You can define forgiveness as accepting pardon from God and pardoning someone else for saying or doing something hurtful or harmful, giving up a desire for revenge, and letting go of anger and resentment. The ability to bravely seek God's forgiveness, request forgiveness from another person, and offer forgiveness to each other all contribute to respect and unity.

Transformation is an interesting blessing that can arise out of asking for and receiving God's forgiveness, and increasing unity between you and others can be part of this transformation:

"Thy generous Lord will assist thee to labor in His vineyard and will cause thee to be the means of spreading the spirit of unity…. He will make thine inner eye to see with the light of knowledge, He will forgive thy sins and transform them into goodly deeds. Verily He is the Forgiving, the Compassionate, the Lord of immeasurable grace."[269] 'Abdu'l-Bahá

Many people notice that their missteps become learning, which then becomes deeds and services that benefit others. It can be powerful to look back at something that has transformed since you failed or sinned. You also may find a measure of serenity in understanding that God can take what went wrong and transform it.

Doing clean-up actions

At this stage, you might be clear that you have asked for and received forgiveness from God. However, if your words or actions harmed someone else or a group of others, that forgiveness may not really sink in until you clean up the issue with them. There are concrete actions for you to take to resolve any issues that arose from your behavior. Ensure, however, that any remedial actions you consider will not cause further harm, including bringing you excessive shame.

Here are some guidelines for how to proceed and what to be careful about:

"Bahá'u'lláh prohibits confession to, and seeking absolution of one's sins from, a human being. Instead one should beg forgiveness from God. … Shoghi Effendi sets the prohibition into context. His secretary has written on his behalf that we '…are forbidden to confess to any person, as do the Catholics to their priests, our sins and shortcomings, or to do so in public, as some religious sects do. However, if we spontaneously desire to acknowledge we have been wrong in something, or that we have some fault of character, and ask another person's forgiveness or pardon, we are quite free to do so.' The Universal House of Justice has

also clarified that Bahá'u'lláh's prohibition concerning the confession of sins does not prevent an individual from admitting transgressions in the course of consultations held under the aegis of Bahá'í institutions. Likewise, it does not preclude the possibility of seeking advice from a close friend or of a professional counselor regarding such matters."[270]
The Kitáb-i-Aqdas, Notes

You and others may pray and consult to understand what was said and done and where there was failure to speak or act in ways that aligned with spiritual principles or laws.

You may find these ways of resolving issues useful, as suggested by the authors of *When Sorry Isn't Enough*:

1. Expressing Regret: "I am sorry."
2. Accepting Responsibility: "I was wrong."
3. Making Restitution: "What can I do to make it right?"
4. Genuinely Repenting: "I want to change."
5. Requesting Forgiveness: "Can you find it in your heart to forgive me?"

The authors suggest that these factors may also be important to consider when offering an apology:

- Your tone of voice and body language must match your words for the receiver to believe that your apology is sincere.
- State specifically what the apology is for and acknowledge the hurt caused.
- Avoid any language (such as "…but…") that communicates blame to the person to whom you are apologizing. Attacks do not usually lead to forgiveness and reconciliation.
- Do not use apology to try to manipulate someone; for example, apologizing in the hope that the recipient will change some behavior.
- Depending on the circumstances and relationship, you may find it most effective to put your apology in writing.

(Summarized from Gary Chapman, PhD, and Jennifer Thomas, PhD, *When Sorry Isn't Enough*)

The next step then, of course, is for you to be clear what behaviors you must work on improving and begin to address these.

Forgiving others

Forgiveness frees us from holding a grudge against a person for what they did. Drs. Les and Leslie Parrott say that forgiving is choosing to reject "vengeance, renounce bitterness, break the silence of estrangement, and actually wish the best" for the other person. They also say, "Forgiveness is not for the faint-hearted. Our sense of justice usually recoils at the thought of this unnatural act. Only the brave forgive."[271] In other words, it takes courage.

Forgiveness is not the same as ignoring the situation or saying that what happened was okay. The initial problem still needs to be addressed—just as we are responsible for our own actions, so are others for theirs. The balance is illuminated by this quotation:

> "The Kingdom of God is founded upon equity and justice, and also upon mercy, compassion, and kindness to every living soul. Strive ye then with all your heart to treat compassionately all humankind—except for those who have some selfish, private motive, or some disease of the soul. Kindness cannot be shown the tyrant, the deceiver, or the thief, because, far from awakening them to the error of their ways, it maketh them to continue in their perversity as before. No matter how much kindliness ye may expend upon the liar, he will but lie the more, for he believeth you to be deceived, while ye understand him but too well, and only remain silent out of your extreme compassion."[272] 'Abdu'l-Bahá

A commitment to unity and an aversion to disunity are part of what prompts people to forgive faster and restore harmony. Forgiveness is directly connected to a sensitivity to unity. The more committed people are to maintaining harmony, the more they will not be able to tolerate disunity for any length of time. Then addressing the issues and promptly forgiving becomes possible.

It's important to be aware that forgiveness needs to be sincere and in integrity. It's not wise to forgive someone automatically just because the situation is difficult, or because you feel unhappy that the other person is regretful. If you say you forgive someone, while you are still holding onto considerable anger, sadness, or pain from the incident, the situation will not be resolved. Some inner healing likely needs to happen first.

Once a situation is resolved, then it's important to leave it in the past and not bring it up again. Reminding someone about the situation can indicate that you did not completely forgive the first time.

Bouncing back afterward

Resilience can be defined as accepting, responding creatively and appropriately to, recovering from, and coping with adversity, misfortune, change, or illness, as well as bouncing back from stressful experiences effectively and in a reasonable amount of time. Here is someone's perspective:

"... [R]esilient people...have three distinguishing characteristics: an acceptance of reality, a strongly held belief that life is meaningful, and an ability to find creative solutions to seemingly insoluble problems."[273]
J. A. Khan

Here are some concrete details:

"A man practices resilience effectively when he:

- Accepts and adjusts to change rather than resisting it
- Acts calmly during crises and takes positive steps to manage them
- Seeks creative and appropriate solutions to problems
- Looks for what he can learn from a current or previous challenge to prevent or respond effectively to future ones
- Adapts to changing circumstances, staying detached enough from what is occurring to respond appropriately
- Stays reasonably optimistic when faced with unwanted events or experiences, but does not engage in serious denial or avoid responding to circumstances
- Withstands, grieves, or quickly recovers from the impact of failures, disruptive events, loss, and disappointments; quickly and confidently re-focuses on goals and resumes action

"A man needs to strengthen resilience when he:

- Grumbles, whines, and complains about unexpected or disruptive events
- Ignores, panics, or responds poorly to problems, often making them worse
- Takes an excessive amount of time to recover from challenges and changes

- Becomes helpless in the face of problems
- Talks pessimistically about all the bad things that are occurring and that might occur in the future"[274] S. M. Alexander

You will notice that when you achieve a significant degree of resilience after a problem or tragedy that people look at your bravery and your power of example, and they want to learn from you and to also be more resilient themselves.

Action

1. Identify something that you did that was a problem and that you have not yet addressed. Study to determine the spiritual principles that apply, or research remediation options as needed. Consult with others as wise. Ensure that anything you do will not cause further or greater harm. Carry out your "clean-up" actions. Reflect on the outcome and determine what will prevent something like this occurring again.

2. Find a messy and disorganized area of your life or that of your family's, such as your bedroom, vehicle, office, garage, basement, storage area, and so on. Seek agreement as needed and then clean and organize the area. While doing it, think about keeping your own life clean, orderly, and in a state of integrity. How do you feel when you're finished, and the area is more organized than it was before? Are there ways this might relate to how you feel when you "clean up" part of your social, work, or spiritual life?

3. Identify one aspect of your behavior that you're unhappy with and ask God to forgive you for it. Choose one or two actions that will contribute to transforming this behavior. Set specific goals that will have you improve. Include your assessment of your progress as part of your daily self-accounting. (See Chapter 5 for more about this daily practice.)

Reflection

1. What is my experience with asking for forgiveness from God? What would help it happen more easily? What would help me believe it had happened? Is there still an effect on me from my choices even after I have asked for God's pardon?

2. What are my experiences with asking for forgiveness from another person? What would make this action happen more easily? Also, is there still an effect on me from my choices even after I have asked for the person's pardon?
3. What do I perceive are current problems, difficulties, and obstacles to my progress?
4. What steps can I take to resolve issues that are troubling me?
5. When I think of a current situation, what will facilitate me learning from the difficulties, recover resiliently, and move forward? What actions will I take in my life for personal improvement?

Part 5: My Bahá'í Community Life—Shining God's Light in the World

19 - Engaging with the Bahá'í Community

Challenge: Sometimes I love being involved with people who are following the Bahá'í teachings; sometimes it seems like all they want me to do is work, work, and work.

Opportunity: I can study the Bahá'í teachings, learn what's involved in community life, and make my own balanced and at times sacrificial choices for involvement and contribution.

Summary:
- No matter what experiences I have had in the past with participating, I can change the nature and quality of my experiences now and going forward.
- My voice is a vital contribution to community consultations.
- It's important to participate in Nineteen-Day Feasts, contribute to the Bahá'í Fund, and serve others as ways of building unity and contributing to universal participation.
- I can strive to have a good relationship with the local and national Spiritual Assemblies, and I can build my capacity to serve on such institutions.
- Bahá'u'lláh, 'Abdu'l-Bahá, and Shoghi Effendi guide and inspire the elected Bahá'í institutions, and these entities are more than just a group of individuals.
- The community and institutions are in the process of maturing, so they won't always function the way I want or think they should; my own responsibility is to build unity and love, as well as grow and contribute my skills, talents, and abilities.

More:

My experiences in community life

For some, community life is fun, spiritually stimulating, and interesting. For others, the response might be "this is boring". You might be participating, or you might sit back in negative judgment about what is happening and just stay away. You might be fully involved in community life, but you have a separate life where you don't follow the teachings. Remember that a spiritual man strives for integrity, where your beliefs and actions align. You are also responsible for influencing your experience of community. If it's not the way you want it to be, or something seems missing, you can reflect on these questions:

- What would you like to see instead?
- What are you going to bravely do to change or influence activity in a new direction?
- What Bahá'í teachings or Universal House of Justice guidance are you going to research and align with?
- Who will you consult with?
- Are you willing to be an active part of the change and invite others to participate?

Here are descriptions of the community:

"They are members of a purposeful community, global in scope, pursuing a bold spiritual mission—working to establish a pattern of activity and administrative structures suited to a humanity entering its age of maturity. Giving shape to the community's efforts is a framework for action defined by the global Plans of the Faith. This framework promotes the transformation of the individual in conjunction with social transformation, as two inseparable processes. Specifically, the courses of the [training] institute are intended to set the individual on a path in which qualities and attitudes, skills and abilities, are gradually acquired through service—service intended to quell the insistent self, helping to lift the individual out of its confines and placing him or her in a dynamic process of community building.

"In this context, then, every individual finds himself or herself immersed in a community that serves increasingly as an environment conducive to the cultivation of those attributes that are to distinguish a Bahá'í life—an environment in which a spirit of unity animates one and all; in which the ties of fellowship bind them; in which mistakes are treated with tolerance and fear of failure is diminished; in which criticism of others is avoided and backbiting and gossip give way to mutual support and encouragement; in which young and old work shoulder to shoulder, studying the Creative Word together and accompanying one another in their efforts to serve; in which children are reared through an educational process that strives to sharpen their spiritual faculties and imbue them with the spirit of the Faith; in which young people are helped to detect the false messages spread by society, recognize its fruitless preoccupations, and resist its pressures, directing their energies instead towards its betterment. The institutions of the Faith, for their part, strive to ensure that such an environment is fostered."[275] On behalf of the Universal House of Justice

"What the friends need to remember in this respect is that, in their efforts to achieve personal growth and to uphold Bahá'í ideals, they are not isolated individuals, withstanding alone the onslaught of the forces of moral decay operating in society. They are members of a purposeful community, global in scope, pursuing a bold, spiritual mission—working to establish a pattern of activity and administrative structures suited to a humanity entering its age of maturity. ... This framework promotes the transformation of the individual in conjunction with social transformation, as two inseparable processes."[276] On behalf of the Universal House of Justice

Universal participation and individual initiative

Individuals find their preferred areas of service and participation over time, and there are also some services that are for everyone to do. Here is some guidance that may assist you to see your roles:

"Every individual believer—man, woman, youth and child—is summoned to this field of action; for it is on the initiative, the resolute will of the individual to teach and to serve, that the success of the entire community depends. Well-grounded in the mighty Covenant of Bahá'u'lláh, sustained by daily prayer and reading of the Holy Word, strengthened by a continual striving to obtain a deeper understanding of the divine Teachings, illumined by a constant endeavor to relate these Teachings to current issues, nourished by observance of the laws and principles of His wondrous World Order, every individual can attain increasing measures of success in teaching."[277] Universal House of Justice

"In addition to teaching, every believer can pray. Every believer can strive to make his 'own inner life and private character mirror forth in their manifold aspects the splendor of those eternal principles proclaimed by Bahá'u'lláh.' [Shoghi Effendi, *Bahá'í Administration*, p. 66.] Every believer can contribute to the Fund. Not all believers can give public talks, not all are called upon to serve on administrative institutions. But all can pray, fight their own spiritual battles, and contribute to the Fund. If every believer will carry out these sacred duties, we shall be astonished at the accession of power which will result to the whole body, and which in its turn will give rise to further growth and the showering of greater blessings on all of us.

"The real secret of universal participation lies in the Master's oft-expressed wish that the friends should love each other, constantly encourage each other, work together, be as one soul in one body, and in so doing become a true, organic, healthy body animated and illumined by the spirit. In such a body all will receive spiritual health and vitality from the organism itself, and the most perfect flowers and fruits will be brought forth."[278] Universal House of Justice

These quotations above indicate that you are a vital and necessary part of the community. Individual initiative, however, also plays a key role in community functioning:

"This challenge, so severe and insistent, and yet so glorious, faces no doubt primarily the individual believer on whom, in the last resort, depends the fate of the entire community. He it is who constitutes the warp and woof on which the quality and pattern of the whole fabric must depend. He it is who acts as one of the countless links in the mighty chain that now girdles the globe. He it is who serves as one of the multitude of bricks which support the structure and ensure the stability of the administrative edifice now being raised in every part of the world. Without his support, at once whole-hearted, continuous and generous, every measure adopted, and every plan formulated, by the Body which acts as the national representative of the community to which he belongs is foredoomed to failure. The World Centre of the Faith itself is paralyzed if such a support on the part of the rank and file of the community is denied it. The Author of the Divine Plan Himself ['Abdu'l-Bahá] is impeded in His purpose if the proper instruments for the execution of His design are lacking. The sustaining strength of Bahá'u'lláh Himself, the Founder of the Faith, will be withheld from every and each individual who fails in the long run to arise and play his part."[279] On behalf of Shoghi Effendi

The community needs your voice and active participation in whatever ways you can offer, and you can find ways to serve that bring you joy. A diversity of action is needed, and that means it's highly likely you can find something that is a good fit for you. As you consult with others, you participate in transforming yourself and your environment. And, you can demonstrate individual initiative and contribute to building community in ways that align with your talents and abilities or with your intention to build greater capacity.

One way you can contribute to the world around you is being involved in consultations aimed at finding solutions to various challenges both within the community and outward as social action. Engagement in this way usually involves having clarity of thoughts and feelings and being able to express both. Here are guidelines for your voice:

"Content, volume, style, tact, wisdom, timeliness are among the critical factors in determining the effects of speech for good or evil. Consequently, the friends need ever to be conscious of the significance of this activity which so distinguishes human beings from other forms of life, and they must exercise it judiciously. Their efforts at such discipline will give birth to an etiquette of expression worthy of the approaching maturity of the human race. Just as this discipline applies to the spoken word, it applies equally to the written word…."[280] Universal House of Justice

Here is also a call to heroic action:

"These, indeed, are the days when heroism is needed on the part of the believers. Self-sacrifice, courage, indomitable hope and confidence are the characteristics they should show forth, because these very attributes cannot but fix the attention of the public and lead them to enquire what, in a world so hopelessly chaotic and bewildered, leads these people to be so assured, so confident, so full of devotion? Increasingly, as time goes by, the characteristics of the Bahá'ís will be that which captures the attention of their fellow-citizens. They must show their aloofness from the hatreds and recriminations which are tearing at the heart of humanity, and demonstrate by deed and word their profound belief in the future peaceful unification of the entire human race."[281] On behalf of Shoghi Effendi

The institution of the Spiritual Assembly

In each locality where there are nine Bahá'ís over age 21, a Spiritual Assembly is elected to guide the community. Here is some guidance to further explain these vital institutions:

"Local Spiritual Assemblies are at the present newly born institutions, struggling for the most part to establish themselves both in the Bahá'í community and in the world. They are as yet only embryos of the majestic institutions ordained by Bahá'u'lláh in His Writings....

"What we find expounded in the writings of our Faith is the lofty station Local Spiritual Assemblies must attain in their gradual and at times painful development....

"Among the more salient objectives to be attained by the Local Spiritual Assembly in its process of development to full maturity are to act as a loving shepherd to the Bahá'í flock, promote unity and concord among the friends, direct the teaching work, protect the Cause of God, arrange for Feasts, Anniversaries and regular meetings of the community, familiarize the Bahá'ís with its plans, invite the community to offer its recommendations, promote the welfare of youth and children, and participate, as circumstances permit, in humanitarian activities. In its relationship to the individual believer, the Assembly should continuously invite and encourage him to study the Faith, to deliver its glorious message, to live in accordance with its teachings, to contribute freely and regularly to the Fund, to participate in community activities, and to seek refuge in the Assembly for advice and help, when needed.

"In its own meetings it must endeavor to develop skill in the difficult but highly rewarding art of Bahá'í consultation, a process which will require great self-discipline on the part of all members and complete reliance on the power of Bahá'u'lláh."[282] Universal House of Justice

"The appearance of a united, firmly based and self-sustaining community must be a major goal of a Spiritual Assembly. Composed of a membership reflecting a diversity of personalities, talents, abilities and interests, such a community requires a level of internal interaction between the Assembly and the body of the believers based on a commonly recognized commitment to service, and in which a sense of partnership based on appreciation of each other's distinctive sphere of action is fully recognized and unfailingly upheld, and no semblance of a dichotomy between the two appears. In such a community leadership is that expression of service by which the Spiritual Assembly invites and encourages the use of the manifold talents and abilities with which the community is endowed, and stimulates and guides the diverse elements of the community towards goals and strategies by which the effects of a coherent force for progress can be realized.

"The maintenance of a climate of love and unity depends largely upon the feeling among the individuals composing the community that the Assembly is a part of themselves, that their cooperative interactions with that divinely ordained body allow them a fair latitude for initiative and that the quality of their relationships with both the institution and their fellow believers encourages a spirit of enterprise invigorated by an awareness of the revolutionizing purpose of Bahá'u'lláh's Revelation, by a consciousness of the high privilege of their being associated with efforts to realize that purpose, and by a consequent, ever-present sense of joy. In such a climate, the community is transformed from being the mere sum of its parts to assuming a wholly new personality as an entity in which its members blend without losing their individual uniqueness. The possibilities for manifesting such a transformation exist most immediately at the local level, but it is a major responsibility of the National Assembly to nurture the conditions in which they may flourish.

"The authority to direct the affairs of the Faith locally, nationally and internationally, is divinely conferred on elected institutions. However, the power to accomplish the tasks of the community resides primarily in the mass of the believers. The authority of the institutions is an irrevocable necessity for the progress of humanity; its exercise is an art to be mastered. The power of action in the believers is unlocked at the level of individual initiative and surges at the level of collective volition. In its potential, this mass power, this mix of individual potentialities, exists in a malleable form susceptible to the multiple reactions of individuals to the sundry influences at work in the world. To realize its highest purpose, this power needs to express itself through orderly avenues of activity."[283] Universal House of Justice

The institutions are also where you turn to as an individual when you have exciting information to share, a problem that relates to the Bahá'í Faith, you observe something that could be harmful to the Bahá'í Faith, or you need guidance or help with something. Diverse examples might include if you:

- Need information about planning a Bahá'í wedding
- Have difficulty in a marriage
- Are excited to share the results of an activity
- Observe someone harming children
- Experience backbiting and gossip among community members
- Have a concern about disunity
- Need to plan a Bahá'í funeral
- Want to publicize an activity
- Have a matter that involves injustice

If you report a problem (which is not the same as childhood tattling!), remember to then detach from it, pray for the situation and the institution, and don't discuss it with others.

Nineteen-Day Feasts—showing up and more

Ideally, the Bahá'í community, its activities, and Local Spiritual Assemblies will be a primary support system for you throughout your life. They will be a safe harbor from the rough waves out in the world. One primary activity for you to be involved in will be the Nineteen-Day Feast. In this setting you can worship, serve, build relationships with community members, and make recommendations to the institutions. It's intended to be an opportunity to regularly spiritually uplift participants and build community unity.

If you struggle at times with your Feast experience, locate quotations about the Feast and study them. You can then raise at the next Feast a discussion about what you have found. You could also offer to host an upcoming Feast, introducing aspects you think would make it something you are drawn to. The importance of you contributing your voice to consultations was mentioned earlier in the chapter. A man says:

"I've struggled with not finding Nineteen-Day Feasts spiritually uplifting at times. Sometimes people make comments, and I feel like they are judging me. Often, though, this is because my self-confidence isn't where I want it to be. When I show up, it's frustrating when I'm asked to take on a responsibility or service that I'm not comfortable doing or really not that interested in, just because there are so few people to do tasks. Sometimes I'd like to just be in community and spiritual places without demanding expectations. Sometimes I'd also like to bring my friends to other activities who are living all sorts of

lifestyles without being concerned about people judging them. The standards in the teachings are high for everyone, but that includes people being friendly and loving as we go through our personal tests."

Here is a small selection of the available guidance about Feasts:

"The owner of the house must personally serve the beloved ones. He must seek after the comfort of all and with the utmost humility he must show forth kindness to every one."[284] 'Abdu'l-Bahá

"To a very large extent, the success of the Feast depends on the quality of the preparation and participation of the individual. The beloved Master offers the following advice: 'Give ye great weight to the Nineteen Day gatherings, so that on these occasions the beloved of the Lord and the handmaids of the Merciful may turn their faces toward the Kingdom, chant the communes, beseech God's help, become joyfully enamored each of the other, and grow in purity and holiness, and in the fear of God, and in resistance to passion and self. Thus will they separate themselves from this elemental world, and immerse themselves in the ardors of the spirit.' … [T]he Feast is rooted in hospitality, with all its implications of friendliness, courtesy, service, generosity and conviviality. The very idea of hospitality as the sustaining spirit of so significant an institution introduces a revolutionary new attitude to the conduct of human affairs at all levels, an attitude which is critical to that world unity which the Central Figures of our Faith labored so long and suffered so much cruelty to bring into being. It is in this divine festival that the foundation is laid for the realization of so unprecedented a reality."[285] Universal House of Justice

"The World Order of Bahá'u'lláh encompasses all units of human society; integrates the spiritual, administrative and social processes of life; and canalizes human expression in its varied forms towards the construction of a new civilization. The Nineteen Day Feast embraces all these aspects at the very base of society. Functioning in the village, the town, the city, it is an institution of which all the people of Bahá are members. It is intended to promote unity, ensure progress, and foster joy."[286] Universal House of Justice

Communities are maturing too

The growth and maturity of the global Bahá'í community is evolving. At different times and if you travel to various localities for education, employment, or service, the communities you encounter may be active and supportive. Others may be struggling. Sometimes you can raise issues and possible solutions, and you will be able to influence a positive shift in the life of a community. At other times, you may only be able to pray for them. It's wise to:

- Resist getting angry about the state of a community
- Contribute your efforts where you can
- Strive to learn from the experience
- Seek further afield for the necessary resources and people to guide you and accompany you with maintaining your spiritual well-being as needed

Below is some guidance for community members:

"Perhaps the greatest test Bahá'ís are ever subjected to is from each other; but for the sake of the Master they should be ever ready to overlook each other's mistakes, apologize for harsh words they have uttered, forgive and forget. He strongly recommends to you this course of action."[287] On behalf of Shoghi Effendi

"The greatest need it seems everywhere inside the Cause is to impress upon the friends the need for love among them. There is a tendency to mix up the functions of the Administration and try to apply it in individual relationships, which is abortive, because the Assembly is a nascent House of Justice and is supposed to administer, according to the Teachings, the affairs of the community. But individuals toward each other are governed by love, unity, forgiveness and a sin-covering eye. Once the friends grasp this they will get along much better, but they keep playing Spiritual Assembly to each other and expect the Assembly to behave like an individual...."[288] On behalf of Shoghi Effendi

"Regarding...the inharmony that seems to exist among certain of the friends...when Bahá'ís permit the dark forces of the world to enter into their own relationships within the Faith they gravely jeopardize its progress; it is the paramount duty of the believers, the Local Assemblies, and particularly the National Spiritual Assembly to foster harmony, understanding and love amongst the friends. All should be ready and willing to set aside every personal sense of grievance—justified or unjustified—for the good of the Cause, because the people will never embrace it until they see in its community life mirrored what is so conspicuously lacking in the world: love and unity."[289] On behalf of Shoghi Effendi

Action

1. Research quotations about the Nineteen-Day Feast. Attend the next Feast in your area and fully participate in all aspects of the experience. Volunteer to host or help with planning another Feast. Does going to Feast feel different when you understand the guidance and when you are an active participant rather than just observing?

2. Set up a system to remind you to carry out your spiritual obligation to give to the Bahá'í Fund every Bahá'í month (every 19 days).

3. Identify one aspect of community life that you wish were different and that you want to contribute time and energy toward. Search for quotations that seem to demonstrate that your idea aligns with spiritual guidance. Reflect on the steps you will take to make the change or get involved. Note the dates by when you want to take each action. Consider who you will consult with and who can help you carry out your actions, especially if you need training. Some activity ideas may include the core activities, such as joining or tutoring a study circle, animating a Junior Youth Spiritual Empowerment group, teaching a children's class, or hosting a devotional. If these are not a fit for you though, perhaps you can volunteer with administrative tasks, start a community service project, clean and organize someone's home, do a social media publicity effort, create a website, find a way to apply your artistic talents, or something else that inspires you.

4. Volunteer to work on an activity that is happening in your community and carry out the tasks you agree to complete. Did contributing to others increase your self-respect? How well did you do on staying humble during your contribution?

Reflection

1. What value is there for me in participating in Bahá'í community life? How can I be consistent with participating?
2. What is the value of the Nineteen-Day Feast for me? For others?
3. What do I not like about participating in community activities? What can I feel empowered to address?
4. In what ways is my voice active and heard in community gatherings? Am I remembering to speak with respect and tact?
5. How are people responding to my participation and suggestions?
6. How could I improve the response of others to my contributions, if needed?
7. When is it good for me to take individual initiative? When might it cause disunity or harm?
8. How could I be more unified with my community?

20 – Making My Community Service Choices

Challenge: There are so many improvements to do world-wide, that I could serve 24 hours, 7 days a week, and it would still feel like an insignificant drop in an ocean of problems.

Opportunity: Serving others is an opportunity to be involved with great people in tackling several community issues at once.

Summary:
- Service is a broad term that encompasses a wide variety of activities of daily life, so I am likely already involved in service; I can also choose to do more.
- The Universal House of Justice provides regular Plans that encourage me to set the priorities for my service; at this time, there are four core activities that are high priority.
- It takes courage for me to be involved in serving others and in sustaining my efforts.
- Who I am as a spiritual being internally must be in harmony with who I am externally and with my words and actions, so I am authentically the same person in all areas of my life.
- It's wise to balance Bahá'í community service with many other aspects of my life, including personal prayer and meditation as well as family life.

More:

Value of service

If you spend about a minute around any Bahá'í, you'll begin to hear about "service", and it's been mentioned throughout. It's hardwired into the teachings and the culture of community life. Chances are by the time you are 15 or are joining or re-joining the Bahá'í community, you will have already participated in some type of service. Here is encouragement:

"An individual must center his whole heart and mind on service to the Cause, in accordance with the high standards set by Bahá'u'lláh. When this is done, the Hosts of the Supreme Concourse will come to the assistance of the individual, and every difficulty and trial will gradually be overcome."[290] On behalf of Shoghi Effendi

Globally there is a system of training institutes that operate throughout most countries. At this time, the materials being used are those of the Ruhi Institute established in Colombia, South America (https://ruhi.org), with an International Advisory Board located at the Baháʼí World Centre in Haifa, Israel. These books include text and quotations to study and practices that result in skill-building and learning-in-action. The purpose of the courses is clarified here:

> "… [T]he courses of the institute are intended to set the individual on a path in which qualities and attitudes, skills and abilities, are gradually acquired through service—service intended to quell the insistent self, helping to lift the individual out of its confines and placing him or her in a dynamic process of community building."[291] On behalf of the Universal House of Justice

Sometimes you will hear people speak of attending a Ruhi study circle. If you have not already, you will likely benefit from participating in a study circle focused on Book 1, "Reflections on the Life of the Spirit". Here are more details:

> "… [T]he training institute…strives to engage the individual in an educational process in which virtuous conduct and self-discipline are developed in the context of service, fostering a coherent and joyful pattern of life that weaves together study, worship, teaching, community building and, in general, involvement in other processes that seek to transform society. At the heart of the educational process is contact with the Word of God, whose power sustains every individual's attempts to purify his or her heart and to walk a path of service with 'the feet of detachment.' The Guardian encouraged young believers to learn through 'active, wholehearted and continued participation' in community activities. Addressed to one young believer, a letter written on his behalf explained: 'Baháʼí community life provides you with an indispensable laboratory, where you can translate into living and constructive action the principles which you imbibe from the Teachings.' 'By becoming a real part of that living organism,' the letter went on, 'you can catch the real spirit which runs throughout the Baháʼí Teachings.' Such wholehearted participation in the work of the Faith provides an invaluable context for the exertion made by young and old alike to align their lives with Baháʼu'lláh's teachings. This is not to say that individuals will not err from time to time, perhaps on occasion in serious ways. Yet,

when the desire to uphold the Bahá'í standard is nurtured through service to the common weal in an environment of unfailing love and warm encouragement, the friends will not feel, in the face of such difficulty, that they have no other recourse but to withdraw from community activity out of a sense of shame or, worse, to cover the challenges they are experiencing with the veneer of propriety, living a life in which public words do not conform to private deeds."[292] On behalf of the Universal House of Justice

Sometimes when people are asked to serve or they initiate their own efforts, there is an inner reaction of not being capable or worthy. Here is some reassurance:

"If the friends always waited until they were fully qualified to do any particular task, the work of the Cause would be almost at a standstill! But the very act of striving to serve, however unworthy one may feel, attracts the blessings of God and enables one to become more fitted for the task."[293] On behalf of Shoghi Effendi

It's also good to remember that you are rarely the only one involved in any activity, and you can look to others for assistance. Here is an example:

"Youth also support each other...coming together in groups to engage in further study and discuss their service, to reinforce one another's efforts and build resolve, looking to ever extend the circle of friendship more widely. The encouragement offered in this way by a network of peers provides young people with a much-needed alternative to those siren voices that beckon towards the snares of consumerism and compulsive distractions...."[294] Universal House of Justice

The earlier in your life you develop a pattern of serving others, the more it's likely to stick with you throughout your life and result in benefits to others and yourself. Consider this viewpoint:

"In essence, generativity is the act of preparing another's garden for spring. It's power in the service of love. It's an act of giving that enables another person to manifest his or her own strengths and gifts through love. It can be as simple as listening and giving support to others—renewing their sense of self and hope. It can be as demanding as raising a child well, or mentoring a student in a difficult and challenging field. ...

[G]enerativity in *high school* predicts good physical and mental health in late adulthood, a time interval of over *fifty* years."[295] Stephen Post

Many service possibilities

The Universal House of Justice provides periodic Plans that guide efforts to address current needs. Whenever possible you can choose to participate in fulfilling the goals of the current Plan. Here is guidance on this topic:

"The call to carry out and support this work is directed to every follower of Bahá'u'lláh, and it will evoke a response in every heart that aches at the wretched condition of the world, the lamentable circumstances from which so many people are unable to gain relief. For, ultimately, it is systematic, determined, and selfless action undertaken within the wide embrace of the Plan's framework that is the most constructive response of every concerned believer to the multiplying ills of a disordered society."[296] Universal House of Justice

There are regular activities you can initiate, such as "fireside" gatherings where people experience your hospitality and learn about the Teachings, or "deepenings", where people study the teachings in-depth. Community-building activities considered most urgent at this time occur at the neighborhood and community level and comprise four "core activities" open to all. Each of them requires organizers, hosts, various service roles, and participants. These are:

1. Children's Classes (approx. ages 5-10)
2. Junior Youth Spiritual Empowerment Groups (approx. ages 11-14)
3. Study Circles (age 15+; designed to build skills for service to others)
4. Devotional Gatherings (all ages)

Devotional gatherings are increasing across the planet, and hopefully you have hosted or experienced them. Remember that you can be creative with what they look like, where they occur, and who participates; the key is being consistent with them. Here is one person's experience:

"I attended a few devotional gatherings in my area, but none of them felt spiritually uplifting for me. I reached out to a few of my buddies to participate, and we went out into the forest near a stream and held a meditative devotional. Someone brought a small drum and another person

an instrument. We raised our voices to the sky and read or chanted prayers. As part of the experience, we each found a piece of wood that we carved to take home as a reminder to do daily prayer and meditation. Now we gather at the beginning of every quarter as the season changes."

The Universal House of Justice makes appeals to youth about their involvement:

"Your earnestness, your energy, your intrepid determination not to shirk the demands of this Day mark you out for this all-important undertaking. Ably trained, spiritually enkindled, and eager for experience, you have arisen to seize the initiative in your immediate surroundings and beyond. The need for you to apply yourselves to service in two capacities in particular—as teachers of children's classes and as animators of junior youth groups—has never been more apparent. Countless parents yearn for the means of developing their children's spiritual faculties that would lay within them the foundations of a principled and upright character. And surely every young person will flourish in a program that helps to form a strong moral identity in the critical years of early adolescence and empowers participants to contribute to the well-being of society. Beyond these specific fields of activity, you must not refrain from acquainting your peers with the potent, the compelling, the world-embracing mission with which you are charged. Which of them would not feel their spirits enriched for contemplating how, through the application of those far-reaching principles enunciated by Bahá'u'lláh, the regeneration of the world can be accomplished and its perplexing crises resolved? Which of them would not be raised to a new consciousness of humanity's capacity to 'carry forward an ever-advancing civilization' by combining their energies with yours and bending them towards this noble aim?"[297]

"The rapid spread of the program for the spiritual empowerment of junior youth is yet another expression of cultural advance in the Bahá'í community. While global trends project an image of this age group as problematic, lost in the throes of tumultuous physical and emotional change, unresponsive and self-consumed, the Bahá'í community—in the language it employs and the approaches it adopts—is moving decidedly in the opposite direction, seeing in junior youth instead altruism, an acute sense of justice, eagerness to learn about the universe and a desire to contribute to the construction of a better world. ... At an age when burgeoning intellectual, spiritual and physical powers become accessible to them, they are being given the tools needed to combat the forces that would rob them of their true identity as noble beings and to work for the common good."[298]

Even if you are not a youth, there are still many roles you can play in support of the core activities.

A wider view of service

Sometimes you may notice that Bahá'ís (or you!) get stuck in what the Universal House of Justice calls a "false dichotomy". It's a form of thinking that is polarized about choices rather than recognizing a coherent and integrated life has many aspects:

> "It is essential then that ever-growing numbers of those in the prime of their lives 'steel themselves for a life of service'[299] (Universal House of Justice) to society. Naturally, many matters occupy their time and energy: education, work, leisure, spiritual life, physical health. But they learn to avoid a fragmented approach to life that fails to see the connections among life's various aspects. Such a disjointed view of life often makes individuals fall victim to the false choices suggested in questions such as whether one should study or serve, advance materially or contribute to the betterment of others, pursue work or become dedicated to service. Failure to approach one's life as a coherent whole often breeds anxiety and confusion. Through service, young people can learn to foster a life in which its various aspects complement each other."[300] (Bahá'í Youth Conferences Participants' Handout)

Here are some examples of false dichotomies:

- Either I can do my schoolwork, or I can teach the Faith to someone
- Either I can go to my job, or I can tutor a study circle
- Either I can take care of grandma, or I can teach a children's class
- Either I can get the laundry done, or I can meet with youth

Below is guidance about the larger view of the Universal House of Justice's Plans.

"Individuals, communities, and institutions are called upon, within the context of a cluster, to create a program of growth involving a vibrant, meaningful, and distinctive pattern of collective Bahá'í life, infused by the spirit of the Creative Word, and open not only to the believers but to those from the wider society. At the core of this community-building process are certain activities—devotional gatherings, the educating of children and junior youth, and the raising up of those who can engage in acts of service—that serve as portals for the participation of ever-increasing numbers. The four core activities are but the nucleus of an organic pattern of life that, as the number of individuals who can initiate activities multiplies, increases in complexity over time, eventually requiring coherence among a range of efforts that also includes visits to homes, social gatherings, Feast and Holy Day observances, deepenings, administration, strengthening the Fund, social action, involvement in the discourses of society, and so on. All these activities are sustained and expanded by the constant endeavors of individuals to reach out to their personal contacts as well as to receptive populations through direct teaching, both personal and collective, and engagement in meaningful conversations."[301] On behalf of the Universal House of Justice

A narrow view of service can sometimes have you feel like you aren't participating when you actually are. If you do something to increase unity in your family, that's service. If you agree to serve on a committee, that's service. If you earn money to support your family, that's service. If you pray and read the Writings each day, that's service. Here is a broad perspective:

"... [E]very aspect of a person's life is an element of his or her service to Bahá'u'lláh: the love and respect one has for one's parents; the pursuit of one's education; the nurturing of good health; the acquiring of a trade or profession; one's behavior towards others and the upholding of a high moral standard; one's marriage and the bringing up of one's children; one's activities in teaching the Faith and the building up the strength of the Bahá'í community, whether this be in such simple matters as attending the Nineteen Day Feast or the observance of Bahá'í Holy Days, or in more demanding tasks required by service in the administration of the Faith; and, not least, to take time each day to read the Writings and say the Obligatory Prayer, which are the source of growing spiritual strength, understanding, and attachment to God. The concept of the Youth Year of Service should be viewed in this context, as a special service that the youth can devote to the Cause, and which should prove to be a highly valuable element in their own spiritual and intellectual development. It is not an alternative to, or in conflict with, the carrying out of the other vital tasks enumerated above, but rather a unique service and privilege which should be combined with them in the way that is best suited to each individual case."[302] Universal House of Justice

Here are comments from participants dedicating their time to a year of service in between high school and college:

"There are often many obstacles we might think are stopping us from offering a period of service, but are often only mental obstacles. ... The heroes of our Faith often arose in the face of what seemed to be barriers in their path. The Cause is never without a great need for more workers, and humanity will continue to be in great need of the unifying force that can free it from the sadness, confusion, and suffering which seem to increase every day."[303]

"My period of full-time service helped me develop a closer relationship with God and the Cause. I deepened my understanding of the history of the Faith and strengthened spiritual habits such as prayer, reading the Writings daily and teaching the Faith. With a greater focus and attention on developing spiritual habits and service to others, I was able to reflect and develop qualities and attitudes that will allow me to better serve humanity in my future job, family, and personal life. It also helped me gain confidence in inviting others on my path of service and in accompanying others with less experience."[304]

The Universal House of Justice provides context for being on the path of service:

"To follow a path of service, whatever form one's activity assumes, requires faith and tenacity. In this connection, the benefit of walking that path in the company of others is immense. Loving fellowship, mutual encouragement, and willingness to learn together are natural properties of any group of youth sincerely striving for the same ends, and should also characterize those essential relationships that bind together the components of society. ... You ... are aware of your part in a mighty, transforming process that will yield, in time, a global civilization reflecting the oneness of humankind. You know well that the habits of mind and spirit that you are nurturing in yourselves and others will endure, influencing decisions of consequence that relate to marriage, family, study, work, even where to live. Consciousness of this broad context helps to shatter the distorting looking glass in which everyday tests, difficulties, setbacks, and misunderstandings can seem insurmountable. And in the struggles that are common to each individual's spiritual growth, the will required to make progress is more easily summoned when one's energies are being channeled towards a higher goal—the more so when one belongs to a community that is united in that goal. ... [D]ivine assistance is promised to all those who arise to serve humankind in response to the galvanizing call of Bahá'u'lláh."[305]

Social and economic development projects led by Bahá'ís are growing exponentially each year. These address areas such as children's education, the empowerment and treatment of women, infrastructure, and medicine. Some of these become businesses or professions for the individuals involved. Some projects are sponsored by a Spiritual Assembly and local community. Yet others are guided from offices at the Bahá'í World Centre in Israel. Here is guidance:

"It is incumbent upon every man of insight and understanding to strive to translate that which hath been written into reality and action. ... That one indeed is a man who, today, dedicateth himself to the service of the entire human race. ... Blessed and happy is he that ariseth to promote the best interests of the peoples and kindreds of the earth."[306] Bahá'u'lláh

You will notice as you serve that whatever you learn to do can find an application somewhere, and the opportunities for service will grow and expand throughout your life. If you learn to serve others thoughtfully and sincerely, you will be a better husband, father, and community member.

Where do you hear the drumbeat of action you resonate with? With perseverance, attention, and action, you will find places to contribute that energize and inspire you.

Coherence—Balancing being and doing

The Bahá'í community often talks about "being" and "doing". With "being", you take care of your spiritual responsibilities and monitor and adjust your behavior based on spiritual principles. You also can relax in leisure activities as needed and do spiritual practices like prayer and meditation. With "doing", you take action that contributes to yourself, your family, and others. Balancing your "doing" with "being" contributes to you having an integrated, coherent life and making choices that align your behaviors with moral and spiritual principles:

> "Service is the magnet which draws the Divine Confirmations. Thus, when a person is active, they are blessed by the Holy Spirit. When they are inactive, the Holy Spirit cannot find a repository in their being, and thus they are deprived of its healing and quickening rays."[307] On behalf of Shoghi Effendi

> "The importance of 'doing', of arising to serve and to accompany fellow souls, must be harmonized with the notion of 'being', of increasing one's understanding of the divine teachings and mirroring forth spiritual qualities in one's life."[308] Universal House of Justice

Sometimes you may notice a pattern of fear arising in your life that paralyzes you and makes it difficult to stay in action. Consider these perspectives:

> "Courage and cowardice are antithetical. Courage is an inner resolution to go forward in spite of obstacles and frightening situations; cowardice is a submissive surrender to circumstance. Courage breeds creative self-affirmation; cowardice produces destructive self-abnegation. Courage faces fear and thereby masters it; cowardice represses fear and is thereby mastered by it. Courageous men never lose the zest for living even though their life situation is zestless; cowardly men, overwhelmed by the uncertainties of life, lose the will to live. We must constantly build dikes of courage to hold back the flood of fear."[309] Rev. Martin Luther King, Jr.

Here is one man's experience:

"I was asked by a Regional Bahá'í Council in my country to play a role in planning an event for a large group. I eagerly agreed and began to actively fulfill the responsibility they gave me. However, I made a mistake, and it resulted in a loss of funds. I felt so bad that I didn't want to keep participating. I became ill as a result and had to drop off the project. However, now I'm finding it difficult to do anything without feeling a lot of fear about the

outcome. I'm getting both medical and spiritual counseling, and they are helping me take small courageous steps back into life. I have also looked back on what I could have done differently. Everyone makes mistakes, and I could have asked God for forgiveness and then done my best continuing to work on the project. I know that once I work through this test, I will do better another time."

As you participate in marriage and family life, a key service you can do for Bahá'u'lláh, it will be wise to remember the importance of maintaining family unity and your home responsibilities in balance with community service. You may do community service on your own, with a relationship or marriage partner, or with family members, but if you sacrifice your family for service, this takes you away from the principles of the Faith. Here is some guidance on this topic:

"... [T]he unity of your family should take priority over any other consideration. Bahá'u'lláh came to bring unity to the world, and a fundamental unity is that of the family. Therefore, we must believe that the Faith is intended to strengthen the family, not weaken it. For example, service to the Cause should not produce neglect of the family. It is important for you to arrange your time so that your family life is harmonious and your household receives the attention it requires."[310] On behalf of the Universal House of Justice

"Surely Shoghi Effendi would like to see you and the other friends give their whole time and energy to the Cause, for we are in great need for competent workers, but the home is an institution that Bahá'u'lláh has come to strengthen and not to weaken. ... Serve the Cause but also remember your duties towards your home. It is for you to find the balance and see that neither makes you neglect the other."[311] On behalf of Shoghi Effendi

[See "Appendix C: Additional Guidance for Youth" for more quotations about service.]

Action

1. Participate in or start a Ruhi study circle. Work with the tutor of the study circle to include hands-on crafts like making or re-finishing furniture, fixing or cleaning a car, or repairing or building a structure. All of these could be in service to someone in need and will build life and work skills.

2. Apply your creativity through creating and performing music or dance for an activity. Consider putting the following quotation to music and sharing it with others: "O My friend, listen with heart and soul to the songs of the spirit, and treasure them as thine own eyes."[312] Bahá'u'lláh

3. Develop a cooperative game (rather than a competitive win-lose one) that you can teach children, junior youth, or youth as part of an activity. Alternatively, work with others to create a new sports activity that teaches the participants how to work together as a team.

4. Train to be a children's class teacher or junior youth animator and begin serving in this capacity, or reach out and invite someone else to participate in one of these roles.

5. Research possibilities for social action and community development projects that you want to be involved in. Make a plan to participate, which may involve funding, travel, skill-building, and more.

6. Hold a fireside, an activity where you offer hospitality and share something about the Bahá'í Faith, and/or a deepening, an activity where you study something from the Bahá'í teachings in depth. What aspects of hospitality are most important to you to demonstrate? How can you incorporate the arts in these activities?

Reflection

1. What do I see as the value of service to others?
2. What is my inner response when asked to bravely arise and serve others?
3. What choices do I make with time and energy to benefit others? What am I learning from doing these acts of service? (Examples: new skills, new attitudes, character development...) What more do I want to learn?

4. What would show that I am paying attention to my "being"? What would indicate that I'm "doing"? What is the link between them?
5. What talents and abilities do I have that I could use to serve? In what areas do I excel where I might be able to be of unique service?
6. What types of service seem like good fits for me? How can I increase my capacity for additional possibilities and opportunities?
7. What do I love about or what makes me happiest about my favorite types of service?
8. What is frustrating, challenging, or stressful for me when being involved in service activities? What could I influence or change? Who could address these concerns? What attitudes or viewpoints could I shift in a positive direction?
9. Are there service choices that are causing disunity or negative consequences in my friendships, other relationships, marriage, or family? How will I address any issues?
10. What joys and challenges have I experienced in serving on administrative bodies, committees, or task forces, whether for a Bahá'í/religious community or a non-profit or civic organization?
11. What are the service needs of my Bahá'í or other religious community? What do I see as my responsibility in meeting them?
12. What are the service needs of the neighborhood, town, city, region, or country in which I live? If I don't know, what could I do to learn more? Am I involved in meeting the needs? Why or why not? Would I like to be if I am not? What specifically could I do?
13. What social action projects designed to make a difference in others' lives are already underway near me in which I could participate? Do I want to participate in one or start one? How could I collaborate with others to learn about the needs and possibilities?
14. For what activities could I serve alongside someone else with their accompaniment so we both strengthen our capacities?

21 - Contributing to Respect, Justice, and Unity

Challenge: It's easy to look at media of all types, and what's happening around me, and think that everything going on is bad #%&!.

Opportunity: It's like taking a refreshing shower in a waterfall to see millions of people taking proactive, positive actions to increase light in the world, just like me.

Summary:
- There's a lot of muck in the world, and it takes a high level of awareness and commitment to a spiritual path to avoid stepping into it and to maintain my self-respect.
- I can act to address social issues.
- The more I bring people together and contribute to them having unified relationships, the better the world will be.
- Backbiting and gossip are highly destructive to unity.
- Saying prayers for protection and urgent aid can be vital during my activities, as can using the power of the Greatest Name as a brief prayer; once I learn to pronounce the various forms of the Greatest Name and memorize them, I have instant access to help anytime, anywhere.

More:

Resisting harm and encouraging justice

Part of maintaining self-respect and being a spiritual man includes being brave and pursuing beneficial choices. You're likely bombarded by media and influences that portray things as wonderful that in fact are not, or they are a mixed experience at best. Figuring out what's harmful through observation, reflection, and discernment isn't easy, so it's good to get input from others. As you discern and resist what can be harmful in your own life, you are better positioned to also protect and benefit others.

There are warnings about becoming mired in the muck of the current world society rather than focusing on what has permanence:

> "Throughout the world, in diverse cultures, Bahá'ís encounter values and practices that stand in sharp contrast to the teachings of the Faith. Some are embedded in social structures, for instance, racial prejudice and

gender discrimination, economic exploitation and political corruption. Others pertain to personal conduct, especially with respect to the use of alcohol and drugs, to sexual behavior, and to self-indulgence in general. If Bahá'ís simply surrender to the mores of society, how will conditions change? How will the people of the world distinguish today's moribund order from the civilization to which Bahá'u'lláh is summoning humanity? 'Humanity,' the Ridván 2012 message of the House of Justice explained, 'is weary for want of a pattern of life to which to aspire.' 'A single soul can uphold a standard far above the low threshold by which the world measures itself,' the message noted. Young Bahá'ís especially need to take care, lest they imagine they can live according to the norms of contemporary society while adhering to Bahá'í ideals at some minimum level to assuage their conscience or to satisfy the community, for they will soon find themselves consumed in a struggle to obey even the most basic of the Faith's moral teachings and powerless to take up the challenges of their generation. 'Wings that are besmirched with mire can never soar,' Bahá'u'lláh warns. The inner joy that every individual seeks, unlike a passing emotion, is not contingent on outside influences; it is a condition, born of certitude and conscious knowledge, fostered by a pure heart, which is able to distinguish between that which has permanence and that which is superficial. 'Wert thou to speed through the immensity of space and traverse the expanse of heaven,' are Bahá'u'lláh's words, 'yet thou wouldst find no rest save in submission to Our command and humbleness before Our Face.'"[313] On behalf of the Universal House of Justice

As you contribute to the well-being of society, you will notice that part of your healthy contribution will be your protective instincts toward the well-being of others. You will be concerned about the safety of those you love and often of others as well. In your behavior toward women, you will respectfully treat them as equals, and not try to dominate, control, or harm them. You will also show kindness to animals. If someone is being bullied or the target of prejudice, you will draw on power and courage as needed to advocate on their behalf or defend them. Sometimes your protective instincts toward others are also part of your everyday life in traffic, at work, or at home. There may also be other times when you are heroic and save someone from severe harm or death. Here is some guidance:

"Blessed and happy is he that ariseth to promote the best interests of the peoples and kindreds of the earth."[314] Bahá'u'lláh

"Be as a lamp unto them that walk in darkness, a joy to the sorrowful, a sea for the thirsty, a haven for the distressed, an upholder and defender of the victim of oppression."[315] Bahá'u'lláh

"O Son of Spirit! The best beloved of all things in My sight is Justice; turn not away therefrom if thou desirest Me, and neglect it not that I may confide in thee. By its aid thou shalt see with thine own eyes and not through the eyes of others, and shalt know of thine own knowledge and not through the knowledge of thy neighbor. Ponder this in thy heart; how it behooveth thee to be. Verily justice is My gift to thee and the sign of My loving-kindness. Set it then before thine eyes."[316] Bahá'u'lláh

"… [F]reedom from racial prejudice must be the watchword of Bahá'ís in the social spaces in which they are engaged for the activities of the Plan. In such intimate settings, people of diverse racial backgrounds encounter the Word of God, and in their efforts to translate the Teachings into practical action, are able to generate bonds of love, affection, and unity, and to learn what it means to establish a true interracial fellowship that is powerful enough to overcome the forces of racism that afflict them and their society. …

"The concept of the relationship of study and service clearly has relevance to the issues of promoting race unity and the growth of the Faith. The friends should study the Bahá'í writings on the subject of eliminating racial prejudice and familiarize themselves with the communications of the House of Justice on the current framework of action for growth. But study must be accompanied by action."[317] On behalf of the Universal House of Justice

Here is a man's experience of advocating for justice for others:

"I was a white man living in an Asian country and training people of various races to be English teachers there. I began to hear the parents of our students often say that they preferred white teachers. They complained when their children were taught by teachers of other races, even though these teachers were excellent and well-trained. I began to systematically speak to the parents, honoring the value of these teachers and encouraging the parents to not show favor to the white teachers or judge any teacher by the color of their skin. The tide of prejudice is very strong in many societies, but at least in our little corner of that city, many parents responded positively, and I started hearing more positive comments about teachers of other races."

Be Brave and Arise

Many issues will arise in your life, in the lives of those you care about, and in the society around you that prompt you to respond: prejudice, economic disparity, well-being of the environment, equality of all types, and many more sensitive and complex matters, none of which can be dealt with in detail here. However, when these occur in your life and around you, here are some factors to keep in mind as you consider whether to act, how strongly to respond, and in what ways:

- Carefully observe and study what is happening and why, attempting to do your best to determine what is true
- Tune into your emotional response and motivations for wanting to act
- Stay aware of the emotional responses of others; often people have painful hurts inside that are affecting their responses in the situation; your compassion will be important even while considering justice
- Act in ways that demonstrate self-respect and respect for others
- Study the Bahá'í teachings that relate to the topic
- Study the current guidance from the Universal House of Justice
- Identify the spiritual principles that apply to the situation
- Pray and meditate for solutions
- Consult with others, including Bahá'í institutions
- Protect the reputation of the Bahá'í Faith, which will include following the extensive guidance on the topic of non-involvement in politics
- Assess your responsibilities, choose your "battles"; assess what to detach from, when to be directly involved, and when to involve others

A man provides his viewpoint:

"To me, my purpose is to educate humanity as best as I can according to my capacity at any given time. I also think there is always room to consider how the virtues of magnanimity, mercy, and compassion can be combined with vigorous pursuit of justice. Sometimes an ignorant or prejudiced person can be open and receptive to learn and can even be transformed by the Word of God regarding the oneness of humanity. Just because someone is ignorant and prejudiced doesn't mean that all bridges have to be burned. If that were the case, humanity will never progress.

"Either way, it's very good to stand up for what is just, fair, right, and against prejudice and ignorance. At the same time, since no one is perfect, we all have the responsibility to reflect on our actions and always consider how and where we can grow or enhance our behavior in the future. If we

always think we do everything just right and perfect, we will stay the way we are and never progress. Last I checked, all humans have imperfections and need to grow closer and closer to God, so staying the same isn't a good option. I believe it's best to question our own actions under any circumstance of moral behavior and weigh them against the Bahá'í teachings. This is vital for me to mature. Some of our best tools for growth are prayer, reflection, and looking at our own actions in light of specific passages from the Writings."

When you do choose to strive for justice as appropriate, this can include turning to appropriate civil or religious institutions and authorities. There may be times when you need to have a voice that aids people in becoming more conscious. A man relates this experience:

"I accidentally made a wrong turn in traffic. A police officer signaled for me to pull over. He crouched behind his car door, pointed his gun in my direction, and loudly yelled at me. I was very scared, but I did my best to stay calm and polite. So did my friends in the car with me. The region I was in has a dark history of racial prejudice and oppression, and it also has a bright history of racial unity and oneness. The light and the dark live right next to each other.

"I turned to the Local Spiritual Assembly, and it asked my permission to follow up with the police department. They were concerned because the incident was unjust and seemed racially motivated. It was good they took this action, as it opened a door for some positive influence of the Faith's institution on the police institution of society."

Defending the Covenant and unity

Remember the content about the Covenant and unity in Chapter 4? A key active role for you in the Bahá'í community is that of promoting and guarding its unity. The Universal House of Justice asks Bahá'ís to be conscious of the "exceptional and glorious stage in humanity's spiritual evolution initiated by the Covenant" and speaks of this consciousness as being "the wellspring of the most exquisite celebratory joy."[318] Universal House of Justice

The challenge to you is to be very aware of when you need to tune up your disunity sensor and stand up for unity. When you see anything happening that will cause division and disharmony between people, you can go into protective mode. Something needs to change course and steps taken to create unity in a situation instead. This can often include turning to a Spiritual Assembly. You can also pay attention to where you can adjust your own behavior or influence that of others. Here is encouragement:

> "In the Impregnable Stronghold be ye brave warriors…. Exercise the utmost care, and day and night be on your guard, that thereby the tyrant may inflict no harm."[319] 'Abdu'l-Bahá

What are some behaviors that cause disunity?

- Backbiting (talking destructively behind other's backs and diminishing them in other's eyes) and gossip (spreading a mix of true and false information)
- Criticizing faults and speaking with cutting sarcasm
- Rudeness
- Manipulation, predatory actions, or bullying
- Ridicule
- Lies

What are some behaviors that create unity?

- Respectful listening
- Speaking only truthfully and kindly to and about others
- Including courtesy along with words and actions
- Consulting with others for wisdom before acting
- Collaborate equally and respectfully when compassionately responding to the needs of others to ensure they agree, are fully heard, and involved in the solutions
- Sincerely encouraging and praising others
- Considering before speaking or taking action how words and actions might make someone feel
- Offering humor that is kind, inclusive, and uplifting
- Engaging those who may feel they are not fully included

Breaking backbiting and gossip habits

As you share information with others, including on social media, consider some protective boundaries to assist you in being respectful. Backbiting, gossiping, or slandering other people are all indicators of character weaknesses. These are common behaviors as people bully, form cliques, or align themselves against others. There is a need for them to strengthen qualities such as respect, acceptance, compassion, friendliness, justice, kindness, truthfulness, and unity.

Here are some definitions to increase your understanding of these destructive behaviors:

- *Backbiting* refers to speaking in a negative, spiteful, derogatory, or defamatory way about a person who is not present. Even when the words are true, the intent and effect are destructive, creating disunity, whether or not the person spoken of finds out what you said.
- *Gossip* involves spreading personal or sensational information that may or may not have some basis in truth, but which is often inaccurate or incomplete. The intent and outcome are often harmful. When you know something interesting about another person, it can be very tempting to share it with others to draw attention to yourself and feel important.
- *Slander*, also known as *calumny*, occurs when you spread clearly false information. This action can damage trust and reputations very severely, and it can cause irreparable harm to relationships between people. It can also result in legal action.

Backbiting and gossip are often key players in destroying reputations and dumping on people's characters. They disunify relationships. You may be tempted to speak in these ways out of a desire to be right about something, or your ego says you can look important in the moment. When you are tempted to justify doing them, ask yourself:

- Is it right?
- Is it wise?
- Would it help or harm your relationship with others?
- Can you think of positives to say about someone instead?
- What would 'Abdu'l-Bahá do?

Backbiting and gossip can happen when you discuss private details about someone or something with friends, family members, neighbors, or coworkers. Whatever private information you know should be considered confidential. You may also be tempted to communicate a complaint about others to someone else to earn sympathy, instead of speaking directly to someone who can do something about the issue. Talking negatively about other's behavior or character even in a casual way is backbiting. If the people you speak to then spread what you said to others, it becomes gossip. The information often becomes distorted and embellished, which may cause harm or embarrassment to you and others. Backbiting negatively affects both the speaker and the listener, as well as the person who is talked about. It's also very important to avoid unreasonably prejudicing others, such as family members, against people in your life that they may encounter.

Bahá'u'lláh says that:

"... [T]he tongue is a smoldering fire, and excess of speech a deadly poison. Material fire consumeth the body, whereas the fire of the tongue devoureth both heart and soul. The force of the former lasteth but for a time, whilst the effects of the latter endureth a century. ...[R]egard backbiting as grievous error, and keep...aloof from its dominion, inasmuch as backbiting quencheth the light of the heart, and extinguisheth the life of the soul."[320] Bahá'u'lláh

To help you think about the implications of backbiting, consider the following quotation and a man's reflection about it below: "Ye have been forbidden to commit murder or adultery, or to engage in backbiting or calumny...."[321] Bahá'u'lláh

"I do not believe anything in the Writings is accidental, and that every word is exactly what it needs to be. So why is backbiting put into the very same paragraph as murder and adultery? And what, exactly, is calumny? ... First, I think that if I were to write a list such as this, I would make it a crescendo, going from the least bad to the worst. It makes a dramatic sort of sense to me. But here, [Bahá'u'lláh] seems to have put it in a reverse order. Or has He?

"Murder, I realized upon meditation of this verse, is the killing of an individual. Adultery is the murder of a family. Despite what we may think with our 'modern values', doesn't that make adultery worse than murder? So what about backbiting? ... Backbiting, from what I have seen, kills the bonds of trust within a community. It is a form of murder on one of the grandest scales.

"And calumny? Well, backbiting is when you say things that are actually true. They may be hurtful, nasty, cruel and so on, but they are true. Calumny is when it is a deliberate lie. It has all the evil effects of backbiting, plus it's a deliberate lie...."[322]

'Abdu'l-Bahá provides this strategy:

"If any soul speak ill of an absent one, the only result will clearly be this: he will dampen the zeal of the friends and tend to make them indifferent. For backbiting is divisive, it is the leading cause among the friends of a disposition to withdraw. If any individual should speak ill of one who is absent, it is incumbent on his hearers, in a spiritual and friendly manner, to stop him, and say in effect: would this detraction serve any useful purpose? Would it please the Blessed Beauty [Bahá'u'lláh], contribute to the lasting honor of the friends, promote the holy Faith, support the Covenant, or be of any possible benefit to any soul? No, never! On the contrary, it would make the dust to settle so thickly on the heart that the ears would hear no more, and the eyes would no longer behold the light of truth."[323] 'Abdu'l-Bahá

Sometimes Bahá'ís don't turn to others because they assume consulting with them about an issue is backbiting. Here is some clarifying guidance:

"You ask in your letter for guidance on the implications of the prohibitions on backbiting and more specifically whether, in moments of anger or depression, the believer is permitted to turn to his friends to unburden his soul and discuss his problem in human relations. Normally, it is possible to describe the situation surrounding a problem and seek help and advice in resolving it, without necessarily mentioning names. The individual believer should seek to do this, whether he is consulting a friend, Bahá'í or non-Bahá'í, or whether the friend is consulting him.

"'Abdu'l-Bahá does not permit adverse criticism of individuals by name in discussion among the friends, even if the one criticizing believes that he is doing so to protect the interests of the Cause. If the situation is of such gravity as to endanger the interests of the Faith, the complaint, as your National Spiritual Assembly has indicated, should be submitted to the Local Spiritual Assembly, or as you state to a representative of the institution of the Counsellors, for consideration and action. In such cases, of course, the name of the person or persons involved will have to be mentioned."[324] On behalf of the Universal House of Justice

"There is a clear distinction between, on the one hand, the prohibition of backbiting, which would include adverse comments about individuals or institutions made to other individuals privately or publicly, and, on the other hand, the encouragement to unburden oneself of one's concerns to a Spiritual Assembly, local or National (or now, also, to confide in a Counsellor or Auxiliary Board member)."[325] Universal House of Justice

Asking Bahá'u'lláh and God to protect me—and others

One of the strongest advocacy and protection tools you can adopt for regular use in your life, especially in difficult circumstances and when you need to be brave and take action to improve something, is the name of Bahá'u'lláh in the Arabic form known as "God's Greatest Name". Here is a description of it:

> "By its use the doors of the Kingdom of God open, illumination is vouchsafed and divine union results. ... The use of the Greatest Name, and dependence on it, causes the soul to strip itself of the husks of mortality and to step forth freed, reborn, a new creature.
> "... The Greatest Name should be found upon the lips in the first awakening moment of early dawn. It should be fed upon by constant use in daily invocation, in trouble, under opposition, and should be the last word breathed when the head rests upon the pillow at night. It is the name of comfort, protection, happiness, illumination, love and unity."[326] 'Abdu'l-Bahá

This same article mentions the potential use of 'Yá Alláh'u'l-Mustagath, O Thou from Whom help is sought most urgently. Here are some additional forms of the Greatest Name that you may find useful to memorize and use as prayers for valuable spiritual entreaty and protective armor:

- Alláh-u-Abhá (God the All-Glorious)
- Yá Bahá'u'l-Abhá (O Thou Glory of the All-Glorious)
- Yá 'Alliyyu'l-A'lá (O Thou the Exalted of the Most Exalted One)[327] Abu'l-Qásim Faizí

Below are other prayers for protection that you may find useful to say and memorize.

> "God sufficeth unto me; He is the One Who holdeth in His grasp the kingdom of all things. Through the power of His hosts of heaven and earth and whatever lieth between them, He protecteth whomsoever among His servants He willeth. God, in truth, keepeth watch over all things.

"Immeasurably exalted art Thou, O Lord! Protect us from what lieth in front of us and behind us, above our heads, on our right, on our left, below our feet and every other side to which we are exposed. Verily, Thy protection over all things is unfailing."[328] The Báb

"I adjure Thee by Thy might, O my God! Let no harm beset me in times of tests, and in moments of heedlessness guide my steps aright through Thine inspiration. Thou art God, potent art Thou to do what Thou desirest. No one can withstand Thy Will or thwart Thy Purpose."[329] The Báb

"God sufficeth all things above all things, and nothing in the heavens or in the earth or in whatever lieth between them but God, thy Lord, sufficeth. Verily, He is in Himself the Knower, the Sustainer, the Omnipotent."[330] The Báb

"O Thou divine Providence, preserve and protect us! O Thou Who art our Shield, save us and defend us! Keep us beneath Thy Shelter, and by Thy Help save us from all ills. Thou art, indeed, the True Protector, the Unseen Guardian, the Celestial Preserver, and the Heavenly Loving Lord."[331] 'Abdu'l-Bahá

Action

1. Identify two actions that you can take with the goal of sincerely increasing unity between you and another person. Reflect on the outcome and plan another action.

2. Identify a social issue that regularly affects your life and begin to educate yourself about it. For example, litter and pollution in your city, children in your neighborhood not having books to read, hunger in your community, or homelessness. If, for example, the issue troubling you is prejudice and racism, and you are wondering about your role in reducing them, you might make a reading list of relevant books such as these listed below and begin your learning process. Perhaps you know of other people to study along with you. Ensure you also study any recent guidance from the Universal House of Justice and your National Spiritual Assembly on this or any other topic you are focused on learning about.

- Promulgation of Universal Peace by 'Abdu'l-Bahá
- Advent of Divine Justice by Shoghi Effendi
- *Power of Unity: Overcoming Racial Divisions, Rebuilding America*, a compilation from the Bahá'í Writings on the unity and the equality of all people
- Lights of the Spirit: Historical Portraits of Black Bahá'ís in North America, 1898-2000, by Gwendolyn Etter-Lewis and Richard W. Thomas
- So You Want to Talk About Race by Ijeoma Oluo
- Stamped from the Beginning by Ibrahim Kendi
- Invention of the White Race, by Theodore W. Allen
- "Race—the Power of an Illusion", provides a global overview: https://www.pbs.org/race/000_About/002_04-background-02-01.htm

3. After going through a learning process, create an opportunity to collaborate with like-minded people or organizations on the topic that you chose, being wise about what activities and approaches align with the Bahá'í teachings.

2. Create an opportunity for a diverse group of people to create a diversity of music with the goal of identifying what music prompts the greatest experience of unity.

3. Memorize the various forms of the Greatest Name. Memorize one of the above prayers for protection.

4. For a few days, consciously avoid being involved as a speaker or listener in backbiting or gossip. This means no negative comments about a teacher or coworker, no passing along information about someone, and no passive listening to backbiting. If you are stuck in a position with a group involved in these activities, you can attempt to change the course of the discussion by raising something positive about the person or a new topic. What are your observations about what happened?

5. Carry out this activity below about backbiting and gossip with a group of pre-teens or youth younger than you. Alternatively, use it during a study

circle on "Reflections of the Life of the Spirit", Ruhi Book 1, Unit 1, for the section about backbiting (https://ruhi.org/).

Materials needed:

- Two clear glass bowls of water
- 1-2 cups of loose dirt in a container
- Attractive natural objects, such as small nuts or pinecones, interesting small rocks, leaves, flower petals, small shells…
- 1 spoon per participant

Instructions:

a. Read this quotation: "… [B]ackbiting quencheth the light of the heart, and extinguisheth the life of the soul." (Bahá'u'lláh, *Gleanings from the Writings of Bahá'u'lláh*, #CXXV, pp. 264-265)

b. Place the bowl of water in the middle of a table and have participants sit around the table (or on the ground or a rug)

c. Give each person a spoon.

d. Pass the container of dirt around to each person and have them each scatter a spoonful of dirt on the top of the water—without stirring. Talk about what happens in people's lives when backbiting (the dirt) occurs about other people and how the water looks with the dirt in it. Reflect on how difficult it would be to take back what was said (clean out the dirt from the water).

e. Ask one person to stir the water. Talk as a group about the damage that gossip (dirty water)—often the spread of information passed through backbiting—can be.

f. Put a second bowl of clean water next to the dirty one. (If you don't have a second bowl, dump out the dirty water and clean the bowl. Refill it with clean water.)

g. Read this quotation: "We can never exert the influence over others which we can exert over ourselves. If we are better, if we show love, patience, and understanding of the weaknesses of others; if we seek to never criticize but rather encourage, others will do likewise...." (Shoghi Effendi, *Lights of Guidance*, #291)

h. Have each participant select a few pieces of the attractive natural objects. Ask them to visualize that these pieces are the good qualities in each other that we can talk about freely. Have them each scatter a few pieces on the surface of the clean water.

i. Ask someone to use a clean spoon to stir up the "good qualities" in the water with "love and encouragement". Discuss whether the water is harmed. How does the water look to them? Talk about how this bowl looks in contrast to the one with the dirty water. What is their response to each bowl?

j. Ask each participant to identify someone to encourage or praise in the coming week. Discuss together the specific words or actions each could use.

Reflection

1. What words or behaviors of mine tend to build unity? What can I increase?
2. What words or behaviors of mine cause disunity at times? What will I strive to improve?
3. How can I be protective of unity in my use of social media? How can I prevent disunity from happening on social media? When is it wiser for me to have a live or in-person conversation with someone?
4. When have I seen people genuinely demonstrating unity and harmony in their interactions?
5. What ways can I contribute to unity among my friends? In a relationship or marriage? In my family? In my community?
6. When I act in an aggressive, predatory, or overly competitive way, what is the effect on unity? How could I re-direct my energy?

7. How can I control disunifying impatience or anger with others or circumstances? What new approaches could I try?
8. When I take action to improve a social condition in my area, how can I demonstrate respect for the people I am interested in serving? How can I be sure my aim is to empower others, and to not be paternalistic?
9. What ways could I contribute to a larger social issue? What teachings or principles are vital for me to include? When can Bahá'í institutions assist with solutions and resources?
10. How does taking action to improve life for others affect my self-respect?
11. What character qualities and approaches enhance my collaborations with others when there are social action projects to carry out?
12. What is my experience of backbiting and spreading gossip about others? What has been the outcome? How can I stop this behavior? What has been my experience of others backbiting about me? How can I respond when something like this happens again?
13. What seems to be the outcome when I share positive words about what someone is doing or offer encouragement to them when they are struggling with a task or project? How do I respond when someone encourages me?
14. When have I turned to prayers for protection? What am I dealing with now where using the Greatest Name or other prayers would be beneficial?

Part 6: Thriving with Others on My Journey

22 - Building Relationships with My Parents and Family

Challenge: It's very difficult at times to see examples of well-functioning and happy families, and sometimes I notice what looks like a good family is messed up underneath the surface.

Opportunity: I can be grateful when there are good things happening in my family, build unity when I can, and take constructive steps to deal with or heal from the bad, so I don't carry on negative patterns to the next generation.

Summary:
- Families are a mix of different people and relationships of varying degrees of closeness, functionality, and unity.
- I can love and appreciate the positive qualities of my family members.
- Qualities such as respect, courtesy, and love can bring my family closer.
- If being with my family feels more traumatic than a unified gathering, I can determine what spiritual principles to apply to protect my well-being.
- I can often influence family members toward unity (when it's safe and healthy).
- I can reach out for help if my family's functioning has negatively affected me.

More:

State of families in the world today

Families are in a wide array of states these days. Some are happy, unified, and involved in community service. Where there is a well-functioning marriage and a stable home life with parents who taught you to make good moral choices, you have a blessing that can benefit you throughout life. The Bahá'í teachings urge families to strive for true well-being and unity:

"Note ye how easily, where unity existeth in a given family, the affairs of that family are conducted; what progress the members of that family make, how they prosper in the world. Their concerns are in order, they enjoy comfort and tranquility, they are secure, their position is assured, they come to be envied by all. Such a family but addeth to its stature and its lasting honor, as day succeedeth day."[332] 'Abdu'l-Bahá

"… [I]f the friends are not able to maintain harmony within their families, on what other basis do they hope to demonstrate to a skeptical world the efficacy of the pre-eminent character of the Revelation of Bahá'u'lláh? What possible influence could they hope to exert on the development of nations and the establishment of world peace?"[333] On behalf of the Universal House of Justice

Many families are troubled rather than unified, and you may find it difficult to live with or be around your parent(s) and sibling(s). Perhaps your family behaves in public like everything is fine, but in private they behave very differently, and you feel like you are living a secret life. You may be or have been experiencing some degree of absentee, neglectful, mentally ill, arguing, abusive, violent, or divorced parents. You may have one functional parent and one not. Maybe you have a good stepparent, or maybe not, and you avoid your parents or stepparents. Maybe your grandparents are treated with love and respect, or maybe they are neglected or dismissed as irrelevant. Here are some men's difficult experiences:

"My parents have stayed together in a relatively good marriage. I can see that this stability has made it easier for me to succeed at school and be more focused on serving as a junior youth animator. However, I've seen many friends get so messed up with their families that they choose to smoke weed, drink, and generally get into trouble. I'm grateful for my own life but troubled about theirs. With working with junior youth, I hope I can be a good role model where they don't have a father to look up to."

"Some days my parents feel so screwed up. All they do is argue or give each other the silent treatment. I've got my learning permit to drive, if an adult driver is with me. One day though I was so fed up with the mess in my house, and so pissed off at never feeling good there, I just grabbed the keys and took off in the car. Three blocks away I ran a stop sign and hit another car. Thank God neither of us was hurt badly. It shook me up though. I need to find better ways to deal with my anger at them."

"My dad didn't have a good example from his father, who was a violent alcoholic. In my early years, he struggled at times with disciplining me too

harshly. However, he never gave up on me or himself. He has had some good mentors, and he has done his best to consistently teach me to make good choices. Now that I'm in my thirties, he and I are close, and he regularly prays and consults with me about my life and work. He's become a really good example of character for me, and I've seen him gradually learn how to have a good marriage and family."

"I left home two decades ago, but I still wake up at night from nightmares. I can hear the yelling and hitting between my father and his latest girlfriend. Some nights she snuck into my bedroom looking for me to treat her better, but it screwed with how I view sex, and pornography at times in my life is now an issue. I've finally begun to see a counselor and thank God it's beginning to help. On my good days I yearn to have a wife and family, but I'm not there yet."

Where a dysfunctional family has been your experience, you will likely find it more difficult to find your way. If your situation is or has been difficult, you may notice how it affects your own moods and behavior. When parents (or siblings) get angry or criticize, no matter how old you are, maybe your head feels like it's going to explode with anger too. It's wise to find constructive ways to reduce your anger and stress level, such as a physical activity or a creative outlet.

[There is more about your relationship with your father in Chapter 4.]

Working through family experiences

You can identify benefits of being part of your family of origin and feel thankful. When you recall special memories, you might remember your family sharing fun activities, a parent comforting you after a disappointment, or a grandparent sharing timeless wisdom. Perhaps your parents have financially assisted with your education. Maybe they are wonderful grandparents to children in the family.

As you reflect, you will discover that you gained both positive and negative learning from your family. Even where there are many negatives, you may now see how you grew or are growing from the difficulties. When you consider your parents, it's wise to recognize that without them, you would not exist.

Each generation learns from the one before, and each one can improve on what happened in the past. Courage and perseverance are needed to move toward healing, to experience gratitude for blessings, and to take thoughtful action to greatly enhance your present and future happiness.

You may have already addressed and resolved mental or emotional issues that resulted from childhood experiences. However, there may still be lingering ones, from which you can still heal, learn, and grow. For example, many adults are affected by their parents' poor relationship and subsequent divorces. If your parents divorced, you may have had to learn that their choice to split up was their decision alone. It was not your fault, and it does not mean there's anything wrong with you. You do not have to follow their path. You may have also experienced violence or abuse as a child, and words or actions in a relationship or marriage partner can remind you of early trauma and trigger a stress or anxiety reaction in the present.

As you resolve and heal, you are less likely to repeat harmful childhood patterns with a partner or your children. You may also more readily recognize where you missed observing healthy parental interactions, and you may choose to observe and get to know other couples for more positive modeling.

Unresolved emotions and harmful thinking patterns tend to re-surface over time, potentially causing negative interactions between you and others. There are, of course, many ways to heal. Effective healing and personal growth depend on your inner strength, circumstances, available resources, and inclination to seek assistance.

The healing actions listed below have assisted many people. You can assess whether each one related to family is wise for you to do or not:

- Pray for the healing of pain or challenges you have from experiences with your family
- Pray for unity with them
- Show love to them through your actions, while keeping yourself healthy
- Appreciate the emotional, material, and spiritual gifts you have received from them, and express your gratitude to them
- Initiate positive communication with them, where this is wise and safe, and seek to understand them
- Stop all negative forms of communication with them
- Spend time with them, if this is likely to contribute to healing
- If interactions with them are very unhealthy, it may be necessary to spend time apart from them

- Pray for forgiveness for them for any of their behaviors that disrupted your life; pray for forgiveness for yourself, if you acted harmfully in situations
- In particularly painful situations, search your heart for reasons to be grateful for the learning and growth that resulted from the experiences, particularly if you see where your learning has benefited others
- Seek professional help where needed
- Write a letter to them; after reflection and if written with wholehearted effort toward increasing unity, prayerfully read it aloud to them and discuss it, or send it to them—if these actions would be fruitful; alternatively, write it and then tear it up or burn it, to visualize the resolution of this issue and provide a sense of closure

Even if your family members are no longer alive, or you are unable to contact them, you may still benefit from trying some of the reflections and activities above.

Many self-help books, websites, videos, and articles can inform and assist you. Expert relationship professionals also offer a safe, confidential place to express and better understand your thoughts and feelings. Their training, objective perspectives, and professional experience with others in similar situations can be highly valuable. Ensure that any professional you rely on is familiar with your beliefs and principles—be they of the Bahá'í Faith or another path—so they don't advise something contrary to your beliefs.

In addition, you may wish to consult Bahá'í institutions, or others familiar with your faith and beliefs. Religious communities and representatives may keep a list of trustworthy, experienced, and competent counselors, or they may offer spiritual counseling themselves.

Spiritual principles to strive for

When you are living with or in close contact with family members, it becomes easy to see each other's faults and failings. Focusing on these can become more dominant than seeing each other's good qualities. You can shift this pattern when you distinguish between a complaint and a criticism and see thankfulness as a balancing quality:

"You will always have some complaints about the person you live with. But there's a world of difference between complaint and criticism. A complaint focuses on a specific behavior or event. ... In contrast, a criticism is global and expresses negative feelings or opinions about the other's character or personality…. Statements that contain complaints are soft start-ups, while those that criticize are harsh start-ups."[334] John Gottman and Nan Silver

"Without thankfulness people would stay focused on negativity. They would do nothing but whine and complain. They would miss the beauty of life and the power of learning, especially during difficult times. … No matter how difficult or dark things become, there is always light. There is something to learn in every painful situation. In fact, sometimes when you look back at a really hard test in your life and realize what you learned, that is when you feel the most grateful of all."[335] L. Kavelin Popov

The Bahá'í teachings talk about the importance of demonstrating positive character qualities toward parents and about the mutual relationship between you:

"Say, O My people! Show honor to your parents and pay homage* to them. This will cause blessings to descend upon you from the clouds of the bounty of your Lord, the Exalted, the Great."[336] Bahá'u'lláh *the definition of homage includes respect and honor

"If thou wouldst show kindness and consideration to thy parents so that they may feel generally pleased, this would also please Me, for parents must be highly respected and it is essential that they feel contented, provided they deter thee not from gaining access to the Threshold of the Almighty, nor keep thee back from walking in the way of the Kingdom. Indeed it behoveth them to encourage and spur thee on in this direction."[337] 'Abdu'l-Bahá

"There should be a spirit of mutual respect and consideration between parents and children, in which the children turn to their parents for advice and direction, and the parents train and nurture their offspring. The fruit of this relationship is that the children grow into adulthood with their powers of discrimination and judgement refined, so that they can steer the course of their lives in a manner most conducive to their welfare.

"Within the framework of this mutual respect, the parents are called upon to show wisdom and discretion when their offspring are developing friendships which might ultimately lead to marriage. They should consider carefully the circumstances under which advice should be given, and conditions under which their intervention would be construed as interference.

"For their part, the offspring should recognize that their parents are deeply interested in their welfare, and that the views of the parents warrant respect and careful consideration."[338]   On behalf of the Universal House of Justice

If your situation with your parents is very difficult, distinguish between respect for them in their role and because they gave birth to you, even if you cannot respect their behavior, choices, or character. There are also times when a parent so crosses a boundary that they may forfeit the right to respect or even lose their parental rights. Consider this guidance:

"Ye have been forbidden in the Book of God to engage in contention and conflict, to strike another, or to commit similar acts whereby hearts and souls may be saddened."[339]   Bahá'u'lláh

"Bahá'u'lláh has placed great emphasis on the duties of parents toward their children, and He has urged children to have gratitude in their hearts for their parents, whose good pleasure they should strive to win as a means of pleasing God Himself. However, He has indicated that under certain circumstances, the parents could be deprived of the right of parenthood as a consequence of their actions. The Universal House of Justice has the right to legislate on this matter. It has decided for the present that all cases should be referred to it in which the conduct or character of a parent appears to render him unworthy of having such parental rights as that of giving consent to marriage. Such questions could arise, for example, when a parent has committed incest, or when the child was conceived as a consequence of rape, and also when a parent consciously fails to protect the child from flagrant sexual abuse."[340]   On behalf of the Universal House of Justice

Steps, halfs, adoptees, and more

You may ask yourself at times, "Who counts as my family?" For example, in stepfamilies, according to M. Scarf, author of *Remarriage Blueprint*, the "insider/outsider" forces are powerful. They often challenge the ideal of family unity and the ability of second marriages to be healthy and stay intact.

People hold loyalties to previous family members, and new members added in can cause polarized positions. Families have cultures and mixing these up into new arrangements can at times cause emotional disruptions, pain, and disunity. Matters like disciplining children, roles and responsibilities, inheritances, money management, and more can be quite complicated in blended families.

Respect, no matter how people are connected to you, is important. So are courtesy and love. Here is some guidance on these qualities:

> "O people of God! I admonish you to observe courtesy, for above all else it is the prince of virtues. Well is it with him who is illumined with the light of courtesy and is attired with the vesture of uprightness. Whoso is endued with courtesy hath indeed attained a sublime station."[341] Bahá'u'lláh

> "When you love a member of your family..., let it be with a ray of the Infinite Love! Let it be in God, and for God! Wherever you find the attributes of God love that person...."[342] 'Abdu'l-Bahá

As you observe your behavior with family members and try to apply respect, courtesy, and love, you can consider such behaviors as:

- Greeting one another rather than ignoring each other
- Respecting personal space with rooms and possessions
- Having visits and meals with each other
- Reaching out consistently with positive communications
- Praying together
- Sharing activities
- Telling stories about positive experiences
- Offering thoughtful service
- Acknowledging and celebrating positive progress
- Having a loving attitude

Influencing family improvement

Your influence on family dynamics will likely depend on your age or circumstances. In a relatively well-functioning family, one of your primary ways to have a voice is to initiate consultation with your parents, siblings, or the whole family. In a family meeting, members can focus on an issue, share thoughts and feelings, and come to a unified agreement for how to constructively move forward. Here is a quotation:

> "Bahá'u'lláh also stressed the importance of consultation. We should not think this worthwhile method of seeking solutions is confined to the administrative institutions of the Cause. Family consultation employing full and frank discussion, and animated by awareness of the need for moderation and balance, can be the panacea for domestic conflict...."[343]
> Universal House of Justice

When parents or other family members are fighting, your urging them to calm down and consult may be difficult, but you may have some influence over them (ensure your safety in the process). Praying for them and their relationship is another way you can help them. Urging them to reach out to a Spiritual Assembly and a professional counselor is another. Your religious community, professionals, and support groups are also resources for you.

For men who have or had abusive parents, you have a choice of going through life viewing yourself as a "victim" and staying focused on what is or was unhealthy or traumatic. You can take your inner storm, succumb to the dark side, and react with anger, depression, fear, and many other natural, human, and understandable emotions. However, you may get stuck there. This can lead to you trying to block out negative thoughts and memories by getting involved with drugs, pornography, alcohol, or other ultimately destructive behaviors. You might also try swearing, lashing out physically, and acting destructively toward others.

It's quite likely you will go through a period of these types of negative reactions, and compassion toward yourself and from others is a natural response to such pain. However, can you often, instead, choose other ways of responding to difficult situations that are more likely to preserve your self-respect and moral integrity? Reflect on your history or situation. Consider which of the following questions might apply to your situation:

- Can you be optimistic about finding help and take positive actions that facilitate your healing and good functioning?
- Can you contribute to your family by praying for unity, saying prayers for healing, and encouraging members toward help and unity?
- If it's wiser or safer for you to be out of the house or out of contact with your family, what arrangements can you make? If you are still living at home, could you live with another family for a while with your parents' permission?

- Can you channel your energy in a more positive direction, such as toward achieving excellent grades, community service, or professional accomplishments?
- When you are tempted to talk back or speak angrily to a parent or other adult, how could you show self-discipline and respect for them and yourself instead?
- Can you channel hormones, excess energy, and rumbling emotions into a sport or martial art?
- If you pray and meditate regularly, does your energy get a positive boost?
- Are there other adults in your life or the Bahá'í community who can be role models that guide you in positive directions?
- Is there a counselor or other professional you can talk to about how you are doing and initiate healing actions with their help?

There are no guarantees in life about families or everyone's spiritual choices. Some people start out life as involved Bahá'ís but later change course. Some people make a mess of their lives and turn to the Faith as part of what sets their lives back on track. Your responsibility is to be vigilant on behalf of your own spiritual well-being, with assistance from others as needed. You are responsible for your own behavior to God. You cannot make excuses for your current and future choices based on how family members or anyone else behaves. The same applies to situations where a parent is not setting or did not set behavior guidelines or limits for you. You can, however, be merciful, gentle, and compassionate to yourself as you look at your situation and strive to improve it.

When you are still living at home, some parents tend toward permissiveness and others more toward setting boundaries and limits. You may need or want more or less of one or the other. You can request a shift from your parents, to which they will likely respond with yes, no, or maybe if your behavior is a certain way. Once you are over 15 years old, you have a great deal of responsibility for yourself:

> "As important as it is for parents to exercise their moral authority in assisting the youth not to make unwise decisions, it is also incumbent on the parents as Bahá'ís to give due consideration to the significance of the spiritual impact of the Faith upon the youth and recognize that the youth must have some latitude to respond to the stirring of their hearts and souls, since they, beginning at the age of 15, must assume serious

spiritual obligations and duties and are themselves alone ultimately responsible to God for the progress of their own souls. The capacity for mature thinking on the part of youth differs from one to the other and according to age; some attain this ability earlier than others; for some it is delayed. Parents are generally in a position to judge these matters more accurately than others and must consider them in their attempt to guide the youth in their families, but the parents must strive to do so in such a way as not to stifle their children's sense of spiritual responsibility."[344] Universal House of Justice

Unity is a concept everyone is trying to understand. True unity includes respect, justice, equality, and the ability to focus on each other's positive qualities, so it's not an easy entity to ensure is present. You may try to foster unity in your family, which is a positive act; however, some members may struggle with the idea. Here is some advice with key spiritual principles you may be able to use in your situation:

"Regarding...the strained relationship between you and your mother-in-law and what you can do to alleviate the situation, we feel you should, with the help and consultation of your husband, persevere in your efforts to achieve unity in the family. From your description of the unfriendly attitude your mother-in-law displays toward you, it is clear that you will not have an easy task. However, the important thing is that you, as a Bahá'í, are aware of 'Abdu'l-Bahá's admonition to concentrate on an individual's good qualities and that this approach to your mother-in-law can strengthen you in your resolve to achieve unity. And furthermore, perseverance in prayer will give you the strength to continue your efforts."[345] On behalf of the Universal House of Justice

Sometimes in very difficult circumstances, it's only possible to contribute to family unity when there is no contact and you simply pray for each other. If it feels impossible at times to pray for difficult family members, you can also ask someone else to pray on your behalf.

Unity in the family is very much linked to the broader unity of the family of humanity. As you look for opportunities to interact in harmony within your family—whatever its strengths, construction, or issues—you can use consultation skills and learn what it takes to stay united. This will contribute to your ability to build unity with others.

Action

1. Reflect about your family, doing your best to clearly see their best efforts and their struggles. Write a list of your grievances about your family and take steps to heal or resolve them, which might include simply destroying the list in some way. Write a list of what you appreciate and respect about each of your parents, siblings, and other close family members. If applicable, also write a list of what you appreciate, or appreciated in the past, about the relationship between your parents.

2. Describe what qualities are important for you to have in an adult mentor, and consider having one, no matter how old you are. It could be a family member, or you might consider a former teacher, a trustworthy neighbor, a sports coach, a manager at work, a youth group leader, or someone else you believe has a level of integrity and wisdom that could be beneficial. Approach someone you think would be a good fit, staying aware that they may have to decline for personal reasons. If they decline because they don't feel worthy to be in this role, you may need to encourage them, or you may simply need to accept their response and go on to the next person on your list. Generally, a mentor interacts with you as a volunteer. Depending on your circumstances, stay aware that at times you may also choose to pay for professional services that can guide your direction, such as a personal coach, career guide, or counselor.

3. Create a video of your family or a collection of photos that represent a mix of the high and low points of your family life. Share it with someone you trust and use the experience to reflect in a balanced way about your experiences. What positive experiences have there been? When did people look happy but were not? What experiences were not photographed? What do you wish was photographed but is missing?

4. Collect a few positive or quirky family stories that reflect your family's culture. Create a family gathering and share them with each other.

5. Think about what type of experience you want the participants to have and then create a meal and serve it to your family.

6. Spend time outdoors or have coffee with a family member you want to have an improved relationship with. What was the result?

Reflection

1. How do I describe my family?
2. What do I like about my relationship with my parent(s) or those in a parental role with me? How can I enhance the positive experiences? What is difficult? How can I address or overcome the difficulties?
3. What are my relationships like with my siblings? Stepfamily members? Others I consider as family?
4. What can I count on my parents to provide in my life? What have I learned that I cannot count on them for?
5. What acts of service can I offer to my parents and immediate family? To grandparents or other relatives?
6. What life skills will I build through being of service to my family and doing needed tasks around the home?
7. What seems functional in my family? What isn't working well?
8. How could I address and/or heal from issues of abuse, neglect, and other serious matters?
9. What gets in the way of my showing respect to parents or other family members? When respect is difficult for me to show due to their behavior, how can I feel and show respect for their role? How could I build a greater level of respectful thoughts, prayers for them, and interactions?
10. What does family unity mean to me? How can I learn more about it? What character qualities and skills do I have that can foster family unity?

23 - Fostering Healthy Relationships with My Friends

Challenge: Sometimes it seems like busy-ness and all our electronic devices and social media make it hard to really connect with friends in person.

Opportunity: I can have conversations on meaningful topics with my friends and with new potential friends, and ensure we encourage each other's best efforts in life.

Summary:
- Friends add richness and enjoyment to my life.
- It's possible for friends to influence me in positive or negative ways.
- I must make a conscious effort and invest time for my friendships to last.
- Building true friendships with others is a key part of the Bahá'í focus on building vibrant communities.
- Friendship is a foundation element for relationships and marriages.
- Avoiding timewasters like excessive screen time or video games can free up time for me to connect with friends and be in action together.

More:

The nature of friendship

You likely have male buddies or mates (depending on what part of the world you live in!). You hang out together, go camping, play sports, create music, study, serve, and much more. You may also have good female friends. When these friendships are healthy and there is a spiritual foundation, you can be part of each other's support team to stay in alignment with the Bahá'í teachings. You likely have other friends who are not connected to the teachings, and sharing your beliefs with them at times flows naturally and at other times isn't as easy. These friends may also try to tempt you at times into behavior that doesn't align with spiritual principles.

You will encounter new people throughout your life where friendship emerges as a possibility:

"One must see in every human being only that which is worthy of praise. When this is done, one can be a friend to the whole human race. If, however, we look at people from the standpoint of their faults, then being a friend to them is a formidable task."[346] 'Abdu'l-Bahá

"Do not be content with showing friendship in words alone, let your heart burn with loving kindness for all who may cross your path."[347] 'Abdu'l-Bahá

Part of your overall health is connected to whether your friends are a positive or negative influence on your life. Some friends may feel like they are easy to be around simply because they don't care about living up to standards, and so they won't in any way call you to be accountable for your beliefs. It takes bravery and perseverance to discover and spend time with friends who know and appreciate you and the Bahá'í teachings. Here is guidance:

"O Friend! In the garden of thy heart plant naught but the rose of love, and from the nightingale of affection and desire loosen not thy hold. Treasure the companionship of the righteous and eschew all fellowship with the ungodly."[348] Bahá'u'lláh

Friendships are also one of the most challenging parts of life sometimes. It's hard trying to figure out who to be friends with, whether someone is a true and trustworthy friend, whether to be with the people who seem more popular, or whether to stick with being with people more like yourself. When someone is disconnected from family and community, friends become more important. Participating in a gang can even seem attractive as a way to connect with others. Of course, gangs usually involve violent and illegal activities that can destroy rather than build a healthy life.

In the complexity of life and friendships, sometimes you notice:

- It's difficult to start friendships with people outside of the circle of friends you already have
- You may feel lonely and insecure when apart from friends
- Being alone seems like the best thing
- You may forget about the importance of maintaining friendships with others when you are in a romantic relationship; it can be easy (and misleading) to think a partner is enough

Keeping friendships strong

Friendships are often built on exploring shared interests, histories, and activities. You can miss some of this exploration and experience when you maintain friendships almost solely through texting, social media, mobile phones, and so on. It's important to have in-person conversations where you can see your friend's face and body language and they can see yours. In a good conversation, you both feel heard, seen, and understood. You increase each other's confidence and empowerment. You are loyal to each other. Here is some guidance:

"The love of God has brought us together, and this is the best of means and motive. Every other bond of friendship is limited in effectiveness, but fellowship based upon the love of God is unlimited, everlasting, divine and radiant."[349] 'Abdu'l-Bahá

"You must love your friend better than yourself; yes, be willing to sacrifice yourself."[350] 'Abdu'l-Bahá

Being friendly and conversational contributes to your interactions with restaurant servers, prospective employers, school staff, coworkers, neighbors, store clerks, and more. Visiting people in their homes and hosting people in yours may expand your opportunity to connect more deeply with others. Having meaningful conversations builds friendships and relationships. The process is synergistic: When you're friendly with others at the neighborhood and community level, you also build useful partner skills for relationships and marriage.

Friendships that go beyond just being social with each other and that build to mutual respect and trust, can be truer and deeper:

- When you notice you are adding value to your friend's life in some way, or you are both better people when you are together, there is a greater connection.
- When you share thoughts about life, God, or whatever is important to you, then mutual understanding builds.
- When you serve others and enjoy activities together it can create lifetime bonds.
- True friendships are mutually respectful, and they include trust, encouragement, cooperation, and fun.

Here is someone's reflection about friendship:

"What I find valuable about friendships is knowing that in good times or bad ones they are always there for me. There's trust, loyalty, honesty, respect, laughter, acceptance, pats on the back, reprimands when I need it, and understanding. Reflecting on all the events in my life, I honestly don't know how I would have made it through my hard times without my friends, and the good times are always better with them. They are the first that I want to call when something happens in my life, they celebrate my achievements, and they offer support when I need it. I guess a simple way to put it is that they make the world a better place, and they make me a better person."

But what if it's your friends who are Bahá'ís that are encouraging you to smoke weed, take a drink, or check out someone's sexy body. It's especially hard to live up to the high standards in the teachings when the people you count on around you are behaving in destructive ways. You may be tempted to go along with them. However, you can also choose to call them out and call them to higher behavior, stop being friends with them, or ask for assistance from a parent or an institution for all of you.

Everyone arranges their friendships in different ways. Some people are happy with mostly interacting on social media; others need quality time together in person. Extroverts might like a lot of social time with a larger group of people, because spending time this way re-charges their personal energy. Introverts might prefer to interact with a small number of people only, and they are more likely to have only a few close friends. They usually need time alone to re-charge their energy. Knowing yourself will guide you to build and maintain friendships in ways that work best for you.

[It may be useful for you to study the material on backbiting and gossip in Chapter 21.]

Building new friendships

One way to expand your circle of friends is to live a coherent life that focuses some of your time and energy on community-building and service. While building friendships through service, you may see the value you each bring to your community and the benefits from participating together. A wide range of social spaces might be considered your "community", including the examples below.

- Neighborhoods
- Parks
- Homes of friends and neighbors
- Volunteer centers and activities
- Community centers
- Religious or spiritual locations, activities, and events
- Non-profit organizations
- Coffee and tea shops
- Local clubs and organizations
- Educational facilities
- Libraries or media centers

Below are some quotations about friendships and having meaningful conversations with those you meet.

"The individual alone can exercise those capacities which include the ability to take initiative, to seize opportunities, to form friendships, to interact personally with others, to build relationships, to win the cooperation of others in common service to the Faith and society, and to convert into action the decisions made by consultative bodies."[351] Universal House of Justice

"... [E]stablish ties of friendship, on the basis of shared understanding, with those previously regarded as strangers."[352] Universal House of Justice

"To the extent that the conversation continues beyond the initial encounter and veritable friendships are formed, a direct teaching effort of this kind can become a catalyst for an enduring process of spiritual transformation." [353]Universal House of Justice

"For the teaching opportunity that is now before the Bahá'í world to be seized to its fullest extent, creative thought needs to be given to the conversations that could unfold with every kind of person. In the course of such meaningful conversations, perception is heightened and hearts are opened—sometimes immediately. In this worthy occupation all find a calling, and of the joy that comes from being engaged in this work none should deprive themselves."[354] Universal House of Justice

A man comments on the process for him and makes suggestions for others:

"Think about where in your own neighborhood(s), building, village, or campus you could possibly meet new people, and get to know some better. Next, pray, sing, strum, drum, deepen, talk, memorize the Writings as you jog side-by-side with them along the sea, island, or meadow. Do what makes you feel spiritually uplifted and connected. Then with all the prayerful courage you can muster, go out to those places for a few hours when there are people around. Walk around or sit in the right places. Find people of any age and type who will just talk to you, even for a few minutes. Listen well. Speak with the confidence that you are being invisibly helped with every thought and divine word. Among them, find those who want a saner and happier world, and authentic connections with other people, starting right here, soon.

"Many yearn to do something about being more connected to others but don't know quite what, how, or with whom. It's been well demonstrated—there are such people in every neighborhood! Then connect with those few who are open to directly applying spiritual principles to the betterment of themselves and their family, community, and society. Find those who are open to interesting new ways, and sit down together to learn about it, as equals, at their place, the park, your place, wherever is best for them. Spend some time every week on that path together—creating spiritual friendships based in today's local social reality: study the divine instructions and take action to better the neighborhood and its families—singles, couples, children, youth, and elderly. Learn from experience, persevere, and grow the friendships.

"Celebrate both the joy and the pain on that journey—that incomparable joy that makes you love to sing, play, laugh, pray, teach, eat, and learn some more, to yearn from the depths of your soul be together. Welcome the inward and outward 'growth pains'—tests that reminds you that nothing lastingly good comes without sustained, faithful effort, inside and out. It really is about that simple, and there are now millions of people all over the world (and not far from you) who have been doing it for years. Ask to be accompanied by someone who has done it, to learn from them along the way, and help you practice for success, using very well-developed courses. They are eager to walk with you."

Hospitality—A gift to friends

In many parts of the world, offering hospitality is an integrated part of the culture. In other places, people resist having anyone in their homes other than family. The Bahá'í teachings value hosting and serving friends. Here is a perspective:

"Sharing is part of hospitality, not only materially but also spiritually: the atmosphere, the qualities of the members of the household. Learning is another aspect: 'peeping in at the window' into another family's way of living is the privilege and benefit of the guests. Offering whatever we can in the spirit of sharing and service, and also of joint experience, is also part of hospitality. Hospitality in the home is a most important way of learning about the outside world. People bring into the home other customs, opinions and ways of doing things, and children as well as adults widen their horizons in increased understanding of the world of human beings." (A. Ghaznavi, *Family Repairs and Maintenance Manual*, pp. 41-43)

Here is a man's experience:

"Our parents raised my brother and I to believe in Bahá'u'lláh and to welcome people into our home as a family. Their guideline was that we had to go around the room and shake everyone's hand and say something to them. None of our friends had to do anything like that, so sometimes it seemed a little strange. Now that I'm moving away from home to university and out into the world though, I'm glad they taught me to be very comfortable with meeting new people and showing them respect."

Here is some of the value that hospitality can bring:

"I beseech God to graciously make of thy home a center for the diffusion of the light of divine guidance, for the dissemination of the Words of God and for enkindling at all times the fire of love in the hearts of His faithful servants and maidservants. Know thou of a certainty that every house wherein the anthem of praise is raised to the Realm of Glory in celebration of the Name of God is indeed a heavenly home, and one of the gardens of delight in the Paradise of God."[355] 'Abdu'l-Bahá

Protecting time and friendships

In a short period of history, many people around the world have adopted technology that provides access to the internet. Some of the resulting activities fuel employment and communication globally. Other devices connect people to social media for contact with friends and relatives. All of this can be positive.

The downside is that many people have become compulsive and constant with the need to look at their devices, and they can interfere with in-person contact with friends and communicating with them. It's almost impossible to carry on a meaningful conversation with someone when one or both of you are looking at a screen. If you feel you cannot go for more than a few minutes without checking your phone for something, begin to test and strengthen your capacity for detachment by trying these or other activities:

- Give your phone to someone you trust for an hour and leave the area, or leave it at home and do an activity
- Plan an activity where there is no mobile phone signal
- Sit through an entire conversation with someone without looking at your phone; do it a second time but with your body relaxed and your mind listening to the person
- Turn the phone face down so you cannot see notifications; silence notifications

Here is some guidance:

"Shoghi Effendi's choice of words was always significant, and each one is important in understanding his guidance. ... [H]e does not forbid 'trivial' pleasures, but he does warn against 'excessive attachment' to them and indicates that they can often be 'misdirected'. One is reminded of 'Abdu'l-Bahá's caution that we should not let a pastime become a waste of time."[356] On behalf of the Universal House of Justice

A man reflects about prioritizing his time:

"Perhaps one way of gaining a sense of someone's priorities is to ask, 'So tell me about what you did last week' and see what they talk about. You could also say something like, 'Tell me something faith (or family or fitness or

work...) related that you did recently', to get an idea what types of things the person is involved in.

"I also notice how people balance priorities and apply courtesy. Personally, if I make a commitment to do something, I like to follow through with it. It's rude when people 'un-commit' to something because something else came up that they simply would rather do, with certain exceptions. For example, a 'family emergency' may be a higher need than a faith event, and could not have been foreseen, however a 'family outing spontaneously organized', I'd have to say 'Sorry, I already have plans', if I already had planned a faith-related event with others in advance. On the other hand, sometimes faith events get 'thrown together at the last minute', when my family had already planned a family party. We unfortunately can't do it all, we have to choose sometimes, and then say, 'I chose what I chose, and I bought my train ticket already'."

If you are uncertain whether you are making good choices for your time or instead wasting it, spend a day or week logging what you do and how much time it takes. Then you will have the facts and can choose to make changes in how you spend your time as needed. Pay careful attention to whether you are using at least part of your time to build friendships.

Action

1. Gather a group of singers and musicians from your area and record a Bahaiblog.net studio session.

2. Set a goal for the next week to have an uplifting or meaningful conversation with someone in your life or someone new you meet. Choose one or two topics to focus on and research the spiritual principles and character qualities related to them. Afterward, reflect on how the conversations went.

3. **Activity reflection:** Where could you expand your activities, perspectives, and friendships? What options do you have access to? Where can you visit or travel to? What opportunity can you create where it doesn't yet exist? What are your goals? Some of the activities listed below could also enhance your life and provide opportunities to meet new people. What appeals to you?

- Facilitate a study session or ongoing group to explore a meaningful or interesting topic
- Host a prayer gathering
- Visit neighbors and friends in their homes or a neighborhood gathering place
- Coordinate or participate in a community service project
- Volunteer your time to support a worthy cause
- Visit or volunteer at an elder care facility or with a children's group
- Offer classes for the moral and spiritual education of children
- Offer friendship, mentorship, and guidance to groups of youth
- Attend conferences or workshops
- Join a committee addressing a civic or social issue
- Enroll in a course at a college, university, community center, or other institution
- Take classes related to the arts
- Volunteer at a museum, concert hall, theater, or library
- Join a book group, hiking group, community theater, sport club or team, game-playing group, or any other group that interests you (*Possible resource:* https://www.meetup.com/)

Reflection

1. What are some key qualities that I've seen in excellent friendships?
2. What do I value about the friendships that I have? What additional elements would enhance them?
3. What friendships do I have that seem mutual and healthy? How can I build more like these?
4. What friendships do I have that seem to lead me into problems? How will I address this situation?
5. How can having meaningful conversations with friends about spiritual topics contribute to our lives?
6. What can I do to strengthen a friendship I currently have? What can I do to keep a friend over time?
7. How can I expand my circle of friends? Why would this be a good action to take?
8. What are my favorite activities to do with friends?
9. What do I do to build trust with a friend? When have I felt a friend violated my trust? How did I feel about this? How did I respond? Could I re-build trust? If so, what made it possible to do so?

10. What are some signs that I would be wise to end a friendship? End a connection with a group of peers?
11. Have I seen a friendship that became a relationship? How did that turn out? What challenges did the couple encounter? How did they resolve them?
12. What value do I see in having friendships with the opposite gender? What would be the benefits of having a marriage with friendship as a foundation element?
13. What value is there in having friendships with people of different ages? Races? Interests?
14. What changes could I make with my use of time, so I invest in and protect my friendships?

24 - Establishing a Happy Relationship with a Partner

Challenge: It's confusing to navigate relationships, and it's often difficult for me to feel like I can succeed at them.

Opportunity: Success in relationships (and marriage) can be possible if I prepare myself, especially my character, and learn from the large body of spiritual and scientific knowledge about what makes them work well.

Summary:
- It's vital for me to focus on key components of relationship success such as character, friendship, and spiritual connection; being skillful with equality and consultation are also essential.
- Spending time with friends can be a good way for me to get to know others as potential partners.
- Dating is a possibility if I care about the person, I'm building a friendship with them, we are practicing chastity, and I'm considering whether they have potential as a marriage partner in the future.
- Courtship is when I get serious about a person, I want to deeply learn about them and them about me, and we figure out together whether being marriage partners is a good choice.
- Cohabitation is common in society, as people often see it as a way to prevent divorce, but "trial marriages"— where a couple lives together without marriage—are not part of the Bahá'í teachings, and these situations can also cause other problems; this unstable situation is particularly risky for any children involved.
- When I'm serious about preparing for marriage by building knowledge and skills, it will prevent problems later and contribute to me having a stronger marriage.

More:

Relationships—Where to focus

There are indicators in the Bahá'í teachings of some key factors in a good relationship and marriage:

A. Character strengths and the couple knowing each other's character

B. Friendship
C. Spiritual connection

Two additional factors for relationship and marriage success are:

- Equality
- Ability to consult as equal partners

Equality was a focus in Chapter 7. One of the best ways to keep a relationship healthy is to be able to consult for understanding and problem solving together. Consultation has been mentioned throughout the book. Here are more details about the first three factors:

A: Thoroughly know the character of a partner—how they behave and why in all circumstances; their character strengths and areas needing growth.

You learned about your own character in Chapter 8, something that enables you to recognize a partner's character strengths and growth areas more skillfully. Below is a selection of quotations about this topic.

> "Bahá'í marriage is the commitment of the two parties one to the other, and their mutual attachment of mind and heart. Each must, however, exercise the utmost care to become thoroughly acquainted with the character of the other, that the binding covenant between them may be a tie that will endure forever. Their purpose must be this: to become loving companions and comrades and at one with each other for time and eternity...."[357] 'Abdu'l-Bahá

> "There is a difference between character and faith; it is often very hard to accept this fact and put up with it, but the fact remains that a person may believe in and love the Cause—even to being ready to die for it—and yet not have a good personal character, or possess traits at variance with the teachings. We should try to change, to let the Power of God help recreate us and make us true Bahá'ís in deed as well as in belief. But sometimes the process is slow, sometimes it never happens because the individual does not try hard enough."[358] On behalf of Shoghi Effendi

> "A couple should study each other's character and spend time getting to know each other before they decide to marry, and when they do marry

it should be with the intention of establishing an eternal bond."[359] On behalf of the Universal House of Justice

As you see others' behaviors and learn about their character, you'll discern which of their attributes, values, and personality traits are complementary to yours. It's generally wise to withhold judgment until you have a broader view of who they are, since pre-conceptions are often misleading. For instance, when you first meet someone, you might observe several superficial aspects about them that you initially think would not make them a suitable partner to live with, based on your understanding of what you're looking for.

As you observe these aspects, you might automatically make judgments about other aspects of the person's life and choices. However, if you get to know the person better, you would probably discover several positive behaviors that could only be seen through a friendship and more time together, such as that they:

- Regularly listen to and spend quality time with you and others
- Always tell the truth
- Pray continuously throughout their day
- Enjoy lively group activities
- Treat everyone with an open, friendly attitude

In other words, everyone is complex, and it's easy for prejudices and assumptions to initially interfere with getting to know someone. The world contains countless multi-dimensional people who defy common assumptions and stereotypes. It takes time to get to know people, to study their characters, and to discover what about them interests, challenges, or delights you. However, there is also a balance to maintain. Sometimes people spend years getting to know someone, ignoring problem areas, and never moving forward into marriage or separate lives.

Transformation is always possible for us throughout our lives. However, trouble occurs when people marry a partner who is very weak in some of the key character qualities that make it possible to live smoothly with them, such as kindness, respect, truthfulness, and thoughtfulness. When someone has weaknesses that regularly cause conflict, couples spend a lot of time on internal relationship repair and then find it difficult to look outward to serving others.

Here is a man's reflection:

"I know one of the very essential lessons I learned from my marriage and divorce was how important it is to become knowledgeable of a partner's character. Compatibility and resolving any potential differences, these also would top my list. Perhaps, even greater would be the person's faithfulness in following the spiritual laws that Bahá'u'lláh brought."

None of us is perfect, all of us have bad days and moments, and we are wise to always to be in self-improvement mode. Before marriage is the only time the teachings talk about fully focusing on knowing someone else's character, though, instead of focusing only on their positive aspects. There is a popular Bahá'í teaching about looking at a person's one good quality and not focusing on their large number of poor ones. However, could you imagine being married to and parenting with someone with only one good quality for every nine bad ones?! So, it's important to pay attention.

B: Develop a strong friendship, with strengths like ease of communication, thoughtfulness, and enjoyment.

Anytime and anywhere, an unmarried person can meet a prospective future marriage partner and begin to develop a close friendship. Getting to know someone can be the same process whether you simply wish to make a new friend, or you think of the person as a prospective partner. Either way, it's good to know if you enjoy each other's company and want to know more about each other.

Early friendship can be relaxed—an interchange in which two people see if they enjoy chatting and getting to know each other. The distinction society has made between how we should get to know a potential marriage partner, versus someone we just want to be friends with, can be misleading. Some people believe that for a relationship to be possible, there must be an almost instant attraction when people first meet. However, many people find that building a close and loving friendship can later cause an attraction to spark. There is no formula or single method for friendships to unfold and relationships to develop, but it's good to include both your head and your heart in the process. Here is this guidance:

> "... [M]an and woman should truly be friends, and should be in sympathy with one another. Their understanding should have a basis in reality...."[360] 'Abdu'l-Bahá

Creating new friendships expands the pool of potential relationships, which enhances the possibility of finding a potential marriage partner. It's often necessary to broaden your perspective of who could be a good marriage partner for you. Sometimes this requires removing or addressing a prejudice or factor that restricts your view—whether it relates to economic level, race, ethnicity, culture, nationality, religious affiliation, physical appearance, personality, lifestyle preferences, geographical location, or any other limiting factor.

Friendships can be beneficial in several ways as you prepare for marriage. They give you opportunities to expand your self-knowledge, strengthen your relationship skills, and develop your character qualities. You can also improve your ability to notice how a friend practices character qualities. When you reflect on how you carry out friendships, you determine which skills and qualities you would benefit from developing further.

C: Build a spiritual connection through prayer, studying guidance, and service

There is much in this book about your own spiritual practices and service to others. In a relationship context, the mission is to explore whether you can smoothly and happily carry these out with each other. Couples can determine their ability to pray together, attend spiritual activities together, and serve together. You don't have to be able to do every type of community service together, but certainly it's good to be able to support each other's service choices as well as be able to do some service efforts together.

Dating—Okay in context

People sometimes say, "Bahá'ís aren't allowed to date", but there is apparently no statement to that effect in the teachings. However, there are boundaries for behavior in a dating relationship and encouragement to be focused on marriage. Here is some guidance:

"... [T]here is nothing in the Bahá'í Writings which relates specifically to the so-called dating practices prevalent in some parts of the world, where two unmarried people of the opposite sex participate together in a social activity. In general, Bahá'ís who are planning to involve themselves in this form of behavior should become well aware of the Bahá'í Teachings on chastity and, with these in mind, should scrupulously avoid any actions which would arouse passions which might well tempt them to violate these Teachings. In deciding which acts are permissible in the light of these considerations, the youth should use their own judgment, giving due consideration to the advice of their parents, taking account of the prevailing customs of the society in which they live, and prayerfully following the guidance of their conscience. It is the sacred duty of parents to instill in their children the exalted Bahá'í standard of moral conduct, and the importance of adherence to this standard cannot be over-emphasized as a basis for true happiness and for successful marriage."[361] On behalf of the Universal House of Justice

"Concerning your wish for a marriage partner to enhance your life and service, you are encouraged to trust in God, pursue your purposes with a joyful heart, and identify opportunities, through your own prayerful consideration or through consultation with others, to meet a man to whom you could consider being married."[362] On behalf of the Universal House of Justice

Here is a reflection on some of the challenges:

"We are often brought up to be nice guys and innocent girls and are very comfortable with ourselves before mate selection becomes an issue. Quickly we find our spiritual values a liability in the world of dating, even within the Bahá'í community, where the same biological and social forces operate as elsewhere. Humble men and modest women frequently find themselves passed over in favor of more dominant or overtly sexual versions of themselves. We feel under increasing pressure to compete, and we feel torn between sticking to our values and selling ourselves short on the dating market, or selling out on our values and adopting flirtatious mannerisms and a provocative style of dress that undeniably achieves results."

Many Bahá'ís discover potential partners who live at a distance from them. Here is a viewpoint on long-distance relationships:

"The concept of long-distance relationships rather than meeting someone in my area is interesting. In many areas the Bahá'í community is small, which is what may drive us toward long-distance relationships. Internet dating, in some ways, has the benefit that when you are talking to someone, the intention is to get to know them as a potential partner, in most cases. Joining social groups in one's own community I highly recommend to people anyway, and of course Bahá'í activities fall in this category. To Bahá'ís, I encourage us to consider at least some groups that are centered

around other interests we might have, as it provides a forum to teach others about the Faith, as well as meet new people.

"That said, sometimes when meeting people in a 'social group' there is that dynamic of 'are we just friends or do we want to date?', and how to manage that while still enjoying being in the social group. It can also be a challenge how to still enjoy going to that social group, centered around a faith or an interest, if it turns out that you don't feel you want to have a relationship with a person you 'dated' there.

"We need to be open to both possibilities (long distance vs. meeting someone who might in fact be our next-door neighbor). Especially in this world where people move around a lot, 'the person now living next door' might have been 'someone who I would have had to have a long distance relationship with' just six months ago, because they just moved into the area. Long distance relationships are probably a more likely necessity for people living in small towns or remote areas though, just because there are fewer people in the area. However, I often wonder along these lines if people living in a small town in one part of the country might more likely get along with people living in a small town in another part of the country, just because both are used to 'small town life'."

A man reflects on many challenges he has experienced in life and his learning:

"Looking back at my relationships with the opposite sex reminds me just how easy it is for society and even our parents to 'help' us make bad choices. Of course, in the end, we are the Captains of our own 'ship' and should claim full responsibility for all choices we make. Here are a few bits of advice I wish my 20-year-old self had known:

1. 'I'm a Bahá'í, and you're a Bahá'í, let's get married and go save the world together.' Don't say this or think this about any woman. Being of the same Faith is very important in my opinion, but it certainly should not be the only deciding factor on whether or not you want to get married.

2. Take your time getting to know a person before dating them. The 'romance' messes with your head and does not allow you to think rationally. If you find yourself being involved sexually with a person before marriage, don't even think you're acting logically. Those hormones are messing with your brain, and you can be assured you will not be making good decisions when it comes to relationships. Getting

into a sexual relationship with a woman before marriage will cause ALL of your wise brain cells to temporarily disappear, and only your hormones will do your thinking for you.

3. If you want to marry someone who is spiritual, good looking (to your eyes), educated, a maidservant of Bahá, potentially a good parent, and has a good job, then you need to be spiritual, good looking (to your eyes), educated, a servant of Bahá, potentially a good parent, and have a good job.

4. Remember that when you decide to marry someone, you are deciding to share your body with that person, and it should only be that one person. If your potential mate does not possess the only body you ever want to thoroughly enjoy, then go find another potential mate. Too many guys out there are constantly thinking about getting into somebody else's body except for their wife's. You'll pay for that mistake in the long run.

5. Be sure to read many Bahá'í-related books to help you become a spiritual being and find a potential mate. Another great book to read is "The Five Love Languages" by Gary Chapman. You learn where other people are coming from and how you can and can't fill up their 'tank' with what they truly perceive as love. Note: The way you want someone to show you love is probably not the way someone else wants you to show them that you love them. And don't be surprised if they cannot accurately tell you how to make them feel loved.

6. Any relationship you are in is going to have some major ups and downs. Knowing when to stop or go forward is a critical part of making a good choice of a mate.

7. If you think being married to the wrong woman is emotionally painful—I picked someone who wanted to be a dependent instead of a partner—I'm here to tell you that you may find it financially painful as well. I have paid out a lot of money in divorce lawyer fees and alimony. Make a good choice the first time around."

Intercultural Relationships

Developing healthy intercultural relationships and marriages is an integral part of developing a diverse international community on its way to creating one unified human family. Globally, community-based unifying activities are leading the Bahá'í Faith community and its friends and collaborators in this direction. When individuals come from different cultural backgrounds, races, or ethnicities, the fundamental principle of the oneness of all people helps them look for points of harmony. The Bahá'í teachings say:

> "Bahá'u'lláh hath said that the various races of humankind lend a composite harmony and beauty of color to the whole. Let all associate, therefore, in this great human garden even as flowers grow and blend together side by side without discord or disagreement between them."[363] 'Abdu'l-Bahá

> "... [F]rom the time of its inception...the Bahá'í world community has been characterized by the integration of the many religious, racial, ethnic, cultural, linguistic and national elements which it comprises. Marriage between persons of different ethnic, and cultural backgrounds, and particularly between black and white Bahá'ís, is warmly encouraged in the Bahá'í scriptures."[364] Universal House of Justice

Couples in a diverse relationship or marriage often have an enhanced appreciation for the beauty of other cultures. It gives individuals the opportunity to recognize and overcome biases, stereotypes, and prejudices in themselves, and to encourage the same process in their family members and community. Intercultural relationships can assist people to overcome the human tendency to believe they are right and others wrong. The way one of you learned to do something may be quite different from your partner, but different is not better or worse, right or wrong.

Dugan Romano, author of *Intercultural Marriage*, says about couples: "They maintain that what keeps life interesting for them is the challenge of continuous discovery, the possibility of reshaping their own perspective as a result of encountering their partner's."[365] Romano comments that it can be a challenge for some couples when they intellectually understand each other's culture but don't have "true emotional empathy". An example given was that of a Japanese wife who giggles when she is upset or frightened and a British husband who explodes when upset. It took them years to stop reacting from their own cultural viewpoint.[366]

Couples who come from different parts of the world often find they travel more than couples who meet in a local area. Even when you meet locally, if you each come from other countries, you might travel there to learn more about each other. You may need to learn each other's language as well, something vital in maintaining communication between you.

When you run into challenges, as every relationship and marriage does, your ability to look for the principles that apply will help keep you on track.

Courtship—A process

Courtship can be considered a time of thoroughly knowing someone and consulting about the potential of marrying each other. It's also a time that can be difficult to navigate. Media has filled the minds of many females of all ages with exaggerated expectations of her special guy as a prince with perfect manners and a muscle-filled physique who falls instantly in love with her, and they live happily ever after. Sometimes this has the women you encounter looking for who will "measure up" (you can't and shouldn't try to!). Throw into that mythical mess the ways relationships are happening in society, and it can all feel like a scary area to avoid. Here's a realistic assessment of one of the fairytale stories:

> "No matter that Cinderella has been socialized to feel at home among the kitchen ashes and would have no idea how to behave in the pomp and circumstance of the royal court. No matter that Prince Charming has grown up in an entirely different culture and acquired its education, tastes, and manners. No matter that the two of them know nothing about each other's attitudes toward the roles of wives and husbands. All they have in common is a glass slipper and a foot that fits it!"[367] Les Parrott and Leslie Parrott

Moreover, Cinderella was raised by an abusive stepmother, dominated by cruel stepsisters, her father died before she matured, and she has had little exposure to a functional marriage and family.

With a more realistic viewpoint, a man says this:

> "I feel that we need to take a more relaxed and natural approach to courtship, to integrate good judgment with instincts, so we rise above the 'head vs. heart' dichotomy. In this way we can meet our need for romance and adventure within marriage rather than outside of it and without repressing these vital aspects of a healthy personality. Marriage has the potential to be the human institution through which the need for passion and romance can best be fulfilled."

It's common for men to have many relationships throughout their lives. At some point, it's likely that a special relationship will develop with someone you realize may be an excellent marriage partner. Hopefully, the friendships you have developed previously built your skills for a friendship-based marriage that includes respectful equality between partners.

As you make choices with the words you use with others and your actions, you gain knowledge and experience with relationships. The more you keep the Bahá'í teachings as the foundation for making those choices, the more likely you are to have happiness, high quality, and stability in a relationship, and then in a marriage partnership.

Here is a letter written by the Universal House of Justice in response to an inquiry from a father about his sons and their relationships:

> "As you know, courtship practices differ greatly from one culture to another, and it is not yet known what pattern of courtship will emerge in the future when society has been more influenced by Bahá'í Teachings. However, there is no indication that it will resemble the practices extant in existing cultures.... In this interim period, the friends are encouraged to make great efforts to live in conformity with the Teachings and to gradually forge a new pattern of behavior, more in keeping with the spirit of Bahá'u'lláh's Revelation. In this context, we offer the following comments.
>
> "Although a Bahá'í may, if he chooses, seek his parents' advice on the choice of a partner, and although Bahá'í parents may give such advice if asked, it is clear from the Teachings that parents do not have the right to interfere in their children's actual choice of a prospective partner until approached for their consent to marry. Therefore, when discussing the issue of courtship with your sons, it would be best to discuss it on the level of principle without reference to individuals.
>
> "In the context of the society in which your family now lives, a society in which materialism, self-centeredness and failing marriages are all too common, your sons may well feel that it is wise to have a long period of courtship in which the prospective partners spend much time together and become thoroughly acquainted with each other's character, background and family. This practice does not in itself contradict Bahá'í law and, as it is not unacceptable in ... [country name removed], it appears to be a viable option. As you are aware, Bahá'u'lláh ordained that Bahá'í engagement should not exceed 95 days, and, although this law has not yet been applied universally, it highlights the desirability of marrying quickly once the decision to marry has been

firmly taken and parental consent obtained. However, in a relationship in which such a decision has not been taken and in which the law of chastity is strictly observed, there is no objection, in principle, to a prolonged friendship in which the two individuals entertain the possibility of marrying each other at some time in the future.

"You have mentioned that your sons like to invite their girlfriends to spend a lot of time with the family and that you are not entirely happy with this situation. Each family member has rights which should be respected, and if you wish to have some time in your home without the presence of non-family members, the other members of your family should take this seriously into consideration. However, we hasten to point out to you that the situation which you describe, in which your sons wish their friends to be involved with your family, is much more in line with the Teachings than the common pattern in Western countries in which many youth virtually exclude their parents from interacting with their peers, sometimes distancing themselves from their families in order to have the freedom to engage in frivolous and even unchaste behavior…."[368] On behalf of the Universal House of Justice

A man talks about what he wants in courtship:

"What I struggle with, is that I want to be 'me', I don't want to be 'changed', I don't want to feel like I am being squeezed into a box, and forcefully re-shaped. Rather, I want to know how to 'grow', or 'grow into' a relationship. 'Abdu'l-Bahá talks about couples improving each other's spiritual lives, but I don't think that means forcing someone to change when they are unwilling and want to be accepted for who they are. Take a tree for example, if you want a tree to grow in a certain way, you shape how the tree grows through gently guiding the branches or trimming the tree to promote new healthy growth. If you try to bend the branches too forcefully, they will break, or if you try to prune the tree too much, you will hinder its growth.

"What I think needs to happen is when people decide they want to be a couple, they talk about where and how they want their couple-ship to evolve, and grow together, while respecting the uniqueness of each person's traits, interests, career goals, and so on, and try to fit them together for mutual benefit. There are many ways to carry this out, so we just have to have a genuine conversation to confirm that our goals align."

Here is an observation on how relationships and marriages could unfold:

"I think that the spiritual goals we are given in the Bahá'í Faith need to be understood in terms of process, rather than as a finished product. The ideal marriage is a goal to be worked toward; it gives direction to our striving. When we look at the ideal marriage as something that we 'should' have, we are likely to feel discouraged, guilty, a sense of futility, and so on. When we understand it to be the goal of a process, which we can move toward regardless of our current situation, and we start working toward it, we can feel hope and encouragement—and that we're making progress. I believe the Faith teaches us that spirituality is a dynamic process, not a static condition. This systematic process applies to marriage preparation and marriage as well."

Challenges of cohabitating

Over the last decades and in many countries in the world, many couples have chosen to live together instead of marrying. It's often a reaction to the high rates of divorce occurring, and many may see it as a way to test whether a marriage could be viable. There has also been a devaluing of the institution of marriage. As social scientists study these trends, they are increasingly finding evidence that marrying is the choice that best leads to strong, healthy couple relationships and to the well-being of children. Some benefits associated with marriage that research identifies are:

- A higher level of commitment; greater confidence in the longevity of the relationship
- Better communication and problem-solving
- Less conflict and violence
- Families and community members offer their wisdom, support, and experience in greater abundance
- Parents who are more likely to include the couple in family events and offer emotional support during difficulties
- Greater family unity
- Children are born into or live in a more stable household and relationship; better child health, well-being, and achievement
- Tendency to be more productive in the workforce and have higher incomes

- Greater physical and mental health and happiness; tendency to live longer
- Families tend to share more of their financial resources with the couple, including financing education
- A higher level of satisfaction, including greater sexual satisfaction; greater motivation to please a partner
- More faithfulness and less likelihood of an affair (contributes to protecting partners from sexually transmitted diseases)[369]

Cohabitation is not part of the Bahá'í teachings, as indicated below.

"The Bahá'í Teachings do not contemplate any form of 'trial marriage'. A couple should study each other's character and spend time getting to know each other before they decide to marry, and when they do marry it should be with the intention of establishing an eternal bond. They should realize, moreover, that the primary purpose of marriage is the procreation of children."[370] Universal House of Justice

Despite this, you may be living together and want to move into being married. Sometimes cohabitating couples develop habits that more align with single life than marriage does. It will be wise to assess your current life for any patterns that don't reflect that of a committed couple and adjust them. For example, in marriage, you would not think of certain furnishings as belonging to only one of you, and finances would be determined together rather than making separate spending decisions.

It will also be good to carefully examine your expectations of marriage and of husband and wife behaviors, as sometimes these won't look like the roles you currently fill. Sometimes when a couple marries that has been living together, their behaviors change because thoughts and memories of what a wife or husband are "supposed to do" or what marriage is "supposed to be like" start governing their actions. Often what arises are behaviors you observed as a child in your parents' marriages. This shift in behaviors can cause disappointment, confusion, or conflict. It will also be wise to ensure you go through a marriage preparation process.

Preparing for marriage

Ideally, each person in the couple relationship is willing to be on a path of growth for a lifetime. You may be someone who thinks this sounds like too much pressure or work or gets anxious about the process and thinks it's easier to stay single (or live with a partner). That could work if life were only about this world, but there are endless spiritual worlds after this. If your mind, body, heart, and soul don't grow and strengthen here, you'll be arriving in the next world terribly handicapped. Relationships and marriages are great places to grow and help each other in this life and be ready for the next one. A marriage is also the best place to raise children to worship God, something that also brings about significant personal growth.

Unity is a key component of strong and happy marriages, which are the foundation of families. These in turn are a building block of ever wider circles of unity in communities, cities, countries, and ultimately the planet. Marriage partners can assist one another to grow spiritually, hopefully serve God and humanity together, and are intended to be companions for eternity.

Your actions leading up to marriage contribute to you creating these strong marriages. When you don't carefully prepare by building knowledge and skills as well as ensure you are complementary with your partner, you can end up in separation or even divorce. This causes disunity, pain, and hardship for everyone concerned. It's important to do some training and preparation for marriage throughout dating, courtship, and engagement. This could include such actions as:

- Consulting with parents
- Meeting with a Spiritual Assembly
- Attending workshops
- Working with a married couple who offers mentoring
- Studying books
- Taking online courses
- Doing a marriage readiness assessment
- Interviewing married couples

This is wise advice: "Careful preparation for marriage is an essential first step in the preservation of Bahá'í marriage."[371] Bahá'í World Centre Research Department

After a couple has made an independent choice to marry, without interference from their parents, Bahá'ís are then required to have their parents' consent to marry. In part, consent is required because it prompts children to be grateful to those who gave them life, and it can build family unity. When Bahá'ís and their partners have consent and begin their engagement, they consult with a Spiritual Assembly about the requirements for the Bahá'í marriage ceremony. See the next chapter for more information.

Resources Note: Preparing for relationships and marriage involves much more than this brief chapter. Books such as *Starting with Me: Knowing Myself Before Finding a Partner*, *Marriage Can Be Forever—Preparation Counts!*, *Fortress for Well-Being*, and *Conscious Courtship* are excellent resources. There are also Bahá'í-based online courses available through www.wilmetteinstitute.org (scholarships are available). Research-based marriage readiness assessments can also be beneficial, such as those through www.prepare-enrich.com. You can search there for some Bahá'ís who offer the service.

Action

1. Read books and online articles about dating, courtship, and marriage, carefully assessing what aligns with the Bahá'í teachings. Start a notebook where you begin to note what you want and do not want in a marriage partner and marriage.

2. Take an online course to better understand and apply the Bahá'í teachings on relationships and marriage.

3. Go out socially with someone and practice self-discipline, staying chaste and not expressing any sexual energy you are feeling. Could you focus on the creative process of building a friendship? How did this feel? Did you feel pressure from the other person to behave against the teachings in any way? What contributed to you staying strong? If needed, how could you be stronger next time? [See Chapters 12-14.]

4. Arrange to spend time with someone in activities such as offering service, visiting with family members or friends of the other person, going to a devotional, cooking, shopping, or playing a sport. What were the differences and similarities between these experiences and simply spending time socially with someone? What increased your ability to get to know the person and their character?

Reflection

1. What is my level of confidence about being successful at a relationship (low, medium, or high)? With marriage? How can I increase my confidence?
2. What are my concerns about dating and courtship? How can I address these?
3. What value do I see in dating and courtship?
4. How can I apply the Bahá'í teachings to these types of relationships?
5. What is important about me that a partner always needs to know?
6. How can I apply "be brave and arise" to participate in dating and courtship?
7. How can I be protective of the well-being and safety of a woman I am in a relationship with?
8. What am I looking forward to in a partner relationship? In marriage?
9. What ways do I think will be most effective for me in preparing for marriage? What are my preferences about interacting with each other's family members?
10. What have I observed in relationships among my family members and friends?
11. What have I observed in my parents' marriage that I want to emulate? What do I not want to use as a model?
12. What does it mean that marriage and family are foundations for global unity?

25 - Creating My Marriage, Fatherhood, and Family

Challenge: I have a lot of skepticism about marriage and see many couples living together or divorcing, so it's tough for me to have confidence and trust in getting and staying married myself.

Opportunity: When I look at the encouragement in the Bahá'í teachings to marry, and when I study the research about its benefits, I feel hopeful I can marry and establish a family.

Summary:
- Ideally, I have a respectful relationship with my parents, and that's a good foundation for when my relationship partner and I ask them for consent for us to marry each other.
- It enhances our success in marriage if we both have excellent characters, a strong friendship, attraction, a commitment to create an eternal union of our souls, and a wish to raise children together.
- As a father, I'm a vital member of the family unit, and I'm responsible for working in partnership with my wife and for ensuring our children are educated spiritually and intellectually.
- I and my wife can create a family that is more than the sum of the people in it, because it's unified, and its members practice kindness, respect, and loyalty.

More:

Parental consent to marry

Once you and a partner independently choose to marry, the Bahá'í teachings have you approach your parents for their consent. Once you have consent, then you can consider yourselves engaged and plan a wedding. Here is brief guidance on the topic:

> "... [M]arriage is dependent upon the consent of both parties. Desiring to establish love, unity and harmony amidst Our servants, We have conditioned it, once the couple's wish is known, upon the permission of their parents, lest enmity and rancor should arise amongst them."[372] Bahá'u'lláh

"Bahá'u'lláh has clearly stated the consent of all living [birth/natural] parents is required for a Bahá'í marriage. This applies whether the parents are Bahá'ís or non-Bahá'ís, divorced for years or not. This great law He has laid down to strengthen the social fabric, to knit closer the ties of the home, to place a certain gratitude and respect in the hearts of the children for those who have given them life and sent their souls out on the eternal journey towards their Creator."[373] On behalf of Shoghi Effendi

Parental consent can be simple or very complex depending on the family circumstances. There are many more quotations than these available, and these do not cover all the possible situations that can arise. Examples of situations where seeking additional guidance is wise could include where there has been adoption, parental abuse, or missing or impaired parents. Couples should turn to the Bahá'í administration for help:

"... [T]he provision of guidance on administrative matters such as the laws of engagement, marriage, and divorce falls under the purview of Local and National Spiritual Assemblies...."[374] On behalf of the Universal House of Justice

Flourishing Bahá'í marriage and family life

The Bahá'í teachings say in honor of marriage:

"And when He [God] desired to manifest grace and beneficence to men, and to set the world in order, He revealed observances and created laws; among them He established the law of marriage, made it as a fortress for well-being and salvation, and enjoined it upon us in that which was sent down out of the heaven of sanctity in His Most Holy Book [*The Kitáb-i-Aqdas*]. He saith, great is His glory: 'Enter into wedlock, O people, that ye may bring forth one who will make mention of Me amid My servants. This is My bidding unto you; hold fast to it as an assistance to yourselves.'"[375] Bahá'u'lláh

Here is one man's reflection:

"A radical change the Bahá'í Teachings call for is in our perspective on the nature and purpose of marriage. We often think of marriage as a 'fortress for [our own] well-being.' This view, definitely the predominant one in our

society, is a self-centered approach. The Bahá'í teachings imply that God created marriage for the betterment of the whole human race. If we do not recognize this, our efforts to make ourselves happy will only lead to our misery.

"In general, a fortress is not a place of peace and tranquility. A fortress is often a stronghold in a battlefield, a particularly strategic spot on the landscape that requires protection from enemy forces. As I understand Bahá'u'lláh's vision for a spiritual World Order, there is no school more important than the family, no teachers more necessary than the mother and father, and no pupils more worthwhile and vital than the children. That strategic spot on the landscape is none other than the future of these kids.

"It is the family's responsibility to secure their children against the manifold forces of evil in the world by imbuing them with the love of God and the knowledge of His teachings for this Day. These children will, in their turn, grow up to be the redeemers of humanity, the dawn-breakers of a peaceful world civilization, the bricklayers of a great peace beyond our wildest dreams. As the challenges and difficulties of the world they inherit from us must increase, so we need to empower them to surmount heights we could never dream of, and surpass us in all the paths of service to God and humanity. That is the primary goal of this 'fortress' for the 'well-being' of the whole human race.

"This fortress, if it understands its role properly, should constantly devote itself to the good of all people. Each member of the family needs to be aware of their mission as servants of God and humanity, and work unitedly with the others to expand the borders of the country of God's Love. A spiritual family will naturally collectively arise to promote spiritual thought and action. Children can be progressively encouraged to share their spirituality with their fellow human beings from the time they are first able to speak and reason. The parents can first lead their children by example, and then systematically instruct them as to how to do what they are doing. Action is the primary text in this school, and words but supplements to it."[376]

Ideally marriage and family are comprised of these qualities:

"The Lord, peerless is He, hath made woman and man to abide with each other in the closest companionship, and to be even as a single soul. They are two helpmates, two intimate friends, who should be concerned about the welfare of each other. If they live thus, they will pass through this world with perfect contentment, bliss, and peace of heart, and become the object of divine grace and favor in the Kingdom of heaven."[377] 'Abdu'l-Bahá

"... [T]he importance of marriage lieth in the bringing up of a richly blessed family, so that with entire gladness they may, even as candles, illuminate the world."[378] 'Abdu'l-Bahá

The reputation of marriage in society has suffered in recent years. It's time to turn that around:

"Marriage is a very sacred institution. Bahá'u'lláh said its purpose is to promote unity. [We] are trying to create a high moral standard, and reinstate the sanctity of marriage."[379] On behalf of Shoghi Effendi

"... [T]he House of Justice feels it most essential for your husband and you to understand that marriage can be a source of well-being, conveying a sense of security and spiritual happiness. However, it is not something that just happens. For marriage to become a haven of contentment it requires the cooperation of the marriage partners themselves, and the assistance of their families...."[380] On behalf of the Universal House of Justice

"Bahá'ís should be profoundly aware of the sanctity of marriage and should strive to make their marriages an eternal bond of unity and harmony. This requires effort and sacrifice and wisdom and self-abnegation."[381] On behalf of the Universal House of Justice

A man reflects on his experience of marriage and parenthood:

"Marriage and having kids is all about sacrifice. Everything is different on the day after marriage regardless of how well you might know your partner. It can be as simple as how each partner brushes their teeth to much larger challenges and differences. The most important thing to know is no matter what size the challenges are, self-sacrifice is needed. We must be willing to admit our shortcomings, change ourselves, and not expect the other person to change for us.
"Having children means you have to elevate the sacrifice level much higher. Besides the obvious changes that come naturally, both parents must be willing to give up so many things that they used to do, such as profession, hanging out with friends, staying out late, and more. So often we meet

parents with young children who still want to hang around their friends late at night, totally ignoring signs that their kids' bedtime has long passed. When our first one was born, my wife, who has a Master's in Business Administration, quit her career to raise him and the one that followed. As a mother, she always made sure our kids' sleeping time came first. Even when we'd visit friends and family, the kids would go to bed at the designated time there.

"These are not sacrifices made only during the first few years. It's a lifetime process. We always watched our two boys like hawks, especially when out at public events. This was not necessarily for protection but to make sure they didn't do things they are not supposed to. So many times, we see kids of all ages grab food that is beyond their consumption capacity and just leave the leftovers behind for someone else to clean up.

"Having a regular schedule for eating together, sleeping, playing, watching TV, and more is so important. We were never afraid of disciplining the boys appropriately so they would learn their limits. On the other side, we always gave them room to make their own mistakes and learn, encouraging them to try new things so they could make discoveries. Punctuality has always been one of my biggest concerns. Our sons often complained about why we were always the first ones to arrive 5 to 10 minutes early, especially when we knew others would be late. Last year when both started part-time jobs, they finally realized the value of always being on time."

Every couple makes sacrifices when they become parents, and when they read the teachings about the roles of mothers and fathers and consult together, this guides them to make their best choices. These choices will also likely change with the age of the children and the family circumstances. Some, like this couple in the story above, might choose to have the wife stay at home as a full-time mother and homemaker. At times, a mother might have paid employment based in the home. In yet other cases, the father might stay at home with the children, and the mother work elsewhere. Both may work outside the home and the children are with caregivers. Other options will emerge through prayer and consultation as well. The choices and combinations are whatever works for the best for your family.

Entering fatherhood and parenthood

Sometimes you may feel strongly attracted to being a father or stepfather, or you may already be one. You may also struggle with taking on this important role and large responsibility. It's also very precious having someone love you and look to you to guide them in positive directions. Fatherhood works best in partnership with the child's mother in most circumstances, but you also have your own unique role. It requires dedication, selflessness, and sleepless nights.

It's beyond the scope of this book to teach you how to be a dad and fulfill your responsibilities. However, the quotations below provide some focus on the importance of being good parents.

> "Teach ye your children so that they may peruse the divine verses every morn and eve. God hath prescribed unto every father to educate his children, both boys and girls, in the sciences and in morals, and in crafts and professions."[382] Bahá'u'lláh

> "Children are the most precious treasure a community can possess, for in them are the promise and guarantee of the future. They bear the seeds of the character of future society which is largely shaped by what the adults constituting the community do or fail to do with respect to children. They are a trust no community can neglect with impunity. An all-embracing love of children, the manner of treating them, the quality of the attention shown them, the spirit of adult behavior toward them—these are all among the vital aspects of the requisite attitude. Love demands discipline, the courage to accustom children to hardship, not to indulge their whims or leave them entirely to their own devices. An atmosphere needs to be maintained in which children feel that they belong to the community and share in its purpose. They must lovingly but insistently be guided to live up to Bahá'í standards, to study and teach the Cause in ways that are suited to their circumstances. ...

> "And now we wish to address a few words to parents, who bear the primary responsibility for the upbringing of their children. We appeal to them to give constant attention to the spiritual education of their children. Some parents appear to think that this is the exclusive responsibility of the community; others believe that in order to preserve the independence of children to investigate truth, the Faith should not be taught to them. Still others feel inadequate to take on such a task. None of this is correct. The beloved Master ['Abdu'l-Bahá] has said that 'it is enjoined upon the father and mother, as a duty, to strive with all effort to train the daughter and the son,' adding that, 'should they neglect this matter, they shall be held responsible and worthy of reproach in the presence of the stern Lord.' Independent of the level of their education, parents are in a critical position to shape the spiritual

development of their children. They should not ever underestimate their capacity to mold their children's moral character. For they exercise indispensable influence through the home environment they consciously create by their love of God, their striving to adhere to His laws, their spirit of service to His Cause, their lack of fanaticism, and their freedom from the corrosive effects of backbiting. Every parent who is a believer in the Blessed Beauty has the responsibility to conduct herself or himself in such a way as to elicit the spontaneous obedience to parents to which the Teachings attach so high a value."[383] Universal House of Justice

"What needs to be appreciated...is the extent to which young minds are affected by the choices parents make for their own lives, when, no matter how unintentionally, no matter how innocently, such choices condone the passions of the world—its admiration for power, its adoration of status, its love of luxuries, its attachment to frivolous pursuits, its glorification of violence, and its obsession with self-gratification. ... May every one of them [the youth] come to know the bounties of a life adorned with purity and learn to draw on the powers that flow through pure channels."[384] Universal House of Justice

S. Truett Cathy spent decades guiding boys to be men. He writes these views in his book, *It's Better to Build Boys Than Mend Men*:

"Children all around us are growing up without strong positive guidance from their parents, who are busy, distracted, absent, or choose to be buddies instead of parents to their children. ... A child needs a new model to break the generational cycle, an adult who will show him or her a better way. ... [C]hildren have plenty of buddies. They don't need an adult—especially a parent—to be another buddy. They need someone they can look up to with respect. That respect begins with the establishment of authority. ... [C]hildren want limits, and they want to be able to respect the adults who set those limits., They want to know where the fence is; that's their security. And, finally, they want to know what will happen when they cross the line. A parent who tries to be a buddy will soon have a tyrant for a child. You don't have to be the world's strongest man to earn the respect of a child or a teenager; you do have to be strong enough to stand your ground against an onslaught of resistance.

"If children have no respect for authority, no amount of punishment is going to change them. One of the best ways to teach children respect for authority is to model our own adherence to the chain of command. Adults can do this by worshiping and respecting God and by obeying the rules of law. It amazes me how many people will cheat on their income taxes, lie to a police officer who stops them for speeding, or take advantage of a clerk who gives them too much change—in clear view of their children."[385]

Here is some more wisdom from S. Truett Cathy:

"When we share our time with children, the little things often become lifetime memories for them."[386]

"How do you know if a child needs encouragement? If he or she is breathing. ... Accountability can reinforce encouragement. ... Appropriate rewards can also reinforce encouragement."[387]

"If our children are to remain pure, we must do three things: pray for them, model purity, and talk to them about remaining pure. This is your responsibility as a parent. It's your job."[388]

"The greatest gift you can give children is a stable home to grow up in. Children who do not have stability at home seek stable relationships with other adults. Live up to your marriage commitment, and children are more likely to trust you and believe that you will not shirk your commitment to them."[389]

"You can't make a child be humble any more than you can make a child love. But you can teach humility to children by serving others and by giving children opportunities to practice humble service."[390]

Establishing a unified family

A family, generally, is a combination of your marriage and your children and/or stepchildren. A stable, unified marriage is the greatest gift you give your children. It supports them in succeeding on all measures and provides them with security and love. Below is some guidance about establishing a family.

"According to the teachings of Bahá'u'lláh the family, being a human unit, must be educated according to the rules of sanctity. All the virtues must be taught the family. The integrity of the family bond must be constantly considered, and the rights of the individual members must not be transgressed. The rights of the son, the father, the mother—none of them must be transgressed, none of them must be arbitrary. Just as the son has certain obligations to his father, the father, likewise, has certain obligations to his son. The mother, the sister and other members of the household have their certain prerogatives. All these rights and prerogatives must be conserved, yet the unity of the family must be sustained. The injury of one shall be considered the injury of all; the comfort of each, the comfort of all; the honor of one, the honor of all."[391] 'Abdu'l-Bahá

A young man married a few years with a young child shares some of his journey:

"I think the most important factor in being a good husband and father was making a conscious decision early on that I wanted to be a good husband and good father someday. This was key, because I didn't have a blueprint of what 'good' looked like. I had a limited father role model growing up because of my father's work schedule, and then my parents got divorced when I was seven. While this did give me some challenges, it also gave me a blank slate to create what the father and husband roles looked like in my mind. I actively sought out what I thought were key elements during my teenage years, so I could pick and choose what I liked about a handful of husbands/dads (who were typically my friends' fathers) to create that social construct together in my head.

"There wasn't any single event that has prepared me to be a good husband or father. It's all a long process, and I think it began with deciding I wanted to be a good person. Then I started defining what the scope of that looked like: wanting to consider other people's feelings, asking for their thoughts, admitting when you're wrong and apologizing, stuff like that. Internal questions arose, like do I want to practice honesty, abstinence, and sobriety? Then if so, I created a talk-track for what to say when my friends challenged or opposed that. I had to ask myself, 'Where do I put my guardrails on the highway of morality?' Then as I moved along over time, I became a better person and was more prepared to be a good husband and father.

"On a practical level, I've found it's easier to be a good husband, and we have found consultation of key value. My wife and I have set up Service Level Agreements (SLAs) around such things as how many pairs of shoes we're each allowed in the hall, who empties the dishwasher on what days, what to do with clothes on the floor, and others. If either of us are in violation of those SLAs, we just remind each other we have an agreement in place. Ultimately what I've found is the Bahá'í Writings have the underlying foundation for what every successful organization does.

"The father role is an ongoing process, just like the Bahá'í Writings say, 'little by little, day by day'. I always tell my friends being a dad isn't like anything you've done before, and there's nothing you can do to completely understand the experience. I usually tell them, 'You can read about skydiving, talk to people who have gone skydiving, or watch skydiving videos, but until you go skydiving yourself, you'll never fully understand the feeling.' In fact, one of my buddies said, 'Yes, it's like that but, more accurately, you first throw the parachute out of the airplane and then jump after it.' And then another one said, 'Yes, in mid-air you have to grab the parachute, put it on, get it fastened, and then make sure it opens in time, all while falling'. I'm still working on the father part. Ask me again when she turns 15, and I'm no longer responsible for her spiritual maturity!"

Dr. William J. Doherty in his book *Take Back Your Marriage* expresses some of his concerns about patterns in life, marriage, and parenting:

"The natural drift of contemporary married life, in our busy, distracted, individualistic, consumer-driven, media-saturated, and work-oriented world, is toward less spark, less connection, less intimacy, and less focus on the couple relationship. Add in the demands of child-sensitive parenting, and you have a pretty good picture of why our marriages decline over time."[392]

"Children are natural and eager consumers of whatever time, attention, and goods and services that parents will provide. It's the job of parents to discern how much is enough, how much is too much, and to enforce the difference."[393]

"Adjustments [to having a child]...are natural and inevitable. But there is a difference between adjusting your marriage to meet your children's needs and losing your marriage to parenthood."[394]

"The greater danger for most of us is to lose our marriage to the demands of parenthood rather than losing our kids to the demands of our marriage (although this happens sometimes in stepfamilies). In a two-parent family, we either fight to create and keep a marriage-centered family, in which the couple relationship is the stable fulcrum of the family and the couple together care for their children, or we become a child-centered family in which the marriage goes on the shelf."[395]

It's vitally important that you and your wife don't let your marriage go on the shelf!

Action (Choose what fits your stage in life)

1. Meet with and interview a couple who has been married between 1 and 3 years and appears to be happy together. Meet with a second couple that has been married for a long time, preferably more than 15 years, and whose marriage you think is a good example to strive for. Discuss with each couple how you could put into action the insights gained from your interviews with them, to contribute to you maintaining a strong, happy marriage. Some suggested questions are (feel free to make or add your own):
    a. How do they express love to one another? What do they do to maintain loving feelings between them?
    b. How does thoughtfully serving each other contribute to their marriage? How does serving others together as a couple contribute to it?
    c. How do they use consultation to build understanding and make decisions?
    d. What other factors enhance the strength of their marriage?
    e. What difficulties have they experienced? How did they address them constructively? What do they wish they had done differently?
    f. How did becoming parents affect their marriage?
    g. What advice would they offer to people thinking of getting married, or to other newly married couples? Was there anything they wish they had known or better understood before they got married?

2. Interview men who are fathers and stepfathers about their experience as dads. What have they appreciated? What has been difficult? What advice do they have for you? Do an activity with younger children and

then with older children, or with your own children. Were you able to implement the advice? What did you learn?

3. Read two books, one about marriage and one about parenting, and assess where the author's perspectives align or don't align with spiritual principles. What did you learn that you can apply?

4. Watch at least two online videos each on being a couple and on being a parent. What did you learn?

5. Take an online parenting course. Two possibilities are through the Wilmette Institute (www.wilmetteinstitute.org) or Positive Discipline (www.positivediscipline.com).

Reflection (Choose what fits your stage in life)

1. What have I seen as the value of parental consent? What could be some challenges? How could these be addressed?
2. What is my view of marriage? How does thinking of it as a divine institution created by God shift my perspectives?
3. In what ways do I think marriage is a "fortress for well-being and salvation"? What does "well-being" look like to me? What do I think "salvation" could mean in this context? What does it look like to mutually look after each other's "well-being"?
4. What are some of the purposes of marriage? Benefits?
5. What do I appreciate about being married? What is challenging?
6. When I look at various types of family formations, what type do I want to create? What am I unwilling to participate in?
7. What do I see as my responsibilities toward a family?
8. How do I feel about being a father or stepfather and responsible for raising a child? What actions am I carrying out? If I'm not in a relationship or marriage with the mother(s), am I still involved with my children?
9. What do I enjoy about fatherhood? What is challenging?
10. What would improve my ability to be an excellent husband? A better father?
11. Who could I mentor to be a better husband or father? How could I make this happen?
12. Where would I turn for help if I have difficulties with marriage or parenting?

Part 7: Bravely Arising to Create My Future

26 - Directing the Course of My Life

Challenge: There seems to be so many choices that I often think it would be easier to just let someone else make the decisions for my life; at other times I rebel, because everyone has an opinion about what I should do.

Opportunity: With the help of God, others, and the gifts of prayer, meditation, and consultation, I can make wise decisions for my life.

Summary:
- I can, with help from God and others, direct how and where my life goes.
- It's easy to get overwhelmed with all the choices for what to do with my life, so it's empowering to prioritize based on spiritual principles.
- I have an inner drive and passion to learn and make beneficial choices.
- I can use prayer, meditation, and consultation for determining my life choices.
- As I make decisions, the power of commitment fuels my ability to bravely carry them out.

More:

Who's in charge?

On your life journey and quest to be a Bahá'í man, you may at times feel as if everyone oversees your life and your choices except you. If you are living at home, your family will have a say in your choices. This is particularly true if you have not yet completed your education, as your parents have a key responsibility to God to ensure you are educated. As an adult you then have the responsibility to pursue your strengths and contribute to the world, and you have more leadership over your choices.

There are always things you can control, from practical aspects like what food to offer to friends in your home to spiritual actions like how and when to do community service. However, in most cases where a decision needs to be made, Bahá'u'lláh's guidance is to engage in prayer and consultation with others. This is a process of discerning spiritual guidance and facts, sharing feelings and thoughts, building understanding, and where needed, making decisions. The participants often arrive at a final choice with clear action steps, and you as a full participant then carry these out.

Using consultation ensures good understanding and decisions for you and others. Here are some examples:

- Should you tutor a study circle or animate a junior youth group?
- Study accounting?
- Save money to buy a home?
- Have a child?
- Plan a vacation?
- Stay in school or get a job? Do both?
- Participate on a sports team?
- Marry a current friend or look elsewhere for a potential wife?
- Change career paths?

In making decisions, you will consult with those you respect and trust. Perhaps these include a relationship or marriage partner, parent, coach, teacher, friends, study circle tutor, junior youth animator, employer, or Bahá'í institution. This quotation may guide you:

> "The question of consultation is of the utmost importance, and is one of the most potent instruments conducive to the tranquility and felicity of the people. For example, when a believer is uncertain about his affairs, or when he seeketh to pursue a project or trade, the friends should gather together and devise a solution for him. He, in his turn, should act accordingly. Likewise in larger issues, when a problem ariseth, or a difficulty occurreth, the wise should gather, consult, and devise a solution. They should then rely upon the one true God, and surrender to His Providence, in whatever way it may be revealed, for divine confirmations will undoubtedly assist."[396] 'Abdu'l-Bahá

Here is guidance about directing the course of your life:

> "Each individual is unique and has a unique path to tread in his lifetime. In espousing the Bahá'í Faith you have defined the direction of that path, for your recognition of God's Manifestation for this Day and your devotion to His Message provide the spiritual and ethical basis for all aspects of your life of service to mankind, while the continuing guidance that He has provided for the community of His followers enables you to know the directions in which the most effort is required at the present time.

"While, during the early years of the development of the Faith, Bahá'u'lláh, 'Abdu'l-Bahá and Shoghi Effendi sometimes gave specific instructions to individual believers on how they should serve the Cause, the Universal House of Justice seldom does this. It is, indeed, the precious privilege of the individual human being to direct the course of his own life. Through exercising this privilege while striving always to conform his conduct to the divine Teachings and devote his talents in the best possible way to the service of the Cause and mankind, a soul deepens his understanding of God and His will.

"This does not mean that you are left to make your decisions without guidance. This you will find from several sources. Firstly, in general, you will find it in the Writings. Secondly, and more specifically, in the teaching plans issued by the Universal House of Justice. Thirdly, in the plans and projects of your own National Spiritual Assembly. All these, it would seem from your letter, you have been striving to follow. Fourthly, with regard to your own personal goals and actions, is the guidance you can receive through consultation—with your wife, with friends of your choice whose opinions you value, with your Local Spiritual Assembly, with such committees of your National Assembly as are concerned with the fields of activity towards which your inclinations lie. Fifthly, there is prayer and meditation.

"You mention that the answers to your prayers never seem to have come through clearly. Mrs. Ruth Moffett has published her recollection of five steps of prayer for guidance that she was told by the beloved Guardian. When asked about these notes, Shoghi Effendi replied, in letters written by his secretary on his behalf, that the notes should be regarded as 'personal suggestions,' that he considered them to be 'quite sound,' but that the friends need not adopt them 'strictly and universally.'

"The House of Justice feels that they may be helpful to you and, indeed, you may already be familiar with them. They are as follows:

> '... use these five steps if we have a problem of any kind for which we desire a solution, or wish help.
>
> [1] 'Pray and meditate about it. Use the prayers of the Manifestations, as they have the greatest power. Learn to remain in the silence of contemplation for a few moments. During this deepest communion take the next step.

[2] 'Arrive at a decision and hold to this. This decision is usually born in a flash at the close or during the contemplation. It may seem almost impossible of accomplishment, but if it seems to be an answer to prayer or a way of solving the problem, then immediately take the next step.

[3] 'Have determination to carry the decision through. Many fail here. The decision, budding into determination, is blighted and instead becomes a wish or a vague longing. When determination is born, immediately take the next step.

[4] 'Have faith and confidence, that the Power of the Holy Spirit will flow through you, the right way will appear, the door will open, the right message, the right principle or the right book will be given to you. Have confidence, and the right thing will come to meet your need. Then as you rise from prayer take immediately the fifth step.

[5] 'Act as though it had all been answered. Then act with tireless, ceaseless energy. And, as you act, you yourself will become a magnet which will attract more power to your being, until you become an unobstructed channel for the Divine Power to flow through you.'

"Also the Guardian's secretary wrote to an individual believer on his behalf: 'The Master said guidance was when the doors opened after we tried. We can pray, ask to do God's will only, try hard, and then if we find our plan is not working out, assume it is not the right one, at least for the moment.'"[397] On behalf of the Universal House of Justice

Are my choices the best ones?

In significant decisions it's wisest to tune into the Will of God for you. [See Chapter 3.] Prayer, intuition, reading, reflection, meditation, and consultation may all play a role. There are no text messages that come from God with exact directions, but there are often confirmations that a choice or decision is on track. You do your best to make a good decision and then watch for confirmations to keep going or indications that you should re-visit the decision and head a new direction. Of course, then there is also the somewhat difficult part to determine: "What if I'm just supposed to learn to persevere?!" Life is not an exact science. However, the quotations below may expand your views on this topic.

"We cherish the hope that through the loving-kindness of the All-Wise, the All-Knowing, obscuring dust may be dispelled and the power of perception enhanced, that the people may discover the purpose for which they have been called into being. In this Day whatsoever serveth to reduce blindness and to increase vision is worthy of consideration. This vision acteth as the agent and guide for true knowledge. Indeed in the estimation of men of wisdom keenness of understanding is due to keenness of vision. The people of Bahá must under all circumstances observe that which is meet and seemly and exhort the people accordingly."[398] Bahá'u'lláh

"God has endowed human beings with more than one way of receiving guidance in the decisions we have to make, as 'Abdu'l-Bahá has explained. There are the Holy Writings, in which are clear directions for the way in which we should live; if an inner voice prompts us to act contrary to the explicit teachings we can be sure that, far from being an inspiration from God, that inner voice is the expression of our own lower nature, and should be disregarded. There is also the gift of intelligence and good judgment—the faculty which distinguishes man from the animal kingdom; God intends us to use the faculty, which can be a powerful instrument for distinguishing between true inspirations and vain imaginings. There is the power of prayer through which we strive to purify our motives, to seek the Will of God and to implore His guidance and assistance. There is also the law of consultation, one of the distinguishing features of this great Revelation."[399] On behalf of the Universal House of Justice

"With regard to your question as to the value of intuition as a source of guidance for the individual: implicit faith in our intuitive powers is unwise, but through daily prayer and sustained effort one can discover, though not always and fully, God's will intuitively. Under no circumstances, however, can a person be absolutely certain that he is recognizing God's will, through the exercise of his intuition. It often happens that the latter results in completely misrepresenting the truth, and thus becomes a source of error rather than of guidance."[400] On behalf of Shoghi Effendi

A man reflects on his experience:

"While I was on pilgrimage to the Bahá'í Shrines in Israel I prayed for and received inspiration for what to do next in my life. The answers were clear and seemed like a good fit for my talents and abilities. On my way home from pilgrimage, I traveled to another country to do service. While there, someone presented to me another possible life plan. I turned again to prayer and assessed the choices. It was clear to me that I should continue with what came to me during pilgrimage. I have carried out that plan, and I have been very confirmed it was the right choice."

The Bahá'í teachings promote establishing the oneness of humanity and service to others for the betterment of the world as integral and necessary parts of leading a fulfilling, purposeful life. Your course in life, including education, employment, marrying, and raising a family, all contribute to the progress of society. Here is this guidance:

> "The betterment of the world can be accomplished through pure and goodly deeds, through commendable and seemly conduct."[401] Bahá'u'lláh

> "... Bahá'í youth can accept—and should be encouraged to accept—a responsibility of their own for moral leadership in the transformation of society."[402] Universal House of Justice

Power of commitment

As you make choices and decisions, it then takes commitment to carry them out. A few authors comment on the connection between choices and commitment and the power of the outcome:

> "... [C]ommitment means making hard choices among alternatives. Many people do not want to give up one option in order to have another, though they will have neither if they do not make a choice. But choices and priorities are intertwined with commitment."[403] Scott M. Stanley

> "The moment you believe you can do something, power seems to stream into you; the moment you believe you cannot do it, you have lost more than half the battle, you seem to be drained of the force necessary to do it."[404] R. Rabbani

"Until one is committed there is hesitancy, the chance to draw back, always ineffectiveness. Concerning all acts of initiative (and creation), there is one elementary truth, the ignorance of which kills countless ideas and splendid plans: that the moment one definitely commits oneself, then Providence moves too. All sorts of things occur to help one that would never otherwise have occurred. A whole stream of events issues from the decision, raising in one's favor all manner of unforeseen incidents and meetings and material assistance, which no man could have dreamt would have come his way."[405] W. H. Murray

Action

1. Identify an issue, problem, or point of decision for you in your life and try out the five steps of prayer listed above in this chapter. What worked well? What was difficult?

2. Identify an issue that involves someone else and invite that person to pray and consult with you. What worked well? What was difficult? Did you reach a unified conclusion?

3. Plan to take a trip to an area in nature. Decide on your destination and how you will get there. Consider all the details that will increase enjoyment in the trip and keep you healthy throughout it, including whether to go alone or invite someone to join you. Then take the trip, doing your best to enjoy the full experience as you go. What happened? What did you learn about yourself and your skills?

Reflection

1. What is scary about taking charge of my life decisions? What is exciting about the process?
2. How do I feel about involving others in making my life decisions? When is it best for me to be brave and invite others to participate?
3. Who or what seem to be my best sources of guidance and assistance?
4. Who could I recommend the decision-making steps in the chapter to?
5. How do I make major decisions in my life?
6. When does fear get in the way of my taking action in life? How can I balance that fear with courage?

7. When do I avoid making decisions or handling issues that arise in my life? Why do I do this? How does this avoidance affect what happens in my life? How could I prevent these negative outcomes?
8. How can I draw on spiritual sources to guide me in making key decisions?
9. When does making decisions with my "gut" intuition work well? When has it misled me?
10. What do I enjoy doing the most? What strengths, skills, and abilities do I have that match what I enjoy doing? Are there others that I want to learn or develop?
11. What do I care about the most? Why?
12. What is important for me to do in bettering the world? What is my passion? Where can I best contribute my time and energy?

27 – Learning and Working As Worship

Challenge: There are thousands of possible degrees and professions, and it's overwhelming trying to make choices.

Opportunity: I know myself well and what interests me, so I'll begin or continue with my education and profession, watch for signs I'm on track with my choices, and see where God, meditation, and consultation with others steer me.

Summary:
- It's vital for me to be literate, learn new knowledge, and tune into what's happening in the world.
- Education of all types contributes to me being successful in my profession.
- Learning what my various aspirations throughout life are, what truly calls me to be in action, is an unfolding process that comes from prayer, meditation, consultation, observation, and experience.
- My work contributes to my family and community and to my self-respect; my work is one way I worship God.
- I can behave ethically with good moral choices in my work and service.
- I respect Bahá'í Holy Days by commemorating them and not working on them.

More:

Progressively learning

Literacy, the ability to read and write, is highly valued in the Bahá'í teachings, in part so that everyone can read the teachings for themselves. Here is guidance:

> "The most immediate access to the dynamic influence of the sacred Word is through reading. The ability to read is therefore a fundamental right and privilege of every human being."[406] Universal House of Justice

A man comments about reading:

"A proper diet is good for your body, and the best books are good for your mind. Your life will be determined by the people you associate with and the books that you read."[407] S. Truett Cathy

The Bahá'í teachings also emphasize the importance of education and work. As you work part-time or full-time, you build attitudes and skills that likely increase your income over time. You also learn to manage money—responsibly budgeting, saving, spending, and contributing to the Bahá'í Funds. Here is encouragement to strive:

> "O loving friends! Exert every effort to acquire the various branches of knowledge and true understanding. Strain every nerve to achieve both material and spiritual accomplishments.
> "Encourage the children from their earliest years to master every kind of learning, and make them eager to become skilled in every art—the aim being that through the favoring grace of God, the heart of each one may become even as a mirror disclosing the secrets of the universe, penetrating the innermost reality of all things; and that each may earn world-wide fame in all branches of knowledge, science and the arts.[408]
> 'Abdu'l-Bahá

A man reflects on this theme:

"A lot of men want to be successful students and successful professionals as well as share the Bahá'í teachings with their peers. The hard part is bridging that gap between the Bahá'í Writings and what's considered contemporary vernacular for college, the workplace, and friends. Creating an 'SLA' (Service Level Agreement), which my wife and I have learned to do, sounds a lot cooler than 'We reflect, have a consultation in unity, and create an honorable agreement that we both uphold.' It's a hard 'sell' for a 17-year old guy going to college to tell his friends, Bahá'u'lláh says, 'Arts, crafts and sciences uplift the world of being, and are conducive to its exaltation. Knowledge is as wings to man's life, and a ladder for his ascent'[409], even though the foundation of its meaning is true. Honestly, I think someone could write a book called, 'Cool ways to say the Bahá'í principles—suggestions for the 16- to 24-year old', and it would fly off the shelf!"

Be Brave and Arise

As you move through life, you can be an active agent in your own ongoing learning process. Learning transforms you and others, and it assists society to forge new patterns more in alignment with Bahá'u'lláh's teachings. If you are not active, there are consequences:

> "Passivity is bred by the forces of society today. A desire to be entertained is nurtured from childhood, with increasing efficiency, cultivating generations willing to be led by whoever proves skillful at appealing to superficial emotions. Even in many educational systems students are treated as though they were receptacles designed to receive information. That the Bahá'í world has succeeded in developing a culture which promotes a way of thinking, studying, and acting, in which all consider themselves as treading a common path of service—supporting one another and advancing together, respectful of the knowledge that each one possesses at any given moment and avoiding the tendency to divide the believers into categories such as deepened and uninformed—is an accomplishment of enormous proportions. And therein lie the dynamics of an irrepressible movement."[410] Universal House of Justice

Education is a prime contributor to your ability to earn an income. Education and work can also synergistically contribute to your ability to improve life for segments of humanity. For example, if you study math and sciences in school and earn an engineering degree, you may position yourself to build roads and bridges in parts of the world with poor infrastructure. Perhaps you decide to learn a trade and work with your hands to build homes for people. If you study anatomy, physiology, and psychology, you might position yourself to coach children in both character and sports or to pursue a career in nursing. Many options are open to you on your first pass through an education system or going back to learn and change the course of your work in a new direction.

Resource Note: Many college students participate in The Institute for Studies in Global Prosperity (ISGP; https://www.globalprosperity.org/), which is a non-profit organization that builds capacity in individuals, groups, and institutions so they contribute to the betterment of society.

Determining my aspirations and profession(s)

From the time you are very young, adults have likely asked you, "What do you want to be when you grow up?" A smart answer these days is "a good man"! The truth is, some people know what work they want to do, and they stay on that course for a lifetime. However, it's also very common for men to change professions and jobs in search for a good fit for them. You may also prefer innovation and new challenges to happen in your work on a regular basis, or you may be a better fit as an entrepreneur.

The teachings encourage pursuing professions, trades, arts, and crafts. Whether you choose to be a teacher, electrician, musician, plumber, doctor, furniture maker, nurse, astronaut, author, computer programmer, manufacturer, consultant, or any other occupation that contributes to others, you are participating in vital work that is part of worshipping God.

Bahá'u'lláh calls you to determine, over time, your "aspiration", and you will likely have more than one throughout your life:

"The All-Knowing Physician hath His finger on the pulse of mankind. He perceiveth the disease, and prescribeth, in His unerring wisdom, the remedy. Every age hath its own problem, and every soul its particular aspiration. The remedy the world needeth in its present-day afflictions can never be the same as that which a subsequent age may require. Be anxiously concerned with the needs of the age ye live in, and center your deliberations on its exigencies and requirements."[411] Bahá'u'lláh

"Man, possessed of an inner faculty which plants and animals do not have, a power which enables him to discover the secrets of nature and gain mastery over the environment, has a special responsibility to use his God-given powers for positive ends."[412] On behalf of the Universal House of Justice

What are you called by God to do that is greater than what focuses on yourself? What is it inside of you that feels like it has a level of urgency and insists you pay attention and focus on fulfilling it? Or have you stopped hearing the drumbeat of what you are to do in life and need to spend time tuning into it? Here is one man's path:

"When I was in my late-teens and early twenties, I worked at a job that looked more enticing than finishing my college degree. It was okay for a while, but I began to lose interest in it. Then I tried a series of similar jobs,

none of which stuck for long. I finally spent time in focused prayer and reflection over a few weeks to figure out what I really wanted to do. With financial assistance and advice from my parents, I started a business that I am very passionate about. It's a great fit for me. It's not easy. Most days I'm putting in long hours. But every day I can tell I'm contributing to the lives of the people I'm working with and serving, and it feels great."

Sometimes parents, teachers, relationship or marriage partners, or others might try to direct your choices in specific ways based on their culture, their own interests and experiences, and their fears. However, while you can and will consult with others affected by your choices, in most circumstances it will be best for you to choose what you enjoy doing that also assists you to serve others and support yourself and appropriate family members. You may not immediately discover an aspiration, or you may have multiple ones over time. You may go back to education sources at times to expand your knowledge and for re-training. The following quotations can guide you in your choices:

"When anyone occupieth himself in a craft or trade, such occupation itself is regarded in the estimation of God as an act of worship; and this is naught but a token of His infinite and all-pervasive bounty."[413] Bahá'u'lláh

"It is understandable that Bahá'ís who witness the miserable conditions under which so many human beings have to live, or who hear of a sudden disaster that has struck a certain area of the world, are moved to do something practical to ameliorate those conditions and to help their suffering fellow-mortals.

"There are many ways in which help can be rendered. Every Bahá'í has the duty to acquire a trade or profession through which he will earn that wherewith he can support himself and his family; in the choice of such work he can seek those activities which are of benefit to his fellow-men and not merely those which promote his personal interests, still less those whose effects are actually harmful."[414] On behalf of the Universal House of Justice

Here is a perspective about work:

"This marvelous capacity we have to do, to produce, is at once the spring of our health and, to a great extent, our happiness in life. Nothing can convey so solid a feeling of satisfaction in this world as something we have accomplished. A job well done, be it making a pie or writing a book or building a bridge, can produce a degree of contentment, a sense of buoyancy and fulfillment, that practically nothing else can. ... Because work is necessary for us, it sets the very essence of our being in circulation, and just as the blood performs so many services in our body essential to health, such as carrying away impurities, re-oxygenizing itself in the lungs, bringing food to the tissues, so work seems to give tone to our whole machine, exhilarates us, and calls forth a new flow of energy."[415] R. Rabbani

How I act in the world

As you interact with teachers, professors, managers, and coworkers, as well as your family, you will strive for a high degree of integrity and honor. Your truthfulness, honesty with handling money and property, responsibility with completing assignments, confidence in offering your skills and knowledge, responsibility, and more will earn respect and be a power of example. People will also grow to respect your principles and beliefs. As they get to know you, they will see you show respect for your religion by striving for excellence, treating women with equality and respect, avoiding backbiting, promoting unity, observing Holy Days, and more. The quotations below illuminate standards to strive for.

> "The light of the Revelation is destined to illumine every sphere of endeavor; in each, the relationships that sustain society are to be recast; in each, the world seeks examples of how human beings should be to one another. ... [T]here are certainly practices a Bahá'í would eschew, such as dishonesty in one's transactions or the economic exploitation of others. Faithful adherence to the divine admonitions demands there be no contradiction between one's economic conduct and one's beliefs as a Bahá'í. By applying in one's life those principles of the Faith that relate to fairness and equity, a single soul can uphold a standard far above the low threshold by which the world measures itself. Humanity is weary for want of a pattern of life to which to aspire; we look to you to foster communities whose ways will give hope to the world."[416] Universal House of Justice

"The nine Bahá'í holy days on which work should be suspended include:

- The Feast of Naw-Rúz (New Year)
- The first day of Riḍván
- The ninth day of Riḍván
- The twelfth day of Riḍván
- The anniversary of the Declaration of the Báb
- The anniversary of the Ascension of Bahá'u'lláh
- The anniversary of the Martyrdom of the Báb
- The anniversary of the Birth of the Báb
- The anniversary of the Birth of Bahá'u'lláh"[417] Universal House of Justice

"The words, the deeds, the attitudes, the lack of prejudice, the nobility of character, the high sense of service to others—in a word, those qualities and actions which distinguish a Bahá'í must unfailingly characterize their inner life and outer behavior, and their interactions with friend or foe.

"Rejecting the low sights of mediocrity, let them scale the ascending heights of excellence in all they aspire to do. May they resolve to elevate the very atmosphere in which they move, whether it be in the school rooms or halls of higher learning, in their work, their recreation, their Bahá'í activity or social service.

"Indeed, let them welcome with confidence the challenges awaiting them. Imbued with this excellence and a corresponding humility, with tenacity and a loving servitude, today's youth must move towards the front ranks of the professions, trades, arts and crafts which are necessary to the further progress of humankind—this to ensure that the spirit of the Cause will cast its illumination on all these important areas of human endeavor. Moreover, while aiming at mastering the unifying concepts and swiftly advancing technologies of this era of communications, they can, indeed they must also guarantee the transmittal to the future of those skills which will preserve the marvelous, indispensable achievements of the past. The transformation which is to occur in the functioning of society will certainly depend to a great extent on the effectiveness of the preparations the youth make for the world they will inherit."[418] Universal House of Justice

When it's tough to choose my course
[See Chapter 26, "Directing the Course of My Life".]

If you are feeling stuck on what education or work choices to make, you may need to pray for inspiration and consult with other people. Remember this guidance:

> "... [W]hen a believer is uncertain about his affairs, or when he seeketh to pursue a project or trade, the friends should gather together and devise a solution for him. He, in his turn, should act accordingly. Likewise in larger issues, when a problem ariseth, or a difficulty occurreth, the wise should gather, consult, and devise a solution. They should then rely upon the one true God, and surrender to His Providence, in whatever way it may be revealed, for divine confirmations will undoubtedly assist."[419] 'Abdu'l-Bahá

Here's what happened when someone followed this quotation above:

"I was ready to leave a job that I'd outgrown and where my managers' ethics stunk. I had a new degree in business, but I wasn't quite sure what to do next. I read a quotation about consulting with others, and so I invited a few friends to come meet with me one evening. We looked at my skills, abilities, interests, education, and experience. We considered whether I should relocate or stay where I was currently living. We assessed my options for work. By the end of the evening we had come up with a viable plan. It took courage to meet with them and courage to then implement the plan, but the outcome was way better than I could have created on my own."

Action

1. Write a statement of your current "aspiration" with your education and/or your work. If you aspire toward something else, or have multiple aspirations, then write an additional statement about it/them.

2. Choose three character qualities to improve your interactions with people at school, work, and in the community, re-looking at Chapter 8 as a resource as needed. Reflect and write down a few specific ways of talking and acting that will demonstrate these qualities. Begin to act and write your observations of the outcomes. Example:

Character Quality of Dependability:

Potential Actions to take:
- I will take the lead on a new school or work project and schedule timely meetings.
- I will offer to play music and/or sing for a devotional gathering and show up on time and well-prepared.
- I will research a topic that a team I participate on needs, and share my learning with them.

3. Do three concrete actions to lead you toward a new education or work choice. Consider one of them being an informational interview with someone in that field or profession.

4. Write a business plan to start a new initiative as a business-owner.

5. Write a few ideas for effective ways to talk about the Bahá'í principles with your peers that they will find attractive. Begin to use and modify them as needed.

Reflection

1. What value do I see in being literate?
2. What value do I see in being educated?
3. How does humility assist me to learn effectively? What else contributes to effective learning for me?
4. Am I able to teach others what I learn? Do I enjoy this?
5. What value do I see in working?
6. What keeps me in a spirit of worshiping God when I am studying or working?
7. Am I able to internally generate the wish to achieve excellence? Does it contribute to me staying focused on my goal if I plan breaks, celebrations, or some small reward? What could increase my internal motivation? Is there someone who could accompany me in staying focused on achieving education and work excellence and goals?
8. How do I blend my learning experiences and sharing the Bahá'í teachings?
9. How do I apply the Bahá'í teachings in my work? What do I want to improve?

Be Brave and Arise

28 - Continuing the Quest for Spiritual Manhood

Challenge: The forces of darkness are powerful, and I often wonder if fighting with my sword of light and inner strength will be enough to resist them.

Opportunity: The more I'm consistent with aligning my choices with the Bahá'í teachings and living a life of integrity on the eternal journey to become my best self, the more my light shines.

Summary:
- Life is a long and eternal journey that requires my best and bravest efforts.
- Part of my quest is to live my life with high integrity and coherence.
- Some services are especially vital for me while I am a youth (15-30 years old), and I can serve in many ways throughout my life.
- When I have a clear mission in life, it empowers and inspires me to be in action.

More:

Life's a spiritual journey

You are on an eternal journey of spiritual growth and spiritual manhood. The journey will include peaks of joy and valleys of despair, times when you feel all is going well, and times when you struggle. These descriptors fit most lives, but when you are living in a spiritual context and with spiritual goals, all aspects of the journey are useful and meaningful.

As you increasingly make spiritual choices, build healthy habits, and create unified connections with others, you strengthen your spiritual muscles. Your spiritual sword made of light glows more powerfully, and you wield it more effectively. You are more likely to speak and act in beneficial ways. Spiritual actions and unified relationships contribute to your happiness and self-respect. You will feel closer to spiritual maturity the more you:

- Have pure and positive thoughts
- Refine your character
- Find purpose and service in the world around you

Hopefully, part of your quest will include a high-quality social life with friends that includes laughter, connections in your neighborhood, involvement in the Bahá'í community, and service in the broader world. As you continue your journey to become the spiritual man that you yearn to be, you will more and more consistently listen to the voices from the realm of light, and less and less often pay heed to the voices that speak from the side of the dark forces. Here is encouragement:

"The friends must, at all times, bear in mind that they are, in a way, like soldiers under attack. The world is at present in an exceedingly dark condition spiritually; hatred and prejudice, of every sort, are literally tearing it to pieces. We, on the other hand, are the custodians of the opposite forces, the forces of love, of unity, of peace and integration, and we must constantly be on our guard, whether as individuals or as an Assembly or Community, lest through us these destructive, negative forces enter into our midst. In other words we must beware lest the darkness of society become reflected in our acts and attitudes, perhaps all unconsciously. Love for each other, the deep sense that we are a new organism, the dawn-breakers of a New World Order, must constantly animate our Bahá'í lives, and we must pray to be protected from the contamination of society which is so diseased with prejudice."[420] On behalf of Shoghi Effendi

"O Fleeting Shadow! Pass beyond the baser stages of doubt and rise to the exalted heights of certainty. Open the eye of truth, that thou mayest behold the veilless Beauty and exclaim: Hallowed be the Lord, the most excellent of all creators!"[421] Bahá'u'lláh

Striving for integrity and coherence

As you deepen your trust in the wisdom of the Bahá'í teachings and institutions to guide you, you will increasingly make good choices. Your words and actions will align with spiritual principles, and you will consult with others regularly. The themes to strive for are coherence and integrity, which are present when you:

- Turn to God and Bahá'u'lláh over and over in prayer for help and guidance, trusting Them to be greater than any issue that arises in your life.

- Tune in through regularly reading guidance and consulting with others to build understanding and make excellent decisions.
- Practice your beliefs and align your choices with the teachings.
- Draw on science and research to inform you as needed.
- Become the same honest person in all the spaces you visit and inhabit.
- Don't try to pretend you are something you are not or hide who you are.
- Consistently keep your promises and commitments.
- Demonstrate a spirit of service to others wherever you are, leaving each person and place better than you found them.

Consistency with these points will contribute to your happiness but achieving them will not be easy. You will often have to remind yourself to "be brave and arise". The worldly social environment, as well as people in your life, will at times not encourage you or hold you accountable for your spiritual and moral actions. Rather, they may take the position that you will simply "grow out" of making harmful choices or make excuses for you. They may not know how to guide you through making wiser choices and initiating better actions. All of this can make striving for spiritual manhood at times more difficult. However, this maturing process is vital, and the tests of life can also forge your transformation.

Remember to take the long view that you are on a spiritual journey. You are taking yourself into account daily, so you are not as dependent on others calling on you to improve. Bahá'u'lláh says:

> "Through the Teachings of this Day Star of Truth every man will advance and develop until he attaineth the station at which he can manifest all the potential forces with which his inmost true self hath been endowed. It is for this very purpose that in every age and dispensation the Prophets of God and His chosen Ones have appeared amongst men, and have evinced such power as is born of God and such might as only the Eternal can reveal."[422] Bahá'u'lláh

You are a powerful member of the army of light:

> "Tear asunder, in My Name, the veils that have grievously blinded your vision, and, through the power born of your belief in the unity of God, scatter the idols of vain imitation. Enter, then, the holy paradise of the good-pleasure of the All-Merciful. Sanctify your souls from whatsoever is not of God, and taste ye the sweetness of rest within the pale of His

vast and mighty Revelation, and beneath the shadow of His supreme and infallible authority. Suffer not yourselves to be wrapt in the dense veils of your selfish desires, inasmuch as I have perfected in every one of you My creation, so that the excellence of My handiwork may be fully revealed unto men. It follows, therefore, that every man hath been, and will continue to be, able of himself to appreciate the Beauty of God, the Glorified."[423] Bahá'u'lláh

"O ye loved ones of God! In this, the Bahá'í dispensation, God's Cause is spirit unalloyed. His Cause belongeth not to the material world. It cometh neither for strife nor war, nor for acts of mischief or of shame; it is neither for quarrelling with other Faiths, nor for conflicts with the nations. Its only army is the love of God, its only joy the clear wine of His knowledge, its only battle the expounding of the Truth; its one crusade is against the insistent self, the evil promptings of the human heart. Its victory is to submit and yield, and to be selfless is its everlasting glory."[424] 'Abdu'l-Bahá

My mission in life

At this point in the book, you have likely developed a strong sense of where you are going, why, and how you might want to get there. What do you now see as your mission in life, your driving purpose(s)? What will fuel your journey, your quest? Consider the following:

"After men have accomplished becoming men, members of the workforce, husband and fathers, they still seek more. Men feel more fulfilled when they are following a vision or on a quest. So after men have conquered the customary roles, they seek and pursue a higher purpose. ... Seeking and discovering higher purpose is a higher stage in the growth of a man. Higher purpose is something that is not meant to benefit you directly, but does benefit other people, society, or some other purpose that is larger than yourself. Being in your higher purpose takes you outside of yourself and into the higher realm of service to others."[425] Howard J. Fox

Be Brave and Arise

The Bahá'í teachings include many calls to action. Here are powerful ones:

"O Son of Man! Humble thyself before Me, that I may graciously visit thee. Arise for the triumph of My cause, that while yet on earth thou mayest obtain the victory."[426] Bahá'u'lláh

"Persevere, however great the obstacles ahead, however dark the coming days. Bahá'u'lláh is your Guide, your Sustainer, and Protector at all times and under all conditions."[427] Shoghi Effendi

"Our motto in these days of world-encircling gloom should be the Words of God addressed to the Blessed Beauty [Bahá'u'lláh] Himself. 'When the swords flash, go forward! When the shafts fly, press onward!'"[428] Universal House of Justice

"… [W]hile we see much to be done, we see many ready to do it. In thousands of clusters, neighborhoods, and villages, fresh springs of faith and assurance are pouring forth, cheering the spirits of those touched by their reviving waters. In places, the flow is a steady stream, in some, already a river. Now is not the moment for any soul to linger upon the bank—let all lend themselves to the onward surge."[429] Universal House of Justice

What will your role be?

Action

1. Go back to the beginning of the book to the "Mapping and Packing for My Quest" section and read all the chapter summaries again. Reflect on your progress and adjust your goals, plans, or map as needed. What is next in your life?

2. Write a mission statement for your life that reflects your learning from throughout the book. Aspects of such a statement could include:

    - The strengths, talents, and skills you bring to your family, work, and service
    - What you base your beliefs on
    - What you intend to create in your life

- What others can count on you for
- Your best character qualities
- What services you intend to offer
- Your goals and aspirations

Put your final statement in a place you will see it regularly for inspiration. Be aware that you will likely edit it somewhat as you go forward. Reviewing it at least annually is a good practice.

3. Create a poster or collage that reflects one or more aspects of your mission. What do you feel and think when you look at it? Does it inspire you? (If you're new to making collages, here's how: Cut out pictures and/or words that reflect a topic or theme from magazines or other sources. Then stick the images and words onto a large piece of paper or cardboard. You can also use markers or crayons to add your own artwork or words.)

4. Create an artistic presentation that reflects one or more of your insights from this book. Gather a group of friends and share it.

5. Organize and facilitate a group study of this book or ask someone else to facilitate it. [See more information in Appendix B.]

6. Write a list of sayings and quotations to guide you in your life. Here is an example:

Guidelines for Life

1. **Tell the truth.**
   "Truthfulness is the foundation of all human virtues." ('Abdu'l-Bahá, cited in Shoghi Effendi, *Advent of Divine Justice*, p. 22)

2. **Be honest with yourself.**
   "Bring thyself to account each day." (Bahá'u'lláh, *Hidden Words*, Arabic #31)

3. **Keep yourself and your surroundings clean and tidy.**
   "Be ye the very essence of cleanliness." (Bahá'u'lláh, *The Kitáb-i-Aqdas*, #K74)

4. **Think and act independently.**
   "See with thine own eyes and not through the eyes of others." (Bahá'u'lláh, *Hidden Words*, Arabic #2)

5. **Do what you say you will do.**
   "Be worthy of the trust of thy neighbor." (Bahá'u'lláh, *Epistle to the Son of the Wolf*, p. 93)

6. **Think of others first.**
   "Blessed is he who preferreth his brother before himself." (Bahá'u'lláh, *Tablets of Bahá'u'lláh*, p. 71)

7. **Find meaning in study, work, and volunteering.**
   "When anyone occupieth himself in a craft or trade, such occupation itself is regarded in the estimation of God as an act of worship." (Bahá'u'lláh, *Tablets of Bahá'u'lláh*, p. 26)

8. **Give to others and don't complain.**
   "Be generous in prosperity, and thankful in adversity." (Bahá'u'lláh, *Epistle to the Son of the Wolf*, p. 93)

9. **Listen and learn from others.**
   Be "a fruit upon the tree of humility." (Bahá'u'lláh, *Epistle to the Son of the Wolf*, p. 93)

Remember: Show, don't tell.
"Let deeds, not words, be your adorning." (Bahá'u'lláh, *Hidden Words*, Persian #5)
(Prepared by Brian Cameron)

Reflection

1. What inspires me generally about the Bahá'í teachings?
2. What and who can support me in my quest for spiritual manhood?
3. What assists me to live according to the Bahá'í teachings and moral standards? When I don't feel as aligned with them as I would like, how can I get back on my quest for excellence?
4. What are some of the benefits from me making good choices and being obedient to the Bahá'í laws?
5. Who would be good to consult with about my choices related to being a spiritual man?
6. What services am I drawn toward fulfilling?
7. What will be some potential outcomes of my efforts to transform my character, my life, my community, and society?

Appendices

Appendix A: What Is the Bahá'í Faith?

The Bahá'í Faith and Its Teachings

The Bahá'í Faith is widespread across the globe, with around 6 million members in established communities in almost every country. Bahá'í communities worldwide work to break down barriers of prejudice and collaborate with other groups and individuals to promote the model of a peaceful global society, beginning at the family and neighborhood level. At the heart of Bahá'í belief is the conviction that humanity is a single people with a common destiny. In the words of Bahá'u'lláh, "The earth is but one country, and mankind its citizens."[430]

Bahá'u'lláh taught that there is one God Who progressively reveals vital messages to humanity through Messengers. Some you may be familiar with are Moses, Jesus, Muhammad, Krishna, and Buddha. Each has contributed to the spiritual development of civilization, bringing the human race to its current state of adolescence, to the threshold of spiritual and moral maturity. Bahá'u'lláh, the most recent Messenger, has brought teachings that address the challenges of the modern world. Humanity is now coming of age—making possible the unification of the human family and the building of a peaceful, global society.

Among the teachings of the Bahá'í Faith are the importance of prayer and meditation, that each person has an eternal soul, and that each individual is responsible for investigating truth for themselves. The Faith is fundamentally committed to the equality of women and men; universal education; the importance of achieving personal, moral, and spiritual excellence; the harmony of science and religion; and the elimination of all forms of prejudice. Its teachings promote the importance of marriage and family as building blocks for a healthy, unified society.

Bahá'ís believe that lasting social change starts at the local level, carried out by individuals, couples, and families. In neighborhoods across the world, Bahá'ís and their friends are engaged in a systematic community building process that cultivates love and translates it into action.

Bahá'u'lláh's teachings include everyone using a process called "consultation" to build understanding and make decisions. It's designed to allow each participant to have an equal voice and express feelings and thoughts in a spiritual atmosphere with the intent of operating in and creating unity and a unified outcome. Consultation is mentioned throughout the book.

This brief introduction merely scratches the surface of this richly diverse, unique, and fascinating global Faith. You can learn more about the Bahá'í teachings and plans for action by visiting any of these websites: bahai.org; news.bahai.org; bahai.us.

Bahá'í People and Entities Included in the Book

Throughout this book are quotations with sources written from the mid-1850's up to the present time. Many are translated from Persian or Arabic, so there is wide variation in language usage. For example, when various words are translated as "man" in English, the original terms almost always imply "humanity", or "man" and "woman", interchangeably. Additionally, you may see words capitalized that you are used to seeing in lowercase letters; this is often to demonstrate that something is significant or sacred.

You may already be familiar with the history of the Bahá'í Faith and the various people and entities that have contributed to the body of its teachings or offer guidance. However, in case this is all new for you, we've included below a brief orientation and pronunciation guide. Throughout the book, you will see source names and notes connected to each quotation, and you can refer to the list below if you want to better understand the reference.

1. **The Báb** (pronounced BAHb/Bob), translates as "The Gate." He founded the Bábí Faith in 1844 in Iran. He prepared people for the coming of Bahá'u'lláh and the Bahá'í Faith.

2. **Bahá'u'lláh** (pronounced Bah-hah-oo-LAH), translates as the "Glory of God". He founded the Bahá'í Faith in 1863 in an area that is now known as Iran and Iraq, and He is sometimes referred to as a "Manifestation" of God. He taught that every human being has a unique purpose to participate in building a unified world, that justice enables each of us to fulfill this potential, and that the inequalities between everyone—including women and men, all races, rich and poor—must be addressed. His teachings span over 100 volumes and are still being translated.

3. **'Abdu'l-Bahá** (pronounced Ab-dool-bah-HAH), was Bahá'u'lláh's eldest son. Upholding unity as the fundamental principle of His teachings, Bahá'u'lláh established the necessary safeguard to ensure that His religion would never suffer the same fate as others that split into sects after the deaths of their Founders. In His writings, He instructed all to turn to His eldest Son, 'Abdu'l-Bahá, not only as the authorized

interpreter of the Bahá'í writings but also as the "perfect Exemplar" of the Faith's spirit and teachings. 'Abdu'l-Bahá wrote extensively and gave talks internationally.

4. **Shoghi Effendi** (pronounced SHOW-ghee, e-FEN-dee; Effendi means "sir") was appointed by 'Abdu'l-Bahá to be the Guardian of the Bahá'í Faith after 'Abdu'l-Bahá's death in 1921. He wrote many letters and books, developed the global administration of the Bahá'í Faith ordained by Bahá'u'lláh and 'Abdu'l-Bahá, and explained many facets of the Faith and its role in advancing civilization. After his passing in 1957, there could be no further individual leaders of the Bahá'í Faith.

5. **The Universal House of Justice** is the international governing council, first established in 1963 and elected every 5 years by Bahá'ís around the world who are members of all the National Spiritual Assemblies. Its offices are in Haifa, Israel. There is no clergy in the Bahá'í Faith. Bahá'u'lláh conferred divine authority upon the Universal House of Justice. It uses a consultative approach to guide Bahá'ís about steps toward the advancement of the welfare of humankind, education, peace, and global prosperity. It is charged with applying the Bahá'í teachings to the requirements of an ever-evolving society, and it is therefore empowered to legislate on matters not explicitly covered in the Faith's sacred texts.

6. **National and Local Spiritual Assemblies** are 9-member bodies elected annually in their corresponding geographic locations. All Bahá'í elections are free of nominations and campaigning. Local Assemblies are charged with promoting the spiritual education of children and young people, strengthening the spiritual and social fabric of Bahá'í community life, assessing and utilizing the community's resources, and encouraging community members to devote their energies and talents to advance collective goals. They inspire and coordinate efforts to contribute to the well-being of the areas where they serve. National Assemblies serve in a similar manner at the national level, coordinating efforts across the country.

7. **The Continental Boards of Counsellors and Auxiliary Board members** are appointed to assist the Bahá'í community to maintain unity and growth, providing moral leadership without the administrative authority vested in the elected institutions. They often consult with individuals

about personal and relationship issues. They also have assigned geographic areas for their service. These appointees serve a set term and are not invested with individual authority.

Appendix B: Forming a Book Study Group

After looking through this book, you may decide you will be most successful at studying its content and carrying out its activities if you involve a few friends or other interested people. They can complete parts of it—or all of it—with you. Informal study groups can assist participants to progress through the material and allow each to gain new insights from the group discussions. Groups can also assist in keeping each other accountable for carrying out agreed activities.

Those in the group may be at different stages of literacy. The group can encourage participants to increase their ability to read and write. Group members may need to accompany each other in the process.

Consult About Ground Rules

At the beginning, before diving into the content, discuss and agree on a few ground rules. It may be useful to write these on a whiteboard or easel pad, so everyone can see them throughout the discussion. This practice allows each participant to feel a sense of ownership for the group and its guidelines. The group refers to them as needed and adds or revises an agreement when required. Try to keep your approach simple. Here are some ground rules your group may wish to consider, if they don't come up naturally in your initial discussion:

1. Uphold confidentiality, through a firm agreement that "what's said in the group stays in the group," and is not mentioned outside the group.
2. Scrupulously avoid the tendency in society to engage in gossip and backbiting—either within or outside of group sessions.
3. Do not use personal devices (mobile phones, tablets...) during group discussions and social time, so as to give full support and attention to the group, out of respect for its purpose and intentions. (Exceptions can be agreed upon, such as using a device for taking notes or in a way that advances the efforts of the group, or arranging breaks where people can check their electronic devices before they put them away again.)
4. Allocate time for prayer, meditation, or other spiritual enrichment activities.
5. Allocate time for social connection and fellowship.

6. Integrate the arts into your group's activities. Expressing ideas artistically often brings vitality to the learning process and enables people to understand a concept in a new, refreshing way.
7. Be respectful and considerate of others. Give everyone time to share, and guard against individuals dominating the conversation.
8. Avoid terminology, jargon, and acronyms—religious or otherwise—that some group members might not understand.
9. Agree on what everyone will read—and do—between sessions. At the same time, if life circumstances and events prevent a participant from fulfilling their commitment, they can still attend sessions, and strive to catch up with the reading and activities, perhaps with another group member accompanying and supporting them.
10. Participants can invite and bring friends to the group, and new people can join the group at any time. (Or, alternatively, once the group begins, no one new should join.)

A Simple Version

1. Opportunity for equal airtime
2. Right to pass
3. Non-judgmental atmosphere
4. Respect self and others
5. Everyone responsible for their own learning
6. Confidentiality
7. Enjoy!

Consider the Logistics

Groups are of course more successful, and function more smoothly, when they agree on some of the logistics and other basic considerations. These questions may serve as useful prompts for your group:

1. How often, when, and where will you meet? (Meeting at least every week or two keeps participants motivated and purposeful.)
2. Who, if anyone, will be responsible for sending the meeting details to the group members? What method of communication will work for all members?
3. Will there be food? If so, who will provide it? Does anyone have a food intolerance or allergy? Will there be any consideration about how healthy the food is?

4. Will anyone facilitate the sessions (recommended)? If so, will it be the same person each time, or will you rotate among the members?
5. Would it be beneficial, for any reason, to take notes of the discussion? If so, who will record the notes and what types of information will they capture from the conversation? Will it be the same person each time, or will it happen on a rotating basis?
6. Do you need or want a group name? How will you talk about the group with others?
7. Will the group share what they learn with others (without sharing personal, confidential information of course)? What opportunities exist for this? Perhaps you could share your learning with a youth group? At a community meeting? With family members? How and when will you carry this out?

Appendix C: Additional Guidance for Youth
(related to those approx. ages 15-30)

"To every generation of young believers comes an opportunity to make a contribution to the fortunes of humanity, unique to their time of life. For the present generation, the moment has come to reflect, to commit, to steel themselves for a life of service from which blessing will flow in abundance. In our prayers at the Sacred Threshold, we entreat the Ancient Beauty that, from out a distracted and bewildered humanity, He may distill pure souls endowed with clear sight: youth whose integrity and uprightness are not undermined by dwelling on the faults of others and who are not immobilized by any shortcomings of their own; youth who will look to the Master and 'bring those who have been excluded into the circle of intimate friends'; youth whose consciousness of the failings of society impels them to work for its transformation, not to distance themselves from it; youth who, whatever the cost, will refuse to pass by inequity in its many incarnations and will labor, instead, that 'the light of justice may shed its radiance upon the whole world.'"[431] Universal House of Justice

"Three great fields of service lie open before young Bahá'ís, in which they will simultaneously be remaking the character of human society and preparing themselves for the work they can undertake later in their lives.

"First, the foundation of all their accomplishments, is their study of the teachings, the spiritualization of their lives, and the forming of their characters in accordance with the standards of Bahá'u'lláh. As the moral standards of the people around us collapse and decay, whether of the centuries-old civilizations of the East, the more recent cultures of Christendom and Islam, or of the rapidly changing tribal societies of the world, the Bahá'ís must increasingly stand out as pillars of righteousness and forbearance. The life of a Bahá'í will be characterized by truthfulness and decency; he will walk uprightly among his fellowmen, dependent upon none save God, yet linked by bonds of love and brotherhood with mankind; he will be entirely detached from the loose standards, the decadent theories, the frenetic experimentation, the desperation of present-day society, will look upon his neighbors with a bright and friendly face, and be a beacon light and haven for all those who would emulate his strength of character and assurance of soul.

"The second field of service, which is linked intimately with the first, is teaching the Faith, particularly to their fellow youth, among whom are some of the most open and seeking minds in the world. Not yet having acquired all the responsibilities of a family or a long-established home and job, youth can the more easily choose where they will live and study or work. In the world at large young people travel hither and thither seeking amusement, education, and experiences. Bahá'í youth, bearing the incomparable treasure of the Word of God for this Day, can harness this mobility into service for mankind and can choose their places of residence, their areas of travel, and their types of work with the goal in mind of how they can best serve the Faith.

"The third field of service is the preparation by youth for their later years. It is the obligation of a Bahá'í to educate his children; likewise it is the duty of the children to acquire knowledge of the arts and sciences and to learn a trade or a profession whereby they, in turn, can earn their living and support their families. This, for a Bahá'í youth, is in itself a service to God, a service, moreover, which can be combined with teaching the Faith and often with pioneering. The Bahá'í community will need men and women of many skills and qualifications; for, as it grows in size the sphere of its activities in the life of society will increase and diversify. Let Bahá'í youth, therefore, consider the best ways in which they can use and develop their native abilities for the service of mankind and the Cause of God, whether this be as farmers, teachers, doctors, artisans, musicians, or any one of the multitude of livelihoods that are open to them.

"When studying at school or university Bahá'í youth will often find themselves in the unusual and slightly embarrassing position of having a more profound insight into a subject than their instructors. The Teachings of Bahá'u'lláh throw light on so many aspects of human life and knowledge that a Bahá'í must learn, earlier than most, to weigh the information that is given to him rather than to accept it blindly. A Bahá'í has the advantage of the Divine Revelation for this age, which shines like a searchlight on so many problems that baffle modern thinkers; he must therefore develop the ability to learn everything from those around him, showing proper humility before his teachers, but always relating what he hears to the Bahá'í teachings, for they will enable him to sort out the gold from the dross of human error.

"Paralleling the growth of his inner life through prayer, meditation. service, and study of the teachings, Bahá'í youth have the opportunity to learn in practice the very functioning of the Order of Bahá'u'lláh. Through taking part in conferences and summer schools as well as Nineteen Day Feasts, and in service on committees, they can develop the wonderful skill of Bahá'í consultation, thus tracing new paths of human corporate action. Consultation is no easy skill to learn, requiring as it does the subjugation of all egotism and unruly passions, the cultivation of frankness and freedom of thought as well as courtesy, openness of mind, and wholehearted acquiescence in a majority decision. In this field Bahá'í youth may demonstrate the efficiency, the vigor, the access of unity which arise from true consultation and, by contrast, demonstrate the futility of partisanship, lobbying, debate, secret diplomacy, and unilateral action which characterize modern affairs. Youth also take part in the life of the Bahá'í community as a whole and promote a society in which all generations—elderly, middle-aged, youth, children—are fully integrated and make up an organic whole. By refusing to carry over the antagonisms and mistrust between the generations which perplex and bedevil modern society, they will again demonstrate the healing and life-giving nature of their religion.

"... We now call upon them [the youth], with great love and highest hopes and the assurance of our fervent payers, to consider, individually and in consultation, wherever they live and whatever their circumstances, those steps which they should take now to deepen themselves in their knowledge of the Divine Message, to require those skills, trades, and professions in which they can best serve God and man, to intensify their service to the Cause of Bahá'u'lláh, and to radiate its Message to the seekers among their contemporaries."[432] Universal House of Justice

"So fundamental are these duties and obligations that to some degree all entities—youth, parents, Bahá'í institutions—share in them, acting in accordance with their respective functions and responsibilities. There is a sphere in which each must make independent judgements and take independent action. A youth must decide on what professional training to pursue and keep a balance between such pursuit and his spiritual obligations; the parents must assist the youth, through material support and moral guidance, to achieve his goal, and must also encourage the youth in the observance of his spiritual obligations; the institutions must promote the Cause of God, endeavor to stimulate action on the part of individual believers in the teaching and consolidation of the Faith, with the full realization that if such action is neglected there can be no hope for the peace of mankind and the future growth of civilization. The institutions cannot, therefore, fail to urge the friends to service and to call their attention to the critical situation of the times and to point out the crucial importance of the action of the individual to the fortunes of the Faith and humanity as a whole.

"Along with all these considerations is the factor of the special role which the youth, with their particular qualities of enthusiasm and idealism, play in the development of the Cause. This has been evident from the earliest days of the Faith and is indispensable to its ultimate triumph. A cursory review of Bahá'í history provides many examples of the heroic deeds of youth, and today's Bahá'í youth cannot help but be inspired by such heroism to also play their part in their own time before they become burdened with the cares of adult life."[433] On behalf of the Universal House of Justice

Be Brave and Arise

Quotation References

My Life Quest

[1] On behalf of the Universal House of Justice to an individual, February 5, 1992
[2] Bahá'u'lláh, *Gems of Divine Mysteries*, #36; #37
[3] Bahá'u'lláh, *Tabernacle of Unity*, #1.14

Mapping and Packing for My Quest

[4] Hal Elrod, *Miracle Morning*, p. 45

1 – Exploring the Current Reality of My Life

[5] Bahá'í International Community, "Toward a New Discourse on Religion and Gender Equality", February 1, 2015
[6] Universal House of Justice, *Framework for Action*, #23.4
[7] Universal House of Justice, *Framework for Action*, #34.3
[8] Universal House of Justice, *Framework for Action*, #16.33
[9] Shoghi Effendi, *Citadel of Faith*, p. 2
[10] Shoghi Effendi, *World Order of Bahá'u'lláh*, p. 171
[11] Shoghi Effendi, *World Order of Bahá'u'lláh*, p. 171
[12] 'Abdu'l-Bahá, *Paris Talks*, #33
[13] Bahá'u'lláh, *Hidden Words*, Arabic #2
[14] Bahá'u'lláh, *Hidden Words*, Arabic #4
[15] Bahá'u'lláh, *Hidden Words*, Arabic #40
[16] On behalf of Shoghi Effendi, *Unfolding Destiny*, pp. 456-7
[17] On behalf of Shoghi Effendi, *Lights of Guidance*, #391
[18] On behalf of the Universal House of Justice, *Lights of Guidance*, #414
[19] On behalf of the Universal House of Justice, *Framework for Action*, #51.4, including a quotation from Bahá'u'lláh, *Tablets of Bahá'u'lláh*, p. 35

2 – Being a Spiritual Man—An Adventure

[20] On behalf of the Universal House of Justice, June 16, 1998, quoted in "The American Bahá'í", January-February 2020
[21] Shoghi Effendi, *World Order of Bahá'u'lláh*, p. 202
[22] Office of Social and Economic Development, Bahá'í World Centre, November 26, 2012
[23] Shoghi Effendi, *Bahá'í Administration*, p. 88
[24] Howard J. Fox, *The Truth About Men*, p. 58
[25] 'Abdu'l-Bahá, *Foundations of World Unity*, p. 77

26 Bahá'u'lláh, *Epistle to the Son of the Wolf*, p. 93
27 Bahá'u'lláh, *Prayers and Meditations by Bahá'u'lláh*, #CLVII, p. 250

3 – Navigating Spiritual Manhood—Some Preparation

28 S. M. Alexander, *Creating Excellent Relationships*, p. 166
29 www.characteryaq.com
30 Bahá'u'lláh, *Prayers and Meditations by Bahá'u'lláh*, #CL, p. 240
31 On behalf of the Universal House of Justice, *Lights of Guidance*, #1228
32 On behalf of Shoghi Effendi, March 19, 1945, quoted in the "Understanding Tests" letter from the Research Department of the Bahá'í World Centre to the Universal House of Justice, July 17, 1989
33 'Abdu'l-Bahá, *Promulgation of Universal Peace*, p. 63
34 'Abdu'l-Bahá, *Bahá'í Prayers*, p. 71
35 'Abdu'l-Bahá, *Paris Talks*, #2
36 'Abdu'l-Bahá, *Paris Talks*, #6
37 Bahá'u'lláh, *Prayers and Meditations by Bahá'u'lláh*, #CLXXXIII, p. 323
38 'Abdu'l-Bahá, *Paris Talks*, #6
39 'Abdu'l-Bahá, *Selections from the Writings of 'Abdu'l-Bahá*, #17
40 'Abdu'l-Bahá, *Paris Talks*, #21
41 Universal House of Justice, *Wellspring of Guidance*, pp. 92-93

4 – Creating a Support System—The Value of a Safety Net

42 'Abdu'l-Bahá, quoted in Shoghi Effendi, *God Passes By*, p. 238
43 Universal House of Justice, *A Wider Horizon*, p. 228
44 On behalf of Shoghi Effendi, *Afire with the Vision*, #79.2
45 Justice St Rain, *Falling Into Grace*, pp. 100-101
46 Bahá'u'lláh, *Hidden Words,* Arabic #13
47 On behalf of the Universal House of Justice, *Lights of Guidance*, #1216
48 Universal House of Justice, *A Wider Horizon, Selected Letters 1983-1992*, p. 226
49 Universal House of Justice, *A Wider Horizon, Selected Letters 1983-1992*, pp. 232-233
50 'Abdu'l-Bahá, https://www.bahai.org/library/authoritative-texts/compilations/prayer-devotional-life/, #6
51 Shoghi Effendi, *Lights of Guidance*, #1845
52 On behalf of Shoghi Effendi, *Lights of Guidance*, #1489
53 On behalf of Shoghi Effendi, *Lights of Guidance*, #1486
54 Rainn Wilson; Bahá'í Blogcast with Rainn Wilson and JB Eckl, Episode 33, January 28, 2019; bahaiblog.net
55 Justice St Rain, *Falling into Grace*, p. 48
56 Howard J. Fox, *Truth About Men*, pp. 3-4

[57] JB Eckl; Bahá'í Blogcast with Rainn Wilson and JB Eckl, Episode 33, January 28, 2019; bahaiblog.net
[58] 'Abdu'l-Bahá, *Compilation of Compilations, Vol. I*, #795
[59] Universal House of Justice, *Framework for Action*, #16.37

5 - Understanding My Best and Building from My Not-Yet-Best

[60] Bahá'u'lláh, *Hidden Words*, Arabic #31
[61] 'Abdu'l-Bahá, *Lights of Guidance*, #1485
[62] Mead Simon, http://onebahai.blogspot.com/2016/11/bring-thyself-to-account-each-day.html#ixzz6FS9fsqMT
[63] Bahá'u'lláh, *Gleanings from the Writings of Bahá'u'lláh*, #LXVI, p. 128
[64] 'Abdu'l-Bahá, *Selections from the Writings of 'Abdu'l-Bahá*, #174
[65] On behalf of Shoghi Effendi, *Light of Divine Guidance*, pp. 69-70
[66] Shoghi Effendi, *Compilation of Compilations, Vol. II*, #2075
[67] Bahá'u'lláh, *Compilation of Compilations, Vol. I*, #766
[68] Shoghi Effendi, *Compilation of Compilations, Vol. II*, #1266
[69] S. G. Bender, *Recreating Marriage with the Same Old Spouse*, pp. 150-51
[70] Stephen M. R. Covey, *Speed of Trust*, pp. 62-63
[71] On behalf of Shoghi Effendi, *Compilation of Compilations, Vol. II*, #1272
[72] Bahá'u'lláh, *Tabernacle of Unity*, #5.7
[73] *Bahá'í World, Volume VIII*, "Bahá'í Youth Activities", p. 551

6 - Developing Spiritual Habits—Connecting to God's Light

[74] Bahá'u'lláh, *Kitáb-i-Íqán*, p. 91
[75] 'Abdu'l-Bahá, *Paris Talks*, #31
[76] Bahá'u'lláh, *Tablets of Bahá'u'lláh*, p. 156
[77] Universal House of Justice, *Messages 1963 to 1986*, #375.5
[78] Universal House of Justice, *Turning Point*, p. 182
[79] 'Abdu'l-Bahá, *Selections from the Writings of 'Abdu'l-Bahá*, #35
[80] 'Abdu'l-Bahá, *Importance of Obligatory Prayer and Fasting*, Section 2, VII
[81] Universal House of Justice, *Framework for Action*, #28.6
[82] Bahá'u'lláh, https://www.bahai.org/library/authoritative-texts/compilations/prayer-devotional-life/, #56
[83] 'Abdu'l-Bahá, https://www.bahai.org/library/authoritative-texts/compilations/prayer-devotional-life/, #57
[84] On behalf of Shoghi Effendi, https://www.bahai.org/library/authoritative-texts/compilations/prayer-devotional-life/, #52
[85] Universal House of Justice, https://www.bahai.org/library/authoritative-texts/compilations/prayer-devotional-life/, #14
[86] On behalf of the Universal House of Justice, *Lights of Guidance*, #1836

[87] Bahá'u'lláh, *Gleanings from the Writings of Bahá'u'lláh*, #LXXIV, p. 141
[88] 'Abdu'l-Bahá, *Will and Testament*, Part 1, bahai.org, p. 5
[89] Shoghi Effendi, *Advent of Divine Justice*, bahai.org, pp. 26-27
[90] Bahá'u'lláh, *Bahá'í Prayers*, p. 4
[91] On behalf of Shoghi Effendi, https://www.bahai.org/library/authoritative-texts/compilations/prayer-devotional-life/, #13
[92] On behalf of Shoghi Effendi, https://www.bahai.org/library/authoritative-texts/compilations/prayer-devotional-life/, #45
[93] Bahá'u'lláh, *The Kitáb-i-Aqdas*, #K18
[94] *The Kitáb-i-Aqdas* by Bahá'u'lláh, Note #16
[95] *The Kitáb-i-Aqdas* by Bahá'u'lláh, Questions and Answers #83
[96] *The Kitáb-i-Aqdas* by Bahá'u'lláh, Notes #7 and #8

7 – Reducing Resistance and Aligning with Positive Action

[97] John Buri, essay "Do You Have a Tail?", included in *All-in-One Marriage Prep*, 2019 ed., p. 74
[98] Bahá'u'lláh, *Hidden Words*, Persian #72
[99] 'Abdu'l-Bahá, *Promulgation of Universal Peace*, #133
[100] Universal House of Justice to Bahá'í youth conferences, July 1, 2013
[101] Les Parrott and Leslie Parrott, *Relationships*, p. 32
[102] On behalf of Shoghi Effendi, https://www.bahai.org/library/authoritative-texts/compilations/prayer-devotional-life/, #10
[103] K. Kingsbury, *Unlocked*, p. 189
[104] Universal House of Justice, *Framework for Action*, #28.6
[105] Collected by A. Honnold, *Vignettes from the Life of 'Abdu'l-Bahá*, #21
[106] Collected by A. Honnold, *Vignettes from the Life of 'Abdu'l-Bahá*, #48
[107] Collected by A. Honnold, *Vignettes from the Life of 'Abdu'l-Bahá*, #85
[108] Dan Popov, quoted in S. M. Alexander, *Creating Excellent Relationships*, p. 40
[109] On behalf of the Universal House of Justice to an individual, February 5, 1992
[110] 'Abdu'l-Bahá, *Compilation of Compilations, Vol. II*, #2116
[111] 'Abdu'l-Bahá, *Paris Talks*, #40
[112] 'Abdu'l-Bahá, *Promulgation of Universal Peace*, p. 134
[113] Chuck Egerton, ABS Poster; https://chuckegerton.files.wordpress.com/2016/08/abs-final-doc-combined-081216.pdf
[114] 'Abdu'l-Bahá, *Promulgation of Universal Peace*, p. 375
[115] Chuck Egerton, ABS Poster; https://chuckegerton.files.wordpress.com/2016/08/abs-final-doc-combined-081216.pdf
[116] Bahá'í International Community, "Toward a New Discourse on Religion and Gender Equality", February 1, 2015

117 Bahá'í International Community, "Toward a New Discourse on Religion and Gender Equality", February 1, 2015
118 On behalf of Shoghi Effendi, *Compilation of Compilations, Vol. II*, #2121

8 - Developing My Character—Increasing My Light

119 Bahá'u'lláh, *Tablets of Bahá'u'lláh*, p. 36
120 'Abdu'l-Bahá, *Selections from the Writings of 'Abdu'l-Bahá*, #2
121 Shoghi Effendi, *Compilation of Compilations, Vol. I*, #162
122 On behalf of Shoghi Effendi, https://www.bahai.org/library/authoritative-texts/compilations/prayer-devotional-life/, #10
123 On behalf of Shoghi Effendi, *Compilation of Compilations, Vol. II*, #1271
124 Universal House of Justice, *Framework for Action*, #16.35
125 Bahá'u'lláh, *Hidden Words*, Arabic, #22
126 'Abdu'l-Bahá, *Paris Talks*, #18
127 'Abdu'l-Bahá, *Promulgation of Universal Peace*, p. 310
128 On behalf of Shoghi Effendi, *Lights of Guidance*, #386
129 On behalf of Shoghi Effendi, *Compilation of Compilations, Vol. II*, #1295
130 On behalf of the Universal House of Justice to an individual, April 22, 2013
131 Sharon Hatcher Kennedy and Andrew Kennedy, "Bahá'í Youth and Sexuality A Personal/Professional View", "The Journal of Bahá'í Studies", Vol. 1, #1
132 'Abdu'l-Bahá, cited in Shoghi Effendi, *Advent of Divine Justice*, p. 22
133 Bahá'u'lláh, *Gleanings from the Writings of Bahá'u'lláh*, #CXXV, p. 265
134 Hooper Dunbar, *Forces of Our Time*, p. 78
135 Nathan Rutstein, *Teaching the Bahá'í Faith*, pp. 87-90, included with permission from George Ronald, publisher
136 Bahá'u'lláh, *Gleanings from the Writings of Bahá'u'lláh*, #XC, p. 177
137 On behalf of Shoghi Effendi, Lights of Guidance, #1709

9 – Striving for My Mental Health

138 Stephen Post, *Why Good Things Happen to Good People*, p. 104
139 WHO: Adolescents: health risks and solutions, December 13, 2018, https://www.menshealth.com/health/a20111514/men-mental-health-awareness-month/
140 On behalf of Shoghi Effendi, *Lights of Guidance*, #675
141 'Abdu'l-Bahá, *Secret of Divine Civilization*, p. 19
142 On behalf of the Universal House of Justice, *Lights of Guidance*, #1206
143 On behalf of Shoghi Effendi, *Lights of Guidance*, #389
144 L. K. Popov, *A Pace of Grace*, p. 93
145 Bahá'u'lláh, *Hidden Words*, Arabic #5
146 Universal House of Justice, *Framework for Action*, #23.14
147 Universal House of Justice, *Messages 1986-2001*, #200.12

148 Justice St Rain, *Love, Lust, and the Longing for God*, pp. 261-263
149 Universal House of Justice, *Lights of Guidance*, #1219
150 On behalf of the Universal House of Justice to an individual, July 24, 1973
151 Bahá'u'lláh, *Gleanings from the Writings of Bahá'u'lláh*, #CXLVI, pp. 315-316
152 Shoghi Effendi, *Advent of Divine Justice*, p. 39
153 On behalf of Shoghi Effendi, *Lights of Guidance*, #291

10 – Striving for My Emotional Health

154 'Abdu'l-Bahá, *Promulgation of Universal Peace*, p. 60, #12
155 Research Department of the Universal House of Justice, "Issues Concerning Community Functioning", section 2, p. 6
156 Summary based on work of John Gottman, PhD, and Nan Silver, *Seven Principles for Making Marriage Work*, 2nd ed, Ch. 3.
157 Marshall B. Rosenberg, *Nonviolent Communication, a Language of Compassion*, 2nd ed, pp. 41-46
158 S. Gammage, *Letting Go of Anger and Bitterness*, p. 13
159 Bahá'u'lláh, *Compilation of Compilations, Vol. I*, #1020
160 'Abdu'l-Bahá, *Promulgation of Universal Peace*, pp. 92-93
161 On behalf of the Universal House of Justice, "Preserving Bahá'í Marriages" 2009, #38
162 'Abdu'l-Bahá, *Some Answered Questions*, 2nd ed., #57.10
163 'Abdu'l-Bahá, *Selections from the Writings of 'Abdu'l-Bahá*, #130
164 Richard Carlson and Joseph Bailey, S*lowing Down to the Speed of Life*, p. 94
165 Justice St Rain, *Love, Lust, and the Longing for God*, p. 218
166 https://www.bahai.org/beliefs/life-spirit/character-conduct/articles-resources/selected-letters-subject-chastity
167 Bahá'u'lláh, *Gleanings from the Writings of Bahá'u'lláh*, LXXX, p. 154
168 Bahá'u'lláh, *Four Valleys*, p. 60
169 S. M. Alexander, *Creating Excellent Relationships*, p. 169
170 'Abdu'l-Bahá, quoted in collected by A. Honnold, *Vignettes from the Life of 'Abdu'l-Bahá*, p. 155
171 'Abdu'l-Bahá, *Promulgation of Universal Peace*, p. 218
172 'Abdu'l-Bahá, *Paris Talks*, #35
173 William B. Sears, "The Prison City of 'Akká", article in *Bahá'í World, Vol. XII*, p. 882
174 On behalf of the Universal House of Justice to an individual, quoted in a Bahá'í World Centre Research Department Memorandum, January 12, 1997, "The Humorist"
175 On behalf of the Universal House of Justice, *Compilations of Compilations, Vol. I*, #138
176 S. Sparks, *Laugh Your Way to Grace—Reclaiming the Spiritual Power of Humor*, pp. 9-10

[177] Stephen Post, *Why Good Things Happen to Good People*, p. 144
[178] Howard Colby Ives, recalling the words of 'Abdu'l-Bahá, *Portals to Freedom*, p. 120, when 'Abdu'l-Bahá was imprisoned with many others in the Holy Land

11 – Striving for My Physical Health

[179] On behalf of Shoghi Effendi, *Compilation of Compilations, Vol. II*, #1777
[180] On behalf of Shoghi Effendi, *Compilation of Compilations, Vol. I*, #1085
[181] Shoghi Effendi before he was appointed the Guardian; "The Function of Sport in Life"; http://bahai-library.com/shoghieffendi_function_sports_life)
[182] 'Abdu'l-Bahá, *Selections from the Writings of 'Abdu'l-Bahá*, #134
[183] 'Abdu'l-Bahá, *Selections from the Writings of 'Abdu'l-Bahá*, #136
[184] 'Abdu'l-Bahá, *Selections from the Writings of 'Abdu'l-Bahá*, #133
[185] 'Abdu'l-Bahá, *Selections from the Writings of 'Abdu'l-Bahá*, #129
[186] 'Abdu'l-Bahá, *Selections from the Writings of 'Abdu'l-Bahá*, #129
[187] On behalf of Shoghi Effendi, *Lights of Guidance*, #1189
[188] https://www.menshealth.com/health/a20111514/men-mental-health-awareness-month/
[189] *The Kitáb-i-Aqdas* by Bahá'u'lláh, Note #144
[190] 'Abdu'l-Bahá, *Selections from the Writings of 'Abdu'l-Bahá*, #129
[191] Universal House of Justice, *Lights of Guidance*, #1184
[192] Universal House of Justice, *Lights of Guidance*, #1183
[193] Universal House of Justice, *Framework for Action*, #27.6
[194] On behalf of the Universal House of Justice, "Issues Concerning Community Functioning"

12 - Striving for My Sexual Health – Some Context

[195] *The Kitáb-i-Aqdas* by Baha'u'llah, Note #134
[196] R. Rabbani, *Prescription for Living*, 1978 ed., p. 87
[197] 'Abdu'l-Bahá, *Selections from the Writings of 'Abdu'l-Bahá*, #84
[198] Tim Alan Gardner, *Sacred Sex, A Spiritual Celebration of Oneness in Marriage*, pp. 4-5
[199] On behalf of the Universal House of Justice to an individual, April 17, 2017
[200] https://www.getlasting.com/marriage-advice
[201] M. W. Davis, *Sex-Starved Marriage*, pp. 11-12
[202] E. Nagoski, PhD, *Come As You Are*, p. 75
[203] Mark Laaser, PhD, from an essay, "The Challenges of Sexual Addiction on Relationships" included in *All-in-One Marriage Prep*, 2019 ed., p. 200
[204] 'Abdu'l-Bahá, *Selections from the Writings of 'Abdu'l-Bahá*, #85
[205] Justice St Rain, *Love, Lust and the Longing for God*, pp. 193-194
[206] Justice St Rain, *Love, Lust and the Longing for God*, pp. 196-197

13 - Striving for My Sexual Health—Spiritual Principles and Challenges

[207] On behalf of the Universal House of Justice to an individual, February 5, 1992
[208] R. Rabbani, *Prescription for Living*, 1978 ed., pp. 88-89
[209] Shoghi Effendi, *Advent of Divine Justice*, pp. 25, 28
[210] S. M. Alexander, *Creating Excellent Relationships*, pp. 159-160
[211] On behalf of the Universal House of Justice, *Framework for Action*, #51.11
[212] On behalf of the Universal House of Justice to an individual, April 17, 2017

14 - Striving for My Sexual Health—Building Understanding and Strengths

[213] Shoghi Effendi, *Light of Divine Guidance, Vol. II*, p. 69
[214] Universal House of Justice, *Messages 1963-1986*, #133.1-#133.3
[215] On behalf of the Universal House of Justice, *Lights of Guidance*, #1216
[216] On behalf of the Universal House of Justice, October 27, 2010
[217] On behalf of the Universal House of Justice, December 22, 2009
[218] H. Hanson, "Sexuality, Self, and the Shape of Society", https://bahai-library.com/hanson_sexuality_self_society
[219] On behalf of the Universal House of Justice, *Lights of Guidance*, #1226
[220] The Báb, *Selections from the Writings of the Báb*, p. 95
[221] Sharon Hatcher Kennedy and Andrew Kennedy, "Bahá'í Youth and Sexuality A Personal/Professional View", "The Journal of Bahá'í Studies", Vol. 1, #1
[222] On behalf of Shoghi Effendi, *Compilation of Compilations, Vol. I*, #14
[223] On behalf of the Universal House of Justice, *Compilation of Compilations, Vol. I*, #128
[224] E. Nagoski, PhD, *Come As You Are*, pp. 229-230
[225] E. Nagoski, PhD, *Come As You Are*, pp. 230-233
[226] On behalf of Shoghi Effendi, https://www.bahai.org/library/authoritative-texts/compilations/prayer-devotional-life/, #10
[227] Universal House of Justice to an individual, January 24, 1979, published in "Bahá'í Canada Supplement", July 1987
[228] 'Abdu'l-Bahá, *Paris Talks*, #26
[229] 'Abdu'l-Bahá, *Selections from the Writings of 'Abdu'l-Bahá*, #190
[230] H. Dobbs, *Spiritual Being: A User's Guide*, p. 198
[231] Raymond Switzer, *Conscious Courtship*, p. 68
[232] S. M. Alexander, *Creating Excellent Relationships*, pp. 169-170
[233] On behalf of Shoghi Effendi, https://www.bahai.org/library/authoritative-texts/compilations/prayer-devotional-life/, #9
[234] 'Abdu'l-Bahá, *Paris Talks*, #54
[235] On behalf of Shoghi Effendi, https://www.bahai.org/library/authoritative-texts/compilations/prayer-devotional-life/, #45
[236] On behalf of the Universal House of Justice, *Framework for Action*, 51.8

15 - Striving for My Sexual Health—Grappling with Dark Forces

[237] Universal House of Justice, *Lights of Guidance*, #1220
[238] Napoleon Hill, *Think and Grow Rich*, Gold Standard Collector's Edition, p. 337
[239] C. S. Lewis, *Collected Letters of C. S. Lewis, Vol. 3*, pp. 758-759
[240] On behalf of Shoghi Effendi to an individual believer, September 28, 1941, quoted in *Messages from the Universal House of Justice, 1968-1973*, pp. 108-109
[241] Mark Laaser, PhD, "The Challenges of Sexual Addiction on Relationships", quoted in *All-in-One Marriage Prep: 75 Experts Share Tips and Wisdom to Help You Get Ready Now;* https://faithfulandtrue.com/, pp. 202-204
[242] Laurie Halse Anderson, January 15, 2019, https://time.com/5503804/ive-talked-with-teenage-boys-about-sexual-assault-for-20-years-this-is-what-they-still-dont-know/
[243] On behalf of the Universal House of Justice, January 24, 1993

16 - Handling the Adulting Stuff

[244] 'Abdu'l-Bahá, *Foundations of World Unity*, p. 9
[245] Universal House of Justice, *Framework for Action*, #35.34-#35.39
[246] On behalf of Shoghi Effendi, *Compilation of Compilations, Vol. II*, #1309
[247] Michael Yaconelli, *Dangerous Wonder*, pp. 78-79
[248] Robert S. Paul, *Finding Ever After*, pp. 235-236
[249] Dale Carnegie, *How to Stop Worrying and Start Living*, p. 24
[250] 'Abdu'l-Bahá, *Lights of Guidance*, #733
[251] Universal House of Justice, *Framework for Action*, #35.46
[252] Paul Coleman, Psy.D., essay "Are We Mature Enough for Marriage?" included in *All-in-One Marriage Prep,* 2nd ed., p. 76

17 – Learning and Growing from Difficulties

[253] 'Abdu'l-Bahá, *Paris Talks*, #14
[254] 'Abdu'l-Bahá, *Paris Talks*, #57
[255] On behalf of Shoghi Effendi, *Lights of Guidance*, #247
[256] Bahá'u'lláh, *Gleanings from the Writings of Bahá'u'lláh*, # CXXXIV, pp. 290-291
[257] Bahá'u'lláh, *Kitáb-i-Íqán*, p. 8
[258] 'Abdu'l-Bahá, quoted in the "Understanding Tests" letter from the Research Department of the Bahá'í World Centre to the Universal House of Justice, July 17, 1989
[259] M. Sefidvash, *Coral and Pearls*, pp. 27-28
[260] On behalf of Shoghi Effendi, *Compilation of Compilations, Vol. II*, #1297
[261] On behalf of Shoghi Effendi, *Compilation of Compilations, Vol. II*, #1322
[262] Universal House of Justice, *Lights of Guidance*, #1209
[263] Universal House of Justice, *Framework for Action*, #54.5

[264] Stephen Post, *Why Good Things Happen to Good People*, p. 114
[265] On behalf of Shoghi Effendi to the Bahá'ís of Kitalya Farm Prison, *Compilation of Compilations, Vol. II*, #1337
[266] Universal House of Justice, *Lights of Guidance*, #589

18 – Cleaning Up My Messes and Going Forward

[267] Bahá'u'lláh, *Gleanings from the Writings of Bahá'u'lláh*, #LXVI, p. 130
[268] J. Picoult, *Change of Heart*, p. 162
[269] 'Abdu'l-Bahá, *Selections from the Writings of 'Abdu'l-Bahá*, #141
[270] *The Kitáb-i-Aqdas* by Bahá'u'lláh, Note #58
[271] Les Parrott and Leslie Parrott, *When Bad Things Happen to Good Marriages*, p. 142
[272] 'Abdu'l-Bahá, *Selections from the Writings of 'Abdu'l-Bahá*, p. 158
[273] J. A. Khan, *Prophet's Daughter*, p. 245
[274] S. M. Alexander, *Creating Excellent Relationships*, p. 200

19 - Engaging with the Bahá'í Community

[275] On behalf of the Universal House of Justice, *Framework for Action*, #51.8
[276] On behalf of the Universal House of Justice, *Framework for Action*, #51.9
[277] Universal House of Justice, *Messages from the Universal House of Justice, 1986-2001*, #48.10
[278] Universal House of Justice, *Messages 1963 to 1986*, #19.5-#19.6
[279] On behalf of Shoghi Effendi, *Compilation of Compilations, Vol. II*, #1333
[280] Universal House of Justice, December 29, 1988, "Individual Rights and Freedoms", p. 16
[281] On behalf of Shoghi Effendi, *Living the Life*, p. 17
[282] Universal House of Justice, *Compilation of Compilations, Vol. II*, #1346
[283] Universal House of Justice to the National Spiritual Assembly of the Bahá'ís of the United States, May 19, 1994; https://www.bahai.org/library/authoritative-texts/the-universal-house-of-justice/messages/19940519_001/1#419867390
[284] 'Abdu'l-Bahá, *Lights of Guidance*, #808
[285] Universal House of Justice, *Compilation of Compilations, Vol. I*, pp. 421-422
[286] Universal House of Justice, *Compilation of Compilations, Vol. I*, p. 419
[287] On behalf of Shoghi Effendi, *Lights of Guidance*, #2037
[288] On behalf of Shoghi Effendi, *Compilation of Compilations, Vol. II*, #1329
[289] On behalf of Shoghi Effendi, *Compilation of Compilations, Vol. II*, #1306

20 – Making My Community-Service Choices

[290] On behalf of Shoghi Effendi, *Compilation of Compilations, Vol. II*, #1334
[291] On behalf of the Universal House of Justice, *Framework for Action*, #51.9

[292] On behalf of the Universal House of Justice, *Framework for Action*, #52.3
[293] On behalf of Shoghi Effendi, *Compilation of Compilations, Vol. II*, #1711
[294] Universal House of Justice, *Framework for Action*, #35
[295] Stephen Post, *Why Good Things Happen to Good People*, p. 47; p. 49
[296] Universal House of Justice, *Framework for Action*, #34.2
[297] Universal House of Justice to the Youth Conference in the United Kingdom, January 1, 2010, *Framework for Action*, #13
[298] Universal House of Justice, *Framework for Action*, #14.16
[299] Universal House of Justice, *Framework for Action*, #22.4
[300] Bahá'í Youth Conferences Participants' Handout, July-October 2013
[301] On behalf of the Universal House of Justice, *Framework for Action*, #55.1-#55.3
[302] Universal House of Justice, European Bahá'í Youth Council, December 7, 1992
[303] https://www.bahai.us/full-time-service-tapping-a-reservoir-of-capacity-to-transform-society/
[304] https://www.bahai.us/full-time-service-tapping-a-reservoir-of-capacity-to-transform-society/
[305] Universal House of Justice, *Framework for Action*, #27.5; #27.7; #27.8
[306] Bahá'u'lláh, *Gleanings from the Writings of Bahá'u'lláh*, #CXVII, p. 250
[307] On behalf of Shoghi Effendi, *Lights of Guidance*, #405
[308] Universal House of Justice, *Framework for Action*, #35
[309] Rev. Martin Luther King, Jr., *Strength to Love*, p. 120
[310] On behalf of the Universal House of Justice, *Compilation of Compilations, Vol. II*, #2160
[311] On behalf of Shoghi Effendi, *Lights of Guidance*, #737
[312] Bahá'u'lláh, *Call of the Divine Beloved*, #80

21 - Contributing to Respect, Justice, and Unity

[313] On behalf of the Universal House of Justice, *Framework for Action*, #51.8
[314] Bahá'u'lláh, *Gleanings from the Writings of Bahá'u'lláh*, #CXVII, p. 250
[315] Bahá'u'lláh, *Gleanings from the Writings of Bahá'u'lláh*, #CXXX, p. 285
[316] Bahá'u'lláh, *Hidden Words*, Arabic #2
[317] On behalf of the Universal House of Justice to an individual, August 6, 2018
[318] Universal House of Justice, *A Wider Horizon*, p. 228
[319] 'Abdu'l-Bahá, *Selections from the Writings of 'Abdu'l-Bahá*, #233
[320] Bahá'u'lláh, *Gleanings from the Writings of Bahá'u'lláh*, #CXXV, pp. 264-265
[321] Bahá'u'lláh, *Kitáb-i-Aqdas*, #19
[322] Mead Simon, http://onebahai.blogspot.com/2009/11/backbiting.html#ixzz6FS2nxJuX
[323] 'Abdu'l-Bahá, *Selections from the Writings of 'Abdu'l-Bahá*, #193
[324] On behalf of the Universal House of Justice, *Lights of Guidance*, #311
[325] Universal House of Justice, "Criticism of Institutions", July 2, 1996

[326] 'Abdu'l-Bahá, quoted in an article, "Canadian Bahá'í News", Issue #117, October 1959
[327] Abu'l-Qásim Faizí, "Explanation of the Emblem of the Greatest Name", with updated diacriticals
[328] The Báb, *Bahá'í Prayers*, pp. 152-153
[329] The Báb, *Bahá'í Prayers*, p. 227
[330] The Báb, *Selections from the Writings of The Báb*, p. 123
[331] 'Abdu'l-Bahá, *Selections from the Writings of 'Abdu'l-Bahá*, #233

22 - Building Relationships with My Parents and Family

[332] 'Abdu'l-Bahá, *Selections from the Writings of 'Abdu'l-Bahá*, #221
[333] On behalf of the Universal House of Justice, *Lights of Guidance*, #740
[334] John Gottman and Nan Silver, *Seven Principles for Making Marriage Work*, 2nd ed., p. 27
[335] L. Kavelin Popov, *Family Virtues Guide*, p. 250
[336] Bahá'u'lláh, "Family Life", #44
[337] 'Abdu'l-Bahá, *Lights of Guidance*, #767
[338] On behalf of the Universal House of Justice, "Family Life", #75
[339] Bahá'u'lláh, *The Kitáb-i-Aqdas*, #K148
[340] On behalf of the Universal House of Justice, *Messages 1986-2001*, #149
[341] Bahá'u'lláh, *Tablets of Bahá'u'lláh*, p. 88
[342] 'Abdu'l-Bahá, *Paris Talks*, #9
[343] Universal House of Justice, *Compilation of Compilations, Vol. I*, #914
[344] Universal House of Justice, *Wellspring of Guidance*, pp. 92-93
[345] On behalf of the Universal House of Justice, *Lights of Guidance*, #735

23 - Fostering Healthy Relationships with My Friends

[346] 'Abdu'l-Bahá, *Selections from the Writings of 'Abdu'l-Bahá*, #144
[347] 'Abdu'l-Bahá, *Paris Talks*, bahai.org, #1
[348] Bahá'u'lláh, *Hidden Words*, Persian #3
[349] 'Abdu'l-Bahá, *Promulgation of Universal Peace*, p. 442
[350] 'Abdu'l-Bahá, *Promulgation of Universal Peace*, p. 218
[351] Universal House of Justice, *Messages 1986-2001*, #216.20
[352] Universal House of Justice, *Framework for Action*, #14.3
[353] Universal House of Justice, *Framework for Action*, #14.4
[354] Universal House of Justice, Ridván 2017
[355] 'Abdu'l-Bahá, *Compilation of Compilations, Vol. I*, #842
[356] On behalf of the Universal House of Justice, *Compilation of Compilations, Vol. I*, #138

24 - Establishing a Happy Relationship with a Partner

[357] 'Abdu'l-Bahá, *Selections from the Writings of 'Abdu'l-Bahá*, #86
[358] On behalf of Shoghi Effendi, *Unfolding Destiny*, p. 440
[359] On behalf of the Universal House of Justice, *Lights of Guidance*, #1269
[360] 'Abdu'l-Bahá, quoted by Universal House of Justice in a letter dated March 26, 1985, in A. Ghaznavi's book *Sexuality, Relationships and Spiritual Growth*, p. 121
[361] On behalf of the Universal House of Justice to an individual, February 5, 1992
[362] On behalf of the Universal House of Justice to an individual, August 25, 2010
[363] 'Abdu'l-Bahá, *Promulgation of Universal Peace*, pp. 68-69
[364] Universal House of Justice, *Messages 1986-1992*, #6.3
[365] Dugan Romano, *Intercultural Marriage*, p. 23
[366] Dugan Romano, *Intercultural Marriage*, pp. 25-26
[367] Les Parrott and Leslie Parrott, *Saving Your Second Marriage Before It Starts*, p. 44
[368] On behalf of the Universal House of Justice to an individual, August 28, 1994, *Marriage Can Be Forever—Preparation Counts!*, 3rd ed., p. 141
[369] Some of these benefits draw on "Why Marriage Matters," Institute for American Values http://center.americanvalues.org/
[370] Universal House of Justice, *Lights of Guidance*, #1269
[371] Bahá'í World Centre Research Department memorandum for "Preserving Bahá'í Marriages" compilation, item 3

25 - Creating My Marriage, Fatherhood, and Family

[372] Bahá'u'lláh, *The Kitáb-i-Aqdas*, #K65
[373] On behalf of Shoghi Effendi, *The Kitáb-i-Aqdas* by Bahá'u'lláh, Note #92
[374] On behalf of the Universal House of Justice to an individual, September 24, 2014
[375] Bahá'u'lláh, *Bahá'í Prayers*, p. 118
[376] David Bowers, quoted in *Marriage Can Be Forever—Preparation Counts!*, 3rd ed., pp. 578-579
[377] 'Abdu'l-Bahá, *Selections from the Writings of 'Abdu'l-Bahá*, #92
[378] 'Abdu'l-Bahá, *Selections from the Writings of 'Abdu'l-Bahá*, #88
[379] On behalf of Shoghi Effendi, *Compilation of Compilations, Vol. I*, #903
[380] On behalf of the Universal House of Justice, *Compilation of Compilations, Vol. II*, #2161
[381] On behalf of the Universal House of Justice, *Lights of Guidance*, #1303
[382] Bahá'u'lláh, https://www.bahai.org/library/authoritative-texts/compilations/prayer-devotional-life/, #94
[383] Universal House of Justice, *Messages from the Universal House of Justice, 1986-2001*, #331.26; #331.28

[384] Universal House of Justice, *Framework for Action*, #16.33
[385] S. Truett Cathy, *It's Better to Build Boys Than Mend Men*; p. 13, p. 17, p. 22, p. 23, p. 28, p. 30
[386] S. Truett Cathy, *It's Better to Build Boys Than Mend Men*, p. 38
[387] S. Truett Cathy, *It's Better to Build Boys Than Mend Men*, p. 41
[388] S. Truett Cathy, *It's Better to Build Boys Than Mend Men*, p. 75
[389] S. Truett Cathy, *It's Better to Build Boys Than Mend Men*, p. 83
[390] S. Truett Cathy, *It's Better to Build Boys Than Mend Men*, p. 105
[391] 'Abdu'l-Bahá, *Promulgation of Universal Peace*, p. 168
[392] William J. Doherty, PhD, *Take Back Your Marriage*, p. 12
[393] William J. Doherty, PhD, *Take Back Your Marriage*, p. 50
[394] William J. Doherty, PhD, *Take Back Your Marriage*, p. 48
[395] William J. Doherty, PhD, *Take Back Your Marriage*, p. 59

26 - Directing the Course of My Life

[396] 'Abdu'l-Bahá, *Compilations of Compilations, Vol. I*, #179
[397] On behalf of the Universal House of Justice, *Messages 1963 to 1986*, #214
[398] Bahá'u'lláh, *Tablets of Bahá'u'lláh*, p. 35
[399] On behalf of the Universal House of Justice, quoted in the "Understanding Tests" memorandum from the Bahá'í World Centre Research Department to the Universal House of Justice, July 17, 1989
[400] On behalf of Shoghi Effendi quoted in the "Understanding Tests" memorandum from the Bahá'í World Centre Research Department to the Universal House of Justice, July 17, 1989
[401] Bahá'u'lláh, quoted in Shoghi Effendi, *Advent of Divine Justice*, p. 20
[402] Universal House of Justice, *Turning Point*, p. 165
[403] Scott M. Stanley, *Power of Commitment*, p. 55
[404] R. Rabbani, *Prescription for Living*, 1950 ed., p. 39
[405] W. H. Murray, *Scottish Himalayan Expedition*, pp. 6-7

27 – Learning and Working As Worship

[406] Universal House of Justice, *A Wider Horizon*, p. 142
[407] S. Truett Cathy, *It's Better to Build Boys Than Mend Men*, p. 113
[408] 'Abdu'l-Bahá, *Compilation of Compilations, Vol. I*, #791
[409] Bahá'u'lláh, *Epistle to the Son of the Wolf*, p. 26
[410] Universal House of Justice, *Framework for Action*, #14.10
[411] Bahá'u'lláh, *Tabernacle of Unity*, #1.4
[412] On behalf of the Universal House of Justice, *Compilation of Compilations, Vol. I*, p. 68, #1.3
[413] Bahá'u'lláh, *Tablets of Bahá'u'lláh*, p. 26
[414] On behalf of the Universal House of Justice, *Lights of Guidance*, #414

[415] R. Rabbani, *Prescription for Living*, 1978 ed., p. 109
[416] Universal House of Justice, *Framework for Action*, #21.7
[417] Universal House of Justice, *Messages 1963 to 1986*, p. 743
[418] Universal House of Justice, *A Wider Horizon*, pp. 38-39
[419] 'Abdu'l-Bahá, *Compilations of Compilations, Vol. I*, #179

28 - Continuing the Quest for Spiritual Manhood

[420] On behalf of Shoghi Effendi, *Compilation of Compilations, Vol. II*, #1314
[421] Bahá'u'lláh, *Hidden Words*, Persian, #9
[422] Bahá'u'lláh, *Gleanings from the Writings of Bahá'u'lláh*, #XXVII, p. 68
[423] Bahá'u'lláh, *Gleanings from the Writings of Bahá'u'lláh*, #LXXV, p. 143
[424] 'Abdu'l-Bahá, *Selections from the Writings of 'Abdu'l-Bahá*, #206
[425] Howard J. Fox, *Truth About Men*, pp. 42-43
[426] Bahá'u'lláh, *Hidden Words*, Arabic #42
[427] Shoghi Effendi, *Afire with the Vision*, #89
[428] Universal House of Justice, *Messages 1963 to 1986*, p. 528
[429] Universal House of Justice, *Framework for Action*, #34.7

Appendices

[430] Bahá'u'lláh, *Gleanings from the Writings of Bahá'u'lláh*, #CXVII, p. 250
[431] Universal House of Justice, *Framework for Action*, #22.4
[432] Universal House of Justice, *Wellspring of Guidance*, pp. 92-97
[433] On behalf of the Universal House of Justice, *Messages 1986-2001*, #141

Acknowledgements

Reading teams provided edits, feedback, and stories throughout the development of this book. As many of them requested anonymity, and some were confidential clients, no specific names are listed here. Please know, however, that this book would not exist without you, and you have my sincere gratitude.   S. M. Alexander

Author Biography and Contact Information

S. M. Alexander is a Relationship and Marriage Educator, author, coach, and character specialist, as well as President of Marriage Transformation®, an education and publishing company. The company's websites are:

- https://www.marriagetransformation.com
- https://www.transformationlearningcenter.com
- www.bahaimarriages.com
- www.bahairelationships.com

Social Media:

- https://www.facebook.com/MarriageTransformation
- https://www.facebook.com/transformationlearningcenter/
- https://www.linkedin.com/in/susannemalexander/
- https://twitter.com/BahaiMarriage

Other details about S. M. Alexander:

- Certified to conduct marriage readiness, marriage strengthening, and parenting assessments with couples through Prepare-Enrich (prepare-enrich.com), and the Character Foundations Assessment™ with individuals through Peirce Group (peircegroup.com)
- BA in Communications from Baldwin-Wallace College
- Meets with individuals and couples globally to prepare them for relationships and marriage or to strengthen their existing relationships, marriages, and families

- Serves as the chair and lead faculty member for the Wilmette Institute's online courses in the Relationships, Marriage, and Family Department (www.wilmetteinstitute.org)
- As a journalist, has written hundreds of articles, including many pieces on relationships and marriage as a contributing writer for bahaiteachings.org, bahaiblog.net, *Simple Marriage*, *Strengthening Marriage*, *Marriage Partnership*, and *First Years and Forever*.
- Collaborates with **Philip L. Donihe** on offering services to individuals, couples, groups, students, schools, universities, and businesses. He assisted with creating Chapters 12-15 on sexual health and gave other input throughout. Phil Donihe (phil.donihe@innovekt.com; +1 423-667-7588) delivers the following:

  - Inntellekt™ online learning platform
  - Character Foundations Assessment™ and Certification of Feedback Providers
  - Innovation Strengths Preference Indicator®
  - Innergize™ self-mastery training and energy empowerment
  - Coaching for men (personal and business) and for couples in business together
  - Consulting for business leaders, teams, and corporations related to innovation, character, team building, and transformation

We welcome hearing from you!

For information, services, app and tool ideas, or to contribute feedback on this book, or to provide stories to add to a revised edition in the future, please email staff@marriagetransformation.com or call, text, or WhatsApp to +1 423-599-0153 (US Eastern time).

www.ingramcontent.com/pod-product-compliance
Lightning Source LLC
Chambersburg PA
CBHW071951110526
44592CB00012B/1057